AntiPatterns in Project Management

William J. Brown
Hays W. "Skip" McCormick III
Scott W. Thomas

Wiley Computer Publishing

John Wiley & Sons, Inc.

NEW YORK • CHICHESTER • WEINHEIM • BRISBANE • SINGAPORE • TORONTO

Publisher: Robert Ipsen
Editor: Theresa Hudson
Associate Developmental Editor: Kathryn A. Malm
Managing Editor: Angela Smith
Text Design & Composition: North Market Street Graphics

This book is printed on acid-free paper. ∞

Published by John Wiley & Sons, Inc.

Published simultaneously in Canada.

This publication is designed to provide accurate and authoritative information in regard to the subject matter covered. It is sold with the understanding that the publisher is not engaged in professional services. If professional advice or other expert assistance is required, the services of a competent professional person should be sought.

Library of Congress Cataloging-in-Publication Data:

Brown, William J.
    AntiPatterns in project management / William J. Brown, Hays W. "Skip" McCormick III, Scott W. Thomas.
      p.   cm.
    Includes bibliographical references and index.
    ISBN 0-471-36366-9 (cloth : alk. paper)
    1. Computer software—Development—Management.   2. Antipatterns (Software engineering)   I. McCormick, Hays W., 1964-   II. Thomas, Scott W., 1957-   III. Title.

QA76.76.D47 B765 2000
005.1—dc21   00-0039235

Printed in the United States of America.

10 9 8 7 6 5 4 3 2 1

This book is dedicated to our families:
Kate, Luke, and Matthew Brown,
Kim, Teddy, and Janine McCormick,
Shara, Ryan, Brynn, and Susan Scott.

I am always ready to learn, although I do not always
like being taught.
—Winston Churchill, British prime minister

All great men make mistakes.
—Lord Randolph Henry Spencer Churchill

. . . this one thing I do, forgetting those things which are behind,
and reaching forth unto those things which are before,
I press toward the mark for the prize . . .
—Philippians 3:13

Contents

Acknowledgments

We wish to thank all the people who made this book possible; those who gave us ideas, encouragement, and help. In particular we wish to recognize:

Brian Bartelt

Brian Bennett

Loren Douglas Dillingham

Joe Faber

Bob Fieldman

Ken Geisinger

Ed Glick

Chris Irwin

Melanie Katz

Lieutenant Commander Doug Kibbey

James W. Moore

Dr. Thomas J. Mowbray

James Stewart

Francis W. Thomas

Of course this book, as all the others, wouldn't have been at all possible without the support of our families who gave us the space and the benefit of their infinite patience. We also extend our appreciation and gratitude to all of those individuals who contributed and consulted on this effort, providing insightful comments and recommendations. Finally we wish to thank our friends at Wiley who made this endeavor possible: Terri Hudson, Kathryn Malm, Angela Smith, and Gerrie Cho.

Preface

It is ironic that the third book in the series on AntiPatterns is being published in the year 2000, the end of the millennium. A year that will undoubtedly go down in history when the world uneventfully survived the "Y2K bug." There is probably no single year previous to this that is more noted for the influence of software programming on our society and planet. Yet with all of the worries, the world survived with little impact. Thanks to the longest running implementation of a refactored solution to ever take place (and probably the most costly), the nature of the problem was identified and the corrective solution defined and implemented. In the case of the Y2K refactored solution many variations were repeated millions of times across critical software worldwide.

Although the world is tired of hearing about Y2K, relatively few have heard about AntiPatterns and as a result our profession of software engineers, with particular emphasis on software project management, continues to repeat the same failures. We promise to end our discussion of Y2K here, but hope to educate you on how to better prepare yourself, as a manager, project manager, or project team member, for the future of software development by understanding the pitfalls of software development through project management. AntiPatterns can't save the software development world, but they can better prepare you for the execution and conduct of a software development project and the problems that are frequently encountered.

In the same manner as the previous two books, *AntiPatterns: Refactoring Software, Architectures, and Projects in Crisis* published in 1998 and *AntiPatterns and Patterns in Software Configuration Management* published in 1999, this book approaches the subject matter from a practical perspective. We hope that this makes our book something that you can relate to, easily comprehend, and implement in your world. We also hope that it sometimes puts a smile on your face as you read about an AntiPattern and recognize your own situation taking place on the pages before you. But mostly we hope that we can help you manage your software development projects in a more effective manner; help you to succeed by recognizing the problems that you have encountered or are about to encounter and by implementing a solution that is capable of overcoming those problems. We recommend that you be versed in the formal practices of software development and project management. The list of books at the end of the Introduction offers much of this knowledge. Kerzner's book *Project Management: A Systems Approach to Planning, Scheduling, and Controlling* provides a tremendous foundation for project management fundamentals that are the hallmark of a solid education. But, if you are a self-taught programmer this book will work just as well for you as it will for the guy who has a Master of Science degree in Computer Science or Systems Engineering. We have assumed that you have a working knowledge of software development but not the route to gaining that knowledge.

This book is aimed at helping you, both individually and corporately, with managing software development projects. This is a very difficult subject to learn and each project brings its own peculiarities. There are so many factors that can and do change. The three primary factors that affect a project are people, technology, and process. If you can learn to manage these three variable factors well, then you will probably succeed in spite of anything else happening around you.

We believe that work should often be fun, and we try to impart some of that in our solutions to the difficult project management problems we present. The AntiPatterns are applicable if you are already a project management guru or development team leader, or have project management as a career goal.

The book can be used either as a tutorial for project management or as a reference guide. The difference is one of using it strategically to avoid many of the commonly repeated, bad practices that exist in software project management or tactically to extricate yourself and your project from the bad practice already impacting you.

Finally, while we don't believe that we can identify the AntiPattern for the next millennium's Y2K equivalent, we do believe that within the pages of the book is a refactored solution to fix it.

Author Biographies

William J. Brown, known as Bill to his friends, is still leading software developments and living in Herndon, Virginia. He describes himself as a technical project manager and is an expert in the art of balancing people, technology, and process to achieve successful software deliveries. He has recently led the deliveries of both a distributed message broker framework and its first implementation in a Web-based insurance claims application integrating to legacy mainframe technology. His strength is in knowing what he doesn't know.

Skip McCormick has a diverse software engineering background in multitier-distributed-component architectures, secure collaboration systems, artificial intelligence, knowledge management, and other related information systems areas. He is the coauthor of two previous AntiPatterns books and is currently consulting to the OBJECTive Technologies Group (www.theOTG.com) as technical director of the Interoperability Clearinghouse (www.ichnet.org), where he is striving to help implement the "Underwriters' Lab" of Software Interoperability and Architectonics. He is also Webmaster for the AntiPatterns Web site, www.antipatterns.com.

Skip holds a B.S. degree in Computer Science from the U.S. Naval Academy at Annapolis, Maryland. He resides with his wonderful bride Kim and two bright-eyed children, Teddy and Janine, in Manassas, Virginia.

Scott W. Thomas is a Senior Product Development Manager at SAGA Software Inc. in Reston, Virginia. He is coauthor of *AntiPatterns and Patterns in Software Configuration Management* (John Wiley & Sons, Inc.). Scott has over 20 years of experience in all facets of the engineering lifecycle. His current focus is on the development of distributed object middle-ware for enabling enterprise application integration. Scott is also an Engineering Duty Officer in the U.S. Naval Reserve. He holds a B.S. in Industrial Engineering and Operations Research, and an M.S. in Systems Engineering from Virginia Tech at Blacksburg, Virginia. He resides in Vienna, Virginia, with his three children, Shara, Ryan, and Brynn, and his wife Susan.

Executive Summary

The primary cause of software development failure is the lack of appropriate project management. This book will address how to improve your software project management and increase the rate of successful projects. All aspects of software development must be managed in a balanced manner to achieve success, including managing people, technology, process, budget, and timescale. Success for a well-planned software development means that the following goals should be met:

- On time delivery
- Costs within budget
- Expected software delivered
- Happy development staff

But achieving this is rare. This is because project management is one of the most difficult activities to perform successfully in any engineering discipline. Recognizing that software engineering has not yet achieved the thorough formalisms associated with construction, airframe, and computer chip engineering means that successful software project management is that much more complex and difficult. Software engineering has often been described as a balance among:

- Formalized construction using predefined components (and in this is very much like construction).
- Rigidly following repeatable processes (as supported by the Software Engineering Institute's Capability Maturity Models) to achieve consistent results.

- Artistic invention of elegant solutions to enable a new mix of technologies.
- Application of clearly identified patterns to solve known problems.

This book is intended to guide the software project manager through the major pitfalls of managing a software development effort and to help master the basic critical techniques that are essential for achieving maturity in the software development processes. The other associated processes, such as software configuration management, are critical but will only succeed if the project management processes permit them to.

Critical Aspects of Project Management

The three key aspects of project management that require careful control are people, process, and technology. Many have properly identified people and process as the key success, or failure, factors but have failed to identify the criticality of technology. Particularly today as more and more technologies become available, more and more different technology systems are created that must be integrated. The result is an open-ended n by n problem when it comes to integrating all of the various systems that use different software technologies within an enterprise. The vaunted golden bullet of Enterprise Application Integration (EAI) does not solve this problem on its own.

It is critical to understand that there is no default hierarchy of people, process, and technology; the interdependencies are often indistinct. Each must be controlled in a balanced manner throughout the software development cycle and this is where the key focus of the project manager must be applied. Everything else is just a by-product of the balance or imbalance achieved: harmonious working, a clear software configuration management process, and understanding how to efficiently implement a technology; or personal enmities, unclear testing process, and failure to successfully implement a technology.

It is critical for today's project manager to be highly versatile and have a thorough understanding of people, technology, and process. If the assumption is made that any of these can be fully delegated then there is no control over that aspect of the software development project. And unfortunately these three aspects of software development have complex interdependencies that are highly dynamic in nature. The only way to deal with any of them effectively is to deal with them together.

This is not to say that a project manager cannot expect the senior project staff to support the management of these critical software development aspects, but there can only be one coordinator to ensure that the correct balance of strategies, tactics, and application of resources is appropriately applied.

Project Management AntiPatterns will help your junior and senior management manage all aspects of software development more effectively by bringing insight into the causes, symptoms, and consequences and by providing repeatable solutions.

Software Engineering as an Engineering Discipline

Many people consider that software engineering is aspiring to, but has not yet achieved, the discipline of engineering. This largely relies on the premise that all software development can be built from referencing a blue book or red book of reusable components using strict repeatable processes. This is certainly partly true, but not completely. If all software development in the world started anew with all the current experience then a more engineering approach would be more achievable.

But consider construction engineering, which is among the pure engineering disciplines. When a building is constructed, whether a house or a skyscraper, the premise of predefined components and repeatable processes is entirely feasible and should be expected. But that certainly does not hold true for maintenance and enhancements that also occur in software engineering. The opposite is true: Most software developers follow the same process for maintenance as for development and tend to use various granularity components to increase maintainability. But home construction maintenance is performed by a widely skilled range of engineers with their own ad hoc approaches, with often little use for anything resembling the original components used to build the structure, but rather component fragments.

So the question becomes, what is required to be an engineering discipline? In software it should be a consistent, repeatable set of software development processes that are rapid and cost-effective to implement. The three key disciplines—software development, software configuration management, and project management—must be addressed to achieve this goal. This book deals with the project management aspects to successfully perform the required software development activities:

- Software concept
- Requirements analysis

- Architecture
- Detailed design
- Coding and debugging
- Testing
- Quality assurance
- Software configuration management
- Release management

Software Engineering AntiPatterns

In all project management commonly repeated bad practices occur, which we call *AntiPatterns*. AntiPatterns are prevalent, recurring software project management roadblocks to successful delivery and are directly caused by the lack of understanding about the correct way to project manage software development. The incorrect approach is commonly repeated in ignorance of understanding. In essence, an AntiPattern will define the bad practice in terms of causes, symptoms, and consequences. A refactored solution is presented that will provide an approach to avoid the AntiPattern as well as to how to extricate a software development already suffering from it.

AntiPatterns can occur in two basic forms:

- Isolated AntiPatterns, which are readily dealt with when they can be identified because they are truly stand-alone with no hidden causes. Chapters 2, 3, and 4 deal primarily with isolated AntiPatterns as they relate to people, technology, and process respectively.

- Interacting AntiPatterns of a hierarchical or sequential nature. These are evident when a project management AntiPattern causes a software development AntiPattern because lack of control is passed down the phase-activity-task hierarchy. This is specifically the focus of Chapter 5, "AntiPattern Collisions."

This book examines key individual project management AntiPatterns in the areas of people, technology, and process. It shows how to refactor the causes, symptoms, and consequences. The more complex problem of hierarchically and sequentially caused AntiPatterns is examined in detail with a pattern solution defined to successfully refactor such occurrences.

AntiPatterns are prevalent throughout the software development process; however, there is a timing factor in solving problems and also an order.

The critical AntiPatterns are those that cause complete failure, often extending beyond the immediate project and resulting in employee attrition, organizational demise, and project failure. This book will help the software project manager identify serious (and even disastrous problems) and provide a refactored solution, which may rescue him or her from additional AntiPatterns. Addressing the software project management AntiPatterns will then help you to identify the next level of AntiPatterns, which are found in more discrete process areas such as software configuration management, architectures, requirements, and testing. Using AntiPatterns will move your software development people and processes into a more predictable, risk-reduced venture. For proof, look at the reviewer comments at Amazon (www.amazon.com), Barnes and Noble (www.barnesandnoble.com), and Software Development Magazine (www.sdmagazine.com, who awarded us a Jolt Productivity Award in 1999) for our first book: *AntiPatterns: Refactoring Software, Architectures, and Projects in Crisis*. We are accused of bringing common sense solutions to complex and dynamic problems in a practical and reusable manner. We have moved somewhat toward our goal of making software more of an engineering discipline by defining repeatable, reusable AntiPatterns. We use these AntiPatterns regularly to make our software development lives easier. We hope that they help lighten your load too!

Introduction

This book takes a long, hard look at the more common project management problems that regularly occur in software development projects using the technique of AntiPatterns to identify these problems and how to avoid them and stop them from impacting your projects. This introduction covers the book's structure and introduces the reader to the concept of AntiPatterns and the AntiPattern template.

AntiPatterns

An AntiPattern is a mechanism to describe a commonly occurring solution to a software development need that generates significantly negative consequences. An AntiPattern examines the causes, symptoms, and consequences of implementing the bad solution and offers a refactored solution that provides a successful method to support the required software development need.

The AntiPattern is a standard format that represents recurring software development problems and their refactored solutions. Both the scale of the problem/refactored solution pair and the applicable viewpoints are important factors that aid in identifying the specific scope of the AntiPattern.

AntiPattern Scale

Scale identifies the level within software development at which an AntiPattern can occur. The software design-level model (SDLM) uses the seven levels shown in Figure I.1:

Global scale. The global level contains the design issues that are globally applicable across all systems. This level is concerned with coordination across all organizations that participate in cross-organizational communications and information sharing.

Enterprise scale. The enterprise level is focused on coordination and communication across a single organization. The organization can be distributed across many locations and heterogeneous hardware and software systems.

System scale. The system level deals with communications and coordination across applications and sets of applications.

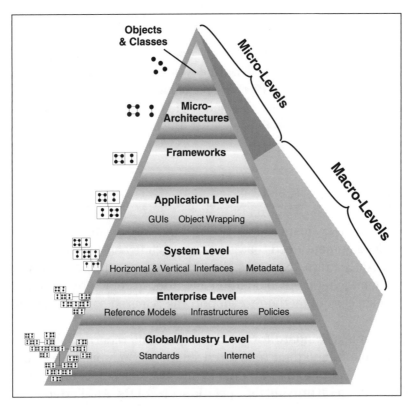

Figure I.1   Software design-level model.

Application scale. The application level is focused upon the organization of applications developed to meet a set of user requirements.

Framework scale. The framework or macro-component levels are focused on the organization and development of application frameworks.

Micro-architecture scale. The micro-component level is centered on the development of software components that solve recurring software problems. Each solution is relatively self-contained and often solves just part of an even larger problem.

Object scale. The object level is concerned with the development of reusable objects and classes. The object level is more concerned with code reuse than design reuse.

AntiPattern Viewpoints

Viewpoints are a position from which a situation can be seen or considered. Viewpoints are critical because they affect how a problem is perceived and subsequently dealt with. They are dependent on the software development role played by the primary decision maker for a given aspect of software development. Viewpoints are usually identified as manager, architect, and developer.

The *manager viewpoint* is restricted to those people who actually manage teams, projects, and programs; with a specific responsibility for planning and scheduling across the software development lifecycle. A project or program manager is also often responsible for the software development lifecycle followed, including the software configuration management.

The *architect viewpoint* focuses on identifying the technology, specifying its configuration in the form of the architecture, and ensuring its correct implementation. Architecture configuration covers logical and physical representations of the architecture and scoping the use of the selected technologies. The implementation role involves ensuring that designs conform to the architecture and updating the architectures based on coding discoveries made during the implementation.

The *developer viewpoint* is primarily focused on the implementation of the software development process. A developer can be an analyst, senior designer, junior programmer, or a quality assurance test engineer. That is, any role in mainstream development implementing the software development tasks, such as requirements gathering, designing, coding and testing, or an associated infrastructure role (e.g., software configuration management or quality assurance).

The AntiPattern Template

The AntiPattern template provides a consistent way to document:

- Common software development problems with their variations
- Ways to extricate ourselves from the impact (symptoms and consequences)
- Methods to avoid the problems, and therefore their causes, in the future

The following template is the standard format and content definition for an AntiPattern.

Name: The AntiPattern name is the key name for the problem that is addressed and is used for future reference to the principles contained in the AntiPattern. Names are critical since they form the basis for an organization's terminology when they are discussing and documenting software and architectures.

Also Known As: This identifies additional popular, descriptive, or humorous names and phrases for the AntiPattern.

Most Frequent Scale: This section identifies where this AntiPattern fits into the SDLM and scopes the dimensions of the solution. Scale is indicated with any of these key words:

- Global
- Enterprise
- System
- Application
- Framework
- Micro-Architecture
- Object

Note that some patterns occur at several scales and different refactored solutions may be presented for each level.

Refactored Solution Name: The refactored solution pattern name is a key reference, particularly when paired with the AntiPattern name for the problem.

Refactored Solution Type: This will identify the type of improvement that results from applying the AntiPattern solution:

- Software, involving the creation of new software

- Technology, solving the problem by the adoption of technology

- Process, providing the definition of activities that are consistently repeatable

- Role, allocation of clear responsibilities to organizational stake-holders

Root Causes: These are the general causes for this AntiPattern:

- Haste, which causes compromises in software quality

- Avarice, which causes greedy decision making and unnecessary complexity

- Pride, the "not-invented-here" syndrome

- Ignorance, the intellectual sloth resulting in failure to seek under-standing

- Apathy, not caring about solving software development problems

- Narrow-mindedness, refusal to practice software solutions that are known to be effective

- Sloth, lazy decision making by seeking the easy answer

- Responsibility, the universal cause

Unbalanced Forces: This section identifies the primal forces that are ignored, misused, or overused in this AntiPattern:

- Management of Functionality, meeting the requirements

- Management of Performance, meeting the required speed and scale of operation

- Management of Complexity, defining abstractions

- Management of Change, controlling the evolution of software

- Management of IT Resources, resource estimating, planning, and control

- Management of Technology Transfer, controlling technology change

- Risk, the universal force

Anecdotal Evidence: Common phrases and humorous anecdotes that succinctly describe the problem.

Background: This section sets the scene for the AntiPattern and introduces the problem under discussion.

General Form: General characteristics of the AntiPattern are identified and an overview of the nature of the problem is presented.

 Symptoms and Consequences: Here we provide a list of symptoms and related consequences resulting from this AntiPattern.

 Typical Causes: This is a list of the unique causes of this AntiPattern, which should be related to corresponding symptoms and consequences where possible.

 Known Exceptions: AntiPattern behaviors and processes may not always be wrong. There are specific occasions when this is the case; this section briefly identifies the primary exceptions to each AntiPattern.

 Refactored Solution: A refactored solution resolves the unbalanced forces, causes, symptoms, and consequences of the AntiPattern.

 Variations: Known major variations of the AntiPattern, with any applicable alternative solutions, are listed. The variations will usually deal with an aberrant form of the AntiPattern, which is unique in some aspect of the problem presented.

 Example: The example is based on a real-world experience of one of the authors or close friend and covers the specific form of the problem, with the refactored solution applied. The refactored solution instance usually varies slightly in its details from the generic refactored solution, providing insight into applying the refactored solution to a real-world occurrence of the AntiPattern.

 Related Solutions: This section primarily identifies and lists any cross-references to other AntiPatterns that are closely related, and explains the differences. If an AntiPattern in the same book is referenced no date is given, but if it is from a previous book in the AntiPattern series then the year of publication is given:

[Brown 1998] *AntiPatterns: Refactoring Software, Architectures, and Projects in Crisis*

[Brown 1999] *AntiPatterns and Patterns in Software Configuration Management*

Patterns and other software development solution sources may also be referenced within the context of the specific AntiPattern.

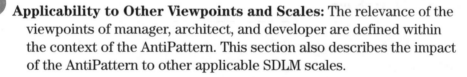

Applicability to Other Viewpoints and Scales: The relevance of the viewpoints of manager, architect, and developer are defined within the context of the AntiPattern. This section also describes the impact of the AntiPattern to other applicable SDLM scales.

All AntiPatterns follow this template to ensure a consistent mechanism for identifying and refactoring the common problems found in the project management of software development. This presentation format presents the nature of the pattern with its negative impact and the associated solution in a logical progression to make the AntiPattern and its refactored solution more easily understood.

Who Should Read This Book

This book is aimed at anyone who wishes to understand how to successfully manage software development. In other words, those people who are directly involved with and whose jobs depend on the failure or success of a software development project. This includes anyone from the developer to chief technical officer (CTO). More specifically it is written for those who manage, or wish to manage, software development. This can be a senior developer who is intent on moving up the team lead/project management ladder.

If you are happy in your current role and have no interest in project management, don't read this book. Many software development staff have no interest in the management aspects of software development and can work in their role without concern or worry about the success or failure of individual projects.

We intend to provide insight into the commonly occurring bad project management practices that abound in software development. You will discover how to avoid these bad practices and how to remove their impact once they occur. Our belief is that problem solving is an essential skill for any management role and we deal with the specific nature of managing problem solving that is inherent in software development.

You should find that this book provides a problem-solving guide to project management problems. We expect that you should be able to gain a strong knowledge of the essential project management skills and understand the pitfalls to avoid. Or in the worst case, how to extricate yourself and your project from the bad problems experienced.

Book Structure

This book is organized into the basic controllable elements of project management—people, technology, and process—rather than focusing on the definition and management of each phase of software development, such as requirements analysis or detailed design. People, technology, and process are the key factors that affect successful software delivery throughout the software development lifecycle and draw together the disciplines necessary to make each phase successful. The theme of this book is refactoring poor project management practices to enable repeatable and successful software delivery.

The book is organized into three parts:

- Part One: Introduction to Project Management and AntiPatterns
- Part Two: Critical Aspects of Project Management
- Part Three: Conclusions and Resources

Part One explains the reason that project management is such a critical discipline to software development success. It is necessary to understand that project management is the *key* to successful software development and is not just helpful.

Part One consists of Chapter 1, "Project Management and AntiPatterns." This chapter introduces you to the state of project management and the critical role it plays in software development success and failure. You'll also learn about the three key elements of people, technology and process that a project manager must manage, as well as the impact that software development standards can play in achieving success or failure of a project. The Standards AntiPattern provides insight into the advantages and disadvantages of adopting standards, whether for people, technology, or process. It examines the need for standards that are effective and bring value to software development and not bureaucracy for its own sake.

Part Two examines the critical aspects of project management. It presents the three categories of project management AntiPatterns: people, technology and process. It is essential to understand the individual facets of each of these aspects and the nature of their interaction to be able to successfully coordinate them. This part contains four chapters:

- Chapter 2, "People Management AntiPatterns," examines people problems within software development and their solutions.

- Chapter 3, "Technology Management AntiPatterns," deals with implementing poorly understood, new, or unstable technologies.

- Chapter 4, "Process Management AntiPatterns," covers the need for pragmatic processes by examining the bad processes that cause project failure and attrition.

- Chapter 5, "AntiPattern Collisions," discusses the problems that can occur when one AntiPattern is the trigger for others and how to deal with multiple AntiPatterns.

Part Three, "Conclusions and Resources," contains three appendixes. Appendix A, "Project Management Best Practices," provides an overview of best practices and lessons learned from the AntiPatterns presented in this book. Appendix B, "AntiPattern Synopsis," provides a brief overview of all the AntiPatterns in a table format. It lists the AntiPattern name, AntiPattern solution, refactored solution, and the chapter in which the AntiPattern was discussed in detail. Appendix C, "AntiPatterns Cross-Reference," is a convenient table that cross-references related AntiPatterns. The project management AntiPatterns are listed, along with the related AntiPattern name and type, and the book in which it appeared.

Depending on why you are reading this book there are two ways to do so. If you already manage projects the best way to use this book is to skim through it to get a general feel for what is covered and then dip in to specific AntiPatterns. Alternately, if you are an aspiring project manager, reading it from beginning to end would be more useful.

Recommended Reading List

The following book list gives a well-rounded view of software development and an understanding of the pitfalls and successful techniques that are part of project management. Additional resources are listed in the Bibliography.

The following books cover both project management as a discipline and general software development. While they are all well worth reading, it is recommended that at least the first five are read to understand the breadth and depth of project managing software development.

Software Project Survival Guide, Steve McConnell, Redmond, WA, Microsoft Press, 1998.

Dynamics of Software Development, Jim McCarthy, Redmond, WA, Microsoft Press, 1995.

Project Management: A Systems Approach to Planning, Scheduling, and Controlling, Sixth Edition, Harold Kerzner, New York, John Wiley & Sons, 1998.

AntiPatterns: Refactoring Software, Architectures, and Projects In Crisis, William J. Brown, Raphael C. Malveau, Hays W. McCormick, Thomas J. Mowbray, New York: John Wiley & Sons, 1998.

Rapid Development, Steve McConnell, Redmond, WA, Microsoft Press, 1996.

Effective Project Management: How to Plan, Manage and Deliver Projects on Time and within Budget, Second Edition, Robert K. Wysocki, Robert Beck Jr., David B. Crane, New York: John Wiley & Sons, 2000.

Managing Software Development Projects: Formula for Success, Second Edition, Neal Whitten, New York: John Wiley & Sons, 1995.

On Time Within Budget: Software Project Management Practices and Techniques, Third Edition, E.M. Bennatan, New York: John Wiley & Sons, 2000.

Object-Oriented Project Management with UML, Murray R. Cantor, New York: John Wiley & Sons, 1998.

AntiPatterns and Patterns in Software Configuration Management, William J. Brown, Hays W. McCormick, Scott W. Thomas, New York: John Wiley & Sons, 1999.

PART

One

Introduction to Project Management and AntiPatterns

CHAPTER 1

Project Management and AntiPatterns

"Rowing harder doesn't help if the boat is headed in the wrong direction."
–Kenichi Ohmae
business-strategy expert

The frequent problem with project management these days is analogous to the project manager being a train engineer. The train track has been laid by the organization and the project manager need only take a train down the track. However, too often the train needs to be taken in different directions than where the track has been laid. The project manager needs to stop the train, get out, and lay track. When this doesn't happen, what lies ahead for the project and the project manager is the great train wreck.

The tracks laid by organizations are the processes, technology, and culture (people) that are steeped within the tradition of the organization. The train tracks represent a pattern of behavior and practice for the project manager. Some of these patterns are good, some bad. Unfortunately, the processes used by organizations become so ingrained that there is a failure to evaluate and reevaluate. In fact, questioning these practices is akin to mutiny. In these organizations you will hear the mantra, "That's the way we've always done it!" What is required is superior leadership by the project manager. The Brawl AntiPattern, in Chapter 2, discusses the need for strong leadership and what is required by the project manager in order to achieve a successful project.

"If you keep doing what you've always done, you'll keep getting what you've always gotten."

—*Scott W. Thomas*
engineer, author

Fortunately, there are organizations that decide that they must change processes to keep up—to redirect the train. However, in the worst scenario possible, these organizations in their attempt to improve can create 100-plus-step processes for the execution of projects. They have thrown innovation out the window and rely on the rigors of the process to save them, rather than the intelligence of their employees. They need to wake up. A process doesn't save anyone, especially when it's a boat anchor around your neck. Hire smart people and give them room to operate. 100-plus-step development efforts only indicate that management has a need to microcontrol the project beyond the realm of reasonableness and that they implicitly don't trust their project managers.

The ultimate objective is to establish a repeatable, mature process that enables successful software development. The concept is similar to the Software Engineering Institute Capability Maturity Model (SEI CMM). The SEI CMM is a set of standards that deal with people, technology, and process. For example, the Systems Engineering Capability Maturity Model (SE-CMM) of the SEI describes the essential elements of an organization's software engineering process that must exist to ensure good systems engineering [SEI 1995]. The section later in this chapter on software development standards lists the SEI standards available. However, like many standard approaches, consistency and repeatability do not differentiate between good and bad software processes.

To be able to achieve a repeatable and mature process, it is necessary to understand the reasons for failure. Project failure is usually attributable to a deficiency in one of the following critical areas:

- A contiguous and well-defined software development process
- Ability to consistently repeat successful software development processes
- Investment of sufficient money and time to deliver
- Sufficient managerial and technically skilled staff
- Mature or slowly changing technology

These deficiencies can generally be categorized into three elements: people, technology, and process.

Programmed to Fail

How many classes and seminars in system engineering, software engineering, and related disciplines have you taken? How many books have you read that tell you how to properly manage a software development effort? If you are like most project managers or developers involved in some aspect of software development, you can probably teach a course or write a book on how to design, specify, develop, test, train, deploy, schedule, and budget your project based on the knowledge you have assimilated through various educational vehicles.

The next question we must ask is, "If we have such well-trained project managers and engineers, why do we still see so many failures or instances of failure associated with these software development efforts?"

The answer is truly simple. It is because no class, seminar, or book can possibly define the thousands of variables that exist for any given project, at any given time. There is no steady state in software development. While each of the prescribed methodologies and processes that are portrayed in a class or book is valid, the approach assumes an otherwise perfect world (an unrealistic world). No professor, lecturer, or author can possibly know what your specific environment is at the time you embark on your project. You have been set up. Failure, of some type, should be anticipated. The approach a project manager should take is prescribed in the books; however, don't expect that all will go as planned. The real question is, "What do I do when something goes wrong and how do I avoid this problem in the future?" That is where AntiPatterns can help.

AntiPatterns are a revolutionary approach to software development. AntiPatterns help you refactor a solution when things go wrong. The concept of AntiPatterns is leveraged from the principle of using patterns to specify a good solution process or working practice and learning from other people's mistakes. AntiPatterns approach problems from a practical and pragmatic perspective. AntiPatterns prescribe a refactored solution for your problem. The refactored solution is not an end-all but rather a point solution for a specific problem in time, from which other variations can be derived.

Software projects fail at an astounding rate. Even those projects that succeed realize some type of failure, at some time. The question is why? The answer is elusive for technically oriented people. Engineers and technocrats expect that all processes, methodologies, people, and technology are binary. Obviously that is not the case and we do not have to look very far in our personal lives to understand this. We live in a random world. While we can predict with some certainty a majority of the variables at any given time, we cannot predict all of the variables, all of the time. It is an indisputable fact.

For example, we can predict with reasonable accuracy the time we will leave for work in the morning. This is achieved by instituting a process, with known relationships to both time and performance. We rely on technology (alarm clock, car) and personnel (us, our spouse) to achieve the process. However, we cannot predict the one morning our cars won't start. However, once we know that our cars won't start, we can refactor a solution knowing the variables at that moment. For example, identifying that the fuel gauge shows empty means that the refactored solution to the problem is to fill the car with gasoline. Alternately, the problem may be more complex where we enlist the help of a mechanic to identify the specific cause of the problem and the required solution, such as replacing a fuel line. Once we survive this instance we can document (in our minds) an AntiPattern and we are aware of how to respond in the future. In fact, we can try to prevent the AntiPattern from occurring once we've mapped the symptoms and root causes. A car, for instance, can usually be prevented from not starting by ensuring that basic automotive requirements are fulfilled, such as regular servicing and sufficient gas supply.

So it is with processes in our software projects. There is randomness and we cannot anticipate every possible failure. However, we can prepare for failure and try to recognize it before it occurs. Imagine that you had the knowledge of all possible failures, their symptoms, root causes, and refactored solutions. While you may not catch every failure before it occurs, you may catch some, and the others you would be better equipped to address when they occur. That is the concept of this book—to document the common software development project management AntiPatterns so that you will be better equipped to prevent and respond to those failures.

People, Technology, and Process

People, technology, and process are the major variables in the failure and success of software development projects. If any one of these three is poorly dealt with, then the software development project will suffer. Steve McConnell identifies some of the more prevalent classic mistakes that occur if the balance between these critical factors, such as those in Figure 1.1, is not addressed sufficiently. Both Jim McCarthy and McConnell are the de facto gurus of software development [McCarthy 1995, McConnell 1996, McConnell 1998]. Any of the mistakes can cause further mistakes to occur and result in the following [Moynihan 1989]:

- Cost overruns
- Premature termination of project
- Development of the wrong product
- Technical failure

Figure 1.1 Drivers of failure.

These critical areas of focus are fully dealt with in the Micro-Management AntiPattern in Part Two of this book.

People

The most difficult aspect of project management ultimately becomes the management of human resources. The management of the project team, support team, customers, and executive management (bosses) all contributes to the most grueling facet of management. Even under the best circumstances there is friction between individuals; this is human nature. When the human function is added to an environment where interaction and cooperation are critical for success, and then this is compounded by a compressed delivery schedule using minimal resources, the complexity and the magnitude of the project are all too frequently overwhelming. Chapter 2 covers the collection of people AntiPatterns.

Software development gurus like Steve McConnell and Grady Booch have focused on social interaction because the sociology of the software development environment is poorly understood, and yet it has such a major impact on even the smallest task. The political aspects of the cliques and hierarchies make up the dynamic fabric in most software development organizations, making it one of the most valuable assets of a software development project manager to master and control.

People interaction occurs in two ways: horizontally and vertically. *Horizontal interactions* are between developers or managers in the same peer group, such as programmers, architects, or team leaders. Horizontal interactions require strong cooperation to achieve shared goals. *Vertical interactions* are between subordinates and superiors within a corporate hierarchy. Vertical interactions require iterative negotiation to ensure that the subordinate(s) own the task that they are implementing and that the manager understands the importance of the feedback from the developers.

Technology

Technical risk factors are attributed to the organization's maturity state as well as its understanding of technology and the maturity of the technology. Both development-time and runtime commercial off-the-shelf (COTS) software, such as a code library or database, can create cost sinks and extreme versioning problems in order to deliver a product. Often COTS software is embedded within the runtime products, creating technical and financial dependencies.

The primary technology areas that require understanding are tailored COTS software and programming environments. This is because often the stability is poor, the interoperability weak, and the rate of codebase change frequent. Competition drives organizations to always push the envelope of technology, and technological products are forced to be dynamic due to product differentiation and product improvements. Of course, the amount of technological advances an organization is willing to undertake is always mitigated by the risk the organization is willing to assume. Compromises limit future functionality with the result being having to replace software based on the earlier decision to use more stable software that is rapidly becoming dated. Chapter 3 covers the collection of technology AntiPatterns.

For example, take distributed object technologies (DOTs), where the Distributed Component Object Model (DCOM) and Common Object Request Brokerage Architecture (CORBA) currently dominate. The interoperability has been initially limited to bridges, which do very little but provide a data integration framework, while the DOTs continue to change not just within themselves but within the associated software and specifications, such as the Microsoft Transaction Service and the CORBA Notification and Asynchronous Messaging Services.

The ability of the organization and the software project manager to manage technology is as critical to success for a software development as technical failure is easy to achieve. Basic software project management techniques such as risk management and proof-of-concept prototyping must be pragmatically used to succeed. Corporate strategies must be balanced with line of business needs for individual projects.

Process

A software development process is meant to be a standard, repeatable set of activities and tasks that produce a required software development deliverable. The problem with processes is that they don't accommodate the variance that occurs with the people and technology. Processes need to be dynamic in supporting these changes. Additionally, they must balance the schedule, skills, technology, organization, and development environment of the project and the project team. Processes must be supported by the appropriate combination of standards, disciplines, and tools that support and enforce those standards and disciplines.

The processes should match the need of the particular type of development. Developing a demonstration does not need the full-blooded processes that are needed to develop a satellite reconnaissance system. The planning, configuration management, and development processes that are extensive and rigid in space shuttle development are greatly reduced and often deliberately not even considered in prototyping production. This is reflected in the various software development lifecycles that are discussed in detail in the Lifecycle Malpractice AntiPattern in Chapter 4.

However, there are some basic software development processes that are critical for any type and scale of development (see Figure 1.2): project management and configuration management. They both need to occur at any level of software development. That does not mean, however, that they have to be as strongly defined and rigorously followed for every type of software development, but the basic principles must be applied in all cases.

Basic planning must include the creation of a schedule of tasks with their interdependencies and estimated effort with planned start and end dates, which is covered by the Planning 911 AntiPattern discussed in Chapter 4. Basic software configuration management must include versioning of critical software development artifacts, such as requirements, design, and most especially code. These topics are dealt with in our previous book, *AntiPatterns and Patterns in Software Configuration Management* [Brown 1999].

Software Development Standards

The best software development processes are standardized so that they can be repeated in an efficient and well-understood manner to give consistent

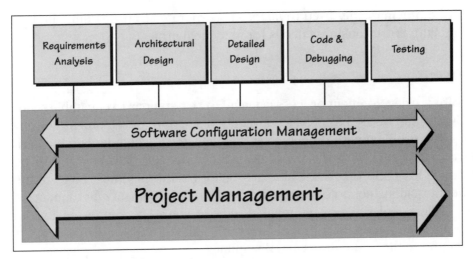

Figure 1.2   Critical software development processes.

high-quality results. Software development standards provide a much-needed template for organizations who are adopting standardized software development processes.

Standards are intended to be a repeatedly implementable solution pattern that enables good practices in software development. This is exemplified by the sterling work of the National Aeronautics and Space Administration (NASA) Software Engineering Laboratory. Software development standards are often tightly coupled to SEI's Capability Maturity Models to measure the effectiveness of software process improvement.

There are four major categories of standards in the computer industry: formal, de jure, de facto, and consortium [Brown 1998]:

- *Formal standards* are those advocated by accredited formal standards bodies such as International Standards Organization (ISO), American National Standards Institute (ANSI), and Institute of Electrical and Electronics Engineers (IEEE).

- *De jure standards* are standards mandated by law and endorsed by a government authority, including such standards as Ada95 and Government OSI Profile (GOSIP.)

- *De facto standards* earn the status through popular use such as in Microsoft Windows and Microsoft Office, Transmission Control Protocol/Internet Protocol (TCP/IP), and the various Internet protocols such as Internet Inter-ORB Protocol (IIOP).

- *Consortium standards* are created by groups of companies supporting a particular cause such as the OMG and The Open Group. Typically, formal and de jure standards are specifications only, whereas de facto and consortium standards may also include an implementation.

Software development standards can directly affect the three major variables of people, technology, and process. Just consider the Software Engineering Institute's management practices models:

- Capability Maturity Model Integration (CMMI)
- Capability Maturity Model for Software (SW-CMM)
- People Capability Maturity Model (P-CMM)
- Software Acquisition Capability Maturity Model (SA-CMM)
- Systems Engineering Capability Maturity Model (SE-CMM)
- Integrated Product Development Capability Maturity Model (IPD-CMM)

Software development standards are ignored, misused, and blamed for many software development failures. But there are two sides to this argument: pro standards and anti standards. Standards actually can provide many benefits, such as SEI's goals in developing CMMs [SEI 1999]:

- Addressing software and disciplines that have an impact on software
- Providing integrated process improvement reference models
- Building broad community consensus
- Harmonizing with standards
- Enabling efficient improvement across disciplines

Standards can also cause many problems for many reasons, ranging from a bad standard to one that is poorly implemented:

- Bureaucratic working practices
- Too much detail to be useful
- Taking focus away from actual software development activities
- Reducing productivity

The next section provides the reader with the Standards AntiPattern that is at the heart of the debate on standards, defining consistent working practices in software development. It is intended to be a tutorial that introduces the nature of an AntiPattern and tackles one of the critical aspects of software development that a project manager must deal with: adopting, deriving, or avoiding a software development standard for people, technology, or process.

The Standards

AntiPattern Name: The Standards

Also Known As: The Necessary Evil

Most Applicable Scale: System

Refactored Solution Name: Back to Zero

Refactored Solution Type: Process

Root Causes: Ignorance, Sloth, Apathy, Narrow-Mindedness, or Pride

Unbalanced Forces: Management of Complexity

Anecdotal Evidence:
   "Standards are bureaucratic and worthless."
   "We'll be okay if we just stick to exactly what the standard says!"

BACKGROUND

Standards claim to be the solution for many development projects by solving the problems of quality and standardization, yet seemingly they never live up to the claim. Project managers use standards as tools that enable visibility into the progress and quality of the development effort, and yet developers often resist implementing standards at every turn, citing too much bureaucracy, gold plating, impediments to progress, and unnecessary work.

When projects attempt to implement standards and fail to achieve the desired result, it doesn't take long for management and project managers to begin to question the effectiveness of standards. For many organizations, standards are discounted and considered only valuable for academics, having little *real* value. It is typically those same organizations that fail to meet schedule, cost, and quality requirements on most of their projects. This AntiPattern will explain why standards fail to address the needs of many organizations and provide a refactored solution.

GENERAL FORM

Why don't standards work? Standards do work if the proper standard is selected and is properly implemented. But when standards are improperly implemented or the improper standard is used, it is easier to blame the standard than assign fault to someone on the project. The following list is a summary of the reasons why standards fail to achieve success on projects:

- Standards receive resistance from developers because they restrict the freedoms of developers.
- Conforming to a standard is perceived as time-consuming, while management is perceived to demand time reduction.
- The proper standard isn't selected or tailored for the project.
- The standard isn't properly implemented.
- The organization isn't committed to implementing the standard.
- The perception is that the organization doesn't value standards.

Developer Resistance

There are two primary reasons that standards are difficult to implement from a developer perspective. One reason is because standards restrict developers in their ability to freely apply "artistic value" to the development effort. The second reason is similar, where the developers feel that they don't require standards. Standards are simply irrelevant, demanding additional time, when time is already at a premium. Developers feel that if they understand the objective, shortcuts will save time with no harm.

In both cases, the developers feel restricted. It is frequently the view of developers that standards limit their freedom [Bennatan 1995]. This resistance makes implementation and its oversight difficult without becoming Machiavellian. The project manager must identify the benefits of standardization and quality to the developers. The standardization or commonality is valuable to a developer's ability to review and understand other developers' code. This is also positive from a project management perspective, because a standard product lessens the value of any one developer: It reduces the truck factor of any one developer. (*Truck factor* refers to the inordinate value of a team member, and when a truck hits that team member, the project is in big trouble.)

Selection and Tailoring of Standards

Another reason that standards don't work is because the wrong standards are selected or standards are improperly tailored for the project. This can be the result of a well-intentioned manager wanting to bring some type of control or quality to the development effort. The manager yanks the first available and seemingly applicable standard off the shelf and throws the standard in the developers' office, telling them to implement. Unfortunately, because the standard wasn't properly understood or tailored to the specific project, some parts of the standard that the developers are forced to implement aren't applicable. The result is that the developers resist the implementation of any part of the standard and, moreover, form the opinion (rightfully so) that the standard requires unnecessary work. Nevertheless, forcing the developers to implement an unnecessary process or the unnecessary requirements of the standard furthers their opinion that all standards are worthless and unnecessary. Whatever the reason, the standards must be properly selected and tailored for the project. Before a standard is selected it is imperative that the requirements for the standard are clearly documented and understood. This ensures that potential standards can be evaluated for their usefulness and fitness for purpose. It is likely that any standard adopted will need to be modified to fit the specific software development culture to be successful.

Implementation of Standards

Assuming the correct standard was properly selected and tailored, it must also be properly implemented to be effective. Often the standard isn't read or understood well enough to be implemented. This can be true of standards that are mandated by the customer. The standard is thrown at the developers and they are expected to correctly implement it without any instruction, previous experience, or consultation from an expert and, like most aspects of software development, experience is all important. Moreover, the word *understanding* should be defined in this context. While it is important for the project team to have thoroughly read the standard, there should be an individual, an expert, who has experience in implementing the standard. Understanding should also refer to standards that are instituted and used throughout the enterprise. They should be supported at the corporate level with the appropriate infrastructure. This includes policies, procedures, tools, and experienced individuals to assist in their implementation. Repeatability is key for the implementation of standards.

One last word about implementation. It is imperative that the development team know in advance what standards are to be implemented. It is not acceptable to have the development team attempt to implement a coding standard once coding has begun. While this should seem all too obvious, it is never beyond the realm of possibility. Imagine a project leader who actually reads the contract and discovers the requirement for the implementation of the standard halfway through the project. All too frequently it's the development team that suffers from this sudden discovery (see Figure 1.3).

Commitment to Standards

One of the most significant factors in implementing a standard is ensuring that the management, project leadership, and development team are committed to implementing the standards. Frequently standards are used as nothing more than a badge, a buzzword, or a check in a box to make the customer happy. Standards require that all members of the organization are committed to successful implementation. Should any one layer in the organization fail to stand by the commitment, the implementation of the standard will likely fail. The implementation of standards requires a great deal of discipline, which is sometimes contrary to the software development environment [Bennatan 1995]. The collateral impact of a failed implementation of a standard is the perception that *all* standards don't work.

Figure 1.3 Standards toss.

Perception of Standards (Organizational Values)

The power of perception within an organization is substantial and must be recognized appropriately. Some perceptions are formed by the organizational policies of a company, others by the attitude of management. Organizational policies sometimes reveal that standards are not valued. This may be true even when standards are in use or have been used in an organization for a substantial period. The standards are taken for granted without realizing their true value. The cost of implementing a standard is often calculable; however, the value is often intangible.

Of course it is possible that in any given instance the standard is costly and ineffective, but this analysis should be carefully reviewed to determine if it is an accurate assessment. It may be that the wrong standard was selected or improperly implemented, but it may also be that the value of the standard is underestimated because it has been in place for so long that the organization no longer realizes its impact. The value of the standard is taken for granted. Essentially this is the "I can't see the forest for the trees" analysis where a manager requests that someone demonstrate the cost-effectivness of implementing a particular standard. If the individual performing the analysis isn't astute or observant enough to look beyond the obvious, the value of the standard may not be uncovered in the analysis. Specifically, the analysis must look at those aspects that aren't directly related to the standard and that may result in cost avoidance for the organization.

SYMPTOMS AND CONSEQUENCES

How can you tell if your program is in the midst of suffering from this AntiPattern? What are the symptoms? The symptoms of this AntiPattern are somewhat transparent since they can be the symptoms of other AntiPatterns, poor program management, and the eminent nature of program failure if the AntiPattern progresses too far. However, in the early stages of the AntiPattern, one of the first symptoms is the initial resistance toward the implementation of standards. Other indications that standards aren't implemented or are poorly implemented may be determined if the project manager engages the staff in discussion about how they are implementing the standards. The project manager should ask specific questions and anything less than a convincing answer should be concern for further investigation. Another method to uncover poorly implemented standards is during program milestone reviews or testing evolutions. Should it turn out during a program milestone review or through testing that substantial failures exist, then there is good reason to thoroughly investigate the cause, beginning with the standard used. This type of investigation may turn out to be inconsequential; however, it may turn out that the standard wasn't fully understood or properly implemented. If these direct and obvious symptoms are missed, a continued disintegration will produce final symptoms that look more like the project death spiral (see The Brawl AntiPattern).

The consequences that can result from this AntiPattern should be apparent from the symptoms. First, the standard is not achieved. This primary result is also reflected in the inability to achieve success within the project discipline for which the standard was to be applied (e.g., configuration control, coding practices, testing). The failure to achieve success within a project discipline can often result in collateral impact to other project disciplines, which eventually leads to project failure or, at minimum, failure of some aspect of the project. Varying degrees of failure may result; nevertheless, it has substantial and fundamental impact on the project. Additionally, the impact to the organizational perspective of standards is affected as well, usually for the worst. Failure of a project that has implemented standards leaves the perception that all standards are worthless.

These same consequences are the result of improperly implementing standards or failing to commit to the implementation of a standard. Of course, failure to use standards at all may have similar results but not necessarily. Not using standards may not result in failure. The ability of the project team, as well as the scope of the project, determines whether a project requires standards at all. The rigor of the project team may overcome the need for standards on a project; however, while immediate project failure is averted, other problems may occur subsequent to deployment. For example, it may be difficult or costly to sustain maintenance of the code if standards weren't used.

TYPICAL CAUSES

Several causes of this AntiPattern have already been discussed. To summarize, the typical causes include:

- Misuse of the standard due to the selection:
  - Hypothetical requirements
  - Badge or checklist mentality of the person performing the selection
  - Requirements for the standard not understood
- Improper selection due to not defining the requirements for the need of a standard
- Improper tailoring due to misunderstanding the purpose of a standard
- Improper implementation due to misunderstanding the culture of the organization that has to use the standard, such as:
  - No management or project team buyin
  - Insufficient funding to implement fully
  - Lazy implementation, resulting in the standard being improperly implemented
  - Inadequate process for implementing the standard, resulting in poor implementation

Misuse of Standards

Misuse of standards is probably the most common cause of the Standards AntiPattern. Misuse stems from project teams viewing standards as a hypothetical requirement only: that standards are used only by academia or government, when in reality standards are frequently used on quality projects by quality organizations.

Misuse of standards also occurs when project teams (with an ample amount of irreverence for a standard) haphazardly attempt to implement the standard, resulting in a less than desirable result, and yet they claim a rigorous implementation. The same result occurs when the project team is merely using the standard as a checklist by which to achieve a contractual requirement or so that they can claim compliance for marketing purposes. There is no intention on the part of the project team to properly implement the standard: It is simply a checkbox to be marked as complete or a line on a marketing brochure. Worst of all, it is difficult for the project manager to discern this cause of the AntiPattern without investigation. The project team will have the outward appearance of having implemented the standard and will likely look the customer square in the eye and state that they have implemented the standard.

Finally, this cause of the AntiPattern occurs when the standard isn't fully understood by the individuals responsible for implementation. So while the project team diligently attempts to comply and implement the standard to the best of their ability, it is still less than successful. This cause can also be true when the standard isn't properly tailored, again because the individual responsible doesn't fully comprehend or have an appropriate level of experience in implementing this standard.

Improper Selection of Standards

Improper selection of the standard by either the project team or the customer is another cause of the Standards AntiPattern. Understanding what you are attempting to achieve and having knowledge of the standards that are available within that domain are critical to making the proper selection. In some cases it may be that a standard isn't required at all. Discerning the need for the standard should be established first. Then there should be a review of the standards that are available within that domain. The person responsible for selection should have some knowledge of and experience with implementing the standard under similar circumstances.

One of the reasons for improper selection of standards is because there are so many standards organizations, and the standards that result from their efforts make it difficult to discern what is appropriate for your project. Because there are so many related standards it is impossible to become familiar with each one, much less become knowledgeable about all of those that exist (see Figure 1.4).

Improper Tailoring of Standards

Next on the list for causes of the Standards AntiPattern is improper tailoring. It must be understood that standards are written to address a wide

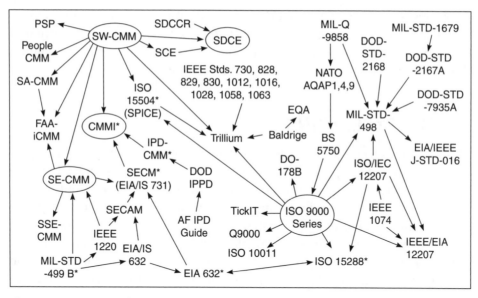

Figure 1.4 Frameworks quagmire.

Source: Drawing by Sara Sheard © 1998 Software Productivity Consortium NFP. Used with permission.

range of environments and circumstances. Without a comprehension of the project environment and the project goals as well as a familiarity with the standard being implemented, it may be difficult to discern which sections of the standard are appropriate for this implementation. It is possible that even the right standard may result in the wrong implementation. Here again, this is where experience comes into play. Having implemented a standard many times under varying circumstances provides a knowledge base otherwise unachievable by just reading the standard. This experience will enable the domain expert to know which sections of the standard are critical and which can be laid aside.

Improper Implementation of Standards

The final cause for the Standards AntiPattern is improper implementation of the standard. Specifically, gaining buyin from both the management and the project team is critical to achieving success in implementing standards, as illustrated in Figure 1.5. Unfortunately, management doesn't always understand that commitment typically translates into additional funding, skilled personnel, and time (schedule) to achieve success. However, no matter how many resources management "throws" at the implementation, if the project manager and the team aren't dedicated to achieving success, the standards may just as well be toilet paper. Finally, there must be a process for reviewing and ensuring that the standards are being implemented properly. If the project manager doesn't initiate reviews that provide insight into the implementation of the standards and are appropriate to the disciplines, there is no need to bother implementing the standards.

KNOWN EXCEPTIONS

The exception to the Standards AntiPattern is standards that are inappropriate for use by the project. These projects are typically smaller in scope and complexity and demand little rigor in the implementation and maintenance. However, the presumption that a standard is not required may precipitate the AntiPattern. Choosing when and when not to implement standards is difficult at best and while in some instances the lack of standards may be overcome by project team finessing, it usually comes with the appropriate amount of problems described by this AntiPattern and others.

REFACTORED SOLUTION

The refactored solution for the Standards AntiPattern is to return to zero, that is, the beginning. This is true whether you are at the beginning of the AntiPattern or smack in the middle. The only difference may be that there

Figure 1.5   Standards buy-in.

needs to be some assessment of how salvageable the deliverables are, for each project discipline, before "trashing" begins. For example, code should not be trashed in its entirety. Rather there should be a determination of what is required in order to have the code achieve the standard, and based on that evaluation it should be determined if the code is salvageable. However, that can only occur subsequent to determining if the appropriate standard was selected, tailored, and properly implemented.

Therefore, notwithstanding the assessment of the status of each project discipline, the first step is to determine if you have sufficient in-house expertise to follow through this process. This is somewhat of a catch-22 since you don't know what you don't know. Nevertheless, the project manager should evaluate the abilities of the individuals responsible for implementing the various standards and determine if they are knowledgeable and capable. If they are deemed acceptable, then proceed; otherwise you will probably need a consultant who is an expert in the project disciplines you are seeking to address. If you choose a consultant, then he or she should lead you through the remainder of the refactored solution presented here.

The next step is to determine if you need standards at all. This determination may be simple and straightforward if there are contractual requirements or a corporate policy, or if you are attempting to achieve a status of compliance (e.g., ISO). Otherwise, the determination is made using criteria that describe the magnitude of the effort and the complexity, reliability, and maintainability of the software. Software that requires a high degree of reliability (e.g., software for controlling nuclear operations) must be developed in an environment that demands a high degree of reliability and confidence through standards. Chances are, if you are developing that type of software you are required to follow specific standards very closely, with a high degree of review and oversight. Beyond high reliability, project complexity as well as maintenance requirements should be evaluated to determine whether standards are useful. The project manager should consult with the individuals responsible for implementing the standards in each of the project disciplines and seek their advice with regards to the implementation of standards. A note of caution must be added since those involved with the development effort often lose sight of the maintenance aspect of software. Determining the need for standards must be accomplished with foresight and with regard to a lifecycle perspective. The project manager may be surprised to learn, after talking with the project domain experts, that standards are already implemented, in which case it must be determined if they are the proper standards and if they have been appropriately implemented.

Determining which standards are appropriate is probably the single most important step in the process. James Moore's book, *Software Engineering*

Standards: A User's Roadmap [Moore 1998], is extremely helpful in comprehending the relationship between standards and your project and determining which is appropriate for your project (see standards sidebar). Aside from contractual, corporate, or compliance, the best bet is to go with IEEE or ISO standards for software development. These standards are widely accepted and are the de facto standards throughout the community.

Moore categorizes standards by these bodies using the following three models [Moore 1998]:

- Context model
- Layered model
- Object model

The context model shown in Figure 1.6 displays the relationships between software engineering and other related disciplines. A layered model (see Figure 1.7) is essentially a hierarchical view of the standards, with the more general standards at the top and more specific standards at the bottom. And finally the object model, Figure 1.8, demonstrates the relationships between key objects. Moore uses these models to map between the standards that adhere to these three models (see Figure 1.9).

SOFTWARE ENGINEERING STANDARDS ROADMAP

Understanding standards and their organization is key to selecting appropriate standards that are beneficial to your software development. The first step for the project manager is to understand that there are various ways in which standards can be organized. One method for categorization is based on the various bodies that issue standards. Some of the more prominent bodies include:

- DOD-STD (Department of Defense Standards)
  MIL-HDBK (Military Handbooks)
  MIL-SPEC (Military Specifications)
  MIL-STD (Military Standard)
- IEEE (Institute of Electrical and Electronic Engineers)
- ISO (International Standards Organization)
- STANAG (Standardization Agreement [NATO])
- TIA/EIA (Telecommunications Industry/Electronic Industries Association)

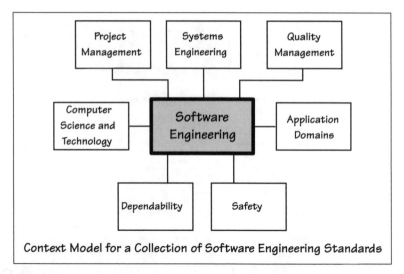

Figure 1.6   Context model.

Source: Drawing by J. Moore © 1998 IEEE. Used with permission.

Moore's book provides a great organization and mapping of the standards. An example of the kind of breakout you can expect is provided in Figure 1.10, which is an overview of the Software Engineering Standards Committee of IEEE (SESC) collection of standards.

Additionally, individual standards are broken down as well. A good example of how the book maps specific standards is demonstrated in the breakdown of the supporting processes of IEEE/EIA 12207.0 (see Figures 1.11, 1.12, 1.13). Moore's book contains 37 figures, 98 tables, and a catalog of 199 standards [Moore 1998]. It should be on the bookshelf of every project manager.

Subsequent to choosing the standards for implementation is tailoring the standards to the specific project. The tailored standard should be commensurate with the project objective (see Figure 1.14). This also applies to the rigor with which it is implemented. Rigor reflects the level of detail, as well as the review and audit that takes place, to ensure that the standards are appropriately implemented. This is a subjective effort and requires that the individual responsible be cognizant and knowledgeable of not only the standard, but also the objectives of the project, to determine what is appropriate for the project.

After successfully choosing and tailoring the standards, the project manager must commit to ensuring a successful implementation. This means that the appropriate funding and staffing are applied to ensure that the standards can be executed. The project manager should be able to identify to his

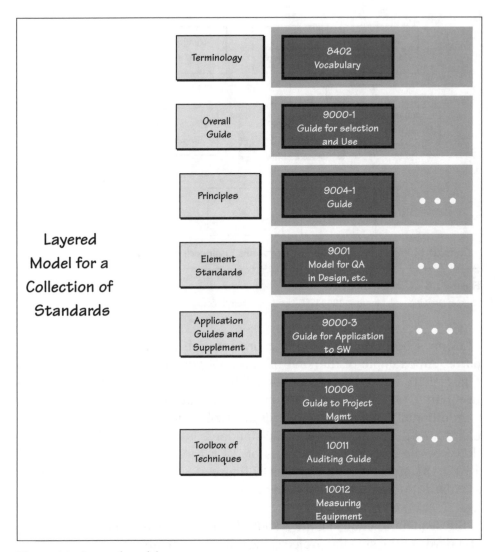

Figure 1.7 Layered model.

Source: Drawing by J. Moore © 1998 IEEE. Used with permission.

or her management what specific and tangible benefits will be achieved through the implementation of the standards. Metrics should be developed and acquired to ensure that the benefits are being derived. If they are not, an analysis should be undertaken to find out why. It may turn out that the standards aren't properly implemented because the project team hasn't been properly trained or made aware of the practices necessary to accomplish the standard. Direct benefits should be identified to management in briefings and reviews as appropriate. The customer or management should have clear insight into what they are getting for their money.

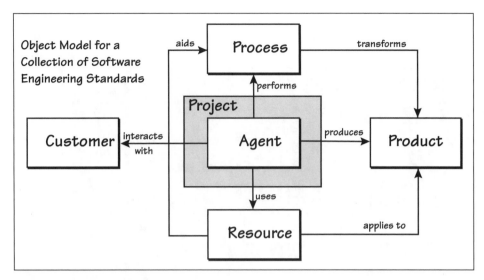

Figure 1.8 Object model.

Source: Drawing by J. Moore © 1998 IEEE. Used with permission.

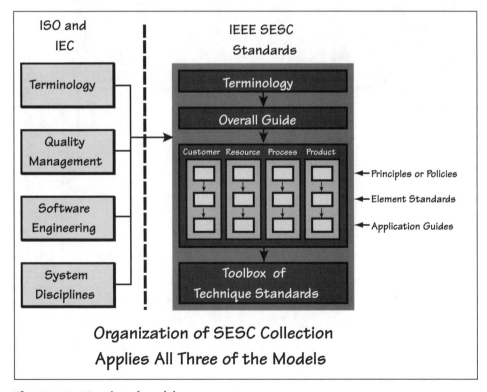

Figure 1.9 Mapping of models.

Source: Drawing by J. Moore © 1998 IEEE. Used with permission.

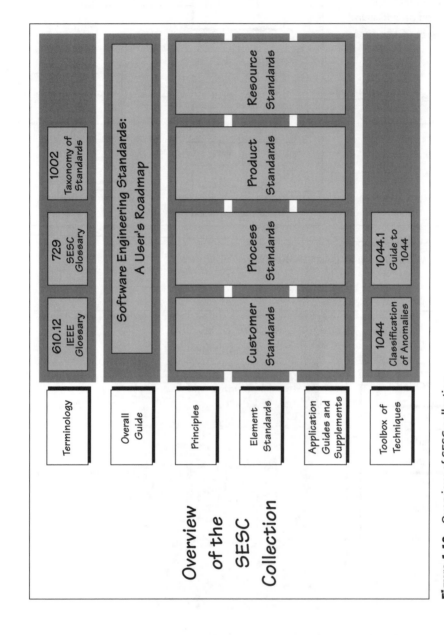

Figure 1.10 Overview of SESC collection.

Source: Drawing by J. Moore © 1998 IEEE. Used with permission.

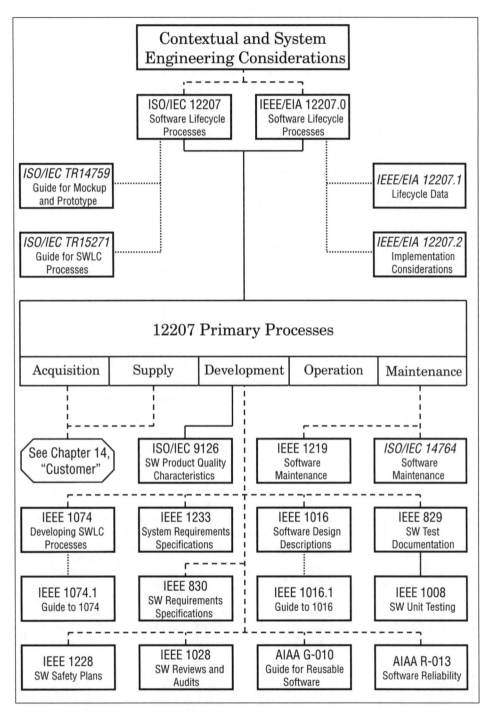

Figure 1.11 IEEE 12207.0 primary processes.

Source: Drawing by J. Moore. © 1998 IEEE. Used with permission.

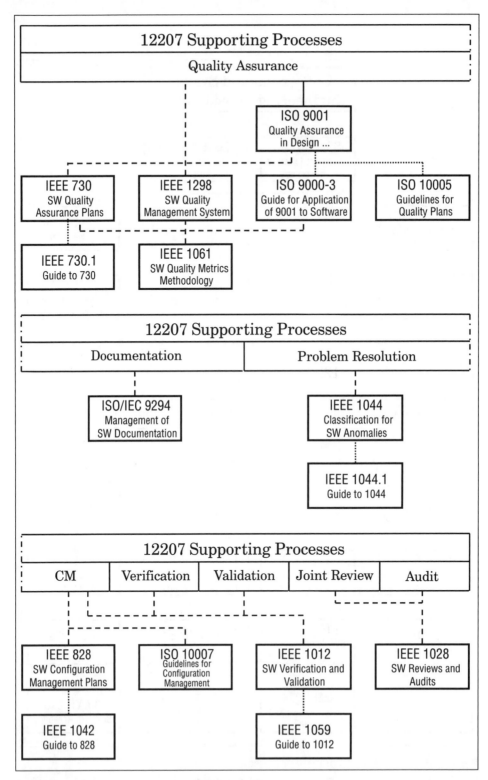

Figure 1.12 IEEE 12207.0 supporting processes.

Source: Drawing by J. Moore. © 1998 IEEE. Used with permission.

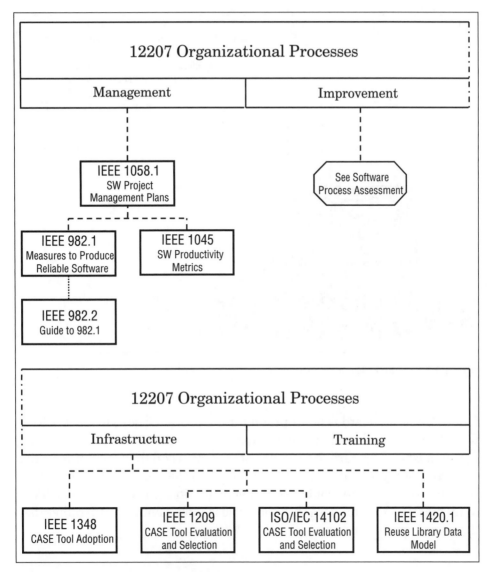

Figure 1.13   IEEE 12207.0 organizational processes.
Source: Drawing by J. Moore. © 1998 IEEE. Used with permission.

VARIATIONS

One variation to the Standards AntiPattern is when so-called experts begin to talk about implementation; you can typically find some deviation in the interpretation of what was intended by the standard. The project manager should be very careful to discern which implementation (read that interpre-

Figure 1.14 Standards commensurate with the project objective.

tation) of the standard is appropriate for the project. The safest bet is to go with the more rigorous implementation.

You must also beware of requiring standards when they are not required. Experts will argue that they are required when the scope and magnitude of the effort don't dictate that type of implementation. The expert is also likely to recommend the standard that she or he is most familiar with, rather than the most appropriate.

EXAMPLE

This is an example of how poorly standards can be used in many ways. It is a story of the development of a configuration management (CM) plan that was initially developed without direction or instruction from the project manager as to what standard to use in developing the plan. It is also the story of how the project manager failed to convey the importance of the plan. A well-developed plan based on IEEE standards was tossed aside for yet another plan that was based on no standard at all. There was no project management buyin and project management didn't value standards in general. This is an example of everyday life in a project.

The project was a software development effort that attempted to develop an initial baseline and then replicate that baseline with slight deviations for several related systems. While reuse of the initial code was expected to be high, it was anticipated that each subsequent baseline would have to be configured and managed separately. Initially a configuration management (CM) expert was called on to write a software configuration management plan for the control and management of the software baseline. The CM plan was to be written against the standards that made sense: DOD, IEEE, or whatever standards could be "pulled off" the Web and coordinated within the context of the project and the organization. The initial result by the CM expert was a mishmash of cut and paste from various CM standards, making little or no sense. After several more attempts by the expert to improve the standard (which resulted in the removal of meaningless boilerplate), the plan was promptly placed in the circular file with all other relevant material. Subsequently, a discussion ensued that identified the real problem. The expert assumed that the plan was merely for completing a contractual requirement rather than actually attempting to create a methodology from which a complex software baseline and its variations could be managed. The expert explained that he really had little time to participate in the project and was trying to help the project leader by putting together something that appeared good enough for completing the contractual requirement.

The story doesn't end there. A real software engineer was then tasked to develop the software configuration management plan. The program manager sat down with the engineer and talked at great length about the purpose and the importance of the plan, as well as the need to anchor the plan with a specific standard that was tailored for the project. The engineer undertook the task of utilizing the relevant IEEE standard for software configuration management. His plan was to develop a single plan for the organic baseline and have another plan for how each of the variations would be managed. This was briefed to the program manager and agreed to by all parties. The plans were developed in great detail with rigor and quality. The plans were submitted for review; however, due to other priorities, the plans never left the inbox. In the meantime the project hired a configuration manager and the software engineer was placed back on the development team. The plans developed by the software engineer were turned over to the newly hired configuration manager.

The newly hired configuration manager was from the old school and had her ways of approaching CM. Her approach was limited to the tool that she was taught to use when she joined the corporation. She had a fundamental understanding of how CM worked, especially in the context of the tool she planned to used. The high-quality, standards-based software configuration management plans developed by the software engineer were promptly placed in the circular file with all other relevant material. The configuration manager pulled an old CM plan from a previous project and proceeded to replace all appropriate information, such that the previous project name was replaced with the new project name. The new CM plan was based on a de facto standard of how the configuration manager operated.

RELATED SOLUTIONS

There are several related solutions to this AntiPattern through the implementation of refactored solutions to other AntiPatterns, such as The Blob, Lava Flow, Golden Hammer, Spaghetti Code, and Cut and Paste Programming AntiPatterns [Brown 1998], that are examples of bad design or development practices that could be avoided by the implementation of standards. Additionally, the Software Configuration Management Expert AntiPattern is a good example of failing to utilize a standard to control the project disciplines. The Failure to Audit AntiPattern is a good example of failing to adhere to the requirements implemented by a standard. The key is to discern which AntiPattern is applicable and apply the refactored solution in combination with the refactored solution presented within this AntiPattern.

APPLICABILITY TO OTHER VIEWPOINTS AND SCALES

This AntiPattern is applicable to the enterprise perspective at nearly every level of the organization. The impact on developers expected to implement a design that may be ambiguous and highly complex is stressful to say the least. Substantial project risk is incurred, and that is reflected in the protracted schedule and increased costs. Perhaps worst of all is the cyclical effect of not implementing standards because they weren't properly implemented, resulting in the Standards AntiPattern.

Critical Aspects of
Project Management

CHAPTER 2

People Management AntiPatterns

This chapter focuses on the People AntiPatterns, in which people are the primary cause of the project management problems. This is probably the most difficult aspect of project management because people are the least constant in the critical ingredients of people, technology, and process. Human nature is so variable that even with a team that has overcome the natural opposing wishes of the individuals within it and has started cooperating (i.e., formed, stormed, and normed), performing is not always smooth and simple. A disturbance in people's lives can have a ripple effect across everything else that they do and other people that they come into contact with, causing others to react and create their own ripples (see Micro-Management AntiPattern).

Optimum people interaction is critical to successful software delivery. Interactions among developers, architects, and managers in the same peer group, and between the managers and the people they supervise, require strong cooperation and iterative negotiation to achieve shared goals. These six People AntiPatterns show the extremes in human nature that can drive a software development to failure or success.

Micro-Management AntiPattern examines the causes of micro-management and the severe symptoms and consequences it can have, with staff attrition and project failure being quite common. Micro-management is often caused by inexperience in one or more aspects of project management: people, technology, or process. In an attempt to compensate for project management inexperience, an imbalance of these factors occurs and drives the project manager to increased micro-management. It is essential to manage people, technology, and process in a balanced way and to identify and mitigate risks as they occur in a pragmatic and consistent manner.

Corporate Craziness AntiPattern reviews the hierarchies and cliques that control the corporate software development environment and the divisive problems that can result. Management cliques are very common and always negatively impact those around them because of the politics involved, causing a dysfunctional work environment. Management hierarchies are often based on personal relationships (so-called old boys' clubs) and managers' favorite views of software development practices regardless of their management skill and experience.

The Brawl AntiPattern discusses the need for both leadership and management from a project manager. Unfortunately, many project managers do not have leadership experience and assume that management is a proscriptive activity. A project death spiral can occur when a critical event is not managed properly, either due to the inexperience and lack of skills of the project manager, or because someone who has not been empowered to make significant decisions acts as a conduit for higher management decisions in the absence of any knowledge of project reality.

Size Isn't Everything AntiPattern assesses the problems associated with allocating the appropriate number of staff to the different phases of a project. Schedule too many staff at the wrong time and the productivity level drops significantly. Schedule too few staff and the deliveries are late. Delivery delays, cost overruns, and technical failure can result from not planning according to the chosen software development lifecycle. The overlap of software lifecycle phases also can have a significant impact on planned deliveries if staffing isn't increased accordingly.

Chaos AntiPattern investigates the need to be able to adapt plans and processes as necessary in order to succeed. Software development plans and processes cannot predict all possibilities that can occur and therefore cannot be followed to the letter to overcome unpredicted problems. A project manager and other managers need to be flexible to ensure that when risks are identified they can be tackled in a flexible, pragmatic, and effective manner. Once chaos starts it is very difficult to restrain. Flexibility of management is the key to resolving this AntiPattern.

Process Disintegration AntiPattern covers the dilemma of how to handle failing processes. Many times we have stood by helplessly as seasoned professionals managed to disrupt otherwise functional processes, preventing success and souring everyone's attitude. Sometimes these people were just corncobs (i.e., difficult people) acting out the symptoms of the Corncob AntiPattern [Brown 1998], and when recognized as such could be appropriately handled. But what is going on when *everyone* seems to have lost it and there is no longer any reasonable hope of continuing without failure? This is where we are likely facing a Process Disintegration AntiPattern. The typical Process Disintegration AntiPattern occurs when several different entities have conflicting objectives and feel that the only way to accomplish their own objectives is to disrupt the process that is somehow benefiting a conflicting entity.

Micro-Management

AntiPattern Name: Micro-Management

Also Known As: Unbalanced People, Technology, and Process, Attrition 'R' Us

Most Applicable Scale: Application

Refactored Solution Name: Macro-Management

Refactored Solution Type: Role

Root Causes: Pride and Ignorance

Unbalanced Forces: Management of IT Resources

Anecdotal Evidence:
"Management don't have any respect for us."
"Management don't know what we're doing; they live in their own little world."
"Not another bloody firedrill! When can we get back to the real work?"
"If we don't tell the developers what to do each day how can we have any control?"
"The developers should do what they're told and if they don't like it, then they should leave!"

BACKGROUND

Many project managers do not understand how to manage people, technology, or process improvement well. They are sometimes excellent technical staff who are promoted or line managers who are given a change of role. Development success should often be attributed to the developers who do the right thing in spite of their management, but such success is often attributed to the project manager's skill, whereas failure can be blamed on the developers' lack of skills.

A project manager must have the skills to work with people, technology, and process as well as the ability to appropriately balance them as necessary to overcome development problems and the different skill levels of their staff. Project managers often overmanage a particular aspect of people, technology, and process, either because they are weak in that particular area and believe that a microfocus will mitigate risks or because it is the one skill area that they have.

GENERAL FORM

Project managers don't always know how to manage people, understand the technology being implemented, or know how to apply pragmatic processes. However, they are driven to make decisions in spite of this and any advice to the contrary. Often this leads to the loss of staff, and the managers responsible are surprised because they never listened to anyone but themselves.

Managers and developers are motivated by and paid for different goals, but managers often assume that everyone else has the same motivation. In practice, some of the management goals are in tension with the development goals (e.g., budget concerns versus quality code delivery), while others are complementary at a more abstract level (e.g., a component-specification design delivery within a multiple-component product delivery). Until the manager understands the necessary developer motivation, there will always be surprises as the developers negatively respond to their manager's actions.

The following failure categories identify the common project management weaknesses and the nature of poor practices that lead a manager to believe that the only apparent solution is micro-management.

People Management Failure

Lack of management focus on people and their issues can cause major disruption to software development. For example, a newly promoted line manager will usually have excellent people skills but no technical skills and often weak process skills, while a recently promoted technical guru or heroic programmer will have excellent technical skills but usually few people skills and marginal developmentwide process skills. The following problems characterize a lack of people management skills and are among the most critical.

Unformed Development Teams

Unformed development teams will not function well. Their productivity will be low, and there will always be dissension within the team until it has formed, stormed, normed, and performed. *Forming* determines the purpose of their specific team and the required roles within the team. *Storming* is the combative interactions between team members to define their own individual responsibilities and level of authority. *Norming* occurs when all of the team members have a common understanding of the goals of the team and their responsibilities within it and start working cooperatively. *Performing* is the stage in which the team has established a clear identity and the team becomes self-managing and proactive. A project manager is responsible for ensuring that all teams go through this process as early as possible to prevent people problems from getting in the way of developing software.

Lack of Clearly Defined Management Roles

Lack of clearly defined roles leads to uncertainty and indecision among senior staff and team leaders. Managers on a project should understand their roles, their relationship to other management roles, and the decision-making process. It is normally expected that the project manager will form the management team and lead the form, storm, norm, and perform process.

Poor Motivation

Poor motivation causes a lack of productivity. People need a reason to do things. If a developer does not want to perform a software development task there is a tremendous risk of low quality, late delivery, and sometimes nondelivery. Lack of team spirit exhibited by poorly formed teams also reduces motivation.

Unrealistic Expectations

Unrealistic expectations can cause frustration and subsequently poor motivation. It is the responsibility of the project manager to establish a realistic project development vision and set the expectations of all the development staff. Too often this does not happen, assumptions are made, and individual expectations are unrealistically set.

Uncontrolled Corncobs

Uncontrolled corncobs [Brown 1998] cause recurring disruption and delays to any software development. They are basically disruptive characters who continually vie to have things done their way and play politics to get their way. A project manager must manage them strongly or remove them from the development.

Encouragement of Heroes

Encouragement of heroes is often another trait of an inexperienced project manager. Every development team needs a hero or two, but to rely on them to continually pull a development through is encouraging disaster and the loss of the heroes. Heroes should lead the process by example and act as role models for the other developers.

Constant Delivery Pressure

Constant delivery pressure, often in the form of unnecessary firedrills, causes extreme frustration to developers who need a controlled environment in which to focus on their software development tasks. Project managers control the level of urgency imposed on developers and need to understand that a constantly high level of urgency benefits no one.

Adding Staff to Speed Up Delivery

Adding staff to speed up delivery is a typical inexperienced approach when managing a software development project. Unfortunately time * people = work done is not true. At a certain point adding people to an activity will cause degradation in delivery performance. A project manager needs to know how to balance staffing levels across the project development phases and activities.

Lack of Technical Respect
for Developers

Lack of technical respect for developers is again a feature of an inexperienced project manager. Many development staff members have successfully delivered a number of systems and their opinions should not only be respected but sought after. Feedback must come from all levels of a software development, not just from the management. If a project manager does not respect the developers, it is likely that the development team leaders also will be infected by this aberrant thinking.

Technology Management Failure

The lack of management focus on technology will usually result in technical failure. When a project manager does not understand the technology, he cannot usefully question or validate any information from technical staff and must rely on someone else's judgment, which introduces risks in technical decision making. The following technical management problems typically cause technical failures of software deliveries.

Choosing Unfamiliar Technologies

Choosing unfamiliar technologies will render a development schedule meaningless because there is no way to accurately account for the learning curve and to predict the difficulties of successfully implementing a novel technology. A project manager must mitigate risk involved in technology adoption and ensure that a project can successfully implement an unfamiliar technology.

Relying on Unstable COTS

Relying on unstable commercial off-the-shelf (COTS) software will cause technical failure in any software development project. A project manager must mitigate all technical risks as they are identified. The project manager must also be able to decide when a technical approach is unacceptable, rather than relentlessly and blindly pursuing it.

Lack of Tools

Lack of tools to properly support development has a critical effect on productivity and quality, particularly in areas such as integrated development environments and testing. However, this must be balanced with going overboard and falling victim to the Silver Bullet AntiPattern [Brown 1998]. A project manager must balance budget spending on engineering tools against their effectiveness in helping developers deliver quality code efficiently.

Overengineering

Overengineering is often a symptom of developers adding "cool" technology features that were not required but easy to do with the technology. This is a dangerous exercise because it may lead to unanticipated development delays, prompting the project manager to micromanage. Usually the micromanagement is applied across the board, not just to the single development team responsible for the delay.

Process Management Failure

Lack of focus on process will cause ad hoc practices within a software development project, reducing quality, adding delays, and raising the risk of delivering the expected requirements late. This causes confusion among developers about what is expected in terms of development artifacts and for managers about how to validate the development artifacts. If a project manager, for example, cannot state the criteria for the completion of requirements, then the requirements and the nature of the software will endlessly change.

Lack of a Planning Cycle

Many project managers do not see the need to produce a plan, incrementally capture work done against it, and refine the tasking detail and estimates over time. The lack of such a planning cycle reduces the amount of accurate schedule information available to a project manager and increases the risks associated with a poor management decision. This often results in firedrills to meet deliveries on dates that are no longer valid.

Inappropriate Lifecycle

Many project managers do not think in terms of lifecycles and their appropriateness to the nature of development unless there is a guiding corporate standard. For example, using a pure Waterfall Lifecycle for a prototype development will overburden the developers with unnecessary process and documentation. A project manager may think then that the developers are not doing their jobs properly and begin to micromanage.

Optimistic Estimating

It is very common to underestimate tasks from a management perspective because it is unusual for a project manager to be able to identify every detailed step in developing software and produce an accurate high-level estimate that has been validated by technical staff. Even when team leaders are producing accurate estimates for their deliveries, a project manager must be able to produce a project plan that removes integration, quality assurance, and documentation bottlenecks, which would cause knock-on delays. These factors can lead to optimistic estimates.

Compressing Schedules

Compressing schedules because of overrunning the allocated time for earlier development phases, and subsequently compressing the time available to later phases so as not to overrun the delivery deadline, is common among inexperienced project managers. Of course, since the earlier phases overran, the later phases probably need more time, not less. When the delays become significant, micro-management is an automatic reaction to get the development deliveries back on track, ignoring the real cause of the problem.

Phase Paralysis

Phase paralysis occurs when development gets stuck in a phase and cannot complete it. Common phases for this are analysis, design, and coding, and usually incur a creep of scope as a subsequent symptom. There are many causes, such as continually changing requirements or architecture. Again micro-management is an apparent solution for a project manager to bring closure to an activity, but it is often perceived with distrust by the developers.

Lack of Quality Assurance

Lack of quality assurance means that there will be failure of one or more deliverables at some point in the development. This often becomes visible at the release end of the development cycle, although the lack of quality is usually introduced during design or early coding. Once delays occur because of upstream quality errors, the project manager again feels that the only solution is micro-management.

Lack of Scope Control

Scope creep can happen at product requirements, product design, and product coding time. A weak software configuration management process will not be able to monitor scope and check traceability throughout the development artifacts. Each creep will cause a proportional delay. Several delays then trigger micro-management as an attempt to avoid further delays.

Lack of Regular and Incremental Deliveries

When a development is allowed to deliver in black-box mode, that is, its state of development is not visible, then the risk of technical failure and associated delivery delays increases because the only time that the software can be evaluated is at the end of the process. This software is continually under construction and cannot be tested until very close to delivery, with no contingency built into the development approach. As McCarthy [1995] and McConnell [1996] both point out, the best way to reduce development risks is to deliver functionality incrementally and frequently. This mitigation approach changes the nature of the delivery schedule. But again, when delivery delays occur because of the lack of regular incremental deliveries, the usual project management response is micro-management.

Balanced Focus Failure

For a software development to be truly successful it is not enough for a project manager to individually tackle the people, technology, and process aspects of software development. It is essential to balance the fluid aspects of all three throughout the software development.

Lack of People Focus

When a project manager does not focus on the developers enough it gives the developers the impression that the project manager does not care about or respect them. The result is frustration and dissension among developers, which in turn reduces any confidence the project manager has in the developers. This can cause the project manager to suddenly focus on the developers and micromanage them in an attempt to halt the delays caused by the earlier lack of communication and trust.

Lack of Technology Focus

Failure to focus on technology will cause some level of technical failure with associated delays. The larger the technical failure, the longer the project delays. A small technical failure is a COTS software feature not properly supported by a third-party vendor, and the associated workaround delays will be in the order of several weeks. A large technical failure such as an architectural strategy not being able to be implemented, because the implementation technology was not properly understood by the architects, can result in many months delay or project cancellation.

Lack of Process Focus

A software development process provides the framework for software development activities. A weak process will lead to ad hoc ways of working and inconsistent results, introducing quality and schedule risks. These risks usually are not visible until later phases of the development project and often result in repeating earlier work because of the poor state of the deliverables.

Lack of Balanced Focus

Figure 2.1 identifies the dangers of a project manager focusing on only one or two of the three critical areas of concern, that is, a lack of a balanced focus on the critical areas of risk. The result will ultimately always be delivery schedule delays ranging from weeks lost to project cancellation. Lack of focus in one area will not be sufficient to mitigate these risks. It will usually result in emergent micro-management of the area(s) not previously focused on.

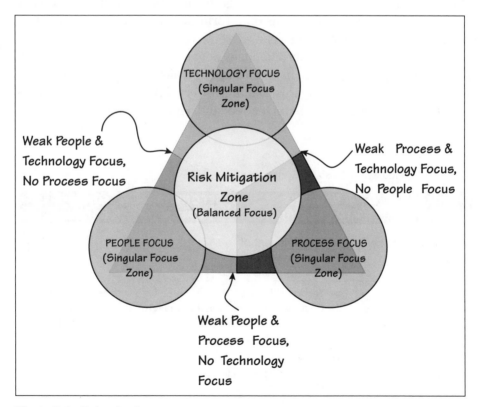

Figure 2.1   Balancing focus.

SYMPTOMS AND CONSEQUENCES

The primary symptom of the Micro-Management AntiPattern is the effect caused by the lack of project manager focus and balanced control of people, technology, and process, which usually yields a lack of quality and schedule delays. The subsequent symptom is micro-management as an attempt to rectify the problem(s) exhibited. Original problems usually are increased by a factor, and the new problems have a knock-on effect. The final consequence is staff attrition with the side effect of project failure. The specific primary symptoms with their related consequences [Moynihan 1989] are defined in Table 2.1.

TYPICAL CAUSES

The ultimate cause of the Micro-Management AntiPattern is a project manager who sees micro-management as a solution for rectifying people, technology, and process problems. The range of micro-management can vary significantly; a firedrill is an occasional form of micro-management, while managing daily developer tasks is an extreme form.

A project manager often micromanages because of a lack of project management skill and experience. In an attempt to make up for lack of skill, the answer for the project manager is to manage very tightly, controlling details that are usually delegated to team leaders and senior developers.

Table 2.1 Related Symptoms and Consequences

PRIMARY SYMPTOM	PRIMARY CONSEQUENCE	SECONDARY SYMPTOM	FINAL CONSEQUENCE
People management failure	■ Development of the wrong product ■ Cost overruns		
Technology management failure	■ Technical failure ■ Cost overruns	Micromanagement	■ Staff attrition ■ Premature termination of project
Process management failure	■ Development of the wrong product ■ Cost overruns		

The micro-management usually has a limited focus, on people, technology, or process; this causes a lack of focus in at least one of the other areas. This then increases micro-management for those areas not under control, even though the type of control is incorrect. The greater and longer such microcontrol is exerted, the larger the negative impact on the software development.

KNOWN EXCEPTIONS

There are some minor exceptions to micro-management being a negative practice; these are valid for limited time periods. The first case is when the development team is new and has not formed, stormed, normed, and performed. The manager can help lead the team through this process and establish a strong vertical working relationship with the development team.

In the second case, the manager has a technical expertise, gained prior to being promoted to management, and needs to closely manage the initial development activities to ensure that the technology learning curve is short. In other words, making sure that zero time is wasted on dead-end approaches and that appropriate technical support is provided.

REFACTORED SOLUTION

The refactored solution is specific to the initial problem as an alternative to micro-management. The discrete, critical problems discussed under the General Form section are refactored here by the following categorized solution activities.

People Management Success

Ultimate software development success depends on everyone working as a team with shared goals.

Catalyze Formation of Management and Development Teams

Rather than hope that development teams will form, storm, norm, and perform on their own and be effective at an early stage of development, it is wise to help them through the process. The best way to do this is for the project manager to act as a catalyst by leading the storming, forming, norming, and performing of the management team (the project manager and the development team leaders) and then getting the team leaders to follow suit with their development teams. The development teams can start storming as soon as the management team has formed (see Table 2.2). This will reduce the delays and make both management and development teams effective early and in synchronization.

Overlapping these stages will solve several problems:

- Unformed development teams
- Lack of clearly defined management roles (and a well-understood decision-making process)
- Uncontrolled corncobs
- Encouragement of heroes
- Lack of technical respect for developers

Involve Everyone in Planning

Producing and updating development plans should involve everyone who will implement them. This, first of all, ensures that developers buy into the estimates under which they are working and that the management experiences the injection of reality into the planning process. Team leaders should update their schedules weekly with a roll-up for support teams to assess their workload and then another roll-up for the project manager to see the weekly snapshot of the development. A good project manager will work with his or her team leaders on the plans. This will help solve the following problems:

- Poor motivation
- Unrealistic expectations

Table 2.2   Forming, Storming, Norming, and Performing Management and Development Teams

MANAGEMENT TEAM	DEVELOPMENT TEAMS
Form	
Storm	
Norm	Form
Perform	Storm
	Norm
	Perform

- Constant delivery pressure
- Adding staff to speed up delivery

Technology Management Success

Technology stability is critical for software to be useful. But it is often necessary to deal with immature technologies.

Perform Runaheads

Areas of technical risk should be dealt with as early as possible. A *runahead* is a critical activity to prove the viability of a technology. The runahead should prove that all the required functionality works as advertised, that the product is stable, and that any available patches and upgrades are regression tested to ensure that the required functionality does not change. This will resolve the following problems:

- Choosing unfamiliar technologies
- Relying on unstable COTS software

Adopt Developer-Friendly Tools

For developers to be efficient they need to use development environment tools that assist them in their work. This means avoiding bureaucratic tools that cause an increase in the workload and choosing those that provide functionality and make developers' work easier, such as the following:

- A CASE (Computer Aided/Assisted Software Engineering) modeling tool that directly supports the programming language constructs and code libraries
- A configuration management toolset with a simple user interface

This will help solve a lack of tools and overengineering.

Process Management Success

Pragmatic Project Management and Controlling the Development

To enable the chances of successful software development by pragmatically planning, it is useful for an enterprise to establish project plan and team plan templates for each type of development. The lifecycle and supporting plan template will vary by the following types of development:

- Prototyping
- New technology development
- Stable/legacy product maintenance

The team plan templates should include tasks for support team activities and nonavailability of developers. The plan should highlight key milestones for each phase. A weekly planning update and review cycle must be established. The project status report should classify the development components of an application or product by traffic light identification: green for on track, amber for drifting, and red for critical. Mitigation activities should be triggered by a component turning amber. This provides fresh information and proactive risk mitigation on a highly regular basis and resolves the following problems:

- Lack of a planning cycle
- Inappropriate lifecycle
- Optimistical estimating
- Compressed schedules
- Lack of regular and incremental deliveries
- Phase paralysis
- Lack of quality assurance
- Lack of scope control

Balanced Focus Success

To balance focus across people, technology, and process it is necessary for a project manager to recognize personal strengths and weaknesses in these three areas, and assess and mitigate the risks in each area in an ongoing manner.

The project manager should not try to be the sole keeper of the problems that arise in these three areas, but rather deal with them as the leader of the management team. Most decisions will be implemented by a team leader and so their involvement in sharing the problem at the right level of understanding, collaborating on a mitigation strategy, and sharing in the management decisions will greatly assist the project manager in effective decision making.

A balanced focus solution requires a performing management team to mitigate the risks (see Figure 2.2). Weekly project manager, architect, and developer team leader meetings should accomplish the following tasks:

- Measure the team progress against the team schedule.
- Assess technology, and process problems and risks.
- Produce mitigation strategies.
- Audit the scope of the development, perform triage, or increase the scope as necessary.

A people decision should ultimately lie with the specific team leader and the project manager, unless it concerns someone outside of the development team, such as a configuration manager or architect. People decisions should be handled very carefully because they will be watched closely by other developers and seen as embodying the attitude of the managers to the developers.

Technology problems should involve the project manager, the architect, and those development teams affected by the problem. Production of a mitigation strategy with fallback options is critical, and progress must be measured at least weekly.

Process decisions ideally should involve a process manager if the role exists; otherwise the project manager with all of the team leaders must instigate their own runtime process improvement across the project, regardless of which team encounters the problem first.

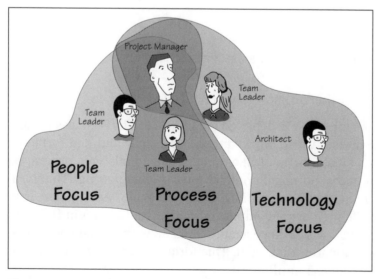

Figure 2.2 Management decision paths.

These refactored activities should mitigate the following risks:

- Lack of people focus
- Lack of technology focus
- Lack of process focus
- Lack of balanced focus

VARIATIONS

An alternate cause of micro-management by the project manager is a lack of trust by the project manager in the development staff. This situation is untenable and either the development staff or the project manager needs to be replaced.

EXAMPLE

This example typifies how micro-management is a reactive tactic by a project manager who does not understand the problems faced.

The Project

A start-up financial product company planned to build the following three Internet-based applications:

- Online trading system
- Alert subscription service for share value changes of a user-specified tolerance
- Service for reporting on subscribed financial news topics

The development structure is depicted in Figure 2.3. The business project manager and the architect had worked together before and had formed a cabal. A *cabal* is a small clique of like-minded individuals who are united secretly for some party purpose, political intrigue, or plotting. This term comes from the names Clifford, Arlington, Buckingham, Ashley, and Lauderdale. These gentlemen were members of the British Cabinet in 1672 and secretly signed a treaty with France against Holland without the knowledge or approval of the monarch Charles II. This form of hierarchy is discussed in the Corporate Craziness AntiPattern.

The initial phase of requirements and architecture proceeded smoothly and each team started their detailed design on schedule. The designs were

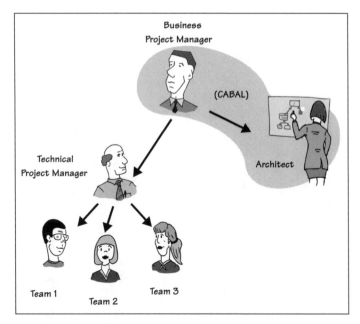

Figure 2.3   Development organization.

expected to take a month and a half to produce. However, there was no defined process for design beyond using the Unified Modeling Language (UML). This was the silver bullet that the technical project manager chose to ensure successful development. Each team leader interpreted this differently (see Figure 2.4).

Process Micro-Management

When the teams presented their designs for review, the reaction of the architect, but not the technical project manager, was very negative. The architect directed each team to produce the following design artifacts that he had in his head:

- Full UML class model
- Heavily documented code for all public interfaces
- Event traces for interface invocation sequence
- Design rationale notes for each interface design to specify performance and scalability

The team reaction to this approach was extreme frustration with the architect for not understanding their design and with the technical project manager

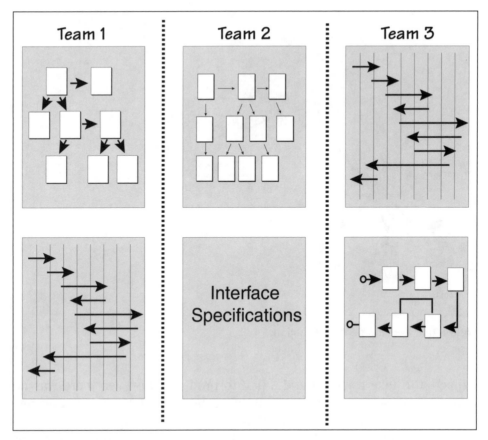

Figure 2.4 Lack of detailed design process.

for allowing this wasteful redesign effort to happen. They believed that while their artifacts were not the same that each team was working at a level of design best suited to itself. The immediate impact was reduced productivity.

The teams reiterated their designs and presented them for review, from three to five weeks behind schedule. The architect then discarded their designs because he did not believe that they were scalable.

People Micro-Management

The business project manager gave the architect direct control of the designers to produce the required design. After another two and a half months of delays and designs that looked reasonably the same as the initial designs, coding was allowed to proceed.

The reaction to this was attrition of two senior developers. The architect voiced that it was better that they leave than continue to produce such "stupid" designs. This worsened the feelings of the team leaders and the developers, who were aware of the politics, and further reduced productivity.

Technology and People Micro-Management

The alert subscription service for share value changes ran into technical problems with Java when trying to concurrently read multiple ticker streams from the Internet and produce asynchronous messages based on user subscriptions. The team leader met with the technical project manager and the architect to assess mitigation strategies. The architect denounced the team as incompetent and stated that it was a truly simple job that should take only a few weeks. Again the architect was given direct control by the business project manager over the developers and the technology to deal with this issue. However, none of the programming language alternatives the architect proposed proved successful and the result was further slippage, at which point the entire development team threatened to resign.

Refactoring a Solution

It eventually became clear to the business project manager that the architect did not understand the correct solutions to the problems and was finally correctly identified as a corncob [Brown 1998] and that their cabal (Corporate Craziness AntiPattern) had caused five months of delays.

Control was returned to the technical project manager and he immediately initiated a mitigation plan for the issues that had resulted from micro-management. He worked with the team leaders to produce mitigation activities to resolve the problems and stop the delays (see Table 2.3).

The management team successfully set mitigation strategies that ensured progress of the software development and stopped the attrition that threatened to prematurely terminate the project. The final consequence of the micro-management strategy was six and half months of delays and the loss of two senior developers. The final consequence of refactoring was retaining the remainder of the development staff and delivering the required software.

 ## RELATED SOLUTIONS

There are several related solutions (most of which are discussed elsewhere in this book) that deal with specific management problems related to an aspect of people, technology, or process.

Table 2.3   Risk Mitigation Strategies

NATURE	RISK	MITIGATION STRATEGY
People	■ Low productivity ■ Developer frustration ■ Senior developer attrition	■ Technical project manager involves team leaders in management decisions ■ Team leaders to involve team in decisions
Process	■ Consistent implementation process for design, coding, and testing	■ Technical project manager and team leaders agree on process and review artifacts for compliance
Technology	■ Design strategy versus programming language defects ■ Internet ticker stream interrupts	■ Delay implementation ■ Investigate programming language workarounds ■ Investigate alternative ticker feeds

The Planning 911 AntiPattern tackles planning and updating development schedules pragmatically, and specifically deals with refactored solutions for the Glass Case Plan, the Detailitis Plan, and the Management Plan.

The Lifecycle Malpractice AntiPattern discusses the impact of choosing an inappropriate software development lifecycle either through ignorance or through the corporate attitude: "being the done thing."

The Batteries Not Included AntiPattern identifies the pitfalls of relying on runtime and embedded COTS programs, particularly those that are unstable and subject to frequent vendor releases.

The Corporate Craziness AntiPattern deals with organizing development hierarchies so that they don't negatively affect the ability to efficiently deliver software.

The Analysis Paralysis AntiPattern [Brown 1998] covers the problem of never quite completing the analysis phase of a development project.

APPLICABILITY TO OTHER VIEWPOINTS AND SCALES

Because micro-management is usually cultural in nature, rather than a characteristic of a rogue project manager, the scale is equally attributable at the system and the enterprise scales.

Corporate Craziness

AntiPattern Name: Corporate Craziness

Also Known As: Hierarchies 'R' Us, Management Dysfunction

Most Applicable Scale: Enterprise

Refactored Solution Name: Garden of Eden

Refactored Solution Type: Role

Root Causes: Avarice and Pride

Unbalanced Forces: Management of IT Resources

Anecdotal Evidence:
"Who the hell's running this project?"
"These roles make no sense!"
"How come there's more managers than developers?"

BACKGROUND

The Corporate Craziness AntiPattern covers the hierarchies and cliques that control the working environment for most developers and discusses how to manage the roles and responsibilities to resolve the craziness emanating from such groups. Many companies form organizational hierarchies based on the senior executive preference of the day rather than on proven organizational models best suited to the size and maturity of the company. The hierarchies are often based on personal relationships and favorite opinions of how the company should manage development, which leads to frequent changes to the organizational management hierarchy and little in the way of consistent management or stable developer support.

 GENERAL FORM

When a company establishes a hierarchy that mismanages software development activities due to the inappropriate structure and roles within that structure, it is implementing the Corporate Craziness AntiPattern. This will impact all software development activities in a negative manner by producing a dysfunctional work environment where nobody wants to work. There are several common hierarchies within software development organizations that can cause a dysfunctional work environment. In many cases corporate craziness can cause a Death March [Yourdon 1997] or a mission impossible project.

Pyramid Hierarchy

A pyramid hierarchy is one in which there are too many layers of management to manage effectively. Nothing can be decided without going through several layers of decision makers (see Figure 2.5).

At best any decision is delayed by the time it takes to get through such a layered decision-making process—where there actually is one! Often managers are afraid to decide by themselves without getting prior approval from their boss in case a bad decision will be blamed on them. The actual information and decision required can go through many stages of translation and the true context can be lost along the way. Finally a manager in the hierarchy may decide to sit on the request because he or she does not want to deal with it. From the perspective of the senior developer asking for a decision the result is the same: the lack of a decision in a useful time period.

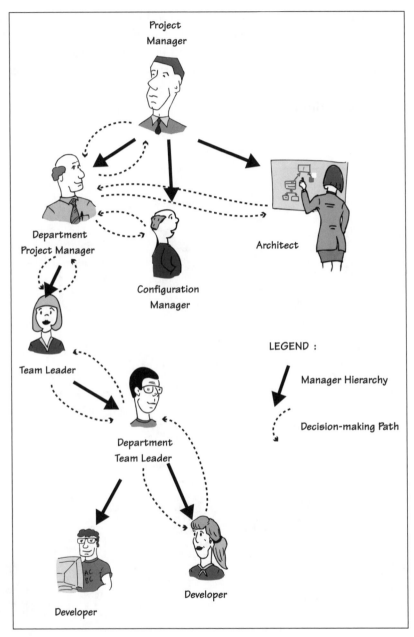

Figure 2.5 A pyramid hierarchy.

Inverse Pyramid Hierarchy

An inverse pyramid hierarchy is one in which there are too many managers in comparison to developers, as illustrated in Figure 2.6. This is a more chaotic version of the pyramid hierarchy because it is not clear who has what decision-making authority and often a request can start a management flail. The result is usually the same as for the pyramid hierarchy where a decision has to go through many managers to be approved.

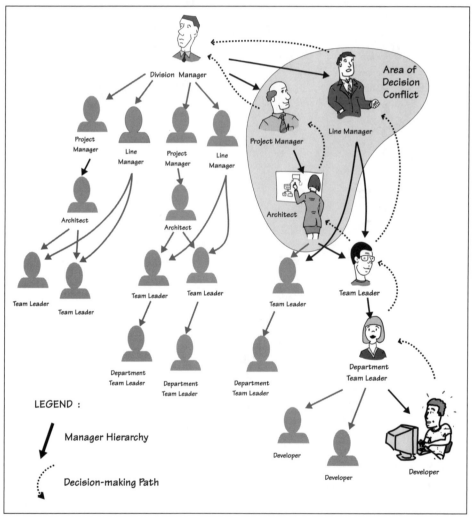

Figure 2.6   An inverse pyramid hierarchy.

One-Dimensional Hierarchy

A one-dimensional hierarchy is a completely flat management structure (see Figure 2.7). This is an even more chaotic version of the pyramid hierarchy that usually reflects the informal sharing of responsibilities between many managers with little regard to role differentiation, which makes it even more difficult to get a decision made. Instead of indefinite postponement of a decision, management flail often results because managers may take alternate stances and make conflicting decisions. This structure is ripe for the Corncob AntiPattern [Brown 1998].

Despot Hierarchy

The despot hierarchy is one in which one person does all the decision making, illustrated by Figure 2.8. One person cannot make rationally balanced decisions. Good decision making involves considering all the perspectives, many of which are in direct tension with others, requiring the need to balance a decision to get the best possible compromise. Deciding the resolution for a software development problem usually requires balancing the tensions of technology, schedule, quality, and developer motivation.

Cabal Hierarchy

The cabal, as stated before, is a small clique of like-minded individuals who are united secretly for some party purpose, political intrigue, or plotting (see Figure 2.9). This type of hierarchy give directions for their own purposes, which are not known to the main body of development staff. This lack of open and honest communication dooms the project from the cabal's inception.

Evolutionary Hierarchy

An evolutionary hierarchy management structure is one that continuously changes, as illustrated in Figure 2.10. Many companies restructure regularly as part of their culture. This regular change of management causes insecurity among managers who then either resist making decisions or don't care what decisions they make. Developers then have a complete lack of confidence in management. Such a lack of confidence prompts developers to ignore management and make decisions themselves, hiding reality from managers who will shortly be gone.

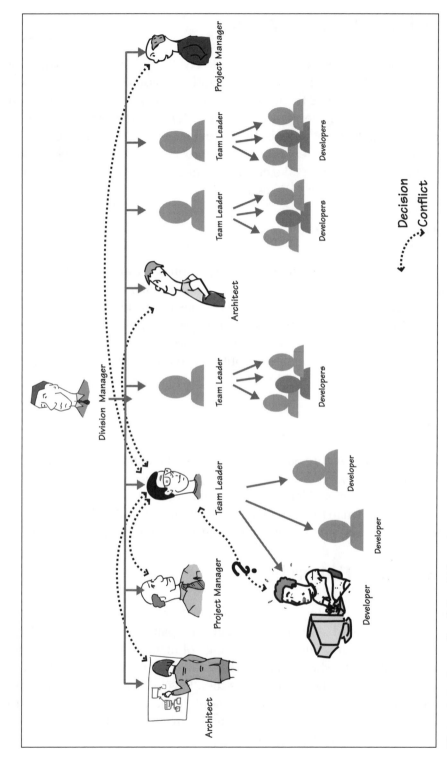

Figure 2.7 A one-dimensional hierarchy.

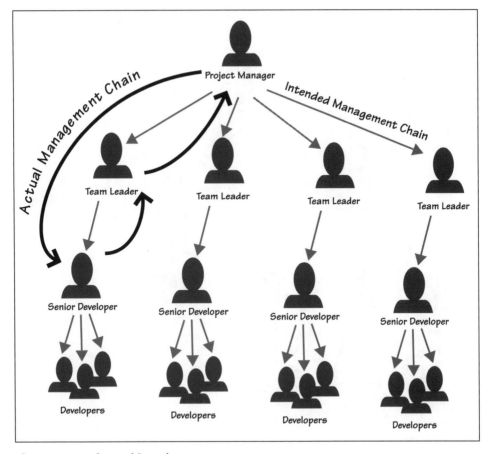

Figure 2.8 A despot hierarchy.

SYMPTOMS AND CONSEQUENCES

The five fairly visible symptoms of the Corporate Craziness AntiPattern and their related consequences are listed here:

1. Dysfunctional work environment that makes developers frustrated and offside with management, creating a divisive culture with a growing lack of trust.

2. Controversial, politically incorrect discussions of management among developers, resulting in a negative impact on development through reduced motivation and lack of trust.

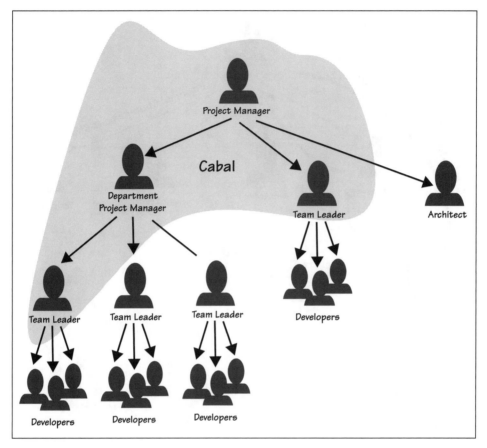

Figure 2.9 A cabal hierarchy.

3. Sick development environment syndrome causes increased reduction in productivity, enjoyment, and sustainability of development work.

4. Lack of timely management decisions, which causes delays and additional development costs by either "working at risk" (without project management approval) on the wrong thing or "sitting on hands" waiting for the decision.

5. Loss of developers seeking a better place to work. The problem usually exacerbates as more developers leave.

TYPICAL CAUSES

Poorly organized management for the size and culture of the organization is the singular cause of this AntiPattern. The management does not have an

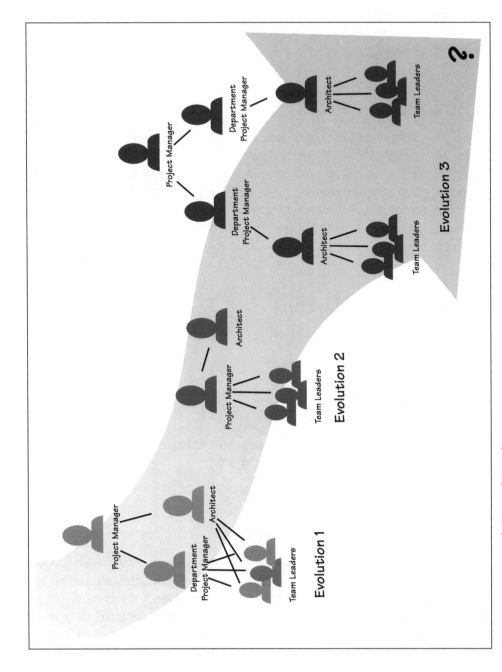

Figure 2.10 An evolutionary hierarchy.

effective hierarchy for decision making or an appropriate understanding of the various aspects of software development that are continually in tension in order to make a balanced decision. This leads to the main symptoms of delayed decisions, lack of effective communication, and staff distrust.

KNOWN EXCEPTIONS

Most management hierarchies can work given the right size and cultural state of company. It is essential that the management needs to be understood in terms of the people, technology, and process being managed because otherwise the management will be inappropriate. For example, a controlled evolutionary hierarchy would actually work if the company was a rapidly growing pre-IPO (Initial Public Offering) that had growing management needs.

REFACTORED SOLUTION

The refactored solution is applicable to all noneffective management hierarchies.

Management Roles

There is a need for management to lead software developments to success by the following approaches [McCarthy 1995]:

- Lead the definition of a winning product.
- Lead the evangelization of the product's vision.
- Lead the team to predictable victory.

McConnell recommends the use of "people-aware management accountability": "The idea behind this long phrase is that managers should be held accountable for whether the organization's human resources emerge from a project strengthened or diminished? Do five developers quit the company at the end of the project? That's a tangible loss to the company and should be held against the manager just as losing $250,000 would be. Does the whole development team emerge from the project with improved skills and incredible morale? That's a tangible benefit to the organization and should be credited to the manager's account." [McConnell 1998]

Belbin's competitive goal experiments with middle and senior managers produced the surprising result that effective management of goal achievements was best realized when the managers were a mix of "undistinguished misfits" rather than any of the "high-performance all-star" teams [Belbin 1976].

Belbin identified eight distinct leadership roles or team functions that team members seemed to play in the most diversified, successful teams. Belbin's leadership roles represent functions needed by a team for peak performance, and they also represent styles in which those leadership functions can be carried out [Constantine 1995].

Belbin identified the following four critical leadership roles:

- Driver, who sets the strategies
- Originator, who comes up with innovative approaches
- Coordinator, the process leader and facilitator
- Monitor, the critical reviewer

Belbin also identified these four critical supporting management roles:

- Supporter, who is the people person
- Implementer, responsible for putting the strategies, innovative approaches, and processes into practice
- Finisher, provides the urgency necessary and ensures completion
- Investigator, researches and acts as the groups interface externally

The need for leadership in various guises is unquestionable. The critical factor is to share the appropriate leadership foci among the management team. Often there are not enough managers to allocate each of Belbin's focused roles to an individual manager. There should be no reason that most managers can't have multiple roles, as long as the roles are not in tension with each other, and as long as they truly have the bandwidth to perform each role sufficiently.

Table 2.4 Traditional IT Management Roles Mapped to Critical Leadership and Supporter Roles

IT MANAGEMENT ROLE	LEADERSHIP ROLE	SUPPORTER ROLE
Project manager	Driver, monitor	Finisher
Process manager	Coordinator	Supporter
Architect	Originator, monitor	Implementer
Team leader	Monitor	Implementer, supporter, finisher

In Table 2.4 four common information technology (IT) shop roles are mapped to Belbin's leadership and supporting roles that are critical to achieve success. The roles also imply relationships and natural tensions between the roles (see Figure 2.11).

Establishing Management Teams

Tuckmann and Jensen introduced the commonly accepted model of the necessary stages of team formation and effectiveness [Tuckmann 1965]. Depending upon the depth of the hierarchy, there may be several management teams at each main level within the corporate hierarchy. In the described types of aberrant management hierarchies the management team(s) have not passed through the third stage of norming yet.

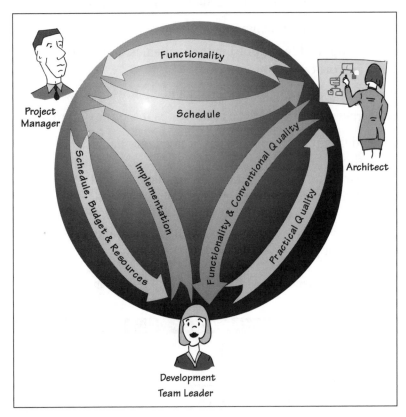

Figure 2.11 Role relationships and tensions.

Forming

Forming is the stage in which the management team determines the purpose of their specific team and the roles required within the team. In a management hierarchy the initial definition of purpose usually comes from the group or individual immediately above the one forming, in terms of chain of command.

Storming

Storming is the combative interactions between team members to define their own individual responsibilities and level of authority. This usually occurs behind closed doors between individuals and at team meetings. Unfortunately, this sometimes results in personal attacks that may cause long-standing differences and noncooperation between individual team members.

Norming

Norming occurs when all of the team members have a common understanding of the goals of the team and their responsibilities within it, and start cooperatively addressing management tasks. There is still an element of establishing clear role boundaries but usually in a less combative manner.

Performing

Performing is the stage in which the team has established a clear identity to those outside of the team, and all of the team members fully understand and accept each other's role within the team. At this point the team becomes self-managing and proactive in its work.

Effective Management Hierarchies

A management hierarchy can be very effective once it suits the size of the organization, suits the maturity of the culture, and has clearly established itself. It is often said that some larger corporations have more managers than any other position. However, this is often not the case. The better companies have clear managerial responsibilities at each level in the hierarchy that allow effective decision making in a well-controlled manner.

The normalized hierarchy controls discrete corporate resources at each level of the hierarchy. Any monetary decisions are made at the highest level because cash flow is critical to corporate survival. Technical decisions are made at the second level because this directly impacts the business users of the technology and the costs incurred. The third level exhibits control over people and the projects in which they participate.

The optimized hierarchy deals with a proportional mix of these roles at each level. The highest level decides on money for sets of projects, broad technology, and a roadmap for application/products. The second level decides budgeting of individual projects, decides specific technology implementations, and has a high-level view of each project. The third level allocates the project budget between phases and development teams, is responsible for implementing the selected technologies, and is concerned with progression of the project through each phase of development with its associated artifacts.

Both management hierarchy models are effective. The normalized hierarchy is more suited to larger, more stable companies, while the optimized hierarchy is better suited to the smaller companies in their first three or so years of existence. However, both are effective ways of organizing hierarchies and can be adapted to work within most companies where software development is the key activity.

 ## VARIATIONS

There are two common variations of the Corporate Craziness AntiPattern that are worth reviewing; they both have different sources but exhibit the same problem.

Marketing Hierarchy

This is a hierarchy that is published as a marketing story for customers and internal staff, but is never implemented. The actual hierarchy is often secret or even undefined.

In the case of a secret hierarchy, those managers who are part of the cabal can apply some rationale controls, though not as much as when the roles and relationships between them are publicized.

In terms of the actual hierarchy of roles and interrelationships being undefined, this is very like the one-dimensional hierarchy where the roles are similarly undefined. It is worse though because the developers know of both the existence of the hierarchy and the place of managers within it, as illustrated in Figure 2.12. They just do not understand the decision-making authorities of any of the managers because (unknown to them) the marketing hierarchy is not real.

Revolutionary Hierarchy

A revolutionary hierarchy is a management hierarchy that changes every time a senior developer complains about the management chain. It often stems from corporate executive insecurity about being able to keep the key developers. They would rather change the middle and lower management structure if a threat of attrition of the key developers is perceived.

Often the revolution chain is from senior or key developers to the executive, resulting in incremental movement of managers from the lowest level upwards. This problem compounds itself in terms of manager insecurity, lack of confidence by the developers, and paranoia from the executives.

 EXAMPLE

A spin-off financial company has four cost centers:

- Insurance
- Mortgages
- IT
- Marketing

The company executive management consisted of a CEO with an executive director from each of the four departments. Each executive was then responsible for organizing their own department, although about 100 staff members moved from the parent company with various expectations of their new positions.

The financial company started off with some applications they had leased from their parent company. The first order of business was to replace the leased systems with their own. This meant three years of sustained development across several projects during which the IT shop went through several stages of evolution. This was primarily an evolution of the management hierarchy driven by ineffective management who failed to deliver the required applications and systems required by the business divisions within expected time and budgets.

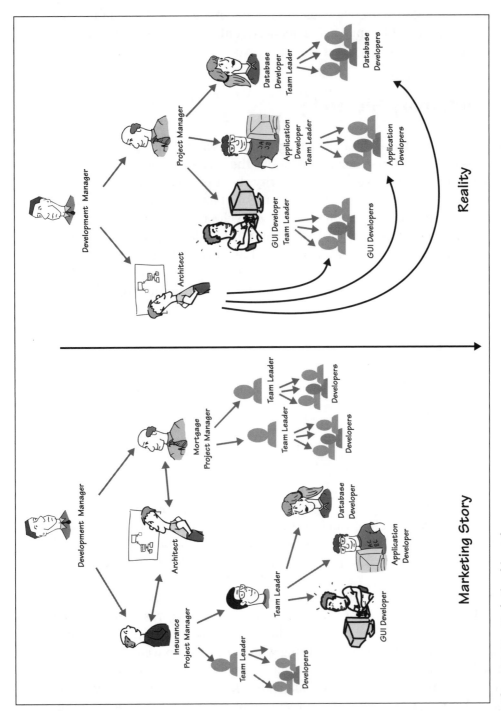

Figure 2.12 Marketing hierarchy.

The Pyramid Hierarchy

New developers were hired until the development staff, including managers, reached 180. The IT executive director wanted to retain tight controls and decided on a skewed version of the normalized hierarchy, but implemented it in the form of an extended pyramid:

1. Top level managers controlled costs.
2. Second level of managers controlled people.
3. Third level of managers controlled projects.
4. Fourth level of managers controlled technology.

This management structure lasted nearly a year before anyone noticed that nothing had been achieved due to a clear lack of a decision-making process and pragmatic chain of command.

The Marketing Pyramid and Evolutionary Hierarchies

Around the end of the first year the company realized that not only could it market its financial services but also potentially sell its applications to other companies, along with consultancy services to modify these applications as required by a customer.

This meant that marketing had to represent the structure for these product-related services to potential customers. This was fine, except that like a used car salesman their story had little in common with reality. Unfortunately, they published their version of the IT management structure internally on the company Web site. This caused much confusion because the same managers were represented but with varying roles and at varying levels of responsibility.

This was in contrast to the reality, which involved constant minor changes to the IT management hierarchy because instant results were not forthcoming. The impact was that several management and developer staff left in frustration, but this was viewed as natural attrition.

The Evolutionary Marketing Pyramid and Cabal Hierarchies

The marketing division continued to portray the application development and consultancy services management hierarchy in a changing variety of ways as an attempt to find one that would help attract a customer for these services.

The IT executive director decided that the current management hierarchy was ineffective because of too many incompetent managers, rather than too many layers and unclear responsibilities. He then proceeded to surround himself with a select group of like-minded senior managers and created a cabal with project and team level managers below that.

This meant that although the cabal managed to form, storm, and norm (but not perform), the lower level managers had no insight into the decision-making process. They perceived the executive management style as a series of firedrills because of the lack of trust between the two levels of management, resulting in more management and developer attrition.

The Evolutionary Cabal Hierarchy

The final twist to the cabal hierarchy was that as individual managers disagreed on critical issues with the executive IT director they were given other roles outside of the cabal because of their disloyalty. Some were glad to be out of the political maneuverings, while others resigned because they had tried their best and had not been supported by their boss (unrequited loyalty).

The Normalized Hierarchy

After about two years the IT executive director had exhausted all options that he personally could think of and decided that as the two business divisions were highly successful he should model his management hierarchy after them. They used versions of the normalized hierarchy, and such a clear chain of command appealed strongly to the IT executive director.

After five months of reasonable stability, but uncertainty, the management team formed, stormed, normed, and performed. This resulted in a major turnaround whereby the IT division started to be far more effective in its developments and responsive to the business divisions.

 RELATED SOLUTIONS

The Corncob AntiPattern [Brown 1998] exhibits similar results although on a much smaller scale because the problem in that case is a single individual rather than an entire management hierarchy. The corncob can be a member of a development team or a senior manager and is an expert at manipulating politics at personal and/or organizational levels. The specific instance is where the corncob either is the despot or is part of a cabal.

The Corporate Craziness AntiPattern usually encourages corncobs to exhibit their worst characteristics and become major roadblocks to completing one or more software development projects. At the extreme this destructive behavior can eventually contribute to project failure and loss of individual staff.

APPLICABILITY TO OTHER VIEWPOINTS AND SCALES

Lack of organized and effective management can also cause the Planning 911 AntiPattern. One of the causes for the Planning 911 AntiPattern is the Corporate Craziness AntiPattern.

The wrong management hierarchies for the size and cultural state of the organization can also cause the Management Malpractice and Project Mismanagement AntiPatterns [Brown 1998]. There is no real limit to the damage this may cause, from project development delivery failure, loss of key technical staff, to high staff turnover (management included), eventually resulting in a company that cannot sustain itself.

The Brawl

AntiPattern Name: The Brawl

Also Known As: The Anti-Patton

Most Applicable Scale: Enterprise

Refactored Solution Name: Leadership 101: Intro to Leadership Concepts

Refactored Solution Type: Role

Root Causes: Ignorance

Unbalanced Forces: Management of IT Resources

Anecdotal Evidence:
> "I must go, for there go my people, and I am their leader."
> —Mahatma Gandhi

> "He's a great manager/engineer/programmer, he'll make a great project manager."

> "This guy has got degrees from MIT and Harvard, he'll make a great project manager."

> "We don't believe you have been taking enough risk with your project. We think you should change the architecture to accommodate the latest thinking in technology. This shouldn't have any impact on the rest of the project."

BACKGROUND

There are at least two distinct aspects to being a project manager: leadership and management. It is important that the two are understood and that good leadership and management skills are applied to achieve success. A poor manager or leader typically results in project failure [May 1998]. However, leadership, more than management, can save a project. Often the battle cry of the engineer or the programmer is, "We need a leader not a manager," or "There is no leadership." When this is the case, development teams muddle about, stagnate, and fail to attain their goals. This festering often results in a brawl where each faction of the development team attempts to position themselves into a leadership role.

Bennis differentiates between leaders and managers:

> Leaders conquer the context—the volatile, turbulent, ambiguous surroundings that sometimes seem to conspire against us and will surely suffocate us if we let them—while managers surrender to it. The manager administrates; the leader innovates. The manager is a copy; the leader is an original. The manager maintains; the leader develops. The manager focuses on systems and structure; the leader focuses on people. The manager relies on control; the leader inspires trust. The manager has a short-ranged view; the leader has a long-range perspective. The manager asks how and when; the leader asks what and why. The manager has an eye on the bottom line; the leader has his eye on the horizon. The manager imitates; the leader originates. The manager accepts the status quo; the leader challenges it. Managers do things right; leaders do the right things. [Bennis 1994]

It is not to say that management is not an important aspect to project management; it is critical. However, it is leadership skills that make the difference. This AntiPattern explores the result of little, poor, or no leadership by the project manager. The refactored solution provides an understanding of the difference between management and leadership, and the foundations of leadership.

GENERAL FORM

If you think of a project as a sphere existing in a homogenous (theoretical or academic) environment there are equal and balanced forces that are applied to the surface that represent the challenges of the project phases (see Figure 2.13). For example, too much or too little staffing, insufficient funding, compressed schedule, changing or new technology, an unidentifiable customer(s), market demands, poorly defined processes, and too much oversight by management (micro-management) are all negative forces that must be corrected. In the homogenous environment the forces are all balanced. The project sphere was designed and planned to accommodate these forces, and it is the leadership that provides the structure that enables the sphere to maintain its intended shape.

Nevertheless, no project exists in a homogenous environment, so when the project sphere is applied to the real world it becomes evident that some of the forces are unequal and unbalanced, which results in deflections in the surface of the sphere, and represents some change to the project (see Figure 2.14). These forces shape the project sphere and eventually affect the final outcome. Planning can accommodate for some of the imbalance in forces; however, some of the variations in forces will be unanticipated and unwelcome, and will vary over time.

It is interesting to note that many of the forces have relationships. These relationships may be directly and indirectly proportional, simple and complex, and time variant. A simple example is the direct relationship a compression in the schedule (increasing the schedule force) has to the funding

Figure 2.13 The project sphere in a homogenous environment.

and staffing. The specific impact for any given project is dependent totally on the project, environment, and timing. Many of the relationships can be mapped out and anticipated [Bennatan 1995]; however, even the best project manager can't plan for all variations. There is always something unexpected that will occur. It is the nature of projects.

The project manager is equivalent to the sphere's skeletal structure, adapting to the forces and adjusting for the extremes. It is the project manager's leadership ability that will enable the project sphere to remain intact over the course of time, to equalize the forces, and eventually to endure those forces that can't be equalized so that the sphere is able to maintain its integrity without collapsing. When the project manager demonstrates poor leadership, the walls of the sphere will collapse and project failure will result (see Figure 2.15).

We hope that the abstract image of a project represented by a sphere helps you envision the concept of the project manager and the forces (chal-

Figure 2.14   The project sphere in the real world.

Figure 2.15 The collapse of the project sphere.

lenges and problems) that come into play with a project. In the real world, project managers are bombarded with problems on a weekly, if not daily basis. They are forced to make difficult decisions, direct their team in the right direction, and achieve their goal.

While many believe that leadership and leadership skills are innate and unobtainable through training, others believe the opposite—that leaders can be formed through training and experience [Hersey 1996]. It seems reasonable, regardless of your position, that a better understanding of leadership skills can enhance your ability to lead and be an effective project manager. Through this discovery it is important to also learn why project managers fail in the leadership position. Figure 2.16 illustrates how the general form of this AntiPattern produces the following three possible failure types in leadership:

Project Manager Leadership Failure. The project manager doesn't understand the difference between management and leadership. He or she focuses on the management of the project and fails to lead.

Mismatched Project Manager Leadership Failure. This failure type has two variations. The first occurs when the project manager is promoted into the position based on technical or academic capabilities without training or experience. The second variation is the case when a good technologist (engineer or programmer) is promoted into a position of project management and leadership.

Figure 2.16 The three faces of leadership failure.

Unempowered Project Manager Leadership Failure. Upper-level management steps in and tries to run the project. This failure type has two variations. The first is characterized by a project manager who is not empowered to be a good leader; he or she cannot effect good leadership skills because the upper-level manager is micromanaging. The second describes a project manager who fails to instill confidence in management and the upper-level managers' attempt to involve themselves.

In each case the result is the same—project failure.

The Project Manager

In the first instance, the Project Manager focuses on the following management processes:

- Planning and budgeting
- Organizing and problem solving
- Process management and process improvement

The project manager doesn't realize or understand the role of a leader and these leadership processes:

- Establishing direction
- Aligning people
- Motivating and inspiring

The Mismatched Project Manager

The second failure type is most common: the Mismatched Project Manager. The first variation of this failure type occurs when an individual acquires the proper credentials to assume the position of project manager, yet has no experience. The second variation of this failure type is the instance where the good engineer or programmer is promoted into the position of project manager based on his success as a technologist. (In the Peter Principle an individual continues to be promoted until reaching their level of incompetence.) In either case the individual is mismatched for the position, either by not having the experience or by assuming the position based on success as a technologist. In the latter, the project manager often fails in both the management and the leadership department and ends up meddling in development (often referred to by engineers and programmers as micro-management). Often the skill sets required by project managers and good technologists are orthogonal to one another. Even in the instance where the engineer or programmer is well organized and capable of accomplishing the management skills, he or she fails to be a good leader because the leadership processes are more instinctive, personality driven, and people oriented. These qualities are more qualitative and less quantitative, which is inconsistent with the traits of most technologists.

The Unempowered Project Manager

The third failure type is also common. The Unempowered Project Manager failure type has two derived variations. In the first, a potentially good project manager is thwarted from pursuing good leadership by being too closely managed and controlled by the next level (upper) manager. This can be the result of another failure similar to the Mismatched Project Manager failure, where a good project manager is promoted to the next level of management and is not prepared to handle the responsibilities. The upper-level manager attempts to micromanage all the projects, perhaps even engineering them. This is an unfulfilling experience for all involved and needlessly ends in disaster. This typically occurs because the upper-level manager doesn't have time to focus on the details and tries to direct the project and major decisions regarding the project (e.g., architecture) without truly understanding the collateral impact on the various facets of the project like cost, schedule, other technologies, and so on.

The second variation of this failure type describes the project manager who fails to instill confidence in his upper-level management. This failing typically comes from repeated status briefings when management walks away with an uneasy feeling about the direction of the project. The project manager has failed to inspire his or her own management. The result is the same as the first variation. The management attempts to run the project and is unable to realize the collateral impact of the decisions made at each of the status meetings when it directs the development team to change directions.

SYMPTOMS AND CONSEQUENCES

The symptoms and consequences of the Brawl AntiPattern are similar for each of the failure types described previously. It isn't difficult to understand that the lack of leadership results in unsuccessful projects and that the symptoms of failure are not altogether different. Still there are other consequences beside the failure of the project and different nuances for each failure type symptom.

The Project Manager

Symptoms for the Project Manager failure type are subtle, and it makes this variant of the AntiPattern more difficult to identify. It may appear that the project is running smoothly and all or most of the administrative actions are documented and accomplished in a timely manner. It may be that a small project or a project that encounters few challenges passes through to deployment successfully. However, it is when the project runs into a difficult situation that the symptoms become more predominate.

The project manager finds it difficult to adapt to whatever change is required and fails to realign personnel to accommodate the necessary changes. This begins the project death spiral (see Figure 2.17). Often this creates a hardship on the staff and morale declines. The development team looses direction. The project manager works the solution out on paper but fails to address the development team so that they comprehend the changes that are required and why. Morale continues to decline and now failures become increasingly more common. Some attrition may be experienced initially and then becomes increasingly more prevalent until staffing becomes an issue. The schedule is frequently impacted at this point, and the project will spiral downward out of control.

Frequently this type of failure is difficult to detect until late in the failure process because the project manager is "managing the hell out of the project" and it appears that nothing else could be done to preempt the problems. For the same reasons, it is difficult to prevent this from occurring again. The project manager blames the initial and subsequent failings on the demise of the project and fails to be identified as having the ability to turn things around.

This type of project manager will exist in an organization for some time before being discovered, or will eventually acquire enough leadership skills to eventually become a viable project manager. The consequences for the organization include not only the failed project, but also attrition of personnel, and a decline in morale.

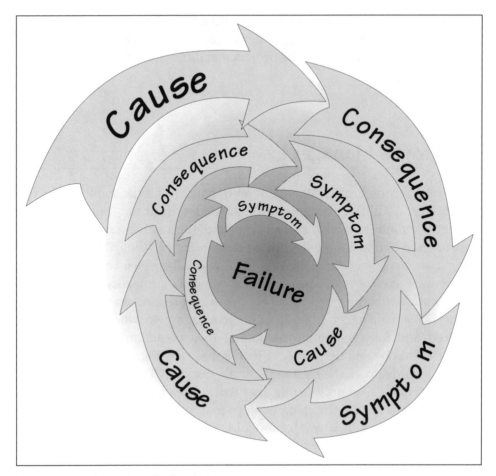

Figure 2.17 The project death spiral.

The Mismatched Project Manager

Many of the symptoms for the Mismatched Project Manager are very similar to the Project Manager failure variation. There are two cases for this failure type as well. In the first case the individual has demonstrated by way of degree or other credentials that he or she is capable of project management and then is promoted to the position, and in the second a good technologist (engineer or programmer) is offered the project manager position as a promotion. When either of these two types of individuals enters project management, failure is just around the corner.

In the first variation, this type of project manager can be referred to as the academic expert, caution is typically the mode of operation and the project

THE PROJECT DEATH SPIRAL

This model reflects the implications of the occurrence of a critical event, the consequence that occurs, and the symptoms that reflect the occurrence. The single occurrence results in a subsequent cause, consequence, and symptoms until the final cycle is achieved (project cancellation). The generic instance for each loop of the model is:

<Cause (critical event)> → <Consequence> → <Symptom>

There are an infinite number of death spirals that can be mapped. This is because a single instance of a critical evident may result in multiple subsequent cycle events. Following is a simple example of the spiral played out through six evolutions:

Cycle 1: <Cause #1: new technology fails to implement as stated> → < Consequence #1: continually redesign and recode by trial and error> → <Symptom #1a: team morale declines, Symptom #1b: incremental schedule delays>

Cycle 2: <Cause #2: lack of ability to be able to implement technology> → <Consequence #2: staff attrition> → <Symptom #2: schedule compression due to decreased staff>

Cycle 3: <Cause #3: project manager leadership diminished by course of events → <Consequence #3: lack of direction of project> → <Symptom #3: team morale declines further and growing cost and schedule over-runs incurred>

Cycle 4: <Cause #4: different technical approach chosen> → <Consequence #4: staff improperly skilled for remaining tasking> → <Symptom #4: task progress halts with no mitigation>

Cycle 5: <Cause #5: technical failure> <Consequence #5: halted development>

Cycle 6: <Symptom #5: project cancelled>

becomes extremely process intensive. The academic expert will ensure that all documentation is prepared and that the procedures are followed. These individuals act as if they are drones, programmed to achieve. They typically do well until some type of challenge is presented to them in which adjustments are difficult. They are unable to adapt, overcome, and succeed just because they haven't been there before. They are unable to quickly realign personnel assets and motivate and inspire as required. They begin to doubt themselves and quickly look to others for reassurance and direction, including from the project team. It is at this point that the project falls apart and goes through the death spiral described in the sidebar.

The second variation of the Mismatched Project Manager is all too common. The programmer is promoted into the position of project manager because of good programming skills. This move is typically done out of desperation (see Typical Causes), but regardless of the motivation, the symptoms are all too obvious. Unless this project manager gets a well-experienced, heavy-duty administrative staff, the first symptom will be little or no documentation. Cost overruns and schedule slippage are likely early on as well. This is because this project manager is spending too much time with the development team trying to figure out a better way. He or she is likely to allow the development team to indulge in technological extravagances, such as pursuing the latest technology or adding gold plating where it isn't required. Upper management may initially be tolerant because they are impressed by the technological innovation that occurs. Nonetheless, it doesn't last long because of cost and schedule problems.

However, even if the technologist project manager is able to evade management's radar, it is short lived when a challenge is thrown at the project and the death spiral soon begins. The types of challenges or forces that invoke these problems are typically managerial or administrative (e.g., cost, schedule, customer, market) rather than technical challenges since the technologist project manager believes any technical problem can be solved given enough time and money.

The Unempowered Project Manager

The final failure type is the Unempowered Project Manager. There are two variations for this failure type. The first variation is the project manager who is heavily micromanaged because the upper management feels it is necessary to involve themselves (for whatever reason). The second variation for this failure type is nearly identical, except for the cause (see Typical Causes). In this case upper management micromanages the project because the project manager, failing to exhibit leadership and instill confidence, forces the management to become overly involved. Either way, this is the wrong approach to project management.

The symptoms are clear in either case. It usually begins with regular project review meetings or briefings where the management, believing they are more aware and knowledgeable about the project effort than the project manager, begins to suggest that specific aspects of the project be evaluated. They may ask the project manager to become more of a risk taker, without fully comprehending the impact. Later, these management suggestions become directives. The frequency of review briefings usually increase and, at management direction, they become more detailed. Sometimes at the request of management, the project leader is asked to have task leaders provide the briefings directly to management.

As management continues to issue directives to the project manager and project team, the project manager's power base is eroded and he or she becomes ineffective. The management directives inflict collateral impact on other parts of the project without the management being aware. This usually causes a domino effect of failure, degrading the already low team morale, and possibly initiating attrition. Usually the best technologists are bailing at this point in the death spiral, realizing what management doesn't. The final consequence is usually the ousting of the project manager. The management team is convinced that if they had done it their way from the beginning there wouldn't be an issue and the only aspect that requires correction is the replacement of the project manager. The new project manager is doomed for failure as well, unless he or she can demonstrate superior technical, managerial, and leadership skills. Even then it is an uphill battle.

Another symptom of this failure type is that management believes that they are experiencing this problem with many of the projects in their purview. Unbelievably (to management) many of the projects are suffering the same lack of proper project management and morale is bad within their entire organization.

Specific symptoms include high attrition among project managers as well as low morale among all of the staff. Additionally, conflict is typical between the project managers and the management.

TYPICAL CAUSES

The causes of the Brawl AntiPattern are similar for each failure type. In fact, there may be primary causes that exist outside of the organization. These external, primary causes drive management to take risks and place young inexperienced personnel into project management positions. A good example of this is a tight labor market, especially when individuals with technical skills come at a premium and must be paid a premium. An organization may feel that spending money on technical skills is necessary, but may skimp on paying for good project managers. The truth is, and has always been, that you get what you pay for—as the old adage states, "Pay me now or pay me later." Perhaps a variation on this would be, "Pay me now or pay me a lot more later." Nevertheless, there are specific causes to each of the failure types of this AntiPattern.

The Project Manager

The typical cause of the Project Manager failure type is management's misinterpretation of an individual's leadership skills, based on the extrapolation of his or her management skills. Fundamentally, this results from management's lack of understanding of the difference between management and leadership. While the individual may in fact have great potential for becoming a good leader, and may survive to become one, he or she lacks the knowledge and experience to become a good project manager.

The Mismatched Project Manager

Just as with the Project Manager failure type, the Mismatched Project Manager failure type is the result of not thoroughly understanding the difference between leadership and management, which results in poor judgement on the part of management. Regardless of the variation of this failure type, management extrapolates a data point to arrive at an illogical conclusion. Specifically, in the case of the individual who is given a project management position as a result of good credentials, management believes that the credentials justify the promotion or hiring. This action may be precipitated by the lack of otherwise qualified personnel to fill the job for the salary offered by the organization. Regardless, it is a poor decision that will more than likely cost more in the long run than if the organization had acquired a more qualified individual.

The cause that results from the second variation of this failure type, where the technologist is promoted into a project leadership position, is typical of organizations that fail to provide well-delineated paths for promoting and compensating technical personnel. The technical personnel are forced to enter management in order to move ahead, both financially and otherwise. Another cause that results from this variation is essentially the same as the first variation: poor judgement on the part of management. It is all too common that good engineers and programmers are promoted and become bad project managers.

The Unempowered Project Manager

The first variation of the Unempowered Project Manager failure type, where management insists on running the project and not letting the project manager do the job, is common when managers are promoted from project management into upper management. They lose the thrill of being a project manager and don't believe that anyone is as good a project manager as they were (otherwise they would have been promoted into this upper-level position, thinks the egotistical manager). These managers are extremely dangerous and must be handled with extreme caution. They believe that they are no longer the project manager for one project but for several. In fact this type of manager can wipe out an organization very quickly. The reality is that the manager can't run the project effectively from this vantage point; that is why they hired a project manager.

The second variation for this failure type is truly the failing of the project manager; however, the response by management is equally failing by constantly overruling the project manager. Nevertheless, the cause of this failure type variation is due to the lack of leadership, commitment, expertise, and (for lack of a better word) marketing on the part of the project manager. The project manager often presents problems without solutions and without instilling enough confidence for management to believe that resolutions are being pursued with an appropriate risk mitigation strategy. The project manager is often perceived as having only problems and no solutions or successes. Additionally, the project manager may not be technically adept at presenting technical solutions; however, because of insecurity, he or she refuses to let anyone provide a briefing. Management is not only unimpressed with the project manager but also with the direction of the project and begins to intervene. This is typically the start of the project death spiral.

 KNOWN EXCEPTIONS

It should be clear that these are specific instances of failure and that the Brawl AntiPattern does not apply in all cases. There are some technologists that (arguably) make tremendous leaders—for example, Bill Gates. Additionally, there are individuals that have the persona and charisma that enable them to succeed in nearly any circumstance, regardless of what deficiencies they may appear to have in terms of leadership ability or otherwise. Persona and charisma are not the keys to leadership skills, but they are strong characteristics that enable some individuals to succeed as leaders.

There are also instances where good, strong managers who do not possess leadership ability still succeed as project managers. These individuals finesse the circumstances and succeed on pure will and hard work. While the end is achieved, the means usually has side effects and the costs are high. These are instances where there can be significant burnout by the staff, and hence attrition.

REFACTORED SOLUTION

The refactored solution is primarily to ensure that a project manager also knows how to lead a project, not just manage it. In addition, the management techniques must be positive and proactive to be successful.

Leadership 101: An Introduction to Leadership Concepts

Understanding leadership is the key to the refactored solution. It is critical that an understanding of the difference between management and leadership be established as well. While the Brawl AntiPattern attempts to identify some of the fundamentals of leadership, it is in no way a complete dissertation on the subject. That said, there are a multitude of texts on the subject matter.

Probably one of the most taught and practiced leadership concepts today was first developed by Paul Hersey and Kenneth Blanchard in the sixties and is called Situational Leadership. The models are based on the premise that there are four different states that followers can exist within, and within each of those states different leadership styles are necessary to achieve the desired results. The model is commonly displayed on two axes divided into quadrants (see Figure 2.18). The model is much more complex than the Brawl AntiPattern is capable of addressing; however, the essence is that there is no singular way to approach leadership. It depends on the situation. Software project managers should familiarize themselves with this approach to leadership, even if they do not subscribe to it. One of the best sources for this information is *Leadership and the One Minute Manager* [Blanchard 1985].

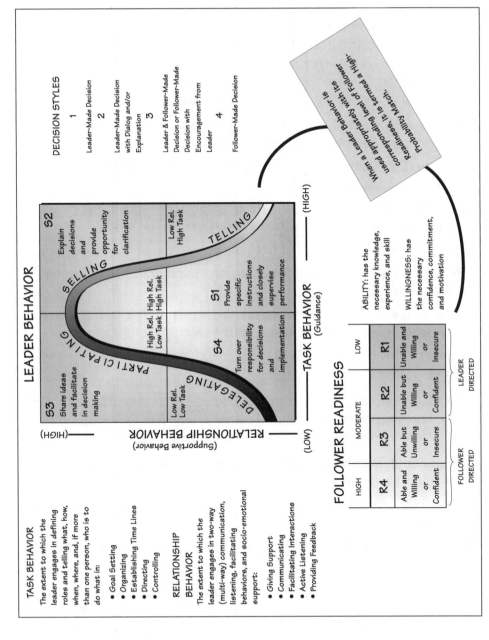

Figure 2.18 Expanded situational leadership model.

Similar to the concept that leadership style is situational and individual, so is the means by which a leader establishes power. This is commonly referred to as the leader's power base. The power base is the power perceived by the followers of the leader. The power base used or exhibited by the leader is indicative of the leadership style characterized by the individual. There is no right or wrong power base, but understanding the perceived source of power is extremely valuable in understanding how to motivate. The power bases of the leader are listed here [Hersey 1996]:

Coercive. Power is derived from the perceived ability to provide sanctions or consequences for nonperformance.

Connection. Power is derived from the association with influential persons or organizations.

Reward. Power is derived from the perception to provide compensation for things that followers would like to have.

Legitimate. Power is derived from the perception of title or position.

Referent. Power is derived from the perception of admiration and personal esteem.

Information. Power is derived from the perception of having access to or being in possession of useful information.

Expert. Power is derived from the perception of education, experience, and expertise.

The final concept presented in this section is an understanding of the three competencies of leadership [Hersey 1996]. The following represent the skills required to be a successful leader, regardless of other strengths:

Diagnosing. Understanding the situation now and what your desired result is for the future.

Adapting. Adapting and finding the resources to accomplish the desired result.

Communicating. Interacting effectively with others to achieve the result.

This introduction to leadership concepts is presented as a means to acquaint project managers with some leadership concepts of which they may not be currently familiar. Additionally, it is intended to be a seed for those not familiar with leadership concepts to further pursue and gain a greater understanding of how to be a good leader.

Just as leadership styles and approach vary with the situation, refactored solutions also vary with the situation. Specifically, the refactored solution depends on where you are in the project lifecycle or if you are in a project death spiral. It is also dependent on many circumstances within the specific organizational and cultural environment of your development effort. Therefore, each solution should be tailored for your specific situation.

Learning to Be a Leader

The first and foremost step to refactoring a solution for this AntiPattern is to establish a project management course that teaches not only project management but also leadership. This is an excellent way to create a common baseline for all project managers to follow. It is an opportunity to share common practices, tools, and guides for project management within your organization. Additionally, it introduces project managers to one another, creating a support base not just to discuss leadership problems but also to share resources via an informal network. A more pragmatic approach is a mentoring program. New project managers should be placed in assistant project manager or other suitable management roles that enable them to learn the ropes under the guidance of an experienced project manager. This part of the solution addresses all three failure types.

Career Path for Management

The second step to refactoring a solution is to establish separate management and technical tracks within your organization, with clearly defined levels of responsibility. This means that there are distinctive positions that are visibly obvious to staff members for achieving the next level and appropriate compensation. Because some organizations compensate project managers more than technologists, and the career path appears to lead to higher positions, many technologists apply for project management positions when it's not truly their desire. When this happens, both the individual and the organization lose because the organization will gain an unhappy, unproductive project manager (and undoubtedly a poor leader), and they will have lost a good technologist. The individual loses because he or she won't be satisfied and more than likely fail in the role of project manager. This part of the solution addresses all three failure types, but especially the second failure type: the Mismatched Project Manager. The remaining solutions are particular to the failure type.

The Project Manager and the Mismatched Project Manager

The Project Manager and the Mismatched Project Manager failure types are the most hopeful of the three. The individual probably requires training and experience, which more than likely will produce a good leader. The exception may be the second variation of the Mismatched Project Manager failure type, where the technologist is motivated to take a management position to achieve greater compensation. A technologist will usually have little experience in leadership or management, making the successful transition to a project management role unlikely.

Nevertheless, given that the project is in the throes of the project death spiral, the project manager should be removed immediately. While this is extremely humiliating for the individual, it is perhaps the only chance of recovering the project. The project manager should be informed that the failure resides with management's inability to properly access the maturity of the individual's capabilities and that management fully intends to provide training and eventually reinstate the individual in a project management position.

The new project manager will need to fully assess the situation and determine if the project is capable of recovering. It is important that he or she arrive at that conclusion independent of management's assessment. In some instances it will be difficult to find a replacement project manager. It should be explained to the incoming project manager that management is aware of the situation and that while they believe the new project manager can recover the project, he or she won't be held accountable if that isn't possible. The incoming project manager should expect to spend a tremendous amount of time to achieve recovery. Existing project schedule, budget, and deliveries will need to be evaluated, adjusted, and negotiated with management and the customer soon after the transition. This type of solution assumes a tremendous amount of risk and is highly dependent on environmental factors like the quality of the development team.

The Unempowered Project Manager

This refactored solution addresses the first variation (micro-management) of the Unempowered Project Manager failure type. The second variation (weak leader) of this failure type can be addressed by the refactored solutions that have been described so far.

This is the most difficult variation of the AntiPattern to refactor. To a great extent it can be resolved by the project management training program discussed previously, which should establish the role of the project manager and the role of management (assuming that management attends the course as well). The project management training program should address specific issues such as micro-management and provide an anonymous 360 degree review, enabling peers and project managers to provide specific comments to management about their techniques. Finally, the training program should assure and reduce any doubt on the part of management about the project manager's abilities.

There is little the project manager can do except confront management about their micro-management techniques. This is a high risk career move and should only be contemplated if the environment is conducive to such a showdown. Generally, micro-management produces a volatile work environment with initially a great deal of confrontation (there is no project big enough for two project leaders). The confrontation generally declines as either the manager feels more confident about the project manager and relaxes his or her grip or the project manager acquiesces to the micro-management.

The other option that can occur is that the project manager leaves. High attrition, especially by the project managers, and low morale are definite indicators of this failure-type variation. Often micro-management is transient because the behavior is the result of a new manager or a new project manager. In either instance the manager is not confident about the abilities of the project manager; however, over time confidence is gained. It is hoped that management can maintain an open and unbiased perspective of themselves and recognize such failings should they occur.

 ## VARIATIONS

The predominate variations have been discussed within this AntiPattern; however, there are less common variations where the lack of leadership leads to similar results.

The Project Manager variation is a person in the role who cannot deal effectively with problems as they arise and allows the symptoms and consequences to rapidly become worse until the project fails completely.

The Mismatched Project Manager is someone promoted into the role with a strong technology background but little knowledge of either management or leadership.

The Unempowered Project Manager is given the position as a token but the immediate superiors take direct control of the project, bypassing the appointed project manager.

EXAMPLE

Sometimes a small project is perceived as highly successful and overnight grows to become an enormous program that includes a research and development effort, as well as an extended deployment of the existing system. In this example, the project grew to over three times its initial size, both financially and in terms of the personnel on the project team. The project was now receiving the highest visibility in the organization. It was popular not only with the users, but also with the management.

The project manager was responsible for the concept on which the initial project was based, which resulted in the success of the project. He wasn't the best manager and relied heavily on subordinates to accomplish the administrative tasks. He also wasn't technically oriented; however, having come from the user community he knew what the user wanted and needed. He definitely wasn't a leader and failed to instill confidence in his management that he was able to execute the larger program for which he was now responsible. However, the project manager was resourceful and had some of the best task leaders working for him and had hired an outside consultant to get the very best technical help.

The project had clear goals and the project manager was highly committed to them. He aligned his staff to the goals and trusted the technical solutions that the technical team presented to him. The added management oversight grew from quarterly to monthly and then weekly meetings. The project manager was unable to defend technical and programmatic decisions personally; therefore, management requested briefings directly from the task leaders. By this point, hostilities and emotions were high. The management was questioning everything the project team had decided on, adding to the hostilities between the team and management.

In parallel with the conflict that existed with the project team, management was promoting the project at every opportunity because they knew their success was tied to the success of the project. Upper management wanted the system deployed as quickly as possible and management was happy to comply. Management's willingness to appease resulted in new goals for the project team, which compressed the schedule and increased functionality requirements. This presented the project team with new challenges. Yet, the success of the first project continued to motivate the project team and they modified the project plan to address the new challenges.

The project team revised the project plan and felt triumphant when they were able to overcome the challenges presented to them. Nevertheless, management was relentless, and began questioning the architectural solution the team had decided on, demanding more cost-effective solutions. Management once again directed the project team to make the change and without relief to the schedule; management assumed the collateral impact was negligible. Again, the project manager did not attempt to contradict the management-imposed direction. The team once again set out to accomplish the task; however, this time with much less enthusiasm. The project manager was angry since now the morale of the team had been shattered. The consultant advised against a reengineering of the architecture at this late point in the schedule; however, management was adamant.

The first casualty was the loss of the lead developer, resulting in increased morale problems. The next loss was the network security specialist. This sent the project team into dismal depths. The project manager attempted to reignite the team, but with no faith in his leadership progress continued to decline. Management continued to put the pressure on the team and acquired a new development leader, but with no relief in the already compressed schedule. Eventually, progress became so minimal and morale so low, the project was declared dead. The project death spiral concluded.

 ## RELATED SOLUTIONS

The Irrational Management and the Project Mismanagement AntiPatterns [Brown 1998] are both relevant to this particular AntiPattern. These are more generic AntiPatterns that deal with larger-scale development environments and deal more directly with management than leadership. Their refactored solutions deal with some of the required project management techniques required to be successful.

 ## APPLICABILITY TO OTHER VIEWPOINTS AND SCALES

The Brawl AntiPattern viewpoint is purely managerial because it deals with project management and leadership from a management perspective, and is directly applicable to the scales of system and application due to the focus being on an entire software development.

Size Isn't Everything

Name: Size Isn't Everything

Also Known As: How To Have a Baby in One Month with Nine Women

Most Applicable Scale: Enterprise

Refactored Solution Name: Trusted Cadre, or Rob-the-Rich

Refactored Solution Type: Role

Root Causes: Haste, Ignorance, Sloth

Unbalanced Forces: Management of IT Resources

Anecdotal Evidence:
> "Good news! I just hired three Java experts for your project! Please get them started in right away—they're expensive, and we can't afford for them to be sitting around, OK? Oh, and by the way, how's the design coming along?"
> "Well, if it will get us ahead we can hire another three teams and put them all on parallel component development and deliver earlier for more money. But it'll be worth it!"

BACKGROUND

The Size Isn't Everything AntiPattern is concerned with how people affect each other as more people are added to complete a project. Theoretically, the more people that cooperate on a single task, the more work that will be accomplished, more quickly (see Figure 2.19).

In fact, when this proves true it is because of a synergetic phenomenon, where each person actually enables the others to do more than they could have done alone. Often one person will not think of all options, hits dead ends, or runs out of steam. When a second person is added this creates alternative approaches and feedback, which somewhat resolves the disadvantages of a single person. Sometimes the two people may take alternative stances and disagree, which results in a stalemate and lack of progress. Adding a third or even a fourth person can add a more balanced approach with broader views and converging consensus.

> **"A cord of many strands is not easily broken."**
> **—Ecclesiastes 4:12**

For example, consider designing a Web site. One designer can only achieve so much, but three or four designers collaborating on the development would be able to cooperatively produce a conceptual design and then

Figure 2.19 The more the merrier.

split the detailed design between them, sharing in the coordination and approval of the detailed design.

Unfortunately the reverse is also a possibility: People can get in each other's way, thereby reducing individual effectiveness. If ten people were put on a task where four people were successfully progressing, chances are that the committee phenomenon would occur, causing endless debate and slowing down the entire progress. All activities require an appropriate number of people with the correct skills to achieve it in an effective and efficient manner.

Using the example above, the ten designers are more likely to waste time endlessly debating details rather than progressing toward a finished product. The sheer number of designers would reduce the chance of agreement because they would form into subgroups with alternative approaches and stop forward progress because of semantic differences. This would be much worse than having only a single designer. Also, some tasks require a certain amount of time to accomplish, no matter how many people cooperate. No matter how many painters you hire, it still takes the same amount of time for the paint to dry. You may be able to speed up related tasks, such as the actual application of paint, but even that process is only scaleable to the extent that painters have enough space to actually work. The same is true with software development. Some basic tasks require a specific amount of time regardless of the number of people applied against it because they are a factor of absolute time, not time per resource.

GENERAL FORM

It is intuitive that the potential production capability of a team is the sum of the potential production capability of the individual members of the team. The graph in Figure 2.20 implies that as long as there are no additional factors affecting productivity, one merely needs to increase the number of producers in order to increase total production.

Unfortunately, as Figure 2.21 shows, the rate of interference between team members increases with the density of the team within a specific domain (or, as you add more painters, they bump into each other more often). This result seems obvious, but the increase of interference and accompanying drop in productivity will vary somewhat and is dependent on the domain space.

There are several factors that modify the interference density within a specific environment. One well-known case is the ever-popular cubicles-versus-offices debate. Cubicles have a lot to offer in modern-day software development because according to Whitaker [1994]:

Figure 2.20 Raw production curve.

- They're cheaper to maintain than offices.
- They're fashionable.
- They foster communication.
- They use space effectively.
- They inspire teamwork.
- They provide visibility to management.

However, cubicles also increase staff density and result in increased interference in the following ways:

- Frequent complaints that noise is preventing people from concentrating
- Increased ad hoc hallway discussions (typically unrelated to production)
- Increased animosity between team members
- Voluntary changes work hours (even against their personal preferences)
- Pressure to answer neighbors' constantly ringing phones (also compounded by the cost-saving reduction in administrative support)
- Conflicts over conference room availability

Figure 2.21 Interference density curve.

The properties of cubical existence result in frequent disruptions in an individual's concentration and can have a compounding effect when a person who is interrupted proceeds to interrupt others (e.g., "Since I can't concentrate, maybe I'll see if it's a good time for that meeting with Jim"). The process is much like a nuclear chain reaction becoming critical. Eventually practically no one can accomplish anything that is even remotely mentally challenging. Meanwhile other aspects of human performance tend to diminish as well, such as patience, cooperation, morale, and ultimately productivity.

DeMarco and Lister point out that as work environment noise increases not only does productivity decrease, but also, after experiencing a physical interruption, it can take up to half an hour for staff to regain the intensity of their concentration for a task [DeMarco 1987].

Thus, the obvious productivity curve is lost as the individual is prevented from producing. If there are enough interruptions, productivity can be completely eliminated (see Figure 2.22).

Somehow, managers must find a way to maximize the raw potential for production while minimizing the impact of staff-density interference. This can be represented as an optimization of curves problem, which can yield a point of optimum size for an organization at any given point in context, as shown in Figure 2.23. In other words, don't overstaff or understaff a project and, moreover, give the developers some privacy to work in so they do not constantly interrupt each other.

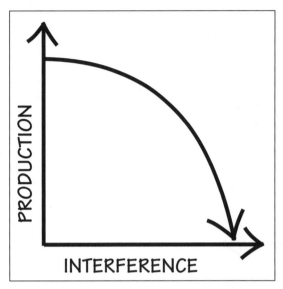

Figure 2.22 Productivity loss due to interference curve.

Too Many Cooks

Figure 2.23 represents a complex justification of the old adage, "Too many cooks spoil the soup." The reasons are interdependent and therefore hard to model in a statistical fashion, but the basic idea is that adding staff to a project isn't always the best thing to do. At certain stages in development it is exactly the worst thing to do. For example, during the time when system design should be accomplished, an oversized design staff will typically produce an initial crude predesign division of the effort into design teams, without true analysis and partitioning of the system. DeMarco writes that since "most projects are effectively overstaffed during the period when design should be done . . . most projects [don't] get any real design done" [DeMarco 1997].

Furthermore, adding staff may falsely *appear* to have been a great idea (sometimes for a surprisingly long time). This is especially true on large-scale projects because process metrics *seem* to improve as the standard process gains rigorous support and "as long as it generates sufficient work (useful or not) to keep everyone busy" [DeMarco 1997].

Too Few Indians

On the other hand, there is indeed a time when the addition of staff is the absolute most prudent thing to do. This is "when the detailed, low-level

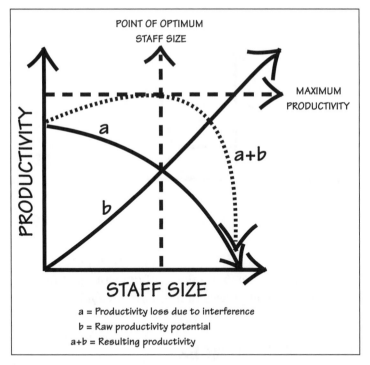

Figure 2.23   Optimization of productivity to staff size curve.

modular design is done, [and] opportunities for splitting up the work explode" [DeMarco 1997]. This is an example where the traditional thinking is wrong and is especially deadly to "aggressively scheduled" projects. Aggressive projects tend to get a lot of resources allocated from the start, to "help them with their challenging schedule," but then they have trouble keeping all those people gainfully occupied during the first two-thirds of the project. The result is that when the project is actually ready for a large staff (if it ever gets that far), upper management is loath to provide additional people since so much staff money has already been spent. In this scenario, everyone loses: the manager, project leaders, and the staff as morale dies on the vine.

Staffing Needs Vary over Time

It is clear then that, in reality, most software development projects require variable staffing based on the nature of work required at each phase. This is because there is indeed an optimal number of appropriately skilled staff for each kind of task (see Figure 2.24).

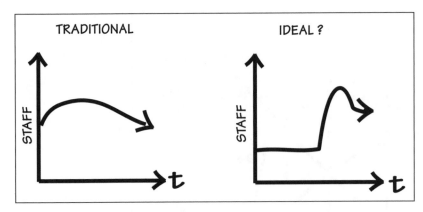

Figure 2.24   Optimization of staffing.

Using a waterfall approach for a new application development as an example, Table 2.5 identifies approximate numbers of development personnel necessary for some of the typical phases of a project lifecycle.

SYMPTOMS AND CONSEQUENCES

The following list of symptoms and their consequences are potential warning signs that may indicate a lurking Size Isn't Everything AntiPattern:

Table 2.5   Variable Project Staffing Levels

SOFTWARE DEVELOPMENT PHASE	STAFFING ROLES NEEDED	TOTAL STAFF
Software concept	1 project manager and 1 analyst	2
Requirements analysis	1 project manager and 4 analysts	5
Architecture design	1 project manager and 2 architects	3
Detailed design	1 project manager, 2 architects, and 4 designers	7
Coding and debugging	1 project manager, 4 designers, and 6 programmers	11
Testing	1 project manager, 4 testers, and 6 programmers	11
Operations and maintenance	2 help desk staff and 1 engineer programmer	3

- Early overstaffing results in forced design shortcuts (to give all those people something to do) [DeMarco 1994].

- Management focused on building staff but unable to describe or assign new staff to specific tasks.

- Frequent "carpeting" of midlevel managers for not using all their project resources effectively.

- Frequent "all hands" meetings called by management to determine the status of the development effort.

- Parallel tasking of dependent activities resulting in frequent deadlocks which are creatively handled by frequent task hopping by teams.

- System design and component breakdown reflects staffing organization more than it reflects any proper systems analysis.

Failure to recognize these warnings or the increasingly frequent consequences will result in incremental delivery delays, cost overruns, and eventual technical failure.

 ## TYPICAL CAUSES

The causes of the Size Isn't Everything AntiPattern are few and simple. Tendencies in the following areas should be carefully checked against the preceding Symptoms and Consequences in order to detect this AntiPattern as early as possible:

- Overstaffing in architecture design phase

- Understaffing in later development steps

- Overzealous hoarding of personnel resources early in project so that resources will be there when needed

- Mistaken belief that increasing staff will increase software delivery rate

 ## KNOWN EXCEPTIONS

There are no real exceptions to the Size Isn't Everything AntiPattern because understaffing or overstaffing always results in problems. The number of resources should be allocated as close as possible to what is truly appropriate for the current phase of a project. Obviously, a small amount of understaffing or overstaffing can be accommodated and may not cause serious software delivery problems right away. But watch out: Long-term impact may be a hidden future result. For example, short-staffed projects may be successful, but the true cost may not be felt until after delivery when your best people flee to lower-stress, better-managed companies, leaving you with an even worse staffing problem.

REFACTORED SOLUTION

The refactored solution to this AntiPattern will vary depending on whether the staff used will work across the software development phases. If so, this constant staffing can have the added benefit of greatly reducing risk because the requirements and architecture understanding will be carried through the full development cycle rather than handed over to another group of staff who must gain their understanding from documentation, company folklore, or software archeology.

Incrementally Growing the Staffing

This version of the refactored solution assumes retention of staff throughout the project. The project manager must identify the software development lifecycle to be followed; this will define what level of overlap between phases must occur. The more overlap required, the more staff required. The initial staffing should be identified for each phase, and then the increase caused by the overlapping phases will be relatively simple to calculate as shown in Table 2.6. Note that the project manager is one of the staff and as such is not counted twice in overlapping phases.

Growing Staffing by Replacement

This version of the refactored solution assumes nonretention of staff throughout the project. If productivity is to be maintained, any new staff must be added to the project early enough to be able to come up to speed prior to taking their primary role in the project. This learning curve can be very steep because modern software projects are increasingly complex and technically very challenging. Just assimilating the project documentation can take weeks before a new staff member is really ready to start performing at near maximum productivity. If people are not given time to assimilate, momentum will probably be lost; there will be dead periods during which

Table 2.6 Overlapping Phase Staffing Levels

SOFTWARE DEVELOPMENT PHASE	OVERLAP	NON-OVERLAPPED STAFFING LEVELS	OVERLAPPED STAFFING LEVELS
Software concept	N/A	2	2
Requirements analysis	N/A	5	5
Architecture design	In parallel with requirements analysis	3	7
Detailed design	1 month with architecture design	7	7 until final month, then 13
Coding and debugging	2 months with detailed design	11	11 until final 2 months, then 17
Testing	2 months with coding and debugging	11	11 until final 2 months, then 21

the new staff are on a learning curve and cannot develop software. One additional problem with this approach involves the challenge of getting new staff members to engage early during an allotted assimilation period and commence tackling the learning curves. Depending on the professionalism of the individual new staff member, you may have to just throw them into the fray right away for a week or two to make them appropriately appreciative of the project's complexity, and then pull them back again for an assimilation period. Although this is a difficult way of tackling the problem of coming up to speed rapidly, it can be effective. Table 2.7 identifies the more rapid increase in staffing levels caused by this approach.

VARIATIONS

The variations of Size Isn't Everything identify the impact of staff with software development experience at extreme ends of the spectrum.

Trusted Cadre and Software Heroes

Where a core team of highly integrated, very skilled, and mutually supportive people already exists, and where that team has some kind of protection

Table 2.7   Impact of Adding New Staff

SOFTWARE DEVELOPMENT PHASE	OVERLAP	OVERLAPPED STAFFING LEVELS	NEW STAFF STAFFING LEVELS
Software concept	N/A	2	2
Requirements analysis	N/A	5	5
Architecture design	In parallel with requirements analysis	7	7
Detailed design	1 month with architectures design	7 until final month, then 13	13
Coding and debugging	2 months with detailed design	11 until final 2 months, then 17	17
Testing	2 months with coding and debugging	11 until final 2 months, then 21	21

by a senior manager from those who would raid the team for their expertise on some other project, a *trusted cadre* can occur. This cadre can have an uncanny ability to effectively manage itself and deal with inappropriate staffing levels internally. This often involves *software heroes* and sacrificial work hours, but if the team's reputation is on the line, pride and esprit de corps will often be sufficient to ensure success. This is risky, however, and can cost dearly since cadres usually stick together and as such will all leave together if abused in this way too frequently.

Warm Bodies

Another variation to the Size Isn't Everything AntiPattern is the Warm Bodies AntiPattern [Brown 1998], which can occur if you add non-productive staff or add staff to any phase too early. Staffing levels are challenging and anything but stable. This is a crucial skill area for a successful software manager to develop: knowing when to add staff, choosing the right staff, and identifying (thereby avoiding) dead wood, that is, developers who are ineffective.

 EXAMPLE

A project that one of us recently participated in involved a very aggressive technological challenge and faced a very near-term must-deliver drop-dead date. Senior decision makers had made promises they were unable to back away from, but the complexity of which they really didn't comprehend. It fell to the design and implementation team that had a decent track record for pulling off such miracles to succeed.

The team was given the following promises:

- You can have whatever staff you need to accomplish this project by the delivery date.

- You can have any available tools and resources necessary to succeed.

- The requirements will not change.

- Final decisions on all outstanding design issues will be resolved by appropriate approval authorities six months prior to delivery and two months before development commences.

Almost from day one, senior management proceeded to add all kinds of staff to the team, thinking that they were being incredibly supportive and helpful. The opposite was true, but the team managed to find things for these people to do to prepare them for the upcoming development push by somewhat reducing the imminent learning curve they would face with the new development environment we were using.

Because the team started out as a trusted cadre, the high-level system design was accomplished and vetted by all approval authorities very quickly. Several critical design decisions were identified that needed high-level directive because they would have dramatic impact on any further levels of design detail. Because of these early successes and excellent products, senior management became overconfident and cocky with their peers and were talked into promising increased system capabilities, which had the compounding effects of increasing overall system complexity, changing the system requirements, and radically changing the high-level system architecture. These changes required extensive vetting of a lower-confidence design with the same approval bodies that had already been vetted the previous high-level design. This, in turn, jeopardized the project's credibility with these boards and resulted in closer scrutiny and a dramatic increase in effort to prepare for and follow up on these briefings.

At this point, a modified schedule was submitted, showing a 30-day slip in delivery date, and senior management literally had a conniption. Expenses were analyzed showing a tremendous rate of project expenditure (all those extra warm bodies waiting for the development phase), and a desperate panic began. Our very carefully laid out project plan was modified in every way imaginable, mandatory overtime was implemented, and the final deliverable was redefined almost weekly.

Finally, senior decision makers asked what else they could do (they were sincere!), and we asked for and were given back enough control of staffing to regain momentum. Three key engineers, with extensive experience on similar projects, were taken off-site to finalize the system requirements and given authority to cast them in stone on their return. Thus, a written requirements specification, incorporating all the absolutely critical requirements and deferring nearly all "nice to haves" was vetted. From this, a different and smaller team comprised of two very experienced developers and one expert technical writer isolated themselves for five days and produced a very detailed system-design document based on the requirements and use cases written to clearly explain the requirements.

A senior level design review was conducted with the proviso that "No additional system functionality ideas or modifications would be entertained (period!)." Then a crack team of developers began to code the design. Other staff assigned to the project were directed to tasks that diverted them from interacting with these developers as much as possible. Some were even let go altogether (one in particular who was a very capable engineer but was found to create turmoil and cause conflict—see the Corncob AntiPattern [Brown 1998]).

In a sense, midlevel decision makers unwittingly implemented a FireDrill AntiPattern [Brown 1998] to clarify the pending disaster and gain the authority over the project staff necessary to succeed.

Other compromises were negotiated, such as the logical assessment that while we could not completely forgo testing (unless there was something produced that needed to be tested), it was pointless to blindly stick to a testing date. So the schedule was adjusted to provide more development time at the expense of 30 percent of the time planned to test. This was risky, to be sure, but the lesser of evils.

 ## RELATED SOLUTIONS

The FireDrill AntiPattern [Brown 1998] exists when project managers drive development by creating false emergencies to break up logjams, usually as an automatic reaction to some external event. The refactored solution is to shelter the project development staff by creating an internal project environment that the development staff works within and an external one where the project manager deals with the customers, bosses, and other external impacts upon the software development. The management reaction to self-caused firedrills is often to indiscriminately add more bodies as a solution to the perceived logjam in development.

APPLICABILITY TO OTHER VIEWPOINTS AND SCALES

The management of staff size affects all people that compose a project's staff resources. When managed effectively, proper staffing benefits everyone. Unfortunately, this is really a top-down concept and must be viewed as such by senior decision makers. They must take on the responsibility of being cognizant and involved enough in the details of a project to accurately assess true staffing needs at any given moment. They must also work hard to anticipate future staffing requirement shifts—they are as certain to be necessary as the rising of the sun. This process takes consistent effort. Unfortunately, it is also work that can be cursorily monitored or even completely sidestepped by lazy managers for a long time before drastic steps will be required.

Chaos

AntiPattern Name: Chaos

Also Known As: The More Things Change, The More Things Change

Most Applicable Scale: Enterprise

Refactored Solution Name: A Sea of Calm

Refactored Solution Type: Role

Root Causes: Haste, Sloth, or Ignorance

Unbalanced Forces: Management of Change

Anecdotal Evidence:
"The only person who likes change is a baby with a wet diaper!"

—Mark Twain

". . . we share Warren Bennis's definition of leadership as the process of creating and implementing a vision. To be a leader, therefore, implies that you must learn to love change because it is intrinsic to the leadership process. Leaders must overcome their resistance to change and become change managers." [Hersey 1996]

"Recently I was talking to one of Japan's best foreign-exchange dealers, and I asked him to name the factors he considered in buying and selling. He said, 'many factors, sometimes very short-term, and some medium, and some long-term.' I became very interested when he said he considered the long term and asked him what he meant by that time frame. He paused a few seconds and replied with genuine seriousness. 'Probably ten minutes.' That is the way the market is moving these days."

—Toyoo Gyohten, Former vice-minister
Japanese Ministry of Finance
Change Fortunes (with Paul Volcker) [Peters 1992]

BACKGROUND

Nearly one third of all software projects are cancelled; two-thirds of all software projects encounter cost overruns in excess of 200 percent and over 80 percent of all software projects are deemed failures [Brown 1998]. In most cases the reason for the high failure rate in software development is not because the project was poorly planned, but rather that the project didn't execute as planned. The project was presented with changes and the inability of the project manager to adapt to those changes resulted in a failure to achieve the goals of the project: cost, schedule, or quality.

Most textbooks and classes instruct students in the proper way to plan and execute a software development project. However, very few, if any, address how to adapt to changes once the project is under way and the pressure is on. The reason is simple: It is impossible to anticipate the many variables and teach all possible changes for planning purposes. This is to say nothing of the combinations of changes that could occur or the time variance of each of these changes. Obviously, the better the plan, the less changes that should occur; minimizing changes should be a primary objective of the plan (risk mitigation strategy). Yet the project manager does not have all elements of the universe under his or her control and, therefore, the chaos that abounds in the world is destined to enter into the project at some unexpected point. Understanding the concept of change and how it affects the project and the project organization is critical to adapting and overcoming the challenge of change.

The U.S. Marine Corps is one of the most successful military organizations in the world. The reasons for their success are many; however, the embodiment of "adapt, overcome, succeed" as the fundamental fabric of their training enables their success. (Some may argue that fighting a battle is no different than fielding software, although the stakes are likely to be less critical.) Nevertheless, it is the ability to adapt and overcome that enables software projects to succeed. The Chaos AntiPattern will address the impact of change on a project and provide a refactored solution for dealing with change.

GENERAL FORM

It is first important to understand what *change* is and the context in which it is presented. However, defining change is difficult and discriminating between change and stability is nearly impossible. *Change* is a process that is ongoing and stability is a state or a stage within that process. The context that change presents itself is in either a planned environment (e.g., we are going to migrate the architecture) or an unanticipated environment (e.g., our lead developer was just killed by a truck). In either of these situations, the change that results can either have strategic (i.e., beyond the project, probably organizational) or tactical (directly related to the project) impact (see Figure 2.25). Regardless, whether change is planned or unanticipated, strategic or tactical, it wreaks havoc on employees, organizations, and projects. Understanding the concepts of change is critical to being able to identify and understand the general form of the AntiPattern. Yet like many broad topics, it is impossible to provide a thorough examination of the subject of change in an AntiPattern. Therefore, the focus for the Chaos AntiPattern will be on the impact of change, since the impact reflects the way that change affects the project and, hence, the project manager. The impact of change can be separated into organizational impact, individual impact, and project impact.

While it remains impossible to separate the impact of change on the organization, individual, or project, for the purposes of this AntiPattern the impact of change will be discussed singularly, from each of those perspectives. It must be recognized that the impact to the individual is ubiquitous regardless. For example, a change to the project, perhaps a slip in the deployment date, has finite and specific results for the individuals working on that project. It is the impact on the individual that should be the focus for the project manager, since this is where the greatest collateral impact will be realized.

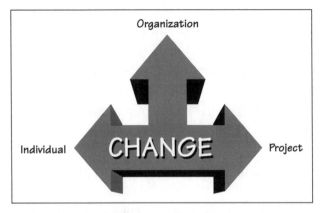

Figure 2.25 The impact of change.

Impact of Change on the Organization

Change that impacts the organization is most likely the result of strategic planning, which is more easily addressed by the project manager as it relates to project and development teams, since it can be predictable and deliberate. In *Managing Strategic Change*, Noel Tichy explains that organizational change is implemented through one of three strategic change models: technical, political, and cultural [Tichy 1983]. He further explains that these models are used to effect change and therefore impact the organization. The ways each of these change models impact the organization are subsequently articulated.

Technical

Technical changes affect the way in which an organization achieves its goals. The nature of the changes is usually one of the following:

- Technology changes that deal with the applications of specific technology within an organization that alter what technical solutions are applied
- Structural changes that deal with organizational structure within software development impacting how projects are staffed
- Strategic changes in software development doctrine that affects the entire software development culture

Political

Political changes affect the way the power base is employed.

- Promotion issues that raise the power (role and responsibility) of selected individuals
- Reward issues that acknowledge select individuals above others within the organization
- Shifts in power centers that shift control of resources and decision making between small groups within an organization
- External control that manipulates organizational decision making without consideration of the impact on individuals working for the organization
- Management changes that cause change within a hierarchy altering the profile and nature of the management

Cultural

Cultural changes affect what is deemed or perceived to be appropriate behavior.

- Performance-related values where a form of role model award is used to recognize contributions to success.

- Decision-making values where the decision criteria are handed down based on a single set of values that do not reflect flexibility in decision making.

- People-oriented values that are the criteria for judging the worth of contributors rather than other forms of success.

- Leadership styles that recognize the style of leadership of an individual to be superior to other styles.

A comprehensive understanding of how changes impact the organization and employees will enable the project manager to better assess solutions for addressing the impact. More important for the project manager is to understand how these changes impact the individual. Individuals represent the greatest variable in achieving project success.

Impact of Change on the Individual

Kenneth Blanchard is one of the world-renowned experts in the field of change management. In addition to his many texts, he provides lectures, and videos on the subject. His very powerful video, *Managing the Journey*, demonstrates the impact of change on individuals by taking the audience through a change exercise. At the conclusion of the exercise he aptly describes what people experience when encountering change:

- People will feel awkward, ill at ease, and self-conscious.
- People will think about what they have to give up.
- People will feel alone even if everyone else is going through the change.
- People can handle only so much change.
- People are at different levels of readiness for change.
- People will be concerned that they do not have enough resources.
- If you take the pressure off, people will revert back to the old behavior.

If you have ever participated in this exercise, it is easy to relate to each of these perceptions and realize the gravity of even minor, insignificant changes. If you have ever gone through a change on a project, you will also be able to quickly recognize the behavior described.

While the individuals working on the project are the most valuable and critical resource that a project manager has available, the ultimate goal must be the success of the project. It is crucial that the project manager understand the significance of both the impact of organizational change and the impact of individual change on the project.

Impact of Change on the Project

The impact of change on the project usually affects one or more of three strategic project facets: schedule, cost, and quality. There are definite relationships between each of these and typically the project manager is asked to ignore them (e.g., "We need the delivery moved up, but don't expect to get any additional personnel or other resources [costs]"). Balancing these three project attributes is perhaps the project manager's most difficult task (see Figure 2.26). A good project manager will recognize that if one element is changed, so must another to maintain equilibrium.

However, to put this in a more tangible context, the impact of change on a project is significant and can be realized through many of the AntiPatterns in this text as well as the two preceding texts by the same authors [Brown 1998, 1999]. Specific examples include compression and expansion.

Compression

Compression applies to any activity that is time based. A subsequent activity has less time available than either planned or required because an earlier activity overran (see Figure 2.27).

Schedule compression. This change may occur for many reasons, and the impact of the change is equally variable. Often when this change is realized by the project manager, all planning is abandoned [*Best Practices* 1996]. This results in the "hack 'n' go" mode of software development or the "just get it done" development approach. Of course a variance of this is an overly aggressive schedule. This variance begs the question, "When is schedule compression not considered schedule compression?" The answer is, "When the compression is accomplished early in the development lifecycle."

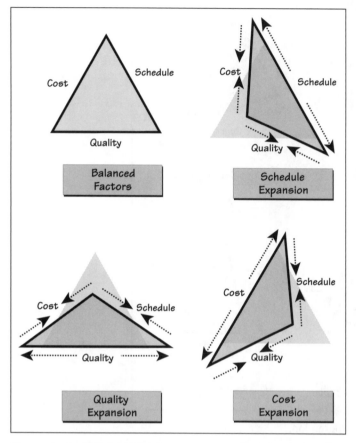

Figure 2.26 Relationships between cost, schedule, and quality.

Quality compression. This change can be brought about in an attempt to reduce cost or schedule; nevertheless, the impact of the change is obvious. Examples include a reduced testing schedule, reduced reviews, or a less than robust test environment. The frequent result is inversely proportional to the desired result, which includes lengthened schedule and increased cost. This is especially true if the quality compression occurs on the front end of the development cycle, where costs to correct problems downstream have been estimated at 50 to 200 times compared to upstream [McConnell 1998].

Cost compression. This change is often realized in many ways as well. However, consider the instance where management is attempting to reduce costs by limiting the development staff. Then at some point realizing their fatal error and the resulting degraded and compressed schedule, they decide to add developers after it is too late. This is a

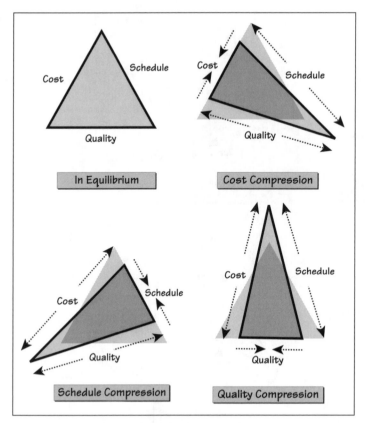

Figure 2.27   Types of compression.

frequent mistake and a change that only produces additional change [*Best Practices* 1996]. Bear in mind Brook's law: "Adding manpower to a late project only makes it later" [Brooks 1995].

Expansion

Expansion is rare for most projects. How many times have you heard, "Take a few extra months to get it done"? However, that is not necessarily the context this type of change implies. Expansion deals with the notional addition of time in the form of schedule, fitness for purpose of the software in the form of quality, and additional funding in the form of cost.

Schedule expansion. However, the context for schedule expansion change is usually after the realization that something has gone awry and the only reasonable solution is to protract the schedule to accomplish the delivery. While this is typically considered a good change, it occurs only after realizing that what was planned must be changed. The result is still change, and it must be dealt with accordingly. Remember that these types of changes will probably impact elements outside of this project, possibly by inflicting schedule compression on other projects. The schedule compression that typically results on outside projects can be caused by numerous factors related to the schedule protraction of the initial project, including reallocation of resources from one project to another to accommodate the change.

Quality expansion. This change can take on many facets; however, consider the AntiPatterns Analysis Paralysis and Requirements Jeopardy. Both of these AntiPatterns incite the expansion of the functionality or the quality of the system. The repercussions typically include both cost and schedule expansion. Nevertheless, there are always those instances where requirements creep takes place as well as a sudden change in testing philosophy that dictates greater rigor in testing of the system.

Cost expansion. This type of change is realized in two cases: the first is cost overrun and the second results from additional funding. While the latter is unusual, there are times when additional funding becomes available to pursue increased system functionality or capabilities. It is also possible that the project was underfunded and additional funding becomes available at some later point. Although many project managers might consider this a positive impact to the project, it is sometimes more complex. Consider an instance where additional funding for personnel becomes available later in the project. It is difficult to bring on new staff late in the schedule, but at the same time management frequently feels they have aided the project manager such that he or she should have no excuses for missing the schedule.

SYMPTOMS AND CONSEQUENCES

The symptoms of change within a project are most easily viewed by understanding the symptoms exhibited by the individuals going through change. Symptoms that are exhibited by the project are frequently the same symptoms that are seen in many of the AntiPatterns that evolve from improperly managed *change*. Individuals going through *change* usually go through four phases [Blanchard 1985]. Project managers must recognize these four phases in order to navigate the project to a successful conclusion. Blanchard describes the four phases:

Denial. A belief that nothing major is occurring.

Resistance. Can range from a negative attitude to all-out opposition.

Adaptation. Change begins to become accepted.

Involvement. Active participation in change, making contributions and suggestions, initiating work, and accepting things as they are.

The consequence of change, if properly managed, is nothing more than the intended result. The consequence of improperly managed change is an AntiPattern. Some examples of change, when it is improperly managed, include the following AntiPatterns shown in Table 2.8.

TYPICAL CAUSES

One of the major reasons that changes occur is that most development efforts are planned in advance of their deployment by as much as 18 months to two years. It is unreasonable to expect anyone to accurately predict the system requirements or organizational and environmental changes that will occur during that time frame. Beside the fact that it is difficult to plan the project in advance, the AntiPattern can result from poor planning, not only from a systemic perspective but also from a risk mitigation and change management perspective.

The second cause of this AntiPattern is the result of the project manager dealing poorly with change once it occurs. A third and final cause is the reluctance of management to respond appropriately to the project manager's requests when a change occurs, especially when management institutes the change.

KNOWN EXCEPTIONS

The Chaos AntiPattern is a universal truth—a law of project management. It builds on other laws of project management. It cannot be refuted. There are no exceptions.

REFACTORED SOLUTION

Defining a refactored solution for an AntiPattern of this granularity is difficult because there are either no specific cases or there are so many cases that it is impossible to define each refactored solution (see Figure 2.27). That said, there are four methods of addressing a refactored solution for

Table 2.8 Examples of Changes to Project Attributes and Related AntiPatterns

CHANGE TYPE	ANTIPATTERN NAME	ANTIPATTERN DESCRIPTION	REFACTORED SOLUTION
■ Quality expansion ■ Schedule compression	Analysis Paralysis [Brown 1998]	Striving for perfection and completeness in the analysis phase leads to project gridlock.	Incremental, iterative development processes defer the detailed analysis until the knowledge is available.
Schedule compression	Death by Planning [Brown 1998]	Excessive preplanning of software projects leads to postponement of development work and useless plans.	Pursue iterative software development process, which includes modest planning with known facts and incremental planning.
Schedule compression	Irrational Management [Brown 1998]	Habitual indecisiveness and other habits result in de facto decisions and development emergencies.	Use rational decision-making management techniques.
■ Quality compression ■ Schedule compression	Requirements Jeopardy [Brown 1999]	Requirements analysis is not performed or isn't properly submitted for configuration control.	Implementation of fundamental requirements analysis and configuration management processes.
Quality compression	Sure Thing [Brown 1999]	Testing is critical to a system, regardless of the size or complexity of the system.	Implementation of testing.
Quality compression	Failure to Audit [Brown 1999]	Failure to perform configuration audit.	Implementation of reviews and audits.

this high-level AntiPattern: (1) preemptive planning, (2) reactive planning, (3) a conceptual understanding of change, and (4) a state of mind that enables flexibility and adaptability.

Preemptive Change Planning

The preemptive planning for the most part is straightforward system engineering. Planning is the first step to minimizing change. Preparing for change is the next step as shown in Figure 2.28.

Planning for Change

It is necessary to plan for change rather than try to react to it because reacting is usually too late to successfully avoid some of the consequences.

- Preparing a realistic schedule with sufficient slack is critical (sufficient slack is an oxymoron). Sufficient slack is approximately 10 percent of the critical path. Anticipate schedule compression and plan how you will address it. Don't assume that an intermediate schedule slippage can be absorbed later [Yourdon 1997].

- Appropriately estimate staff and other resources. This should be accomplished in the context of your organization. "Structuring an organization for change is much harder than designing a system for change" [Brooks 1995].

- Develop a software development plan and stick to it.

- Regularly reevaluate the system size, staff effort, and schedules.

- Identify high-risk project areas and risk mitigation strategies. Specific dates that identify when a risk item is no longer viable for the project to pursue and still meet the schedule. These dates should be strictly adhered to.

Preparing for Change

Developing a change management process is critical to dealing with change. This is not the same as a configuration control. The change management process addresses all aspects of the project, technical and administrative, and depending on the size of the project may simply involve the project manager or a staff selected by the project manager. The process may be formal or informal but should be documented. This is extremely valuable later because should your decision to deal with change be challenged, you will

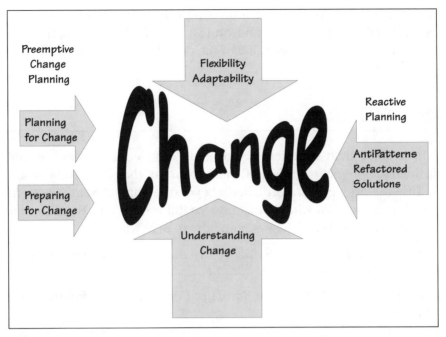

Figure 2.28   The significance of change.

need to recall your rationale and the environment at the time the decision was made. The change management process presented here is derived from *Effective Project Management* [Wysocki 1995].

- No change is insignificant. Recognize that you are probably dealing with only the tip of the iceberg when evaluating a change.

- Document every change that impacts the project. This should include not only the event, but also who and what precipitated the event, the environment in which it occurred, and the rationale behind the change.

- The project manager or team, as appropriate, must evaluate the potential impact of the change to the project. Creative responses must be formulated and considered (this is where flexibility and adaptability are important). Thinking out of the box is critical to success, and it is often desirable to garner outside, objective opinions. It is also very important to consider the impact of project response within the context of the larger organization or system. No project is an island.

- The project response to the change (if any) and the rationale for the response must be documented. If the presented change is one that could be selected for implementation, a project impact must be prepared. Finally, if the impact is beyond an identified threshold, management may need to be notified of the decision, with alternatives prepared as backup.

Reactive Planning

This is little more than experience and book knowledge. Beyond having gone through the project gauntlet and being aware of the pitfalls that await, there is little the project manager can do beyond reading about the experiences of others. The following books give useful insight into the different aspects of change, its consequences, and how to deal with it:

- *AntiPatterns: Refactoring Software, Architecture, and Projects in Crisis* [Brown 1998]
- *AntiPatterns and Patterns in Software Configuration Management* [Brown 1999]
- *Death March* [Yourdon 1997]
- *Constantine On Peopleware* [Constantine 1995]
- *Peopleware: Productive Projects and Teams* [DeMarco 1987]
- *The Soul of a New Machine* [Kidder 1987]

Understanding Change

This part of the refactored solution is more ambiguous and academic. However, understanding the process of change is beneficial to implementing changes to the project. Following are the condensed steps predominately identified in *Management of Organizational Behavior* [Hersey 1996]. These steps provide an insightful summary methodology for understanding the phases for accomplishing project change successfully.

1. Establishing a need for change.

   Dealing with denial. Denial is a coping skill that initially numbs individuals and groups to the changes they do not wish to acknowledge.

   Dealing with resistance. This is the most difficult stage. Considerable attention must be given to this stage.

2. Change process.

   Unfreezing. Motivating the individual or group to change.

Changing. Providing individuals or groups with new patterns of behavior.

Refreezing. Establishing the newly acquired behavior as patterned behavior.

VARIATIONS

There are no variations to the Chaos AntiPattern.

EXAMPLE

A small project team from the Information Technology (IT) Department, unnoticed within the organization, was involved with the development and deployment of a productivity tool for use by an internal group. Given the magnitude of the project, it received little attention from management. Management regularly ignored the project manager who requested additional resources to accomplish the project. Because of numerous complications, including requirements creep, the project slipped past its initial deployment date, eventually meeting the third rescheduled date. This apparent inability to meet the project delivery created less enthusiasm for the project by management, with no perceived responsibility for not having provided the resources.

However, once the project was deployed it received substantial recognition by the user base. Soon many other similar organizations were interested in learning about the system. The result was to have a developer create a briefing and establish a demonstration of the current system and also to begin mocking up a demonstration of the next release. Removing this individual from the development team part-time to perform this activity had substantial impact on the development team of two, which was also in the process of correcting errors from the initial release. The briefings and demonstrations created even greater demand for more briefings and demonstrations. Management interest in the project was now substantial since this was creating a wealth of projects and means to expand the domain of the IT Department. Management was regularly committing to more deployments of the tool without consulting the project manager.

Management believed that this was a cookie cutter operation by the project team, such that the software could be tailored quickly, enabling rapid deployment of multiple systems. However, management failed to consider the service release, the briefings and demonstrations, and the ongoing development of the next major release of the tool. At the same time, the project manager had been insisting on more resources to accomplish the near impossible.

The change in the strategic deployment of this system to multiple organizations eventually was met with increased resources; however, many of the resources were delivered late in the project cycle—too little, too late. Additionally, many of the staff became burned out as a result of the burdensome and compressed schedule. While this example identifies many problems, it is the number of changes to the project that were improperly handled that resulted in the occurrence of this AntiPattern. The project eventually failed to make the high-intensity delivery schedule and the project manager, despite early success, was removed and blamed for the project failure.

RELATED SOLUTIONS

Related solutions identified earlier in this AntiPattern in Table 2.8 cover both compression and expansion caused by change:

- Analysis Paralysis [Brown 1998] deals with quality expansion and schedule compression by introducing incremental, iterative development processes.

- Death by Planning [Brown 1998] also deals with schedule compression by the implementation of an iterative software development process and incremental planning.

- Irrational Management [Brown 1998] deals with schedule compression by rational decision-making management techniques.

- Requirements Jeopardy [Brown 1999] deals with quality compression and schedule compression by implementation of fundamental requirements analysis and configuration management processes.

- Sure Thing [Brown 1999] deals with quality compression by implementing reviews and audits.

APPLICABILITY TO OTHER VIEWPOINTS AND SCALES

The Chaos AntiPattern affects all viewpoints; however, its focus is the management viewpoint because it deals with project management issues.

Process Disintegration

AntiPattern Name: Process Disintegration

Also Known As: The Process Club

Most Applicable Scale: Project, Organization

Refactored Solution Name: The Major Technical Collaboration
Initiative

Refactored Solution Type: People/Technology

Root Causes: Sloth

Unbalanced Forces: Management of Complexity

Anecdotal Evidence:
"They [management] don't even understand the impact of what
they're demanding! Dang it! This schedule is impossible, and unreasonable. Forget it! Who gives a flip!?! Not me. %@#%$#
them!"

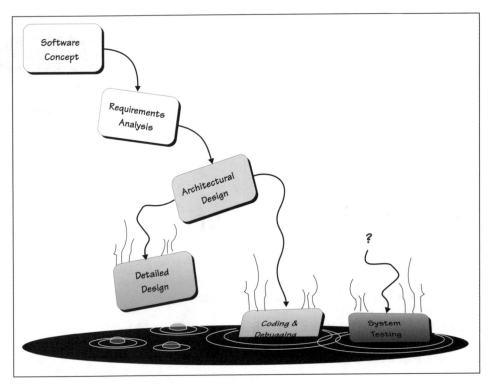

Figure 2.29 Process disintegration.

 # BACKGROUND

Despite its name this AntiPattern is primarily a people-caused AntiPattern that has process consequences. As process advocates in a seeming process-resistant world, we are often faced with the dilemma of just how to handle situations in which a group of professionals is determined to pull defeat from the jaws of victory, and all in the name of principle. The typical situation occurs when several different contractors are collaborating on a common, very ambitious project for a large organization. It is usually a case where no one is the obvious leader in the specific combination of technologies being used; therefore, each is reluctant to sign up for the dubious honor of being in charge and risk being the easy scapegoat if it all "comes apart in flight." However, everyone involved is also keenly aware that whoever does manage to be in charge, if and when success is reached, will receive enduring recognition and general fame (and, of course, a lot of future contracts and therefore a lot of money). Thus begins an uneasy mutual collaboration among avowed enemies, subordinate only to a weak project manager whose only power is in controlling bonus award money and future contracts. (See Figure 2.29.)

As the project proceeds, separate interests typically spark heated criticism of nearly anything any other person proposes, resulting in a filibuster-like logjam in the essential flow of ideas and concepts. This is when the specifications are heaved in as the authority, and everyone is forced into a very carefully planned, if not highly inefficient, dance macabre of requirements, process checks, and review boards for everything from system architecture-design issues to interface button icons and colors. In short, it's "Process to the Rescue!"

At this point, the process is the enemy. The players commence a foundational attack, misusing the process to gain ascendancy and control over each other and sidestep the elements that they cannot figure out, even pasting in hundreds of pages from other project's documentation to complete their portion of the massive amounts of documentation required by the process.

Thus, as you should plainly see, the Process Disintegration AntiPattern is not a process AntiPattern at all. Rather, it is a people AntiPattern, since it is caused by people, usually maliciously. What isn't as obvious, however, is the role of technology in this AntiPattern. As you will see in the following section, technology plays a key role in refactoring this AntiPattern.

GENERAL FORM

In spite of its name, this AntiPattern really is not a process AntiPattern. While it does manifest as a process breakdown, the roots develop deep down as a people challenge long before the more visible symptoms become apparent. People use tools to accomplish their desires and modify their environment. In software project management, processes are tools too. Just as people can use hammers to create good things, they can also misuse them by striking other people and causing grave bodily harm; process experts can use processes to ensure success, or misuse processes to intentionally inflict pain, anguish, and even mortal wounds (from a business perspective) on others by intentionally preventing the steps that must be taken to succeed. Where processes cause failure, we often find the Process Disintegration AntiPattern lurking, ready to attack naive, unsuspecting software professionals.

Nevertheless, this AntiPattern is likely to be realized in a process-intensive organization. That is a polite way of stating that the organization has lost focus of the objective, and now the focus is on the process. You will typically find a consultant onboard analyzing every detail of the organization's process, recommending evaluation upon evaluation and introspective analysis of how things could be done better, and on, and on. The result is a mind-melting 100-step organizational process designed to ensure success—so claims the consultant. Those managers that are weak of mind and short on experience believe every word and soon they'll be at the helm of endless review boards that chastise project managers for missing process steps. Quickly then the process is the project and success is gauged by the project manager's ability to navigate review boards and gain approvals for the next phase.

In the midst of this process quagmire are poor managers and worthless leaders. They have no practical experience and probably are not technically oriented, but rather brainless bureaucrats that want to feel the rush of power by finally getting even with the "techies." So it is, even the process fails. Slowly the process disintegrates, everyone gives up on the uncountable number of steps and the meaningless plans and documentation used merely for checking a box on a review board checklist. Finally, the power-hungry boards, looking to weld power over the project manager since they have no power themselves, define their own ad hoc processes. It is a baroque, noir setting that takes place in the dungeons of large corporations and governmental organizations. The conference room is the torture chamber where the inquisition begins, and no one leaves unscathed. The chair of the review board sits on high, stretching an arm out, hand clinched, and thumb positioned to turn down if he or she dislikes your presentation or up if you have appropriately passed this phase of the gauntlet.

It becomes no different at the project level. Ever fearful of being called before the next review board, no one wants to step forward. Projects become leaderless, and no one takes on risk. The more risk free, the more likely success. Yet on any given project review, heads will roll, careers are crushed, and egos pummeled. The only hope is to refactor the organization.

So, like the AntiPattern, the refactored solution to the Process Disintegration AntiPattern also falls outside the process realm. The most practiced solution to the Process Disintegration is best found in people and technology.

SYMPTOMS AND CONSEQUENCES

The symptoms and consequences to this AntiPattern provide an abysmal perspective for most project managers and their teams. They include:

- Ignorant, egotistical managers with no experience in project management.
- Consultants defining processes.

- Excessive use of standards and checklists.

- Focus on process and boards, rather than projects.

- Inordinate number of process steps for achieving anything.

- Leaderless projects; little or no initiative on the part of the project team.

- No risk taking on projects.

- False reporting—everything is okay and always will be because we know the consequences.

- Ignorance of the true state of project activities and deliverables.

- People leaving in droves, citing intense dissatisfaction with the way things are run.

- Deadlines are missed and those responsible just don't seem to care about any resulting impact elsewhere.

- A state of apathy has overcome the organization.

- Increasingly stern threats concerning arbitrary deadlines and drop-dead dates.

TYPICAL CAUSES

The ultimate cause of the Process Disintegration AntiPattern is managers who have little or no experience as technical project managers. They fail to demonstrate leadership and are so fearful of being found out that they wreak havoc to maintain the illusion that they know what they are doing. This is the Wizard of Oz situation. The great Oz knows all—but it's really just some silly old man behind a curtain. Beyond this ultimate cause, listed here is a compendium of causes that result in the AntiPattern:

- The state of apathy is largely the result of increasing recognition that the business process has become far more important than the resources performing the process.

- Corporate changes that bolster an already growing feeling that the organization increasingly views employees as challenges or necessary evils that must be tolerated.

- Failure of process consultants, planners, implementers, and managers to recognize errors in the plan. Nor do they support reasonable changes in the processes that could more easily accommodate human situations and needs because it threatens their power structure.

- Senior management vendettas or quests to accomplish some kind of spectacular feat by some unreasonable (or flat-out impossible or arbitrary) deadline, which overrides any reasonable need to nurture or cultivate the work force for longer-term or continued success.

KNOWN EXCEPTIONS

The only known exceptions to the Process Disintegration AntiPattern is when the process is tempered by knowledgeable and experienced leadership that comprehends and understands the reality of project management. However, under those circumstances the AntiPattern probably will not be realized.

Beyond reasonable management, a project manager who spans both the technical world and the clique of the management domain may be in a favorable situation. This situation alone stands to provide an exception to the Process Disintegration AntiPattern.

REFACTORED SOLUTION

In spite of the typical reaction to seeking a technological (easy) solution to a people (difficult) problem, the Process Disintegration AntiPattern provides a unique situation where such a fix can truly be effective and very simply implemented. The key is to go all out and completely implement it, without short cuts (see Figure 2.30).

The key point is that the process is disintegrating because it is perceived to be impossible, inflexible, or out of touch with the people it's designed to manage. They have lost faith that the project can be completed *at all* [McConnell 1998], or that management cares about their staff's concerns or needs.

Connecting People or "Power to the People"

People grow disillusioned or even surly toward their leaders, and this bleeds over into a growing callousness toward each other. The result is a cocooning process that promotes increasing distant social ties between the human beings that work in the organization. However, humans are the very reason that this distance is such a problem to begin with and provide the critical means toward its resolution. Humans need social interaction. They are social entities. Therefore, any sincere effort to truly acknowledge and

Figure 2.30 There are no shortcuts to the shortcut.

recognize these powerful human needs can increase the human interaction and revive people's concern for and awareness of each other. This can in turn revive the humanity of the team. There is likely to be an initial period of skepticism on the part of the project team, but clear human recognition and relationships are such a strong motivator that this period can be as short as a few days while things get rolling.

What we are referring to is a *web collaboration* initiative that rewards individual creativity and imagination while also increasing people's interhuman connectivity. The project is an internal one, supported by internal dollars and eventually leveraging bootleg time from other projects (once they are back on their feet again). It must be perceived by everyone as sacrificial on the part of the management and have a grass roots sort of support, where there is a common belief among developers that this is the correct approach.

One company that has successfully followed this prescription developed a corporate intranet that has become a world-class example of quality knowledge engineering and one that is a major factor in the company's readiness to compete on nearly any front. The people that have contributed the most to the project found a unique outlet for their creative efforts that earned them special, and very powerful, recognition from other team members who found their contributions to the intranet highly useful.

A successful internal effort that doesn't come under the scrutiny of the process may provide some insight for the tyrants at the helm. While this threatens their continued power hold over the organization, it may be enough of a paradigm shift for someone at a higher level to reconsider, especially if the project gains visibility within the organization. If the project is successful enough, the power shift center may be relocated with the concentration of resources.

VARIATIONS

A variation is a "great work," which can also have the same unifying effect as power to the people, by providing a focus because of the immensity of the undertaking. However, since the work itself is not personally beneficial to the workers, it must be perceived as incredibly significant and worthy of their personal sacrifice to accomplish it. These kinds of cases are typically legendary, such as the early Microsoft days as the fledgling corporate founders struggled to live up to the mighty task of developing the operating system for IBM's new personal computer. Other examples abound in the new Internet galaxy. Such bright examples as Yahoo.com and Amazon.com provide excellent great work case studies (see Figure 2.31).

EXAMPLE

This is an example that directly reflects the refactored solution. The organization for this example was stagnant and drenched in a tradition of process and formality. Morale remained low and management had a strong hold over the direction of projects. Project managers were fired quickly if they didn't react and adhere to the demands of processes that had been created.

In the background of this organization was a small cadre of individuals (mostly younger) who were stealing away time and energy to further a technology that was on the leading edge. Little was it known that all over the corporation similar and related efforts were taking place. This continued for well over a year before it was discovered that these pockets of individuals were pursuing such efforts.

The success of the individual efforts were quickly recognized by the next level of management. They were quick to insulate the small project teams

Figure 2.31   A great work.

from the institutional grip of the process. The management efforts slowly began to prosper and some recognition was forthcoming from the higher levels of the organization. The midlevel managers began to talk among themselves about how they could leverage these efforts into a single project. The result was a corporate knowledge management system, based on the corporate intranet that had been created.

Initial capabilities were limited but, as time went on, the capabilities grew. The highest levels of corporate management began to realize the success of the independent efforts, as well as the potential. Funding came from corporate management to pursue expansion of the effort with connectivity to the entire corporation. The project teams insisted on independent management control, citing their initial renegade actions as the basis of their success. This was the beginning of the end of the large corporate stranglehold on projects.

Nearly ten years later, a fully robust knowledge management, intranet environment was available. While the capability was landmark, the critical aspect of what had happened was transparent. The seemingly cold bureaucratic organization based on strict adherence to processes had transformed into an organization that focused on the fostering of small projects and project teams that pursued innovative technologies, independent of the greater organization. The culture of the organization actually changed. The focus was on the ability to share knowledge and collaborate on projects and corporate efforts.

There are a lot of forces at play in this example that have nothing directly to do with the refactored solution. Nevertheless, it is the singular desire to independently create, to have freedom to experiment, that engenders success, and success brings about change. People want to be associated with successful team efforts. It is the breaking down of barriers at the lowest level that will enable the organization to change at the higher levels.

RELATED SOLUTIONS

Several related AntiPatterns may provide helpful refactored solutions.

- Myopic Delivery deals with an inappropriate project management focus on delivery at any cost, which forces people to follow bad and weak processes in an effort to speed up delivery.

- Corncob [Brown 1998] deals with countering troublesome people who try to manipulate others for their own ends, often using processes as the vehicle for control.

- Irrational Management [Brown 1998] deals with project management indecisiveness and its negative impact on staff and processes.

- Project Mismanagement [Brown 1998] deals with the lack of management of the software development processes.

APPLICABILITY TO OTHER VIEWPOINTS AND SCALES

The applicability of this AntiPattern is at the enterprise level, affecting the entire software development organization. Occasionally it may occur in an isolated manner on a large project where most of the organization's staff are working, causing the same impact.

CHAPTER 3

Technology Management
AntiPatterns

Technology AntiPatterns exist when technologies are the primary cause of problems. Technology risks increase dramatically as soon as there is a lack of understanding about a technology and/or a lack of maturity of the technology.

When there is a lack of understanding of a technology, the architects and designers will make false assumptions about the capabilities of the technology and the project manager will make poor decisions based on errors in estimates. This will lead to delays due to the learning curve and rework that results because of the false assumptions.

In immature technologies the stability is often poor, the interoperability often weak, and the rate of codebase change often frequent. Even when this is known and the technology is still chosen because of its promised future advantages, problems will inevitably occur. Workarounds must be made, and they may need to change as new versions are released.

Technology management is one of the weaker project management practices. It is usually assigned to architects and designers. But what can't be understood clearly can't be managed correctly. The six Technology AntiPatterns show the dangers of poorly understood technology to successful software development.

Batteries Not Included AntiPattern examines the severe development and maintenance problems that can be caused by choosing immature commercial off-the-shelf (COTS). COTS is a U.S. government term for packaged software that can be bought off-the-shelf. Immature COTS will not work as advertised, will be unstable, and will have frequent bug fix releases. Each new version requires that the software under development or existing application be modified. This leads to development that shows little sign of finishing and has endless and expensive maintenance. Even when the COTS is isolated by an abstraction layer, the lack of backward compatibility and changing feature support can cause major difficulties in moving to the next version of the COTS.

Distributed Disaster AntiPattern deals with resolving the issues of using distributed object technologies (DOTs) when integrating new and legacy systems across the enterprise. The problem is how to integrate the applications written in different languages that use different data typing and associated functionality in an integrated manner with the DOTs. Even when the DOTs are restricted to a middleware (middle server tier) framework, they are complex to use without considerable abstraction to hide their complexities, which also reduces the features available. Managing the technical framework of languages and DOTs is critical to success in enterprise applications and middleware frameworks.

Gilding the Lily AntiPattern examines the additional requirements or design attributes that are sometimes "piled on" during the design and development cycle of a project, but especially during the requirements analysis and the design phase. When the addition of requirements and design attributes occur in the extreme, either in quantity or in scope, the result for the project can nearly be catastrophic. Often the process of piling on is referred to as *gold plating* or *gilding the lily*. It is important for the project manager to know when to stop enhancing the system and when to start development. This AntiPattern will explain how the Gilding the Lily comes about, how to nip it in the bud, and how to recover from near disastrous results.

Wherefore Art Thou Architecture AntiPattern discusses managing the implementation of an ever-evolving reference architecture and its impact on software development project schedules. Often architecture can impact multiple projects not only in the form of technical requirements and the design approach, but in a more overbearing way by causing the evolution of both requirements and design because of another good architectural idea. This can take a form similar to the Analysis Paralysis AntiPattern [Brown 1998], but has a much greater impact. The evolution of the architecture and its implementation in software development projects must be carefully managed if it is to be beneficial, rather than increasing software delivery risks.

Killer Demo AntiPattern covers how demonstration software can take on a life of its own. Software developers can spend increasing amounts of time extending a demonstration rather than developing the fully functional code that is required. The AntiPattern is manifested when the needs of the demo begin to outweigh the original intent. The more impressive the demo, the more likely that this AntiPattern will manifest. This is because demand to show off the demo increases each time it is shown, and as the demo's reputation grows so does the status level of those sponsoring the demo. Eventually, top executives are involved, sending the new demo team all over the map to show off the Killer Demo; thereby directing the use of key resources in ways that are completely orthogonal to any actual system development process.

One-Shot Deal AntiPattern deals with special case projects. As they look back on the many projects that comprised their career, many people realize that most of their projects were treated as special cases and were typically expedited to meet some kind of unrealistic deadline. If they were brutally honest they would probably even admit to directing the expediting themselves! It is a sad but typically true fact that a large percentage of software projects fit into a category that might be called one-shot deals, for which the developers often had no intention of being around to maintain once produced. More typically they just didn't have time for all that project management bureaucracy because they had to get the job done before running out of funding or time (or both).

Batteries Not Included

AntiPattern Name: Batteries Not Included

Also Known As: Some Assembly Required

Most Applicable Scale: Application

Refactored Solution Name: Read the Instructions Carefully

Refactored Solution Type: Technology

Root Causes: Haste, Ignorance, and Narrow-Mindedness

Unbalanced Forces: Management of Change and Management of IT Resources

Anecdotal Evidence:
"Whose stupid idea was it to use *that*!"
"I know it's popular but it doesn't fit with what we're doing."
"The corporate architecture office tells us what programming languages for GUIs, non-GUI client software and server side software, and database development to use, so we don't need to worry about that."

BACKGROUND

The Batteries Not Included AntiPattern covers the impact of poorly choosing development-time and runtime COTS. Unreliable COTS vendors can cause users to have to cope with version management of erratically evolving software and the embedded costs of the continued inclusion of these COTS in new applications or products.

Development-time COTS include programming language environments, middleware toolkits, and code generators. Runtime COTS include databases, bridges, and gateways between different technologies, as well as application technologies such as accounting packages and utility technologies including network software and antivirus software.

Both development-time and runtime COTS can create cost sinks and extreme versioning problems in order to deliver a product. Emerging programming environment COTS used for runtime development are susceptible to frequent changes. COTS embedded within the runtime product create technical and financial dependencies.

COTS is a key technology area that requires serious risk assessment by the project management and senior technical staff because their stability is often poor, their interoperability is often weak, and the rate of codebase change is often frequent.

Compromises in the adoption of COTS limit the future product functionality. This often has the result of replacing the initial COTS software with more stable COTS software.

GENERAL FORM

The general form for the Batteries Not Included AntiPattern is broken down by the two different types of COTS implementations: development-time and embedded runtime. The general form for the development-time COTS is the scenario in which the developer organization selects an emerging technology, such as an integrated development environment for Java, as a way to fast-track the development of product software for the marketplace. All the way through early development the COTS vendor releases frequent upgrades and patches. The development team finds that it continually has to redo earlier development work to keep their solution viable. This cycle is often exacerbated by the lack of essential documentation causing the developers to hit dead ends during early implementation.

The general form for the embedded runtime COTS exists when a system integrator purchases a COTS product without evaluating its compliance to the requirements or the technical difficulties of embedding it with an application. These problems lead to an unexpected effort in making it compatible within the developed software solution. The business organization using the software now has a critical dependence on the embedded COTS of which they are probably unaware.

Then, when an upgrade release from the COTS vendor is adopted by a systems integrator, the application needs to be updated as well to still use the modified COTS functionality to support the business requirements.

This is an enforced cost on the business organization. This cycle of upgrade due to critical dependence on COTS continues at the discretion of the COTS vendor, or the system integrator finds that it cannot upgrade the applications that use the COTS!

There are instances in which a system integrator chooses to stay with an older version and inherit the problems that come with that decision, including maintaining a legacy system that becomes less and less functionally useful because of its dependency on a legacy COTS version.

SYMPTOMS AND CONSEQUENCES

The symptoms and consequences for development-time and embedded run-time COTS are dealt with separately in Tables 3.1 and 3.2.

TYPICAL CAUSES

Market forces drive divergence of COTS products, leading to proprietary features in the rush to stay ahead of the competition. The proprietary features are usually those used most, and then the user is caught in the web because they depend on the specialized features of that product. For example, how many developers use a relational database and use only the purely

Table 3.1   Development-Time COTS Symptoms and Consequences

SYMPTOM	CONSEQUENCE
Frequent vendor releases	Retesting software with each new release
Changing functionality supported	Changing design and code, as well as retest
Lack of supporting documentation	Design and code dead ends, workarounds, and inability to support required functionality

Table 3.2 Run-Time COTS Symptoms and Consequences

SYMPTOM	CONSEQUENCE
Changing functionality supported	Failed interoperability with application
Embedded within a critical application or product	Reliance on a specific COTS version
Lack of supporting documentation	Consultancy/experience required to implement

standard functions that are common to all Relational Database Management Systems (RDBMSs)?

The Software Engineering Institute (SEI) concludes that the level of COTS vendor competition "leads to a marketplace characterized by a vast array of products and product claims, extreme quality and capability differences between products, and many product incompatibilities, even when they purport to adhere to the same standards" [SEI 1999].

Product Differentiation

The interoperability between COTS is precarious due to the fact that market forces drive product differentiation and hence preclude interoperability. This leads to growing customer dependency on the COTS vendor driving the rate of change. COTS are not stable because vendors are continually improving the functionality so that the product continues to be more marketable and the vendor can sell the newest versions.

Time to Market

Since the primary cause is that the vendor is rushing a product to market to beat the competition, the software is not the result of a rational software development process. Instead, the process is more of a "code and fix" lifecycle [McConnell 1996] where the importance is placed on the release of the software rather than the method by which it is achieved.

This prompts the systems integrator to continually correct defects that result from the collateral impact of the last round of maintenance, which in the meantime was released to appease the customer base. This usually results in a vicious cycle.

Marketability

COTS vendors must differentiate between versions to ensure that there is a need for the customer to upgrade. When significant new features are added that can be mapped to supporting specific business and technical needs, the COTS upgrade is posed as essential. It is in the interest of any COTS vendor to release versions regularly with increased functionality.

A final twist of this cause is when a COTS vendor declares certain features as no longer backward compatible, causing more pressure on the user of the COTS to keep up with the versions as they are released.

COTS Acquisition

The ultimate cause from the perspective of the development team using the COTS is a lack of choice. Often COTS are part of an architectural strategy which is assessed and agreed to on paper, but never implemented to validate the true effectiveness of the COTS. The essence of this cause is that the assessment exercise is managerial rather than technical, resulting in poor business and technical decisions. A weak architectural process will ensure the selection of poor quality COTS.

A strong architectural process, such as that specified by Bennett, ensures that COTS are matched to the functional and data requirements [Bennett 1997]:

External Requirements Tasks. Establish product (COTS) targets and evaluation criteria.

System State Task. Establish requirements for the software.

Behavior Identification and Allocation Task. Identify components and their interactions/relationships.

Software System Architecture Task. Design the functional scope of a development-time COTS and the integration of embedded COTS.

 KNOWN EXCEPTIONS

A common exception to the Batteries Not Included AntiPattern is when a vendor's COTS, such as an Oracle RDBMS, are used for the majority of functionality within an application and the technology is stable. This used to be more the norm but now is more the exception, unfortunately.

REFACTORED SOLUTION

COTS selection is simpler for development-time COTS because they will be used as they are, not embedded in an application or enhanced. The refactored solution deals primarily with runtime COTS.

The Software Engineering Institute has developed the COTS-Based Systems (CBS) approach, "focused on improving the technologies and practices used for assembling previously existing components (COTS and other nondevelopmental items) into large software systems, and migrating systems toward CBS approaches" [SEI 1999].

The SEI suggests a move away from the traditional software engineering approach of system specification and construction with one that is replaced by a component focus. The SEI CBS steps are:

1. Identification, for defining requirements and the measurable acceptance criteria.

2. Qualification, where the candidate COTS are evaluated against the requirements and measurable acceptance criteria.

3. Adaption, in which the architecture for embedding the COTS is defined.

4. Integration/assembly, where the COTS integration coding tasks take place.

5. Upgrade, dealing with the evolution of systems that are dependent upon COTS.

Note that the first two steps of identification and qualification specified by the SEI are relevant to both development-time and runtime COTS.

Assessing COTS

The first stage is to state the requirement for the COTS in a measurable way so that candidate COTS can be effectively evaluated. This corresponds to the SEI CBS step of identification and qualification (see Figure 3.1).

Define the Purpose for the COTS

What problem is the COTS going to help solve and how does it fit into the solution? For example, is it a rapid storage mechanism for Binary Large Objects (BLOBs) or scaleable persistence for complex data sets? Or is it a programming language to assist with developing ActiveX controls or portable graphical

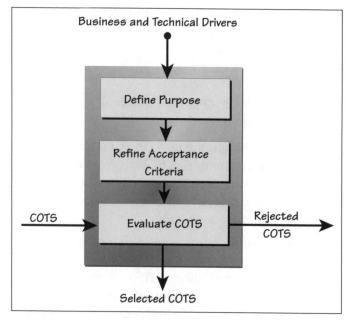

Figure 3.1   Assessing COTS.

user interfaces (GUIs)? The answer will help focus on the specific acceptance criteria that need to be derived. The answer consists of two parts:

- What is the feature it will provide or assist in supporting? These are high-level business and technical requirements.

- What other logical components will the COTS interact with? This identifies the interfaces required from an architectural perspective.

Define the Acceptance Criteria for the COTS

How can the COTS solution be measured against the requirements? There is a need to specify the exact requirements that the COTS must fulfill (see Figure 3.1).

- What are the derived technical requirements? Derive individual requirements from the COTS's purpose statements and make them as measurable as possible. Avoid terms like *fast* for performance or *large* for scaleability since they are meaningless, but rather define dimensions based on the intended use.

- What are the interface specifications? A programmatic interface specification will ensure that the desired functionality and data type support can be tested.

- What levels of costs is the company willing to fund? Maximum costs for purchase, development, and maintenance must be set.

Evaluate the COTS

How is the best-fit COTS identified? This step must physically prove that a COTS can sufficiently support the requirements.

- Compare the derived technical requirements to the COTS technical specifications and other marketing material. SEI suggests that vendors who comply with ISO 9000 are preferable because they use "well-defined practices and procedures," but often that does not in itself make them an effective software provider.

- Compare the interface specification to that published by the COTS vendor. Note that not all vendors publicize the COTS interfaces but offer only a vendor proprietary solution with their COTS embedded. Hands-on evaluation identifies such mismatches, "alternatively called architectural mismatches by Garlan, Allen, and Ockerbloom, and interface mismatches by Wallnau, Clements, and Zaremski" [SEI 1999].

- Test the COTS by developing the required application or product-side interfaces and run tests for all the required functions and data type support.

- Assess the results in terms of trade-offs for functionality, maintainability, and overall costs.

Implementing COTS

How can the chosen COTS be properly used or embedded as part of the required solution? This stage details the process for integrating COTS into an application or system and corresponds to the SEI CBS steps of adaption and integration.

Adaption

What additional code must be written for the COTS to meet the requirements? From the results of the evaluation stage, if a COTS has survived we know the deltas between the:

- Derived technical requirements and the COTS technical specifications
- Architectural and interface mismatches

- Required and actual "ilities" (performance, scalability, maintainability, availability, etc.)

These results define what adaption needs to be performed to use the COTS in the required manner:

- Deciding (designing) which COTS functions are invoked
- Adding functionality to the application or product software to make up for that missing from the COTS
- Wrapping the COTS so that the interface mismatch is hidden

The COTS should be included not only as part of the architecture but also as part of the design. The specification design will deal with the latter two items from the adaption definition list. The COTS is not included in implementation design.

Integration

The integration step is where the rubber meets the road and the adaption is put into practice, that is, where the physical integration takes place. This is somewhat different from a traditional code and test exercise due to the architectural uniqueness caused by wrapping and then adding external functionality to the COTS. The software directly interacting with the COTS needs to be built in these incremental steps:

1. Code the additional COTS functionality.
2. White-box test the COTS with the additional functionality.
3. Code the wrapper for the COTS and additional functionality.
4. Black-box test the wrapped COTS.
5. Integrate with components that access the COTS wrapper.
6. Integration test the subsystem.

Maintaining Embedded COTS

How is the COTS maintained as part of the application or system? And what impact will upgrading the COTS have on the application or system? The following steps to maintaining the application that has the COTS embedded corresponds to the SEI CBS steps for upgrading and involves repeating the testing from the integration step (see Figure 3.2):

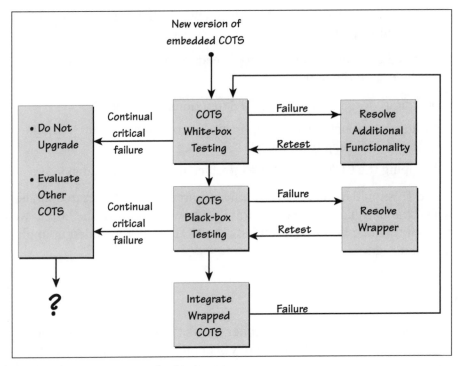

Figure 3.2   Maintaining embedded COTS.

1. Make any modification necessary to the functionality of the externally added COTS.

2. White-box test the COTS with the additional functionality.

3. Make any modification necessary to the wrapper for the COTS and additional functionality.

4. Black-box test the wrapped COTS.

5. Integrate with components that access the COTS wrapper.

6. Integration test the subsystem.

The critical testing is that of the COTS with the additional developer-provided functionality. The rest of the testing is for confidence to confirm that it fully works as expected.

Any failure investigation should start with the interface of the new COTS version. It may be that the interface has had functionality removed, the type parameters have been changed, or the required interface invocation sequence has been modified.

Once the specific problem has been identified the additional functionality must be redesigned/recoded. In addition, the COTS side of the wrapper may also need to be redesigned/recoded.

Ensure that the COTS, additional functionality, wrapper, and tests are all under change control to ensure that controlled regression to previous code and COTS versions is available. The functional delta between the currently used COTS version and the new one that the vendor just released may be significant. In that case the organization may decide to stay with the older version and postpone upgrading until there is a better business advantage to doing so.

VARIATIONS

A variation of the Batteries Not Included AntiPattern occurs when there is a significant financial impact of using too many COTS to help fast-track a product development but with the downside of reducing the profit margin and passing on problems with licensing dependencies to your customers.

EXAMPLE

A development-time example of implementing a programming language is given, followed by a runtime example of embedding a database.

Programming Language

A 1999 example of the Batteries Not Included AntiPattern is the Microsoft Visual J++ development environment that was being used to develop Distributed Component Object Model (DCOM) server services. Because the product was relatively new, Microsoft was issuing new releases approximately every two to four weeks during 1999. Unfortunately the use of J++ was a customer requirement and so each version release drove design and coding, and retesting occurred frequently. This worked reasonably well for a while, with the only serious problem being the lack of published documentation.

Then the release versions started to exhibit enough subtle product differences to cause failure of previously working code. This caused code investigations, redesign, and recoding on a frequent basis, resulting in schedule slippage and growing concern over the feasibility of the technical approach. The customer was alarmed to the extent that the programming language requirement was waived if a viable alternative could be found that would stop the increasing delays.

After working with Microsoft support staff for several weeks it was decided that a more proven approach was to switch programming languages to Visual Basic, where both the language and the DCOM integration was stable and mature (see Figure 3.3).

Once the language switch had been made from Microsoft J++ to Microsoft Visual Basic, the coding task became much easier and some of the lost time was made up by the better understood programming environment. This was because Microsoft Visual Basic was a stable development-time COTS with extensive available documentation and stable support for ActiveX and COM.

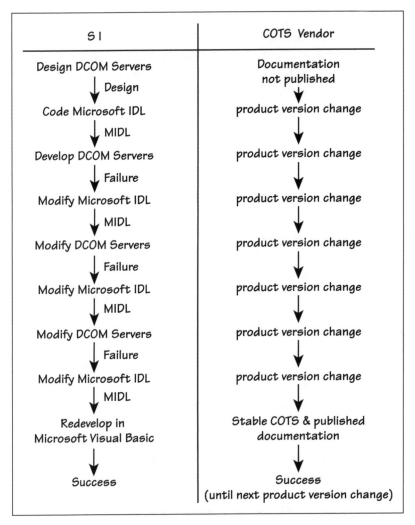

Figure 3.3 A story of development COTS.

Database

A financial company wanted to standardize a centralized database for all of their customer record keeping. Initially it used a variety of databases across the various client-server financial applications: Microsoft Structured Query Language (SQL) Server, Microsoft Access, Sybase, and Oracle. It was decided to unify the technical solution by focusing on a single COTS product. This resulted in the decision to incrementally transition to an Oracle database solution and replace all of the current databases. The company chose to replace Sybase first, followed by Microsoft SQL Server and finally Microsoft Access. The replacement database applications were installed for use as they were delivered.

During the transition a number of problems were uncovered. The first problem was the implementation differences between the proprietary functionality of the Sybase and Oracle databases. The Sybase proprietary features had been used because the original database implementations had been developed as stovepipes, stand-alone applications with no interoperability with any other applications, with no restriction on what database features were used as part of the legacy stovepipe applications. The company managed after some trial and error to replace all of the implementation features of the Sybase systems by developing additional software and a wrapper to give a coherent, single interface to be used by all applications. This effort resulted in an informal process for transitioning the databases.

Now that the company had an informal process for this work it went much smoother for the Microsoft SQL Server replacement. However, the next problem surfaced when the company tried to integrate the two Oracle replacement implementations. The added functionality and wrappers for the Oracle replacements of the Sybase and Microsoft SQL Server had each been designed in a stovepipe manner. This incompatability resulted in a failed integration. It turned out that during the design phase for each replacement database type the added functionality had resulted in stovepipe wrapper designs that were incompatible.

The company then had to backtrack and redevelop additional software and retest across all systems. This proved extremely frustrating to the IT and business users because of the delays caused by reinstalling the replacement applications.

The company then started replacing the Microsoft Access databases with much more confidence since they had overcome all obstacles. What wasn't anticipated was a major upgrade release from Oracle that the company wanted to take advantage of. The development team halted the final database replacement until they could understand how to avoid the problem of being forced to make database system changes to effectively use the new features in the current and future releases of Oracle. Their assessment was that they were at the mercy of the database vendor if they wanted the new feature(s) and that if they decided to postpone upgrading for multiple versions they would be creating a larger change problem in the future. This created a dilemma for the company and, in an effort to reduce the scale of the problem, they redesigned the wrapper to handle structured parameters (see Figure 3.4).

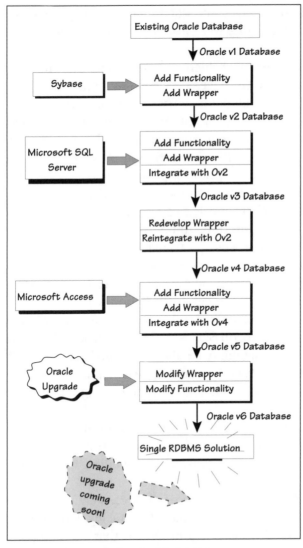

Figure 3.4 A story of embedded COTS.

Finally the company had a single technology for their customer records across all financial client-server systems that they could now exploit to full advantage with confidence that they were not hostage to a single vendor.

RELATED SOLUTIONS

Vendor lock-in is a direct symptom of the Batteries Not Included AntiPattern. The Vendor Lock-In AntiPattern deals with adopting a product technology and becoming completely dependent on it. "When upgrades are done, software changes and interoperability problems occur; and continuous maintenance is required to keep the system running. In addition, expected new product features are often delayed, causing schedule slips and an inability to complete desired application software features" [Brown 1998]. The refactored solution is to create an isolation layer with a proprietary interface to the specific product technology and an abstract interface for the developer user. This reduces the required maintenance and associated costs while giving a level of independence from the specific vendor and version of their product.

APPLICABILITY TO OTHER VIEWPOINTS AND SCALES

The Batteries Not Included AntiPattern and its variations sometimes can apply to both system and enterprise scales. In fact, in the case of the Vendor Lock-In AntiPattern variation [Brown 1998], it is applicable to an enterprise wishing to use a single embedded COTS as a way to completely converge to a single technical solution.

Distributed Disaster

AntiPattern Name: Distributed Disaster

Also Known As: Middleware Muddle

Most Applicable Scale: Application

Refactored Solution Name: Technocracy

Refactored Solution Type: Technology

Root Causes: Haste, Pride, and Ignorance

Unbalanced Forces: Management of Functionality and Management of Change

Anecdotal Evidence:
"CORBA is the only *useful* distributed technology."
"We're a DCOM shop, we don't need anything else to build enterprise applications."
"We believe in mixing CORBA and DCE for scaleable and secure enterprise solutions."
"Who cares how many languages and distributed layers we have, it's only software!"
"What's the problem with accessing CICS from Java over an MQ Series gateway and spraying the results on a Web server for users to query ad hoc? The logical architecture identifies only seven layers which are hardly complex; just look at the conceptual design!"

BACKGROUND

The Distributed Disaster AntiPattern deals with resolving the issues surrounding programming languages that run over multiple distributed object technologies (DOTs) when integrating new and legacy systems across the enterprise. Most organizations have at least two or three significant currently used programming languages; whether it's COBOL, C, and SQL or C++, Java, and Visual Basic. Also both DCOM and Common Object Request Brokerage Architecture (CORBA) are highly prevalent DOT solutions. In both cases the problems are the same: how to integrate the applications written in different languages that use different data typing and associated functionality in an integrated manner with the DOTs. Recent COM/CORBA bridges offer a server-side solution in a proprietary manner, but this does not resolve the critical client-side application use of the underlying technologies. Managing the technical framework of languages and DOTs is critical to success in enterprise applications and middleware frameworks.

GENERAL FORM

The selection of compatible technologies is critical to building scaleable and performant enterprise systems. Normally technology is selected in one of the following three ways:

- There is a single corporate architecture that mandates all of the technologies in an attempt to deal with all possible software implementations.

- Each software development project decides its own architecture in whatever manner it is able.

- The line of business customer dictates the technologies used, without the constraint of the technologies chosen by any other corporate lines of business.

The drawback with a corporate architecture approach is that a single technology approach cannot adequately deal with a wide range of technical problems that involve legacy and new software.

If a software development project decides its own architecture, it usually is based on either the existing skills of the developers or the skills they want to gain. Either way it leads to inconsistencies enumerated by the number of projects.

A line of business customer will consider only their line of business, not the other corporate lines of business. This causes technology diversion when usually the corporate goal is to share information, not make it harder to access.

The final result of these approaches is solution failure, specifically the lack of interoperability with other associated forms of technical failure.

Like all other aspects of software development, the selection and implementation of an architecture must be managed at both the micro (project) level and macro (product or corporate) level. Otherwise ad hoc or constraining solutions will inhibit the achievement of the required functionality.

SYMPTOMS AND CONSEQUENCES

There are two alternate primary symptoms that eventually lead to a single final consequence. There are also several interim, more specific technical symptoms and consequences as identified in Table 3.3.

TYPICAL CAUSES

The initial cause is the *approach* used to decide the architecture, as stated earlier in the General Form:

Table 3.3 Distributed Disaster Symptoms and Consequences

PRIMARY SYMPTOM	PRIMARY CONSEQUENCE	SECONDARY SYMPTOMS AND CONSEQUENCES	FINAL CONSEQUENCE
Restricted applicability of the architecture to the problem.	Incompatible programming languages and DOTs reduce achievability of technical requirements.	Inability to support required functionality vertically through all software layers resulting in reduction of functionality supported and associated workarounds. This in turn leads to lack of scaleability and performance.	Technical failure
Inconsistent solutions.	Incompatible programming languages and DOTs prohibiting full integration with other applications.	The creation of line of business-based stovepipes, leading to the inability to provide functional and data access to other systems across the other lines of business; i.e., the lack of interoperability.	Technical failure

- A single corporate architecture that mandates all of the technologies, which leads to the symptom of restricted applicability of the architecture to the problem.

- Each development decides its own architecture, which leads to the symptom of inconsistent solutions.

- The line of business customer dictates the technologies used, which again leads to inconsistent solutions.

KNOWN EXCEPTIONS

The main exceptions to the Distributed Disaster AntiPattern are when the purpose of the software development exercise is a demonstration, prototype, or proof of concept. This is because technical failure or lack of interoperability may be a valid result, although the expectation will always be that the intended software development should be successful.

In reality there is no exception for doing a poor job of engineering software, regardless of the development lifecycle artifact. A poor engineering approach is just that; and it can happen only because the management planning and control failed! Most software development successes and failures can be attributed to the quality of project management!

REFACTORED SOLUTION

How can a project manager deal with highly technical issues, many of which concern a novel technology? How can planning, control, and risk mitigation be applied to the implementation of one or more poorly understood technologies in conjunction with several better-understood dependent software technologies?

In fact, it is certainly possible to deliver a scaleable enterprise solution assuming that there is reasonable flexibility in the architecture approach and sufficient time for proof-of-concept activities.

Planning an Architecture

Architecture planning is a component of project planning. Not only must a schedule be produced but so also should the architectural standards concerned with mitigating the risk of technical failure, including the lack of interoperability. The architecture, whether defined by the project or more centrally, must state the programming languages and the DOTs and their intended purpose and scope of use. The schedule must define the timeline for the production and review of the architecture and its relationships to the phases immediately before, after, and parallel to it.

Architecture Schedule

There are four essential activities within the architecture-definition phase [Bennett 1997], which are also identified in the Batteries Not Included Anti-Pattern:

External Requirements Tasks. Establish product (COTS) targets and evaluation criteria.

System State Task. Establish requirements for the software.

Behavior Identification and Allocation Task. Identify components and their interactions/relationships.

Software System Architecture Task. Design the functional scope of a development-time COTS and the integration of embedded COTS.

Figure 3.5 is a schedule template for the four essential architecture-definition tasks. Note that the tasks must synchronize with the software configuration management process for configuration identification and audit.

The next step is to identify the interdependencies between the architecture tasks and the software project development tasks of project management and configuration management (see Figure 3.6) and design (see Figure 3.7).

The key points of any phase activity, such as architecture definition, with respect to project management is to identify the triggers for replanning to ensure that the estimates of effort, cost, progress, and time to complete are adjusted and validated whenever a significant event occurs. This is in addition to the normal capture of actuals and schedule adjustment that should occur every week.

The interdependencies between architecture, design, and coding are complex. The architecture sets design strategy and constraints against which the design must be revalidated at every step. Also because architecture will never manage to predefine all answers to design questions that will arise from coding problems, there will always be the need to have a flexible architecture and proactive architects working hand in hand with the development teams.

Architecture Standards

The architectural framework should outline a conceptual model of all of the component partitioning, interfaces, and connections [Shaw 1996]. This gives a readily understood context for the architecture. The conceptual

ID	❶	Task Name	Duration	'99 T W T F S S	Jun 27, '99 M T W T F S
1		External Requirements	1 day		
2		Identify Existing Required	1 day		
3		Functionality Provide	1 day		
4		Data Types Handled	1 day		
5		Public Interfaces	1 day		
6		Define Business Problem	1 day		
7		Business Functions to be Support	1 day		
8		Business Data to be Supported	1 day		
9		Critical Success Factors	1 day		
10		Internal Requirements	1 day		
11		Produce Viewpoint Scenarios	1 day		
12		End User Scenarios	1 day		
13		System Integrator Scenarios	1 day		
14		Software Scenarios	1 day		
15		System Administrator Scenarios	1 day		
16		Security Administrator Scenarios	1 day		
17		Document Technical Requirement	1 day		
18		High Level Requirements for Each	1 day		
19		Overall System Requirements	1 day		
20		Evaluate Technical Requirements	1 day		
21		Evaluate Consistency	1 day		
22		Evaluate Scope	1 day		
23		Refine Technical Requirements	1 day		
24		Define Details of Scenarios and R	1 day		
25		Re-evaluate Consistency and Sc	1 day		
26		Architectural Context	1 day		
27		Define Conceptual Design	1 day		
28		Components	1 day		
29		Component Structure	1 day		
30		Component Interactions	1 day		
31		Component Transactionality	1 day		
32		Component Interface Specifict	1 day		
33		Define Critical Objects	1 day		
34		Object Hierarchy	1 day		
35		Object Management	1 day		
36		Object States	1 day		
37		Component Interface Specifica	1 day		
38		Document Design Strategy	1 day		

Figure 3.5 Schedule template for architecture production.

model must cover all aspects of the system, product, or application being defined, including all external dependencies.

The required use of the DOT and associated services must be clearly defined. This should include any abstraction or wrapping of the DOT services. The implementation objects of a DOT are usually restricted to those objects that need to be distributed rather than all of the application objects being distributed, because of the additional overheads produced by the distribution technology. For example, in many CORBA-based systems many objects are C++ rather than CORBA objects since they need no distributed

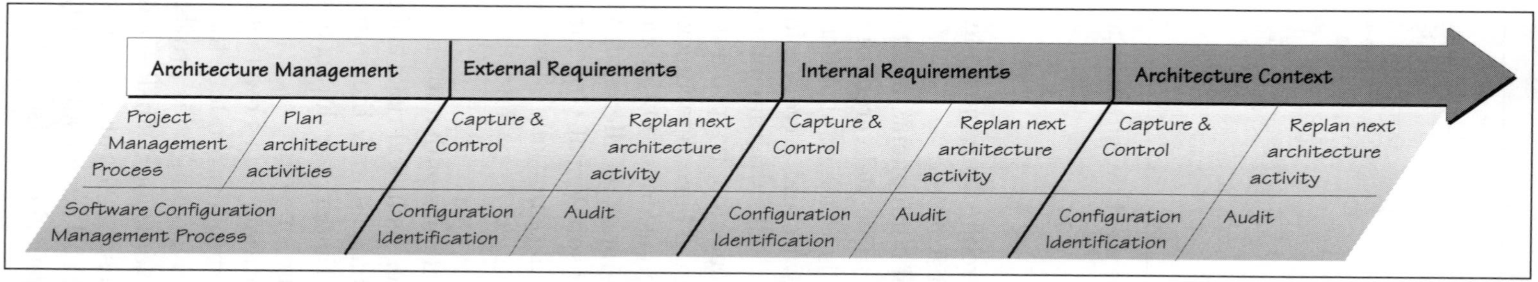

	Architecture Management	External Requirements		Internal Requirements		Architecture Context	
Project Management Process	Plan architecture activities	Capture & Control	Replan next architecture activity	Capture & Control	Replan next architecture activity	Capture & Control	Replan next architecture activity
Software Configuration Management Process	Configuration Identification	Configuration Identification	Audit	Configuration Identification	Audit	Configuration Identification	Audit

Figure 3.6 Architecture schedule, project management, and configuration management process interdependencies.

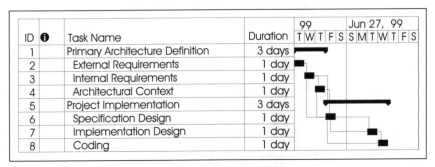

Figure 3.7   Schedule interdependencies between architecture, design, and coding.

object characteristics. The architecture must identify the pieces of the system that are required to be distributed.

The nature and location of components must also be identified. The differences between software to be delivered as an executable, a dynamic library, or as a static library is of major significance; just as the difference between client-resident software and server-resident software is important.

The scope of the use for each programming language must be clearly defined to guide the implementation. If a programming language is used for something other than its planned use, a technical risk is introduced, which may have unforeseen repercussions. Often multiple programming languages are used side by side, such as Microsoft Visual Basic for client-side GUI and services and Microsoft Visual C++ for server-side services, and changing the use of either will potentially cause technical risk. This is why having scope and usage defined as part of the architecture reduces the technical risks.

Finally, all known technical risks with mitigation options must be defined in as much detail as possible. Technical risks are defined during the definition of the architecture and also during the software development project implementation. Many risks that appear during design and coding are architectural risks that were never foreseen.

When the architecture introduces a new technology or novel use of a technology, it is not sufficient to just produce the architecture standards. It is critical that the innovation introduced is proven via an architecture runahead activity. The goal is to develop a small-scale prototype with the innovative technology. This means that the architecture and specification design and code must be produced and tested sufficiently. Otherwise the architecture is no more than a theoretical exercise.

An iterative system architecture approach using viewpoints [Hilliard 1996] provides a different approach to the refactored solution, from architecture inception to project implementation, which is referred to as the Goal-Question-Architecture (GQA), analogous to the Goal-Question-Metric approach to software metrics [Kitchenam 1996]. The following list defines the steps to GQA:

1. **Define the architecture goals.** What must this architecture achieve? Which stakeholders, real and imaginary, must be satisfied with the design and implementation? What is the vision for the system? Where are we now and where are we going?

2. **Define the questions.** What are the specific questions that must be addressed to satisfy the stakeholder issues? Prioritize the questions to support view selection.

3. **Select the views.** Each view will represent a blueprint of the system architecture.

4. **Analyze each view.** Detail the architecture definition from each viewpoint. Create the system blueprints.

5. **Integrate the blueprints.** Verify that the views present a consistent architecture definition.

6. **Trace views to needs.** The views should address the known questions and issues. Discover any gaps not addressed by the architecture specifications. Validate the architecture with respect to formal requirements. Prioritize the outstanding issues.

7. **Iterate the blueprints.** Refine the views until all questions, issues, and gaps are resolved. Utilize review processes to surface any remaining issues. If there are a significant number of unresolved issues, consider creating additional views.

8. **Evangelize the architecture.** Make an explicit effort to communicate the architecture to key stakeholders, particularly the system developers. Create lasting documents (such as a video tutorial) that will provide valuable information throughout the development and maintenance lifecycle.

9. **Validate the implementation.** The blueprints should represent "as-built" design. Determine any deltas between the blueprints and the system implementation. Decide if these differences should result in system modifications of updates to the blueprints. Upgrade the documentation for consistency.

Controlling an Architecture

Once the architectural planning stage is complete the more difficult activity of implementing the planned activities begins. This is very difficult when at least one of the technologies is novel or being used in a novel way. Novelty increases the risk of some aspect of the implementation going wrong, whether it is in design or coding.

The controls occur at the software development project level in the relationship between the software project schedule and the architecture evolution. The architecture evolves at both the macro level of where a new version of the reference architecture is formally released and the micro level that is usually project driven (see Figure 3.8).

Controlling architecture is largely being concerned with ensuring that the implementation adheres to the reference definition of the architecture via the software configuration management process. Each step in the software configuration management process is applicable to both the evolution of the architecture and the software development project implementation of the architecture.

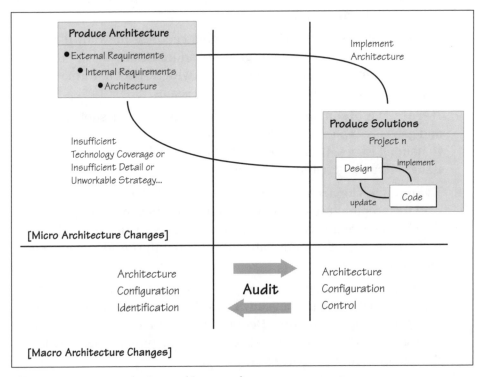

Figure 3.8   Macro- and micro-architecture change management.

Configuration Identification

This is identifying the formal version of the architecture and its components and their inter-relationships for a software development project to use. This is the baseline that it must adhere to. Because architecture will evolve at both the macro and micro level, such configuration identification is critical. Microlevel configuration control poses the greatest risk as these changes usually happen because the software development project implements the architecture.

Configuration Control

The evolution of the architecture at the macro and micro levels must be carefully controlled to ensure that only formally agreed to changes are made and, prior to the decision, that sufficiently detailed impact analysis has occurred. This will help mitigate risk of ad hoc architectural decisions causing cost increases, delivery delays, and technical failure.

Status Accounting

The status of the evolving architecture definition and its implementation status in each software development project must be identifiable at any point. Each step in the architecture process and phase of the development process should have start-up and completion milestones with associated audit criteria. This will enable the status to be readily identified.

Audit

The criteria associated with each milestone for each step in the architecture process and each phase of the development process provide the information that allows the architecture production and implementation to be audited. The audit will ensure that the architecture has been defined (and is sufficient for its purpose) and implemented as planned.

 # VARIATIONS

There are many minor variations to the Distributed Disaster AntiPattern, all of which have an insufficient formal architecture definition and implementation process at the core. Unless the architecture is formally defined and controlled in its implementation, some level of inconsistent solutions and lack of inter-operability, with associated increased cost and delivery delays, will result.

EXAMPLE

Several years ago a European bank decided that it would embrace CORBA as a distribution technology. The architecture was owned by a corporate architecture team who was not involved in actual software development projects. The branch system upgrade project was selected for the first implementation. The technology set for the project (see Figure 3.9) was Microsoft Visual Basic, OLE 2.0, Microsoft Visual C++, and Object-Oriented Technologies DOME object request broker.

The Microsoft Visual Basic scope was:

- GUI navigation
- Field-type validation
- Workflow front-end control
- Document image processing presentation

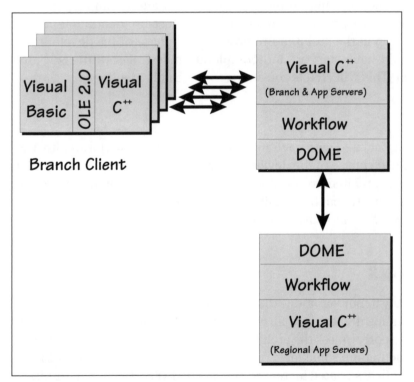

Figure 3.9 Branch banking system theoretical architecture.

The Microsoft Visual C++ scope was:

- All application processing logic on clients and servers
- Validation of received data
- Workflow business logic

Object linking and embedding (OLE) 2.0 servers were to be used to expose VC++ object interfaces so Visual Basic could access multiple Visual C++ objects simultaneously because the complex GUI forms contained fields that were attributes of different Visual C++ objects.

The plan was to use DOME (Distributed Object Management Environment) solely on the server side of the branch system to invoke objects residing on other servers using standardized interfaces such as Object Management Group or Interface Definition Language (OMG, IDL). Its purpose was to provide location transparency.

Both OLE 2.0 and DOME were new technologies and there had been no architectural run-ahead activities to prove that the architectural theories would work as expected. This initially manifested as a problem during early coding, stemming from insufficient design detail and assumptions that the architecture was correct.

The first coding problem found was Visual Basic to Visual C++ communication. OLE 2.0 did not work as expected. Because of the lack of a proven architectural example, the client development team fell into a black hole of iteratively reinventing the design and code in an attempt to get the OLE server code working.

The next problem in the code proved to be the implementation of the CORBA interfaces. The architecture had not specified what objects were to be distributed, the interfaces needed, or the interface sequence required. This left the server development team to their own invention. They assumed that all server-side objects needed to be CORBA objects.

The hidden problem that did not become visible until later was that at that time Visual Basic, Visual C++, and DOME did not support a technically equivalent set of functions and data types. This caused the inability to support required functionality vertically through all software layers resulting in a reduction of the required functionality.

The visible symptoms were repeated technical failures and associated delays. After six months it was decided that a more pragmatic architecture was necessary if the system was to be delivered in a useful time period.

Two architects from the corporate team were added to the project in an effort to refactor the technology strategy. It was critical that the problems with the architecture be resolved because other strategic development projects had been mandated to adhere to it.

The first step was to understand the problems that had arisen to date. The architects quickly discovered that the architecture lacked the required level of detail to ensure that an effective design was produced. It did not provide a coherent technical strategy for successful implementation. The drawback was that no architectural runaheads had been performed in the two primary areas of technical risk, aside from the development teams doing so by accident in their attempt to implement the technologies.

Although much had been learned by the mistakes already made in the use of the technology, it was decided that an architect would work with each team to:

- Define the architecture to a sufficient level of detail
- Produce a detailed design of a single functional thread
- Prove the design through working code

The client development team initially worked on designing and coding a working example of one multiple-field Visual Basic form connected by an OLE server to one Visual C++ class. At this point the design was produced to link from the Visual Basic form to three Visual C++ classes and the code was extended. This now proved that the architecture would work.

The server development team designers worked with the architect to invent the guidelines for when a business object should also be a CORBA (distributed) object. This meant designing the location of components and their required interaction. It became evident that only remote interacting objects and services between the services required distributed (CORBA IDL) interfaces. The architecture standards were then updates with the required use of the DOT and associated services. The design was redefined with the nature and location of components and objects.

The scope of the use for each programming language, which had previously been defined in the architecture prior to the project starting, was refined in line with the proven use of OLE and DOME. This was because the manner in which OLE was used affected what was implemented in Visual Basic and Visual C++; and that the use of DOME, its distributed services, and the nature of the CORBA objects affected how Visual C++ was used on the server side.

Finally the architecture correctly documented the technical risks encountered. This was a list of technical approaches that did not work with the mitigation because of how the problem had been solved. The resulting architectural standard provided a proven successful basis for adoption by other software development projects.

RELATED SOLUTIONS

The Wherefore Art Thou Architecture AntiPattern is a related solution because it deals with refactoring an uncontrolled architecture. Such an enterprise architecture would include the strategy for implementation of DOTs and programming languages, and so stops the Distributed Disaster AntiPattern from occurring.

The Enterprise System Fable AntiPattern [Brown 1999] details the approach to enterprise systems so that they can successfully achieve reusable enterprise components and integrated views across their systems. This solution defines the need for defining architectural components and mechanisms to properly support the enterprise.

The Stovepipe AntiPattern [Brown 1998] and the Enterprise Stovepipe AntiPattern [Brown 1998] examine the problems posed by stovepipe systems and the refactored solutions required to enable interoperability. This identifies the nature of the required solution, including the need for DOTs.

APPLICABILITY TO OTHER VIEWPOINTS AND SCALES

While the Distributed Disaster AntiPattern is identified at the application level, it is equally applicable to the system and enterprise scales because DOTs are often used to integrate new and legacy systems across an enterprise for the purpose of information sharing. It is even arguable that it primarily occurs at the enterprise scale because such a controlled architecture process is usually adopted only by mature software organizations.

Gilding the Lily

AntiPattern Name: Gilding the Lily

Also Known As: Gold Plating

Most Applicable Scale: System

Refactored Solution Name: Better Is the Enemy of Good Enough

Refactored Solution Type: Process and People

Root Causes: Ignorance, Sloth, Narrow-Mindedness, or Pride

Unbalanced Forces: Management of Complexity

Anecdotal Evidence:
    "Know when to say 'when.' "
    "Oh, oh, I know, let's add. . . ."

BACKGROUND

Sometimes during the design and development cycle of a project, but especially during the requirements analysis and the design phase, additional requirements or design attributes are piled on. When requirements and design attributes are piled on in the extreme, either in quantity or in magnitude, the result for the project can be catastrophic or nearly catastrophic. Often the process of piling on is referred to as *gold plating* or *gilding the lily*.

Gold plating is often associated with government procurements where it is perceived that excessive standards are invoked, which results in equipment that is overbuilt or overspecified for its intended use. Often it is the collateral results of piling on that impact the project more than the over-specification of the system. More than likely the project will have overrun schedule and costs. However, gold plating happens in the commercial world as well, and it happens when well-intentioned managers, architects, developers, and users decide to make the product "a little bit better." Sometimes it remains unnoticed and other times it results in an AntiPattern.

A recent HBO movie entitled *The Pentagon Wars* provides a perfect example of this type of AntiPattern. The movie portrays the development of the Bradley Infantry Fighting Vehicle, an army troop carrier/scout vehicle that, in its final redesign, is effectively a deathtrap for its occupants. The movie depicts several generals involved with the design of the vehicle requesting and implying additional requirements until the integrity and purpose of the system are jeopardized and its usefulness questionable. One of the characters from the movie, Air Force Colonel Burton, states, "So, what we've got is a troop carrier that can't carry troops, a scout vehicle that's too slow, and it cannot engage a tank but carries enough firepower to wipe out half of downtown Washington." This movie provides a most dramatic and vivid portrait of the Gilding the Lily AntiPattern (see Figure 3.10).

It is important for the project manager to know when to stop enhancing the system and when to start development. This AntiPattern will explain how Gilding the Lily comes about, how to nip it in the bud, and how to recover from near disastrous results.

GENERAL FORM

Excessive and exorbitant requirements or design attributes may not appear to be that excessive or exorbitant, at least initially. Suggestions or requests for improvement may appear as well-intentioned, good ideas. The project

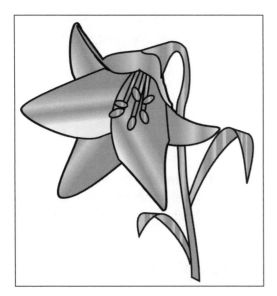

Figure 3.10 The Gilding the Lily AntiPattern.

manager must recognize good ideas and use them if appropriate; however, he or she must also keep in mind the objectives of the project. Typically, the primary objectives of any project is to deliver a system that achieves the requirements in a timely manner, within a reasonable cost. Sometimes discerning what meets requirements can be difficult, yet achieving requirements can never be the final criterion for success. If major functionality has been missed and identified sometime later in the design or development process, it may be prudent to maintain the current baseline and incorporate the missed functionality into the next release. However, missed functionality isn't really the essence of the Gilding the Lily AntiPattern. Of concern here is the functionality or design attributes that are nice to have or "icing on the cake" and are forced onto the system.

Often the project manager will realize this AntiPattern when designing the user interface, because while there is quantitative design criteria for user-interface design, there is also a lot of subjective judgment about how it should look and feel. People will come out of the woodwork with opinions about user-interface look and feel, frequently increasing the requirements and design attributes.

In reality, Gilding the Lily is one of the oldest forms of project mismanagement, having potentially catastrophic results. It is often difficult for a project manager to prevent because the individuals that are guilty of causing this type of AntiPattern are not usually malicious, but rather have the best intentions. They also tend to be stakeholders with some type of leverage with the project (see Figure 3.11). Specifically, the guilty parties that cause this AntiPattern are:

- Management
- Users
- Architects
- Developers

The Gilding the Lily AntiPattern consequently derives its specific causes, symptoms, and consequences by the software development role that primarily caused it. The following sections examine the details for each of these roles.

Management-Created Gilding the Lily

A management-created Gilding the Lily AntiPattern typically is the result of managers that:

- Have too little to do
- Were previously and often recently architects or developers
- Are micromanagers
- Are previously and recently from the user community
- Are just too damn enthusiastic about the project

Often managers that are guilty of the Gilding the Lily AntiPattern are gifted with keen insight into what would be a valuable enhancement to the system. However, because they are not directly responsible for meeting schedule and cost, they often lose focus of the schedule and cost and are more interested in leaving their mark on the project by having some revelational idea implemented. Later they can point to the product and proudly state, "Yeah, I designed that!" Management can have another potential motivation, which is to ensure the success of the product. Again, this sometimes clouds their perception of schedule and cost, yet they firmly believe that they know what is going to make this system the next "killer app" and without implementing their suggestion the project will never achieve that status, much less achieve user acceptance. A variation to the killer app motivation is the need to incorporate the latest technology that is being touted by trade magazines to increase market share.

Avoiding and recovering from the management-created Gilding the Lily AntiPattern can be difficult, if for no other reason than management has a

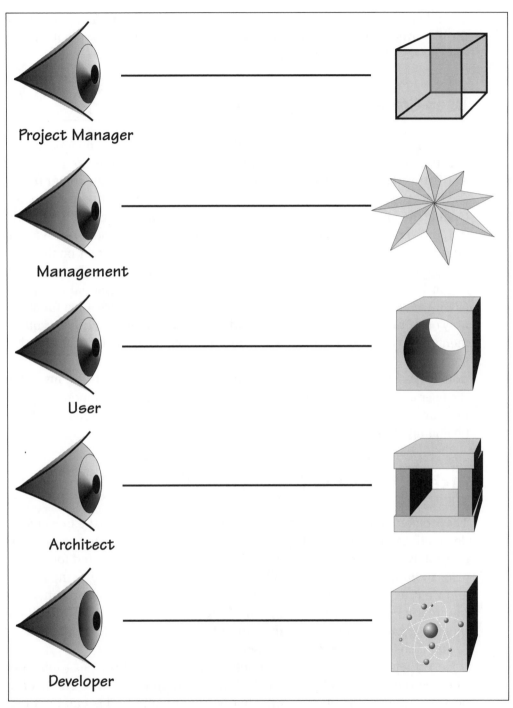

Project Manager

Management

User

Architect

Developer

Figure 3.11 Gilding the Lily-Created AntiPatterns.

great deal of leverage over the project manager. This is a definite land mine for the project manager and working your way through this type of Gilding the Lily AntiPattern can be difficult.

User-Created Gilding the Lily

The user-created Gilding the Lily AntiPattern is perhaps the most pervasive because the user is typically considered the customer (see the Customer AntiPattern) and the project manager is trying to make the customer happy (i.e., the customer is always right). The other reason that the user-created Gilding the Lily AntiPattern occurs is because the user has very little insight into the significance of changes to a system. Frequently users believe that because a product uses object-oriented technology, the functionality can merely be plugged in or pulled out, without collateral impact. The user paradigm is similar to loading application software on a personal computer (PC). You can either choose to load or not load the software, turn functionality on or off. This may be the case if this was one of the functional requirements; however, frequently it's not a requirement, yet it is assumed that software development has become so modular that manipulation of functionality is simple. The project manager must be persistent in convincing the user of the impact of changes to the system. In fact, agreements regarding how changes to the system will be made should be discussed at the beginning of the project.

Architect-Created Gilding the Lily

The architect-created Gilding the Lily AntiPattern is perhaps the most easily detected and corrected. This is because the project manager usually has control over the architects, and the design is typically presented for review prior to implementation. Typically architects take great pride in their work and want to be remembered for their latest achievement. They often strive for greatness even with the simplest of projects. However, it is difficult for them to create a Gilding the Lily AntiPattern without explicitly attempting to maliciously alter design attributes.

Nevertheless, in order for architects to do their job, they must interpret the requirements. It is the interpretation of requirements that can lead to design attributes that go beyond what is truly required. This can be a real sticking point for architects and result in hotly contested and passionately debated concepts. Architects take ownership of their design and often take issue with critiques, especially over design attributes that are perceived as being extravagant or exorbitant. The worst thing the project manager can do in this instance is to offend the architects, so tactful relations are suggested.

Another instance of the architect-created Gilding the Lily AntiPattern may occur during requirements analysis. Again this type of Gilding the Lily AntiPattern occurs because the translation of user needs into requirements is taken beyond what was intended. For example, the user may request that a capability be provided to enable user-to-user communication in a virtual environment. What isn't stated in that need is whether the communication be synchronous or asynchronous. If the requirement is established that synchronous communications are necessary, then further delineation is necessary to discern if this is text, audio, or visual based. A good analyst is necessary for this job, and it is important that he or she translates needs to requirements literally without placing personal paradigms on what should be incorporated.

Developer-Created Gilding the Lily

The developer-created Gilding the Lily AntiPattern is perhaps the most difficult to detect since it can be the most transparent to the project manager. Developers like architects want to add their touch to the project. Sometimes it's adding the neat thing they learned on the last project or sometimes it's overriding the software architecture and design because they can implement another feature. In either case, the developer has much more control and power than most of the other members of the development team and, therefore, measured control should be implemented to ensure that only the requirements are being achieved.

The developer-created Gilding the Lily AntiPattern is especially difficult to detect on smaller projects with single developers. Design reviews and testing occur less often (if at all) and it is difficult to gain meaningful insight into the work being accomplished. Often with smaller projects the schedule is such that the first look by the user and project manager is with the deployment of the final project. It can also happen on smaller projects that the architect and the developer are the same person. This can be particularly tricky because there are no checks and balances. The only mitigating factor under these circumstances is that smaller projects usually don't produce career-ending results—but not always.

Summary

Of course, only in a perfect world will these types of Gilding the Lily-created AntiPatterns be realized in a singular way. In reality, the project manager will more than likely have to contend with each of these types of Gilding the Lily AntiPatterns, and it probably goes without saying that the complexity increases substantially because each individual group builds on the gold plating created by others. There is a definite synergy created by building on others' gold plating, and it sometimes becomes very difficult to remember what the real requirements and objectives were. When testing occurs it is difficult to find the requirement that establishes the existence of specific functionality.

SYMPTOMS AND CONSEQUENCES

The symptoms and consequences for the Gilding the Lily AntiPattern cover the spectrum of system engineering disciplines and product lifecycle. It is difficult to attribute each of the following symptoms to every occurrence of the AntiPattern, since the symptoms are somewhat dependent on the cause and severity of the AntiPattern. Nevertheless, here are the more commonly occurring symptoms for the Gilding the Lily AntiPattern:

- Delayed development due to never-ending discussions about the baseline requirements versus desired or suggested enhancements.

- Design and implementation issues are constantly reintroduced in the analysis phase.

- Analysis exceeds schedule with no predictable end point.

- The complexity of the analysis results in intricate implementations making the system difficult to develop, document, and test.

- Frustration, resulting from the inability to baseline the system and begin development.

- System deployment is delayed and increased costs are incurred due to increased development time.

- Users are dissatisfied with the system functionality because the development team was unaware of the actual or agreed-to requirements versus gold plating implementation.

- Inability to deliver the desired features to the user. These include:
  - Unstable system
  - Insufficient documentation to perform operations and maintenance

- Documentation not consistent with the implementation
- Inability to document system requirements, design, and test documentation
- Unable to perform requirements traceability
- Inability to achieve interoperability or reuse
- Replication of functions (including those provided by commercial software)
- Inability to manage risks

It is possible that the Gilding the Lily AntiPattern results in no immediate negative consequences, but it is unlikely to remain true for the long term. The only typical exception to a favorable long-term result would most likely occur on smaller projects where the magnitude of the gold plating was minimized and the ability to maintain the system unimportant. It may also be that the maintenance is provided by the developer, which minimizes the risk of problems. However, it still may be possible that there are additional, collateral problems down the road, such as interoperability and code reuse, even for smaller projects.

 ## TYPICAL CAUSES

In the General Form, four groups were identified as being responsible for each of the variations of the Gilding the Lily AntiPattern. Yet these individuals or groups are not the actual cause of the AntiPattern. This AntiPattern occurs primarily when the project manager fails to properly handle each of the four groups and address their requirements. The root cause for the Gilding the Lily AntiPattern lies with the project manager and his or her ability to lead (see The Brawl AntiPattern) by maintaining configuration control of the baseline. The root cause has secondary implications that are listed here:

- Poor project management leadership
- Inexperienced and unknowledgeable project manager
- Poor configuration management implementation and practices, which include:
  - Failure to baseline
  - Failure to control the baseline
  - Failure to audit
  - Failure to create a requirements traceability matrix

- Code reviews and software inspections do not map requirements to functionality
- Insufficient or inadequate testing
- Ineffective risk management
- Poor communications with or between the project manager and:
  - Management
  - Users
  - Architects
  - Developers
- Lack of management and insight into the project schedule and costs

KNOWN EXCEPTIONS

The Gilding the Lily AntiPattern is a relative AntiPattern. It is not black and white and is relative to the environment in which it occurs. The degree of damage or severity to the project, resulting from the AntiPattern, is relative to the magnitude of the added functionality and design attributes that are piled on. So, one small added feature (in most cases) will not bring a system to a grinding halt (see Figure 3.12). It is also true that the severity of the

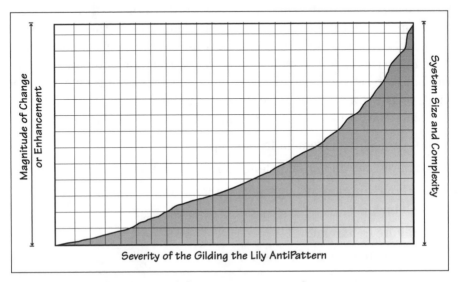

Figure 3.12   Gradient impact of change versus system size.

damage is relative to the magnitude of the project, which means that a larger, complex project may well be impacted by a single change outside the boundaries of the baseline requirements. Therefore, there can be numerous exceptions to the Gilding the Lily AntiPattern if taken in the strictest sense; however, by definition, the AntiPattern won't occur until the magnitude of the change is substantial enough to impact the system.

REFACTORED SOLUTION

The refactored solution for the Gilding the Lily AntiPattern is entitled "Better Is the Enemy of Good Enough." This concept must be constantly maintained by the project manager, since this is the idea he or she will be forced to sell to others who request gold plating. The project manager will be forced to use two things to achieve the refactored solution. The first is the skill for high-grade interpersonal communications. The second is a firm configuration management infrastructure, including a tyrannical configuration manager.

The solution can be broken down into two phases, depending on how far the AntiPattern has progressed. The first phase begins when the project manager is being pressured to implement gold plating. This can occur at any point in the lifecycle; however, it is most prevalent in the early stages. The second phase occurs when the damage has already occurred and the project manager is attempting to recover by performing damage control.

Pressure Phase

This phase is initiated when the project manager is approached by anyone with ideas (see Figure 3.13). The project manager must respond positively by stating, "Gee, that is really a *great* idea! We'll have to *implement* it in the next release. We will submit a *request for change* and review it at the next engineering review board. We will be sure to get back to you on the cost and schedule impact that results from implementing *your* idea."

The concept is simple:

- First, you acknowledge that the individual has a good idea.

- Second, you affirm that it is your intention to incorporate the idea (in the next release).

- Third, you establish that you have a process for implementing changes and that this change, like all changes, will be reviewed at the next review board.

■ Fourth, and finally, you acknowledge that there is a cost and schedule impact to performing the change to the system.

These words will go a long way to assuring the individual that they have been heard and that the project manager will take action on the idea. If the individual is persistent, don't fight the battle then. Don't let management or users bully you into accepting a change to the system without renegotiating the contract for delivery (meaning cost and schedule). Reply to the individual that you will return with the impact to the schedule and the cost, and then ask them if they are willing to accept a schedule slip, provide additional funding, and in some instances gain approval from other stakeholders (see The Customer AntiPattern). Often, this is enough to end the discussion permanently. Nevertheless, the project manager still needs to reply with the impact (see Figure 3.13).

Architects and developers tend not to be put off so easily. This is where "the configuration manager from hell" comes in. Often the architects and developers must be physically prevented from making changes. This is accomplished by baselining the requirements and the design. Tight configuration control of the baseline for the product or application is imperative, as well as basic version control of the individual software artifacts. The proj-

Figure 3.13   Project manager in the pressure phase.

ect manager must be extremely careful not to overlook configuration control, for soon thereafter the architects and developers will rule. This can result in potential anarchy, with a high probably that the Gilding the Lily AntiPattern will manifest itself (see Example).

Damage Control Phase

How do you recover from the damage that has been done by changes that have been implemented? This depends on several things:

- How good your configuration control is
- How tight your schedule is
- How tight your budget is
- How flexible your design is

If your configuration control is poor, cash in your chips and go home, game over. Basically you'll have to start all over and you probably won't make it. If your configuration control is good, then perform and audit and assess where the baseline stands. If you have a good grip on what functionality is there, what is not there, and what is added, then you must determine if a minimum set of requirements have been met in order to continue with development. If they haven't, you need to assess costs and schedule to determine if you have the latitude to implement or go home. If either you can absorb the additional costs and schedule that comes with performing recovery development or you have a critical mass of functionality, then keep the added functionality and go forward.

This is a difficult situation and will be highly stressful, as well as risky. Control must be recovered and renegade architects and developers must be eliminated (you'll probably consider "taking them out" one evening as they are walking across the parking lot). Project managers must explain to management and users that the system is baselined and that there will be no more changes until after the initial delivery. Finally, keep a close eye on all activity and perform regular code reviews and integration testing to gain additional confidence.

 VARIATIONS

Two variations are defined in previously published texts on AntiPatterns. Requirements Jeopardy [Brown 1999] deals with controlling requirements that would result in Gilding the Lily. Analysis Paralysis [Brown 1998] covers the symptom of never completing analysis, which also contributes to Gilding the Lily.

EXAMPLE

This example illustrates a developer-created Gilding the Lily AntiPattern. While there were other forces that attempted to influence the project (in particular, management with the user interface), the most egregious was caused by the developer. In fact, this AntiPattern would most likely not have been realized if not for the developer. All other gold plating would more or less have been consumed without major impact.

It is difficult to imagine that a developer could actually sidestep direction from the project manager and take control of the system design, implementing his or her own desired attributes, but it happens, and this is an example of how it happened. To understand how a developer can take control of a project and implement those aspects of the design he or she chooses, it is important to understand the series of circumstances that lead to this point.

The project begins with a compressed schedule and because management wanted the latest, bleeding edge technology implemented, there was only one qualified developer available. (Most intelligent project managers would have run away at this point, recognizing all of the symptoms of about 20 AntiPatterns and one new AntiPattern, The Terrorist Developers.) The sole developer convinced the project manager that with only one additional developer the project could be accomplished on time. The qualified developer agreed to mentor and instruct the second developer in the new technology. This appeared to be a reasonable and prudent act; however, the qualified developer was much more sinister.

Jumping ahead in time, the system requirements were completed and the system was quickly entering the system-design phase. One of the design attributes that the qualified developer wanted to implement was installation and maintenance wizards for system administrators. The first round of the design phase had the wizards as a key component of the system. However, after several reviews, which incorporated the aspect of schedule, it was decided that the wizards could be deferred until a later release of the system since the functionality could be implemented manually (albeit more difficult for the system administrators). The qualified developer was not happy with the turn of events since he was particularly interested in accomplishing this aspect of the design himself.

Several weeks passed and it appeared that development was taking longer than anticipated. The project manager called together the two developers and began to question them on the progress of the effort, breaking down the system modules assigned to both of them. As it turned out, the qualified developer had taught the second developer all that she needed to know to accomplish everything but the wizards, while the qualified developer worked diligently on the wizards. The project manager was furious and demanded an explanation. The qualified developer rather coyly explained that he believed that the wizards were critical to the success of the system and had proceeded to work on them. The project manager regained composure and explained the project's compressed schedule, giving the qualified developer a direct order to cease and desist all work on the wizards and work on assigned modules.

Unbelievably this scenario reoccurred two more times, until the project manager gave up. The project manager felt as though he was held hostage since there was no one else to replace the only qualified developer and the delivery date was quickly approaching. At that point in the schedule, even if another developer could be found, he or she would not be able to come up to speed quickly enough to finish the project on schedule. So the project development continued with considerable delay, resulting in extreme compression in the test schedule.

Once testing began, a critical flaw in the design logic was uncovered that affected global directories. This design flaw had a direct impact on the wizard implementation and many of the wizards had to be corrected to implement the revised design. This effort put the project over the delivery threshold; however, testing continued. Unfortunately, testing uncovered additional flaws in the wizards. The developer had substantially changed the design to incorporate the wizards and when it was time to pull the wizards to allow the basic functionality of the system to be delivered, additional errors were realized. The developer was eventually fired. The project manager, who never had the opportunity to implement the refactored solution, was reprimanded and placed in an administrative role.

RELATED SOLUTIONS

There are numerous related solutions to the Gilding the Lily AntiPattern because it can affect many system engineering disciplines over the project lifecycle. If you believe that your project is experiencing the Gilding the Lily AntiPattern, it would be advised and prudent to review the following AntiPatterns and their respective refactored solutions before proceeding. They are all contributory to Gilding the Lily in terms of causes; therefore, their solutions are also required where that is the case. (Note that unless a reference follows the AntiPattern, it is in this book.)

- The Brawl AntiPattern demonstrates that if a project manager cannot lead as well as manage the project will spiral out of control.

- Chaos AntiPattern is an inability to deal with change, resulting in unforseen consequences on the software development.

- Micro-Management examines how project managers cause the software development problems, by directing at a task level to compensate for their inability to properly control people, technology, and process.

- The Customer AntiPattern identifies the customer as essentially a conglomeration of internal and external people who all add requirements that can result in Gilding the Lily.

- Developer-Software Configuration Management AntiPattern [Brown 1999] exists when developers run their own software configuration management process and find that the software configuration is out of control.

APPLICABILITY TO OTHER VIEWPOINTS AND SCALES

The Gilding the Lily AntiPattern affects all three viewpoints, managerial, architectural, and developer because they each can contribute to the problem; however, the primary focus of the refactored solution is at the managerial and architectural viewpoints. It is predominately realized at the system and application levels because that is where the main impact occurs.

Wherefore Art Thou Architecture

AntiPattern Name: Wherefore Art Thou Architecture

Also Known As: Asynchronous Architecture

Most Applicable Scale: Enterprise

Refactored Solution Name: Managed Enterprise Architecture

Refactored Solution Type: Process

Root Causes: Ignorance and Narrow-Mindedness

Unbalanced Forces: Management of Change and Management of Complexity

Anecdotal Evidence:
"The developers don't understand the bigger picture and just want to rush ahead and develop code without concern for how it all needs to fit together. They'll have to wait until we figure it all out! It's not easy like programming. We do all the hard work and they just implement it and even then they manage to screw it up!"—an architect

"The architects don't understand the reality of implementing software. It's hard! All they do is write white papers from which we have to produce detailed technical requirements and design from. Then they come and tell us that we did it wrong, because they don't understand it. If they specified a real architecture and stopped messing with it all the time we would have delivered by now!"—a developer

BACKGROUND

The Wherefore Art Thou Architecture AntiPattern deals with managing the implementation of ever-evolving reference architecture and its impact on software development project schedules. Often architecture can impact multiple projects not only in the form of technical requirements and the design approach, but in a more overbearing way can cause the evolution of both requirements and design because of another good architectural idea. This can take a form similar to the Analysis Paralysis AntiPattern [Brown 1998], except in this case it is the architecture that is never finished but has a much greater impact on the remaining software development. The evolution of the architecture and its implementation in software development projects must be carefully managed if it is to be beneficial rather than increasing software delivery risks.

GENERAL FORM

Architecture should address the technical requirements and the design strategy for software development. It usually drives the derived technical requirements and conceptual level and interface-specification-level designs. The conceptual design must identify the application or product components and the nature of their interaction and relationships. The specification design must specify the interfaces for each component and the interface sequence in a formal manner, such as using the International Standards Organization (ISO) Interface Definition Language (IDL).

An architecture team often operates independent of individual software development projects. This means that the architecture evolves over a much longer time period than the phase allocated for it in a project schedule. An ever-evolving architecture will not always address required technology strategies and tactics at the required time.

The architecture acts as a direct constraint to progress because without it the design and subsequent code deliveries will not meet the technical requirements defined in the architecture. Yet because the architecture evolution cycle and the software development project architecture phases are not synchronized, delays of varying magnitude occur.

An errant architecture can pass through two major cycles (see Figure 3.14) from a software development project perspective: that of being insufficient applicability to support the technology being used and that of specifying multiple approaches to the technologies it covers.

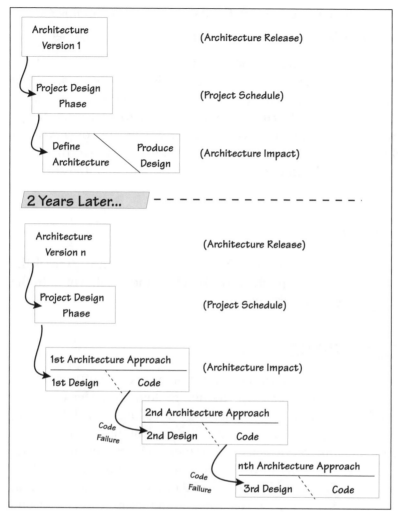

Figure 3.14 Evolving architecture cycle.

From an enterprise perspective the problem is an uncontrolled architecture that cannot be easily implemented and causes software development delays and degradation of interoperability of systems.

SYMPTOMS AND CONSEQUENCES

The common symptoms for an unmanaged enterprise architecture are:

- The architecture does not specify the technical requirements or design strategies.

- The architecture does not specify the use of chosen technologies.

- The architecture is produced in an informal and ad hoc manner.

The main consequence is that the development team is left to invent the missing architecture artifacts in a vacuum. This action usually causes a flail between the developers and architects when the architects disagree with the developer-invented architecture. This then leads to recurring delays where final consequences can be survivable or fatal. The cost of survival is alienated and frustrated developers, and cost and schedule overruns. The cost of failure is technical failure or premature termination of the software development project.

 ## TYPICAL CAUSES

The singular cause of the Wherefore Art Thou Architecture AntiPattern is the lack of a managed enterprise architecture. This becomes visible at both the definition and implementation stages.

 ## KNOWN EXCEPTIONS

There are no known exceptions within application or system software development since even a small company with a single system should have a stated architecture for that system. The difference is the level of detailed documentation, which may be less and proportional to the scale of the system.

Prototypes and demonstrations can be produced with no regard to architecture, but then they are truly throw away and cannot be considered for any proof of concept. This would be a wasteful exercise in most cases that could have benefited from using a reference architecture to guide it and achieve a more useful result.

 ## REFACTORED SOLUTION

To avoid the problem caused by the lack of a properly defined and managed architecture it is necessary to understand the solution to architecture definition and management.

Architecture Definition

Enterprise architecture evolves at its own pace because it is driven by the emerging business requirements and the functionality of the technologies available, while at the same time being constrained by the existing legacy technology systems. Enterprise architecture must be subject to strict configuration management so that a software development project will always use a formal version. There should only ever be a single version of the overall enterprise architecture available for general use by software development projects.

The next generation of the architecture will evolve at two levels. Primarily it will be at the enterprise level that a strategy for adopting the next wave of technologies, such as message queuing and Enterprise JavaBeans will be developed. At the project level integration of technologies, such as Web access to a CICS (legacy mainframe) system, is the objective. This will drive changes to the formally released version of the architecture as software developments find gaps and inaccuracies within the architecture.

Architecture can be used at five places in the software development lifecycle [Bennett 1996]:

- Addressing the emergent properties of a system via technical requirements and design
- Representing the system in a viewable form
- Identifying and planning component reuse via design strategy
- Allocating component development across development teams
- Estimating the size and cost of the system

An enterprise architecture must define all of the technical requirements and the design strategy for software development to ensure that there is no need to locally invent solutions because the architecture was insufficient. It normally consists of:

- Enterprise components, objects, and containers
- Enterprise, system, and application-component-interface specifications
- Existing system and application-interchange formats
- Platform specifications
- Architectural patterns
- Implementation guidelines for projects (see the Distributed Disaster AntiPattern)
- Enterprise COTS (see the Batteries Not Included AntiPattern)
- Enterprise security
- Partnership interconnectivity/integration

Architecture Management

Architecture must be managed at two levels: corporately for its generic definition and by project for its implementation. These two levels must be fully synchronized and subject to software configuration management.

It is inevitable that a centrally produced architecture will not be fully sufficient for all software development projects. So it is necessary to drive extensions and changes to the architecture from individual software development projects.

Projects and lines of business must not be allowed to invent their own architecture undermining these benefits that can only be gained from enterprise architecture:

- Interoperability of systems across lines of business
- Centralized data access across lines of business
- Compatible systems
- Component and object reuse

Management of production and implementation of an enterprise architecture, along with the required planning and scheduling, are discussed in the following sections.

Management of the Production of an Enterprise Architecture

A full reference version of the enterprise architecture must be produced before any projects can attempt to implement it. This must include proving that the technology functions as specified and is compatible with the associated technologies. Because technology adoption generally happens in five- to ten-year cycles, there are many legacy systems with a variety of technologies that must be included in the overall enterprise architecture, in addition to the new ones being adopted. This leads to a complexity that must not only be managed but also proven to work in advance when new technologies, or new combinations of technologies, are intended to be implemented corporately.

The first step in the production of an enterprise architecture is being able to model what exists in current systems. The next step is to model required future systems, including those projects already under way. From these two views a single enterprise architecture must be produced, which will require carefully managed refinement. The following sections detail these steps.

Modeling the Current Systems

Modeling the existing systems and applications and identifying components, interfaces, and interchange formats will help to identify the specific nature of existing systems and any software reuse. This will form the initial enterprise architecture from which the next generation of technology applications and systems can be added to complete the enterprise view. The architecture model of existing systems must ensure that the following details are captured:

- Functionality provided with application and system components
- Public interface specifications
- Data types supported
- Transactional nature

Modeling the Next Generation Systems

Modeling the next generation systems is the production of the architecture for new technology applications and systems, such as an established financial company that wishes to implement a relationship management system using new technologies and integrate it with their existing legacy systems. The following architecture definition is discussed further in the Distributed Disaster AntiPattern.

The architectural framework of next generation systems should outline a conceptual model for all component partitioning, interfaces, and connections [Shaw 1996]. This gives a readily understood context for the architecture. The conceptual model must cover all aspects of the system, product, or application being defined, including all external dependencies:

- The required use of the DOT and associated services must be clearly defined. This should include any abstraction or wrapping of the DOT services.

- The nature (static library, dynamic library, or executable) and physical runtime location of components must also be identified.

- The scope of the use for each programming language must be clearly defined to guide the implementation. If a programming language is used for other than its planned use, a technical risk could be introduced that may have unforeseen repercussions.

- All known technical risks, identified during the definition of the architecture and also during the software development project implementation with mitigation options, must be defined in as much detail as possible.

- When the architecture introduces a new technology or novel use of a technology, it is critical that the innovation introduced is proven via an architecture run-ahead activity. The goal is to develop a small-scale application or product version with the innovative technology.

Producing the Enterprise Architecture

The enterprise architecture must be iterated further to fully integrate the legacy and future views of the corporate systems. This will show the critical corporate components within the enterprise and across all Line of Business (LOB) applications and systems in the form of:

- Reusable enterprise components
- Application modifications to use enterprise components
- Single-view connectors and containers
- New applications

Management of the Implementation of an Enterprise Architecture

However high-quality the enterprise architecture is, the key to success is the quality of the implementation and is completely subject to the effectiveness of the management of the implementation. This is a technical management activity, mixing the skills of a project manager and an architect. A small management team is usually the most efficient way to be effective; one role is that of a project manager with extensive technology experience and the other two are highly experienced architects with leadership skills.

Implementation starts with an enterprise architecture roadmap to define the implementation sequence. The reusable components should be developed early in the roadmap to gain early benefits. Interoperability between new and legacy systems should be a key focus of the roadmap to enable information sharing.

Producing an Enterprise Architecture Roadmap

Prior to any software development proceeding under the control of the enterprise architecture, it is necessary to produce a roadmap that identifies the application development projects that will be the vehicles for reusable component production, system interoperability, and any application replacement required.

The roadmap will specify the sequence and priority for all software development projects that come under the enterprise architecture umbrella. By necessity there will always be the exception to the rule, but these should be kept to the minimum or the enterprise architecture will fail.

Implementing Reusable Components

The roadmap will identify the priority of reusable component development. Only a few of these should be planned for development at one time due to the bandwidth of the architecture management activity. For each reusable component to be developed at least two application developments must fully validate the interface specification in a highly formal and detailed manner during their design stage. Then either one of them builds the component or a smaller third project is initiated to build it.

Implementing Interoperability

To develop interfaces at the system and application levels, particularly between new and legacy technologies, interface layers with conversions between the required data formats must be created. The interoperability will be in the form of data interchange or function invocation between the specified applications.

As input each application development project will be given detailed technical requirements stated by the architecture:

- Component specification
- Component interface definition
- Interchange formats for data conversion

Application/Addition/Replacement

New applications are developed for two reasons. The first reason is that a new set of business functions are required that are logically independent of the existing applications business functions. In this case the new applications will likely need to interoperate with some of the existing applications. The second reason is that existing (legacy) applications are migrated, often incrementally, to new technologies to aid in the addition of new business functions.

Planning and Scheduling Architecture Implementation

All of the above architecture implementation management activities must be planned and scheduled. The architecture implementation schedule must be synchronized with the associated software development projects. This is not a trivial task because projects rarely run to schedule because of a myriad of reasons not fully under a single point of control.

The first activity must be the production of the enterprise architecture roadmap, but there is no preset order to the following activities:

- Implement reusable components
- Implement interoperability
- Add/replace application

From an enterprise perspective interoperability of existing systems will usually be the highest priority. Implementing reusable components may not be a critical consideration if cost is not a primary driver, except in new systems where if invested in, it is easier to achieve if required. Application addition/replacement is only critical from an enterprise perspective because of the business need to support new functionality and to extend the life of the legacy systems by interoperating with them.

VARIATIONS

While the Wherefore Art Thou Architecture AntiPattern focuses on unmanaged enterprise architecture, the same problems are true for architecture that are produced for individual applications, products, or components:

- Architecture does not specify the technical requirements or design strategies.
- Architecture does not specify the use of chosen technologies.
- Architecture is produced in an informal and ad hoc manner.

The level of impact is less, but the problems are the same. The refactored solution is simpler because there are fewer other technologies (legacy and future) to consider.

EXAMPLE

An insurance company in the United Kingdom had five stovepipe insurance applications. Four of them were legacy-based COBOL on minicomputers, and the fifth was client-server-based (Microsoft Visual Basic and Microsoft SQL Server). Interoperability was achieved by flat-file transfer and data reentry. The company decided that it needed to improve the way its business was run with the critical need being to provide a single customer view across all applications. The company did have a business architecture that drove this initiative, but did not realize that for the initiative to be successful it would also need an enterprise technical architecture. A single project was formed to implement the single customer view. The approach selected was to implement the querying of the data first, followed by multiple-system-update capability, as shown in the following sequential activity list:

1. Single view querying (see Figure 3.15).
   a) Develop presentation services
   b) Develop data gathering and filtering services
   c) Develop connectors to stovepipe applications

2. Single view updates.
   a) Extend presentation services
   b) Add data location and update services
   c) Extend connectors

The querying approach chosen was to marshal the separate data sets from the stovepipe applications, combine them, and filter the response for each user query. It initially concentrated on providing the presentation services on the front-end server and client machines. The analysis took three months and the project immediately went into an iterative design and coding process. The technology used was Microsoft Visual Basic and Microsoft SQL Server. The front-end system was built in the following five months with few problems.

The next stage of the project was to develop the data gathering and filtering services but the lack of an architecture strategy caused the Analysis Paralysis AntiPattern [Brown 1998]. The project and business managers decided that in an attempt to move forward they should implement the connectors while the data gathering and filtering services were analyzed further.

The technologies for the connectors had not been defined, nor proved, because of the lack of the architecture. The project chose Microsoft Visual C++ because they had some staff skills in that area, leading to a rather ad hoc technical architecture (see Figure 3.16). Unfortunately they had no idea about how to build a connector. This stage suffered from design and coding paralysis. The project was suspended after an attempt to produce any further working software failed five months after the delivery of the presentation services.

The company now realized that it needed a technical equivalent of the business architecture and that they needed to bring in external staff to

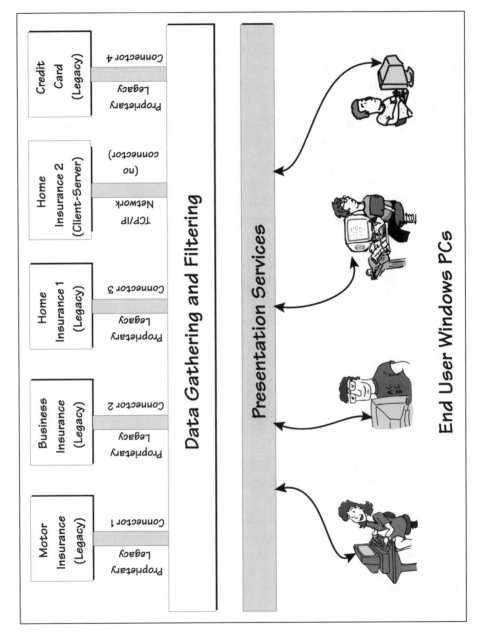

Figure 3.15 Abstract architecture.

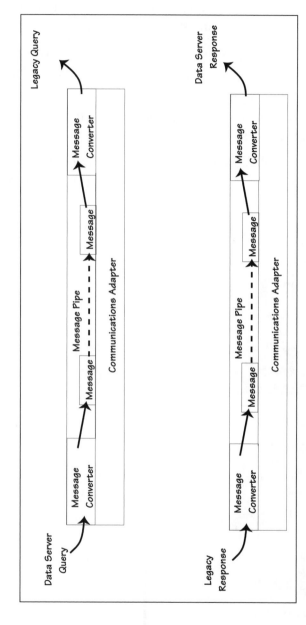

Figure 3.16 Ad hoc connector architecture.

achieve this. They hired two architects, one of whom had skills in building financial systems with modern technologies and the other had worked on gateways to legacy systems. The first step was to sequentially produce a full enterprise architecture combining the views of the:

- Existing legacy systems data, functionality, and interfaces
- Integration technology to connect the single customer view application with the legacy systems
- New single customer view application with data location, gathering, and filtering services

The technologies of Microsoft Visual Basic, Microsoft Visual C++, and Microsoft SQL Server were retained but their scope was changed (see Figure 3.17).

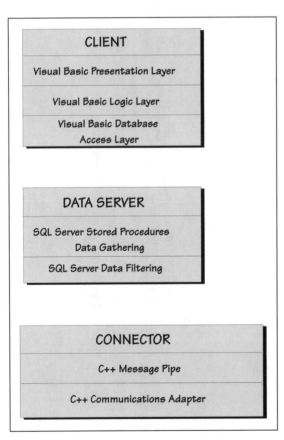

Figure 3.17 Technical architecture scope.

Implement Single Connector
- Legacy Adapter #1
- Connector
- Data Server Adapter
- Test with Data Server

Implement Single Connector
- Legacy Adapter #2
- Test with Data Server Stub

Develop Minimal Data Server
- Data Gathering
- Test Evaluated Connectivity
- Data Filtering
- Test with Clients

Develop Connector #3
- Legacy Adapter #3
- Test Functionality

Develop Connector #4
- Legacy Adapter #4
- Test Functionality

Extend Data Services
- Data Gathering
- Data Server Test
- Data Filtering
- Client Test

Figure 3.18 Software development schedule outline.

The architecture run-ahead activities that were intended to prove that the architecture could be successfully implemented were included in the software development project as the lead activities, as shown in Figure 3.18. The run-ahead (proof-of-concept) activities were:

- Implement a single legacy connector with minimal data location.
- Implement a second connector with extended data location.
- Develop minimal data gathering and filtering services.
- Add the remaining connectors.
- Extend the data gathering and filtering services.

RELATED SOLUTIONS

The Enterprise System Fable AntiPattern [Brown 1999] discusses the failure to achieve enterprise architecture and how to refactor the failed approaches in order to gain the benefits from enterprisewide systems. It demonstrates the need for an enterprise architecture.

The Distributed Disaster AntiPattern examines the problems associated with managing the implementation of complex technologies and how to mitigate the risks of technical failure. Such data and functional distribution must be identified within the enterprise architecture process.

APPLICABILITY TO OTHER VIEWPOINTS AND SCALES

The Wherefore Art Thou Architecture AntiPattern will always primarily occur at the enterprise scale, but the initial visible impact will be at the application and system scales. The enterprise problems take longer to appear because of the latency involved in developing enough stovepipe systems prior to trying to make them interoperate.

The primary viewpoint throughout this book is managerial, but this AntiPattern is also valid from an architectural viewpoint. It is hard to separate the viewpoints here because the real viewpoint is architecture management, a necessary combinatory viewpoint to achieve success.

Killer Demo

AntiPattern Name: Killer Demo

Also Known As: Death by Marketing

Most Applicable Scale: Enterprise

Refactored Solution Name: Isolation and "Binning," Burn the Ships!

Refactored Solution Type: Role

Root Causes: Greed, Ignorance, Arrogance

Unbalanced Forces: Management of IT Resources

Anecdotal Evidence:
> "Look, I know you guys are busy, but we need you to make a few changes to the demo before tomorrow's big briefing for the CEO. It's gotta be perfect, Okay?"

BACKGROUND

It has been said that only a small minority of people can truly conceptualize an idea without some kind of concrete example. Knowing this, savvy software concerns often build the most impressive prototype demonstration that they can manage as a means of representing the future product they are trying to sell. These demonstrations are often referred to as *Killer Demos*, using the word *killer* in its more recent vernacular to imply that it is very, very impressive. While Killer Demos are common and make a lot of sense from a marketing and internal conceptualization perspective, there are cases where a Killer Demo begins to become more important than the actual and eventual product that it was originally built to demonstrate. When this happens, the word *killer* tends toward its more traditional meaning, and we find our project dying under the weight of a deadly Killer Demo AntiPattern.

Also consider that the word *demo* means different things to different people, and it is these semantics that create the problem:

To the end user, a demo is proof that required business processes are supportable in a useful manner. In other words, a proof-of-concept prototype of a series of GUI forms that show the correct access to functionality and data required by the required business processes.

To the software manager, a demo proves that an acceptable solution is provided within time and budget constraints. User and technical acceptance is the goal, where a working prototype is produced.

To the architect, a demo is a technical solution that is achievable and sustainable in terms of fully functional software that can be extended.

To the developer, a demo is a technology solution that can be implemented as intended and demonstrates the ability to support the required business processes, but is not extensible.

It is this nature of confusion that can lead to the Killer Demo AntiPattern. When is a demo not a demo? When there is an expectation that it is something more!

GENERAL FORM

The general form of the Killer Demo AntiPattern centers on a slick prototype or demonstration program that represents some future state of a product yet to be developed (see Figure 3.19). This demonstration is a key marketing or support-garnering tool used by management to convey the

Figure 3.19 The sleeping monster.

value of the product to be developed. The AntiPattern is manifested when the needs of the demonstration begin to outweigh the original intent of the demonstration. Supporting the demonstration begins to draw key resources away from the necessary functions required to actually build the future product, such as design and development of the actual system itself. The more impressive the demonstration, the more likely that the Killer Demo AntiPattern will manifest itself. This is because demand to show off the demonstration increases each time it is presented, and as the demonstration's reputation grows so does the status level of those desiring a presentation. Eventually, top executives are involved, sending the new demo team all over the map to present the Killer Demo, thereby directing the use of key resources in ways that are completely orthogonal to any actual system development process.

Unfortunately, once this happens, it is typically irreversible unless the senior decision makers are able to realign system development resources and schedules to support the demonstration as a separate entity that does not impact design and development staff. If successful, the only remaining challenge is in managing the very real potential for feature creep as feedback from the now separate demonstration staff affects the system requirements.

SYMPTOMS AND CONSEQUENCES

The consequences vary based on the symptoms, and often the two are tightly intertwined, as the following list shows:

- The project fails to shift from marketing phase to design/development phase because all technical resources are completely tied to keeping a demo or prototype running, or making improvements/ modifications to it.

- During design or development, the prototype is not baselined and frozen.

- System architecture or design is driven by the demo.

- There is no design documentation. Instead, people are directed to the demonstration for design information.

- Resources critical to the ongoing success of a project are gradually drawn away from actual production in order to maintain the Killer Demo. This is usually accompanied by classic crisis management symptoms.

- Long-term viability is sacrificed to support short-term "critical or else there'll be no long term" crises concerning demonstrations or customizations of the demonstration in key briefings.

- Senior-level executives are constantly sending the demo team all over to show it off, which effectively removes the demo team from the resource pool.

- At some point it is recognized that actual product development has been sacrificed, and desperate managers will make the incredible decision to field the demonstration. Invariably, some naive developer will propose this and claim that it just might work. Depending on the job market, others might even stick around to attempt such a miracle.

TYPICAL CAUSES

The cause of the Killer Demo AntiPattern is easy to understand. It is human nature to focus on the more enjoyable or immediately gratifying activity of building exciting demonstrations than all the boring configuration management, documentation, or any of the other burdensome activities critical to any large-scale production development. Upon examination (if examined at all) one would expect to find that a decreasing percentage of available resources should be required to support a demonstration as the actual project gets under way and the demonstration is baselined. This, sadly, is not what we find in real life. What we do find is that the resources necessary to support the demonstration increase over time as do efforts to enhance it, and other hangers-on latch on to what becomes a defacto demo team. This is further exacerbated as the demonstration grows in complexity and is therefore increasingly brittle, requiring even more specialized staff to support it. What's worse is that these specialized staff must be on hand at every demonstration in case it breaks (see Figure 3.20).

As Figure 3.21 illustrates, it's not overly difficult to represent the impact of a Killer Demo AntiPattern.

In the Killer Demo AntiPattern, the ratio of effort expended on the demo does not decrease. In fact, it often increases over time as more is expected of the demonstration and more versions of it exist until an organization and management issue for the demonstration is born (see Figure 3.22).

Furthermore, it's a quick way to gain wide praise from senior management and peers alike. However, the longer term, disciplined effort necessary for a sustainable production requires a lot of work and produces little flair or excitement.

Figure 3.20 The Killer Demo away team.

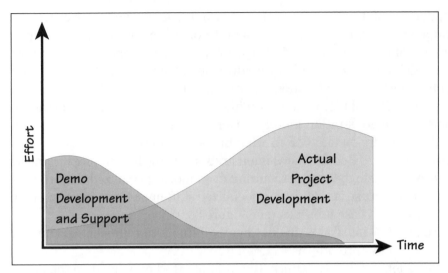

Figure 3.21   Normal project effort curve.

 ## KNOWN EXCEPTIONS

Companies whose primary business is the development of promotional demonstrations or marketing packages, that is, GUI focused, must produce killer demonstrations to succeed. These companies have the huge advantage of not being responsible for the long haul and can therefore ignore it.

However, when the demonstrations begin to deal with interconnectivity between applications, in addition to whatever GUI requirements exist, the company must then consider the wider implications caused by the additional criteria placed on the demonstration.

 ## REFACTORED SOLUTION

Preventing the Killer Demo AntiPattern requires careful preplanning and may leverage one of several sneaky methods. The safest approach is to manage expectations very carefully from the beginning. This requires knowing in advance the goal to be attempted and exactly what the role of any demonstration is to be, as well as what any demonstration's limitations will be.

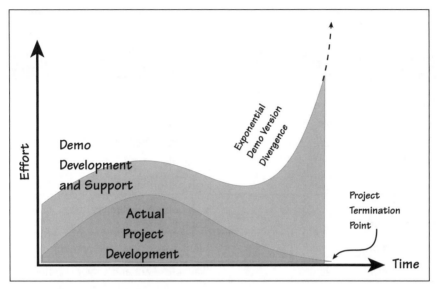

Figure 3.22 Abnormal project effort curve.

Prevention Strategy: Isolation and "Binning"

Obviously, one cannot know everything in advance, but the real brain effort of planning ahead must be expended as far as possible. Managing expectations means that the prototyping effort is clearly delineated in a project schedule and budget. It is best to include the prototyping tasks in the project schedule, but group them independently. This will allow you to manage development and other resources more realistically and provide you with some ammunition should you need to justify any future reluctance to extend the demonstration beyond its real purpose, without additional resources to support such a task.

The principle mechanism for preventing the Killer Demo AntiPattern is to establish a clear demarcation zone between any code developed for a demonstration and any code developed for actual production, as shown in Table 3.4.

The criteria lead to the natural conclusion that the demonstration software would often be best developed using a different programming language than that of the normal application development software. The distinctions are critical and the Killer Demo AntiPattern usually occurs because of the demonstration programming language characteristics. The programming language chosen must be fit for its purpose, and the purpose must be clearly defined.

Table 3.4 Criteria Comparison for Demo and Application Development Programming Languages

DEMO PROGRAMMING LANGUAGE CRITERIA	APPLICATION PROGRAMMING LANGUAGE CRITERIA
Very rapid development	Rapid development
Low level of feature complexity	Complexity appropriate for nature of implementation feature
Nonscaleable	Scaleable
Low performance	High performance
Adequate stability (compile and run)	High degree of stability (compile and run)
GUI interaction only	Client and server development
Available graphical libraries	Available client and server libraries

There is an implicit assumption here that all demonstrations are basically graphical in nature and aimed at end users. Different criteria would be applied if the nature of the demonstration were connecting a legacy application to a user-available desktop application package, such as Microsoft Excel. In this case, while it is expected that the Microsoft Excel macros would need to be written, the main work would be the connector technology. Table 3.5 differentiates the programming language criteria dependent on whether the demo is GUI based or connector based.

The solution is often the use of a COTS gateway or messaging product; which, while expensive, is only a fraction of what the cost would be to build it.

Of course there are situations when a richer demonstration would need to have the superset criteria from Table 3.3. This may still require more than a single programming language to achieve. However, there has to be a clean line drawn between demonstration and working code, otherwise we fall back into the trap.

A demonstration is either a sample or proof-of-concept delivery. The sample demonstration is GUI-focused software. The proof-of-concept demonstration requires some interconnectivity. It may be that in addition to the interconnectivity the proof of concept requires some GUI development. Note that because of the research nature of the work, proof-of-concept activities may prove that concepts are not feasible for a range of technical reasons, many of which relate to the adequacy of the selected

Table 3.5   Criteria Comparison for GUI Demo and Connectivity Demo Programming Languages

GUI DEMO PROGRAMMING LANGUAGE CRITERIA	CONNECTIVITY DEMO PROGRAMMING LANGUAGE CRITERIA
Very rapid development	Very rapid development
Low level of feature complexity	Low level of feature complexity
Nonscaleable	Nonscaleable
Low performance	Medium performance
Adequate stability (compile and run)	Adequate stability (compile and run)
GUI interaction only	Gateway interaction only
Available graphical libraries	Available client and server libraries

programming language or COTS. This leads quickly to the view that there may be a need to create a third category of software development that lies between a demonstration and full development code: proof-of-concept prototype. Table 3.6 adds the programming language criteria for proof of concept demos.

Table 3.6   Criteria Comparison for GUI Demonstration, Application Development, and Proof-of-Concept Programming Languages

DEMONSTRATION PROGRAMMING LANGUAGE CRITERIA	APPLICATION PROGRAMMING LANGUAGE CRITERIA	PROOF-OF-CONCEPT PROGRAMMING LANGUAGE CRITERIA
Very rapid development	Rapid development	Very rapid development
Low level of feature complexity	Complexity appropriate for nature of implementation feature	Low level of feature complexity
Nonscaleable	Scaleable	Scaleable
Low performance	High performance	Medium performance
Adequate stability (compile and run)	High degree of stability (compile and run)	Adequate stability (compile and run)
GUI interaction only	Client and server development	Gateway interaction only
Available graphical libraries	Available client and server libraries	Available client and server libraries

Recovery Strategy: "Burn the Ships!"

In the spring of 1519, a Spanish fleet set sail,
Cortez told his sailors this mission must not fail.
On the eastern shore of Mexico they landed with great dreams
But the hardships of the new world made them restless and weak.
Quietly they whispered, "Let's sail back to the life we knew"
But the one who led them there was saying,
Burn the ships, we're here to stay.
There's no way we could go back now that we've come this far by faith.

—(Stephen Curtis Chapman)

About 2000 years ago, Julius Caesar, Proconsul to Rome, set out across the sea to conquer England. Caesar had had many battles with the 'Gauls' in France whose allies, the 'Celts', inhabited England at the time. England was a terrible place for a Roman soldier. It held an aggressive and dangerous enemy; for the Celts were known for their skill in war and especially for their skill with the chariot. The Romans were vastly outnumbered—about 50,000 Roman soldiers to half-a-million Celts. Worst of all, any retreat to Rome and friendly territory was across the channel—they were cut-off from any quick re-supply or relief. As the Roman fleet drew near the coast, hordes of Celts could be seen lining the Cliffs of Dover, their battle gear glinting in the sun, ready to do battle. Caesar turned down the coast, away from the cliffs, and after a fierce battle in the surf with the enemy, established a small beach head. They were landed in England all right, but held only a small purchase on the land—entirely surrounded by Celtic armies. Legend has it the Caesar then did an incredibly daring thing for his men. He knew he had a commitment problem with his soldiers. As long as the Roman ships remained on the coast line, there was hope of retreat back to familiar country. So he burned the ships, their only means of escape, so as to make it perfectly clear to his men that there was to be no retreat, that if they were pushed back in battle it would be into the sea itself. There would be no retreat across the sea's wide expanse, only death if the battle were lost. He needed commitment from his soldiers to victory, commitment to conquer, and this is how he assured it. They needed to realize, and he needed them to realize it quickly, that they were here to stay.

—http://home1.gte.net/psneeley/MrpMan.htm#Burn the Ships!

When Caesar ordered the ships to be burnt, he removed any temptation for desertion or retreat. His troops won. You may have to take a similarly drastic step. Delete the demonstration! Just say no! You'll probably want to keep an archive somewhere, but don't tell anyone about it except your supervisor (you may also want to explain your reasons first . . .). If the demonstration code *can't* be altered, then *voilà*, the staff standing by to do so are now reavailable for the actual system development effort.

If Caesar had failed, he also would have been dead and therefore not around to endure any postburning demotion parties, but you will still be around after the fact if you take this drastic measure and it doesn't work. So if your career might be severely jeopardized by deleting the demonstration, maybe you can get someone more senior to authorize taking the demonstration offline in order to proceed with development.

Hands Off

This solution can be called Hands Off. The trick here is to assign a fresh young engineer to assist the senior demonstration developer. After the young engineer has learned enough to take over, find a crisis (see the Firedrill AntiPattern [Brown 1998]) that demands the senior developer's immediate and complete attention and require the new engineer to take over for a while. Then, move the senior developer to actual development as soon as the crisis has been handled since the young engineer is handling the demo just fine.

 ## VARIATIONS

Multimedia anything. Today there is a loud cry from all fronts to produce slick Web sites with very cool things on them. This typically means animated Graphics Interchange Formats (GIFs), movie files, and neat Java applets and Java-scripted interfaces. Everyone is out to impress each other and often lose sight of the initial purpose of an organization's Web presence altogether.

As people grow more familiar with the Web and its cool eyeball candy, they are increasingly selective about their browsing and are seeking sites that offer true utility and value to their lives, in addition to pure entertainment. Our advice is that you do not overdo the sensual impact at the expense of true functional utility. Otherwise, like the killer demo, your killer Website will bleed your resources dry before any return on the investment is likely to be realized.

 ## EXAMPLE

The following two examples demonstrate the basic nature of the Killer Demo AntiPattern. In both cases connectivity for purposes of information sharing was a primary architectural goal.

Demo One

This large project involved the integration of several very large, massively expensive legacy systems by wrapping them with middleware interfaces and accessing them from thin integrated clients. The project lasted for several years and by about the third or fourth year had produced a very slick demonstration that actually accessed five separate servers, and through event-driven user interaction provided an integration that we were all very proud of and were asked to demonstrate constantly.

As the demonstration grew in popularity with each showing, the project team found themselves continually setting up at various places to demonstrate it to higher and higher officials and executives. At first this was a real kick because the team gained companywide recognition and was able to head up a very popular and growing consortium comprised of many other cool companies and organizations.

Gradually, the demonstration and its setup (which involved launching several massive legacy systems and their wrappers) began to take its toll on the fairly small staff and limited budget. They ran out of money several times and only stayed alive for the last two years with funding from additional legacy system sponsors in exchange for the added integration of their system into the demo, which by now was a true killer demo.

Additionally, this occurred at a time when budgets were being cut. Thus, the killer demo became increasingly important to management as a marketing tool and, therefore, had to be ready to go in a moment's notice. Increased high-level participation in the project also led to additional mandatory periodic status reports and attendance at monthly project briefings, typically requiring eight hours of preparation and practice briefing time prior to the actual briefing, which cost half a day.

In the end, the project's sponsor decided to pass the project off to a different shop where its evolved configuration was more appropriately located. Unfortunately, this new shop did not share the original sponsor's vision of what the demonstration provided and after unsuccessfully trying to leverage it to bolster one of their already bloated projects, it was finally dropped altogether.

Demo Two

A systems integrator intended to develop a proof-of-concept demonstration for a Wall Street trading house that illustrated how end users could access legacy system data via their Web browser and in-house Web server. The initial scope was to allow a single batch file produced from the regular overnight run of a legacy system to be accessed on demand. This was to show a list of customer account numbers and allow the customer to selectively retrieve their details. The architecture was developed for a wider

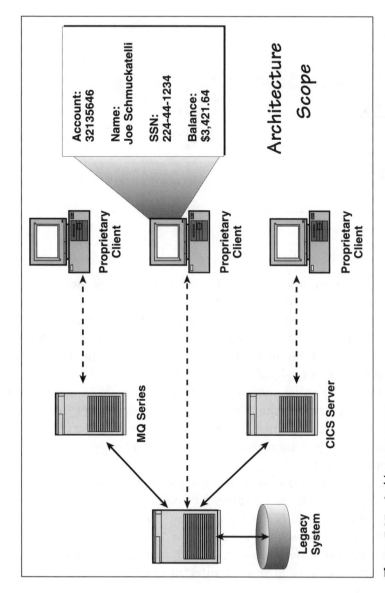

Figure 3.23 Architecture scope.

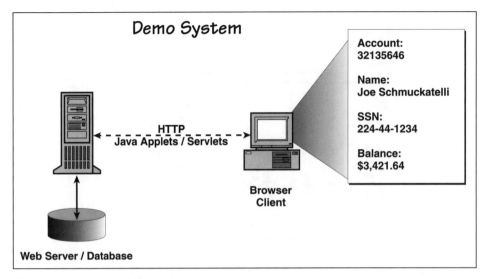

Figure 3.24 Demo scope.

range of interconnectivity including CICS and MQ Series (see Figure 3.23) to show the potential information sharing capabilities.

The demonstration implemented Java applets and servlets in Visual Café as shown in Figure 3.24. It was anticipated that this effort would take three weeks. The delta between the scope of the architecture and the demonstration implementation was significant.

The demonstration was successfully developed and shown to business managers at the customer site. The business managers were very positive about the demonstration; however, the architecture was also presented and the business managers immediately wished for extensions, hinting at a development contract.

The next stage was to access three legacy files from overnight batch runs and allow dynamic Web-based query of combined and filtered customer data. This was considerably more complicated and had to be completed in another two weeks: a customer set deadline. This was barely achieved and moved the software down shortcuts to achieve the rapid delivery, which moved it away from the layered architecture and isolated access mechanisms (see Figure 3.25).

This demonstration version was also highly successful and drove the business managers to make more promises of potential future work if more of the promised architecture was proven. But the only proofs yet to be made were for CICS and MQ connections. The business managers set three months as the time line for the CICS demonstration extension.

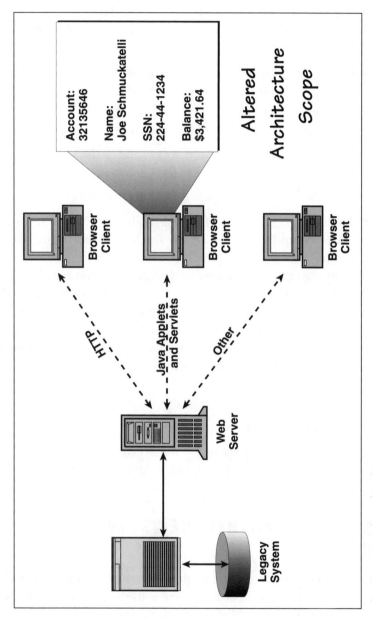

Figure 3.25 Altered architecture.

This immediately caused the developer team lead to question the unrealistic schedule to deliver fully functional code on the basis of the following required tasks:

- Analyzing the CICS system to identify a useful transaction for compatible customer information to integrate with that already provided by the batch files

- Technically evaluating a CICS gateway product to use with (preferably) a Java programming language interface

- Reprogramming some of the second demonstration version to the architecture so integration would be possible

- Building the functional extraction software for the CICS transaction data

- Integrating the CICS and batch file extraction software

The team leader recognized that this was at least a five-month task, but his manager was completely focused on the promised future work that could be achieved by delivering the next version of the demo.

The result was that the team leader and senior programmer left the company in the face of such an unreasonable attitude. Management used other resources, somewhat less skilled, who at the end of three months had not come close to delivering the demonstration. After another month of delays, the business managers concluded that the systems integrator was incapable of delivering and dissolved the relationship.

RELATED SOLUTIONS

Gilding the Lily AntiPattern is strongly related to the Killer Demo AntiPattern because in a sense that is what the killer demo becomes.

APPLICABILITY TO OTHER VIEWPOINTS AND SCALES

Architects tend to ignore, and even disdain demonstrations, seeing them as nuisances and wastes of time that risk encouraging management to overlook the real need to architect the eventual product.

Senior management, being devoted to garnering support for the project, is usually the strongest force behind creating a killer demo in the first place. Managers who are closer to the project, such as the actual project leader, are easily lured by the quick rise in status that a really neat and popular demonstration can win, but are also (or should be) most aware of the resource costs associated with the demonstration that may save them if they can force themselves to take a longer-term view.

Architects have the objective of creating a sustainable solution and when tasked to develop a demonstration will architect a fully functional and extensible solution that goes well beyond the intent of any demonstration. Demonstrations based on a viable architecture will leave themselves open for further development activity that is promised by the architecture. However, if only a demonstration programming language is used in the development of the demonstration, and not in some semblance of the actual operational environment, failure can result because the recipients of the demonstration won't believe the viability of the demonstration.

Developers, like project leaders, can also be lured by the instant fame and recognition to be earned by creating a very impressive demonstration. However, this quick fame can easily lead to a recurring and expanding nightmare of keeping the demonstration available and constantly adding to it if the demonstration becomes a killer demo.

One-Shot Deal

AntiPattern Name: One-Shot Deal

Also Known As: Quick'n'Dirty

Most Applicable Scale: Enterprise

Refactored Solution Name: Aim Before You Shoot

Refactored Solution Type: Process

Root Causes: Sloth, Haste, or Ignorance

Unbalanced Forces: Management of IT Resources

Anecdotal Evidence:
> "We don't need a major production here, this is a quick and dirty effort that we won't need to maintain later."
> "Look, if we don't deliver this piece of crap this month, there won't be a *next* month!"
> "Hey, we don't need any documentation, just leave enough clues in your code in case we need to make some changes later."

BACKGROUND

As they look back on the many projects that composed their career, many people realize that most of their projects were treated as special cases and were typically expedited to meet some kind of unrealistic deadline. If they are brutally honest, they would probably even admit to directing the expediting themselves! It is a sad but typically true fact that a large percent of software projects fit into a category that might be called one-shot deals for which the developers often had no intention of being around to maintain once produced. Or, more typically, they just didn't have time for all that project management crap because they just had to get the job done before running out of funding or time (or both).

In all likelihood, the One-Shot Deal (see Figure 3.26) has been around longer than you have. Just about every project management text of any merit whatsoever addresses the dangers of sacrificing process management tasks on the altar of expediency. This book does not differ. However, the mere fact that the issue is widely addressed indicates a pattern or in this case, since it is repeated with results that should be avoided, an AntiPattern. With this in

Figure 3.26   One-shot deal.

mind, we offer up the One-Shot Deal AntiPattern to constructively extend the lexicon so that everyone can now refer to the occurrence as a One-Shot Deal.

A grizzled guru of 1960s development days shared this amazing but all too believable story with the authors as we researched this book. This particular guru, who we'll call Ed, explained that back in the early 60s he was working as a software developer to develop databases for a government contract. He said that most of his products were last-minute conceptions, needed for some emergent analysis or another, and were not expected to be used beyond the immediate crisis. Ed also explained that many of these quick kludges are still in use today, almost 40 years later.

The products that they developed contained many date fields, which are typically defined to include all four digits of the year. Ed said that he clearly remembers discussing how many bytes to use for the year, predicting that unless four bytes were used there would be problems in the year 2000, which was nearly 40 years away but would still arrive nevertheless. However, the project team was assisted by a new government-mandated standard for data fields that specified two-digit date fields for their contract. The mandatory directive mistakenly assumed that software would not still be around after 30-odd years, and since memory and storage were expensive, it was prudent that the government *require* contracted developers to use the new abbreviated date format.

Ed shuddered as he contemplated the expense that has been laid out since then to maintain his so-called one-shot deals. We did too.

GENERAL FORM

The One-Shot Deal AntiPattern is typically found in the following three instances:

- The Demo
- The Tool
- Retrofit

The Demo

In the first instance of this AntiPattern a quick demonstration is required. Perhaps something that isn't even functional but has the look and feel of the functional application. When the demonstration is successful, management then requires something that is functional, and it is often required in short order. The common misperception is that since the demo is completed most of the work is completed. You might hear management demand, "All you have to do is make it work! You've already done the rest."

This version of the One-Shot Deal AntiPattern is realized when the users find the demonstration to be exactly what they wanted. The marketing staff promises the world, both in terms of time (read that as compressed delivery schedule) and added functionality (read that as it wasn't even part of the demonstration screen). The marketing squad returns to demand a fully functional version of the demonstration with slight changes. Little do they understand that no changes can be made since the actual product doesn't exist.

The Tool

The second instance of the One-Shot Deal AntiPattern is found in organizations where systems that originated as in-house tools and utilities are created by developers to help with larger problems (see Figure 3.27). It should be obvious that anytime there is a justification for bootlegging time from a larger project to build the tool or utility, a reasonable amount of effort should take place to implement a systems engineering process with project management control, specifically if the tool or utility is worth developing because it is actually *needed* and therefore marketable. If it is marketable, it will eventually be

Figure 3.27 Making your own tools.

marketed and therefore must be supported, which in turn justifies at least some basic level of proper systems engineering process.

Unfortunately, there may be another force at work in this AntiPattern. This force may be the reason that the developers have to develop their own utilities greed. If a utility is available that can accomplish what the one-shot deal utility would do, then it is usually more economical in the long run to just buy it and get on with carrying out the real business objectives. The obvious exception to this occurs when such a tool is not already available, or may be available but is inadequate.

The Retrofit

The One-Shot Deal AntiPattern also occurs when the development team is forced into a quick and dirty solution that will address a legacy environment. Consider an architecture that is soon to be overhauled, yet the demand for functionality remains in the near term. The development team is tasked to perform the development effort quickly, and without serious documentation, because soon the architecture will be replaced. It is believed that the product won't be around long and won't require support by anyone other than the development team. However, for sundry reasons, the architecture remains in place for an unexpected period of time. What is left is the One-Shot Deal.

SYMPTOMS AND CONSEQUENCES

The symptoms and consequences are the same regardless of the variation of the One-Shot Deal. A summary list of the symptoms for the One-Shot Deal AntiPattern follows:

- Quick tasks, outside of the ordinary grind but deemed useful in helping perform the ordinary grind more efficiently, easier, or better
- Self-developed utilities, quick fixes, or data converters that are only needed for a one-time process
- Projects with no hard set of requirements, or a set of requirements that has grown over time by accretion
- Direction to "ignore all that process crap" and just toss something together for the "meantime"
- Mistaken belief that there will be support later to redo it properly
- Little or no requirements specification
- Loose, evolving system architecture

- Inordinate amount of in flux or to-be-replaced code
- Dead code
- Unexplained interfaces
- Uncommented code
- Analysis Paralysis AntiPattern
- Requirements Jeopardy AntiPattern

Consequences are typically not realized until later in the lifecycle when it becomes apparent that appropriate control and processes were not applied. The consequences for the One-Shot Deal AntiPattern are typically not fatal, but rather, draining of critical resources. This may be considered a slow death. Consequences for the One-Shot Deal AntiPattern are identified in the following list:

- Unreliable performance.
- Poor performance.
- Duplicate tools are developed for the same purpose, since the development of the One-Shot Deal tool is informal and other developers are unaware of its existence.
- Applications don't scale, perform poorly, and are not interoperable (i.e., stovepipe).
- System or product architecture is described by a COTS product.
- Closed architecture.
- Duplication of commercial products; functionality provided in commercial products, either in total or in part.
- Inadequate support for configuration management.
- Maintenance is nearly impossible.
- Continued development and maintenance produces poorly coded applications and results in more poor programming practices by future programmers.

TYPICAL CAUSES

Some of the causes of the One-Shot Deal AntiPattern have been discussed in the General Form; however, a more complete list is provided here. Causes are typically affiliated with one of the three specific variations of the AntiPattern, and some are duplicative for each.

The Demo

- Lack of strategic vision
- Assumption that the code will be developed from scratch, Greenfield development [Brown 1998]
- Previous successes using the same approach
- Ignorance of the difference between a demonstration and a fully developed application

The Tool

- Strong resistance to formal projects
- Developers who are intimidated by the real work they face and, instead, manage to convince their management that they should first "develop some critical tools we'll need," which will allow them to continue developing products or using tools that they are already comfortable with
- Developer organizations that are too lazy to seek out professional utilities already developed and widely in use
- A software development company that is too lean (cheap) to purchase world-class developer tools and chooses rather to develop their own tool sets
- Failure to communicate between development projects
- Project isolation
- Previous successes using the same approach
- Single developer

The Retrofit

- Strong resistance to formal projects
- Software shops who need to convert one format of data into another to be able to transition to a new RDBMS, or in order to support a new customer or delivery platform
- Failure to communicate between development projects

- Previous successes using the same approach
- Focus on the delivery schedule (Myopic Delivery AntiPattern)
- Focus on the bottom line (cost, greed)

KNOWN EXCEPTIONS

Prototypes are an appropriate exception to the One-Shot Deal AntiPattern. The key to working with prototypes is to ensure that they *never, never, never, ever* get rolled into a development system. McConnell points out several things you can do to ensure that this never happens:

- Develop prototypes in a different language than the production (especially one not scaleable). If the project is supposed to be shipped as a C++ or Java application, "develop the prototype in Microsoft Visual Basic so that it would be impractical to use it as the basis for the real software" [McConnell 1998].
- Manage expectations. This is uniquely challenging because of the two-edged-sword nature in underselling so that you can overdeliver versus losing by overselling to present a positive and favorable impression and foster a can-do attitude.

If there is any likelihood that your prototype will be rolled into a production system, plan ahead by including skeleton process hooks in your development processes and environment that allow a more formal software development process to be rapidly migrated to, such as:

- Automated source code control [McConnell 1998]
- Formal defect tracking [McConnell 1998]
- Formal system interface definitions (recommend the use of OMG's IDL—*It's not just for CORBA anymore*, it's an ISO standard)
- Regression testing with documented findings (informal for now, but *very* useful later.)

REFACTORED SOLUTION

There are two refactored solutions. The first is intended to prevent the One-Shot Deal AntiPattern, while the second is intended to cure the problems once encountered.

Aim Before You Shoot (Prevention)

"Plan for the future and invest wisely." It sounds like sage advice that one might find in a fortune cookie, but it is never more appropriate than when facing the One-Shot Deal AntiPattern. The critical point is that any shot is worth aiming before shooting, especially if you've only got one shot to fire! Experience shows that any successful demo, utility, or retrofit project will probably prove useful far beyond the initial need. In fact, the need for a particular useful utility was often the initial spark of some of today's most popular software development companies. For example, consider Peter Norton's file undelete and disk editor tools not the property of the Symantec corporation.

Whenever you find yourself developing something that is not part of an actual deliverable, suspect that you might be building a One-Shot Deal. If there are no requirements for the thing you are building (or it's being created for a single use, but you secretly plan to save it because you are quite sure that it will come in handy again soon), get *very* suspicious! Consider the implications of success for a moment. Ask yourself some of the questions in Table 3.7.

Enough "yes" answers to these questions should tip you off that perhaps a business case could be made to support the development of this tool as an actual product versus a One-Shot Deal.

Table 3.7 Criteria to Establish the Implications of Success

CRITERIA FOR IMPLICATIONS OF SUCCESS	YES	NO
Am I creating this for me so I can do my real job better?		
Are there others who would really like it, and would it help them do their job better?		
Will I need it again?		
Is this tool not really available somewhere else (or at a reasonable price)?		
Would someone pay for this demo or tool?		
Is it likely that the demo will become a product?		
Would we have paid for this tool if it were available?		
If I were to show others this tool/utility, would it raise my self-esteem?		
Is it likely that the legacy system will exist for more than one year?		

Look What We Found! (Cure)

So how do we stop the One-Shot Deal AntiPattern once we realize we're deeply in it, and promises have been made, work has been redirected, and *something* must be shown for the effort? Your best bet may be to schedule a briefing to senior management to present a "wonderful discovery." The discovery is that you have identified a terrific new market and marketable product that the company ought to consider pursuing for the following reasons:

- Developers everywhere could do their jobs better!
- They really need it, would surely like it, and want it!
- They will need it over and over again!
- It isn't available anywhere else, or it's way too expensive elsewhere.
- People will pay for this demo (implementation of) or tool—we know because *we* would have paid for it if it was available somewhere!
- We will be using this (legacy) system for more than a year, and so will others. We can market our solution.
- Our company/division/group will be *famous!* We'll all be *rich!*

If you can sell them, and your hunches prove right, you may find yourself in a much better corporate position very soon! You may be creating an entirely new line of products or even be responsible for an paradigm industry shift. Don't laugh, just read about the Mark Andreesons, Bill Gates, Amazon.coms, and Peter Dells of our day.

VARIATIONS

Carpentry shows on television often advise viewers to create intermediate products to help line up several pieces more easily or to help them get two components to join squarely. These items are called *jigs*. While jigs fit most of the criteria of a One-Shot Deal, they are often not retained beyond a particular project and are therefore not as enduringly constructed. This is because they are typically easy to make and of limited utility, often lasting only until some special series of repeated steps have been accomplished in creating the final work. Jigs are also often disposed of once their utility has passed because they can take up a lot of space in a workshop and their parts may be needed for another jig.

This analogy can apply as well to software; however, storing old software jigs usually does not take up significant space in the workshop. Thus a case can be made that if there's any chance the jig will come in handy later, there's no major cost in just saving it.

One major problem with this mentality, however, is that finding old software jigs later can be harder than just creating new ones, and therefore the old jig really is just wasting space on a hard drive somewhere. Much of the difficulty with software reuse fits into this area.

 ## EXAMPLE

This is an example of the Tools variation of the One-Shot Deal AntiPattern.

While consulting with large government agencies, a developer was asked to assist a small group who needed some data collection assistance. What they were trying to do was put together a quick and dirty tool for remote sites to post information to a central location. This information was then to be used to assemble special reports, in one case a massive inventory database and in the other a quick daily status report.

In the first case, a starting system was provided in the form of a highly specific Lotus Notes database application (which itself was a previous One-Shot Deal) that was being used already by a similar organization and only needed some simple modifications to work in the new context.

The second case required a temporary Web-based data collection utility that would be used for only a couple weeks and then shut down. Personnel on-site had already been experimenting with Microsoft office products (Microsoft Access and Microsoft FrontPage) to assemble a prototype that proved to be absolutely unscaleable and insecure (but it did have a very pretty interface).

Both applications met the selected One-Shot Deal criteria listed in Table 3.8.

Table 3.8 Responses to the Selected Criteria

CRITERIA FOR IMPLICATIONS OF SUCCESS	YES	NO
Am I creating this for me so I can do my real job better?	X	
Are there others who would really like it, and would it help them do their job better?	X	
Will I need it again?		X
Is this tool not really available somewhere else (or at a reasonable price)?	X	
Would someone pay for this tool/Would we have paid for this tool if it was available?	X	
If I were to show others this tool/utility, would it raise my self-esteem?	X	

In answering question number 1, the applications were not considered to be products and therefore they were not being developed. Rather, they were considered to be in-house utilities to be used to gather data to support the organization's real job, which was providing specific reports to senior administrators.

In answering question number 2, the organization was using someone else's local tool because it was really liked and was perceived to be helpful elsewhere. The second "yes" was less obvious.

The answer to question number 3 was also clearly "yes," since both of these group's functions were unlikely to change, and therefore they would also have an ongoing repeated need for the same tools later.

Question numbers 4 and 5 were definitely answered "yes" since the organization had looked for a better way and then decided to pay my firm to do the work.

Finally, the answer to number 6 was the most revealing answer and a dead giveaway for a One-Shot Deal AntiPattern. The personnel in charge clearly anticipated receiving accolades from their superiors for their brilliant and forward-thinking use of technology to provide wonderful efficiency in gathering data. In fact, the user interfaces for these systems were given extra attention in anticipation that they would be showcased to the management when asked how the data had been gathered so amazingly fast. The pressure to make the applications look cool was incredible and had a negative impact early on by inappropriately affecting exploratory system development decisions.

However, as it happened, both applications resulted in only limited success. Tools were created that looked very nice, but failed to live up to their perceived importance. And once an accounting of the cost was made, those responsible quickly blame-stormed their way out of sight, covering their tracks and burying the tools, never to be seen again.

 ## RELATED SOLUTIONS

The Myopic Delivery AntiPattern shares much of the One-Shot Deal's context in that both occur in environments where short-term thinking is the accepted norm and, in particular, the focus is not on proper project management, but rather the delivery schedule.

The Killer Demo AntiPattern also has a lot in common with the One-Shot Deal. The key difference is in what the *intended* product of a development staff is and who the intended customer is. For the Killer Demo, the product is initially the actual demo, whereas the One-Shot Deal is typically a tool or utility thrown together in order to assist in the development of the real product. As far as customers, Killer Demos usually start as a marketing tool designed for persons outside of the organization, whereas One-Shot Deals start out as tools designed and built by developers for themselves.

APPLICABILITY TO OTHER VIEWPOINTS AND SCALES

The One-Shot Deal AntiPattern is rare outside of developers and local management. Any consideration at the architecture or senior management level would have probably resulted in a decision of either "don't go there; it's a waste of time and too risky" or "hey, this has market potential; let's do it right"—the appropriate response in either case.

Process Management
AntiPatterns

With Process AntiPatterns processes are the primary cause. Processes suffer from the same advantages and disadvantages as standards do. A useful process is a clearly stated set of integrated steps that are repeatable and provide a pragmatic mechanism to produce a necessary software artifact. A poor process is primarily concerned with production of associated documentation rather than the software artifact itself and is bureaucratic in nature, causing extra paperwork with no real software development benefit to those having to follow it. This results in staff not following processes at all or a drop in productivity because staff do not believe they should have to follow inadequate processes.

On the other side, a consistent way of developing software moves software incrementally towards an engineering discipline. This means that sometimes a software developer must follow a process partly for a future benefit, one that they will not fully accrue during the first implementation of the process. Take design, for example, which defines specifically how the code will function (implementation design) and integrate with other software via application programmer interfaces (specification design). This is useful both for the initial developer and the eventual maintainers. Software managers and developers need a software lifecycle perspective to appreciate the benefits that a set of pragmatic processes can bring. These six Process AntiPatterns illustrate the dangers of not having pragmatic, well-understood processes for all aspects of software development.

Planning 911 AntiPattern discusses three forms of poor software development planning: the Glass Case Plan, the Detailitis Plan, and the Management Plan. These deal with lack of planning, overplanning, and false planning respectively. Software planning is intended to be the representation of the reality of software development. Many projects fail from either overplanning or underplanning; in other words, an inappropriate level of planning will ultimately lead to growing risks, delays, and often failure to deliver at all.

Lifecycle Malpractice AntiPattern deals with nine major software development lifecycles and their suitability to the three main types of software development: prototyping, new product delivery, and stable product maintenance. Lifecycle model agility is the key to successfully delivering the three types of software in a cost-effective manner. This requires that management understand the impact of implementing the various software lifecycles in their development culture and technology environment. A dogmatic adoption of a single lifecycle approach across all types of projects will result in delivery delays and cost overruns, and will lead to technology malpractice and reduced competitive edge due to extended time to market.

The Customer AntiPattern occurs when the project is pushed and pulled in multiple directions by multiple organizations, each attempting to further their interests. Worst of all is when the interests of these organizations are orthogonal to one another or even uncorrelated. Each of these organizations can be identified to the project manager as the customer. The project manager often finds it difficult to make anyone satisfied, directing the project first in one direction and then another to satisfy the customer de jour. It truly becomes a lose-lose situation. Often the project manager must sell his or her soul in order to make everyone happy. Sometimes the cost is project failure, but then the definition of failure depends on whose interests you didn't satisfy.

One Size Fits All AntiPattern details the negative impact of a monolithic software development process that has been designed for all possible projects. It has been invented to ensure consistency of software engineering practices, deliver earlier, and save money. Such a monolithic process is too bureaucratic for smaller projects and can never cover all possible process variations required by larger projects. Often such a beast will be ignored and this can cause as much, if not more, damage than following it.

The Domino Effect AntiPattern covers the problems met when moving critical resources between projects. Project managers who treat the resources for each project for which they are responsible in a collective manner, blur project boundaries causing a domino effect of problems. The need to continually move the critical resources to cover gaps left by moving them from a previous project leads to software delivery delays, developer frustration, and lack of confidence in management, with the extreme being developer attrition and project failure.

Myopic Delivery AntiPattern covers slipped schedules that are faster than can be controlled, generating project compression. Project compression creates a gap in the space-time continuum, which allows the incomprehensible to be accomplished in the minds of management. It causes all logical, pragmatic, rational, reasonable thinking to fly out the window. Management will do anything to meet the delivery date. No one's life is unexpendable. Everyone will suffer. Nothing is more important than the delivery date. This AntiPattern will discuss what happens when the schedule slips and management continues to demand the original delivery date.

Planning 911

AntiPattern Name: Planning 911

Also Known As: "The best-laid schemes o mice an men gang aft agley"
    In proving foresight may be vain:
    The best-laid schemes o mice an men
    Gang aft agley,
    An lea'e us nought but grief an pain,
    For promis'd joy!

    Still thou art blest, compar'd wi me!
    The present only toucheth thee:
    But och! I backward cast my e'e,
    On prospects drear!
    An forward, tho I canna see,
    I guess an fear!
                —*"To a Mouse"* by Robert Burns, 1784

    Being able to predict the future may not work:
    The best plans of mice and men
    Often go astray,
    Leaving us with nothing but grief and pain
    Instead of that which we planned to gain!

    Still you are blessed, compared to me!
    The present only affects you:
    But oh, when I look back,
    On poor prospects!

> And forward, though I cannot see,
> I guess and fear what may be!
> > —loose translation by William J. Brown (another Scot), 1999

Most Applicable Scale: Application

Refactored Solution Name: Planning for Success

Refactored Solution Type: Process

Root Causes: Ignorance and Sloth

Unbalanced Forces: Management of Change and Management of IT Resources

Anecdotal Evidence:
> "I have a cunning plan." (Baldrick from Black Adder)
> "We can't get started until we have a complete program plan."
> "The plan is the only thing that will ensure our success."
> "What do you mean you haven't finished it yet, you must send out the requirements document tomorrow!"
> "I own the management plan and your delivery schedule must be in line with it! If you need a copy I'll e-mail it to you."

BACKGROUND

A project management plan is extremely broad and high level. It states the strategies for all aspects of a development. It addresses software development strategies at a topical level and then references the discrete process plans for the specific details. It is programmatic, including cost, schedule, and organization, and also outlines how the other software development aspects should be addressed, such as the testing approach and the software configuration management mechanisms.

NASA uses the term *Software Development/Management Plan* [NASA 1990] and the Software Engineering Institute's Capability Maturity Model for Software uses the term *Plan Technical Effort* [SEI 1993] to refer to the project management plan.

The sidebar outlines NASA's Software Development/Management Plan. It clearly enumerates the necessary topics that must be dealt with to effectively plan and manage a software development project. Use this outline as a project plan template.

Software planning is the representation of the reality of software development. Many projects fail from either overplanning or underplanning; in other words, an inappropriate level of planning will cause an inappropriate level of management that will lead to growing risks, delays, and often failure to deliver at all.

The Planning 911 AntiPattern deals with how to plan your way out of trouble when no one knows what the reality of delivery is because of poor project planning, whether it is because of too little or too much detail. It explains how to plan your way out of the Detailitis Plan [Brown 1998], the Glass Case Plan [Brown 1998], and the Management Plan situations. In the Detailitis Plan the project schedule attempts to capture too much detail throughout the development. In the Glass Case Plan the project schedule is produced prior to beginning development but never captured against during the development. In both cases it is impossible to use the project schedule to visibly assess the actual status of the development. In the Management Plan, the software development schedule is completely produced by senior management who have no direct, day-to-day contact with the senior development staff and therefore no real information about the state of the software development. The management then attempts to deliver by surprise firedrills defined by milestones in their management plan that are out of synch with the team development schedules.

NASA SOFTWARE DEVELOPMENT/MANAGEMENT PLAN

1. Introduction
   1.1. Purpose
   1.2. Background
   1.3. Organization and Responsibilities
       1.3.1. Project Personnel
       1.3.2. Interfacing Groups

2. Statement of Problem

3. Technical Approach
   3.1. Reuse Strategy
   3.2. Assumptions and Constraints
   3.3. Anticipated and Unresolved Problems
   3.4. Development Environment
   3.5. Activities, Tools, and Products
   3.6. Build Strategy

4. Management Approach
   4.1. Assumptions and Constraints
   4.2. Resource Requirements
   4.3. Milestones and Schedules
   4.4. Metrics
   4.5. Risk Management

5. Product Assurance
   5.1. Assumptions and Constraints
   5.2. Quality Assurance
   5.3. Configuration Management

6. References

7. Plan Update History [NASA 1990]

While each of these poor planning cases is common, the best management approach is to produce a published plan whose detail is appropriate for the phase of development and then capture progress, replanning as necessary on a weekly basis for each development team.

The basic problem centers around project planning. To fully understand the project planning problems and for those readers who have not read the Death By Planning AntiPattern [Brown 1998], which contains the Glass Case Plan and Detailitis Plan, we briefly cover each in the sections that follow. The Management Plan is a new addition.

GENERAL FORM

Each of the project management situations results in delays, staff attrition, and project failure if not dealt with sufficiently. Having said that, they each exhibit specific differences by which they cause the same result.

Glass Case Plan

Often a plan is produced at the start of a project and despite the fact that it is never updated, it is always referenced as if it is an accurate, current view of the project. This is fairly common since it gives the management an idealistic view of the software development. Management assumes that because there is a plan, delivery will follow automatically, exactly as the plan specifies with no intervention (or management) necessary. However, because the schedule is never tracked against actual progress, it becomes increasingly inaccurate over time (see Figure 4.1). This false view is often compounded by the lack of concrete information about the progress. Often the lack of progress only becomes apparent after a critical deliverable slips and the project continues to fall behind its planned deadlines for delivery milestones.

Detailitis Plan

Sometimes the goal of effective delivery is assumed to be best achieved by a high degree of control via a continuous planning exercise that involves most of the senior developers and managers. This approach often evolves into a hierarchical sequence of plans that show increasing levels of detail. The high level of detail promotes the perception that the project is fully under control and proceeding according to schedule (see Figure 4.2). However, to produce and update the plan requires effort from those who should be implementing it, not supporting it. Management are usually ignorant of this, hence the problem persists.

Management Plan

The Management Plan is where two plans exist: a formal, published plan by the management and the hidden, actual work plan of the developers. Poor

Figure 4.1 A Glass Case Plan.

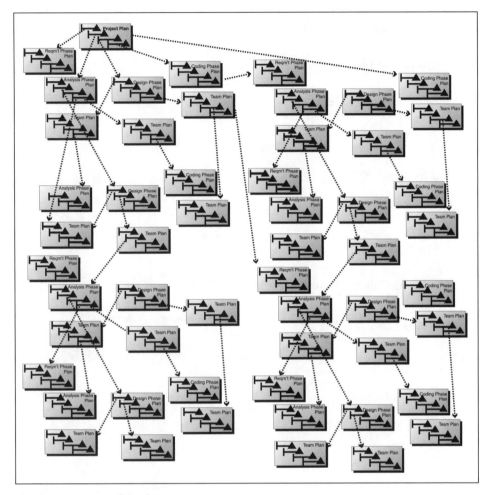

Figure 4.2   A Detailitis Plan.

and nonexistent planning does not control the chaotic nature of software development. This creates a significant disparity between the management's planning models and actual development activities. Architects and developers often have to live double lives. On the one hand they need to visibly cooperate with management's plans for the project. At the same time developers must confront the actual status of the software and associated development artifacts, which do not resemble the Management Plan (see Figure 4.3), and ensure that the software delivery is made a reality by following their own plan.

The plan is often used to pressure developers into working on development artifacts out of sequence and for declaring such artifacts complete

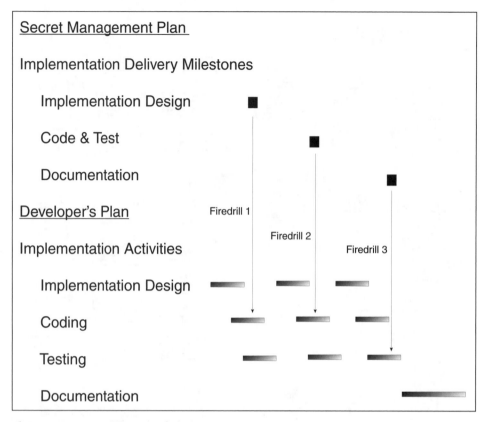

Figure 4.3 A Management Plan.

before they are mature, causing problems downstream. This is because the managers have produced optimistic estimates and delivery milestones without any developer input. So there is no injection of reality into the plan.

SYMPTOMS AND CONSEQUENCES

Each type of poor project plan has its own symptoms and consequences, although the final consequences are often the same.

Glass Case Plan

The primary symptom of the Glass Case Plan is the lack of an up-to-date project plan that accurately shows the current state of software development artifacts against a timeline of milestones for critical internal and external delivery points. The secondary symptom is really an extension of the first in that the Glass Case Plan becomes more and more out of date. This increases the difference between management expectations and reality.

The consequences of the Glass Case Plan are:

- Lack of knowledge by anyone on the project about the status of the development. The plan has no meaning and control of delivery lessens as time goes on. The project may be well ahead or behind of its intended delivery date but no one would know.

- Failure to deliver a critical deliverable.

These consequences grow incrementally until finally the project overruns with the usual options of:

- Further investment
- Crisis project management
- Project cancellation
- Possible loss of key staff

Detailitis Plan

The main symptom of the Detailitis Plan is that more time is spent planning, capturing progress, and replanning than is spent on delivering software and its associated artifacts.

The consequences of this plan are intertwined and feed off each other:

1. Each planner has to monitor and capture progress at the level shown by its plan and reestimate continuously.

2. The domino effect of this endless planning and replanning causes further planning and replanning.

3. The objective has shifted from software delivery to continually delivering a set of plans.

4. Continual delays to software delivery and eventual project failure.

Management Plan

The main symptom from a developer viewpoint is a series of firedrills that are both unnecessary and untimely. A secondary symptom that sometimes occurs is micro-management of the development by the project manager because the management plan milestones are continually missed.

The main consequences of a series of surprise firedrills to meet the management plan schedule are disillusionment and diminished morale of the development team(s) when they are blamed for missing a firedrill date. The final consequence is attrition of staff.

It is possible that the development team rises to the occasion and is able to successfully accomplish demands of the management-created firedrill. These types of efforts dampen the morale of the developers because they had to put in extra effort to complete the management task that was a major distraction from the software development activity they were already undertaking. Moreover, it burns out the development team. Additionally, if the purpose of the firedrills is only to provide management with the perception that the team is making progress and the true essence of the firedrill does not provide a critical advance in the development schedule, then management walks away with the perception that the development has been moved forward. In fact, the firedrill has made no impact at all except to run the development team into the ground. Worse yet, management feels empowered to effect additional firedrills to achieve additional perceived results. And no matter how good a development team is, it is highly unlikely to successfully deal with endless management firedrills without suffering attrition.

 **TYPICAL CAUSES**

The causes of the three types of management situation are usually fairly specific. They each have their own cultural and management drivers that vary by company and individual project manager.

Glass Case Plan

There are three common causes of the Glass Case Plan:

- A tool used for contract acquisition with no intended follow-through
- Overzealous initial planning in an attempt to enforce absolute control of development
- Ignorance of basic project management principles

Detailitis Plan

There are five common causes of the Detailitis Plan:

- Overzealous continual planning in an attempt to enforce absolute control of development
- Planning as the primary project activity
- Customer-forced compliance (i.e., micro-management via planning controls)
- Executive-management-forced compliance (i.e., micro-management via planning controls)
- Enough political-power-based greed to commit to any detail as long as the project continues to be funded

Management Plan

The primary cause is that the senior management have their own plan that is not shared with the project development staff but is used to drive the production of artifacts. In those cases where the development project is successful, the developers are experienced and know that the plan is worthless, and ignore it.

KNOWN EXCEPTIONS

Software development projects can succeed despite poor planning practices. Some developments, such as short demo and prototyping exercises, often can be left to the discretion of a handful of experienced developers who do not need a plan but rather requirements they understand and a deadline that they have some say in.

REFACTORED SOLUTION

There are basically two refactored solutions. The first is applicable to both the Glass Case Plan and the Detailitis Plan, while the second is specific to the Management Plan.

Glass Case and Detailitis Plans

The refactored solution for the Glass Case and Detailitis Plans is to produce a schedule with the correct level of detail that reflects the software development plan. Scheduling is usually the generic term used for:

- Creating a schedule of related development tasks defined by a software development lifecycle
- Estimating the tasks in terms of effort and elapsed time
- Capturing the progress of tasks for an elapsed time period
- Evaluating the captured against the project plan
- Updating the captured against the project plan

To better understand how to plan to the correct level of detail each of these steps are examined with reference to the lifecycle phase of a software development.

Creating a Schedule

To create a schedule involves several sequential steps:

1. Choose a software development lifecycle.
2. Develop a template.
3. Create a balanced plan.
4. Establish a baseline.

A project schedule should primarily show the progress of a software development lifecycle through the phases. It captures the steps required to achieve the final delivery, and includes the estimated delivery schedule and the state of the artifact development activities, that is, actual progress.

The phase artifacts are defined by the chosen software development lifecycle, which should suit the nature of the development:

Pure Waterfall. Suited to strong management control, stable product specification, and stable technologies.

Spiral. Suitable when risk is high and cost is less of a factor than successful delivery.

Sashimi. A rapid version of the Pure Waterfall requiring strong continuity of development staff throughout the project.

Waterfall with Subprojects. Allows different components to be developed separately and relies on fixed requirements and architecture.

Staged Delivery. Delivers functionality incrementally.

Evolutionary Delivery. Suited to vague requirements and customer collaboration.

The project schedule should identify all activities and tasks in sequence, their dependencies, and the artifact delivery milestones. A template of a project schedule should be created and reused for all developments of the same nature, as shown in Figure 4.4. The template should be refined as process improvements occur. The project schedule is best represented as a Gantt Chart, in which the information is readily absorbed as a visual snapshot to illustrate deliverables, associated dates, and interdependencies of both planned and achieved tasks.

McCarthy suggests using *natural* milestones. Natural milestones are significant points that should be part of the normal delivery process like archi-

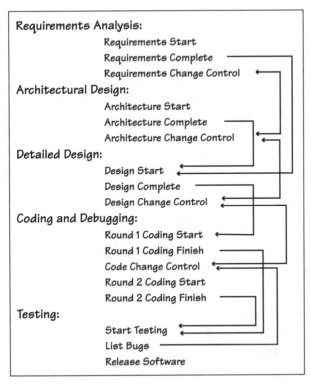

Figure 4.4 A template plan schedule.

tecture delivery, rather than an invented point such as design iteration three. McCarthy further suggests "schedule a milestone somewhere between every six weeks and every three months. With smaller, feature, teams (say, 10 to 20 people total), you can have more frequent milestones because smaller teams reduce the overhead of a milestone" [McCarthy 1995].

Creating a balanced plan is necessary to achieve delivery of the required features for an agreed to budget and delivery schedule. Investment in earlier development phases reduces the cost and risk of later development phases. Assume a notional formula of `features = cost * schedule`. While this isn't exactly true, it will do for the purpose of assessing the impact of increasing or decreasing any of these three factors in the production of a software development plan:

- Increasing features requires cost and/or schedule to be increased: `features = cost * schedule`
- Reducing cost requires a reduction in features for a fixed schedule: `cost = features/schedule`
- Reducing schedule requires a reduction in features for a fixed cost: `schedule = features/cost`

Establishing a baseline will enable a snapshot of the schedule to be used to quantitatively measure progress. A baseline is a version of the schedule against which you track progress. Once the estimates are produced and are considered by the implementors as the best current thinking and approved by the required managers, the schedule should be baselined. This will then ensure that all changes are visible. Most project management tools do this automatically and are a handy aid for determining whether the project activities and tasks are on schedule.

By tracking against the baseline schedule tasks the following states of deliverables will be immediately obvious in a Gantt Chart (see Figure 4.5):

On Schedule. The task started on the planned date and the progress to date matches the estimate for the time period.

Early. The task started earlier than planned, with an estimated new delivery date that is earlier than planned.

Late. The task started later than planned, with estimated new delivery date that is later than planned.

Delivered. Shows the date the task was 100 percent completed, regardless of whether it started or finished early, late, or as planned.

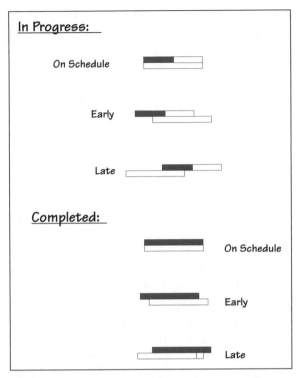

Figure 4.5 Actuals against a baselined schedule.

Estimating the Tasks

There are many complex factors to consider when estimating the time it takes to complete a large number of both tightly and loosely related tasks. The best approach is to deal with the complexity incrementally. Produce an outline schedule and iterate its evolution to the required level of detail. To estimate software development tasks well means dealing with several variable factors and avoiding the following known pitfalls:

- Dealing with development dependencies
- Optimistic scheduling
- Nondevelopment activities
- Estimating guidelines
- Contingency planning
- Time boxing
- Prohibited scheduling approaches

Development interdependencies need to be well understood. They occur because of dependencies between software development activities and their artifacts. Minimize dependencies because they are not under development team control [McCarthy 1995]. This means that the underlying risks appear vague and are liable to result in significant delays due to waiting on someone else; either another team in the same project (or another project) or a vendor. Synchronize dependencies that are critical and unavoidable, such as dependencies against a program of projects, customer schedule, or business schedule.

Optimistic scheduling generally occurs because of pressure to deliver and straight-line thinking. Management frequently applies pressure for rapid results. This in itself would be reasonable if the scale or quality of development was proportional, but it usually is excessive for the specified delivery period. Adding developers does not proportionally reduce the time required to deliver. It depends on the manner in which the specific tasks and work structure can be shared. If the work-breakdown structure allows parallel activity then the addition of developers is a useful tactic; but if the tasks are sequentially dependent then adding developers purely adds overhead for no gain. After a point adding more staff starts to slow delivery down because of complexity in communications: Too many cooks spoil the broth.

Optimistic scheduling also occurs naturally because often those estimating do not understand the complex set of interrelated development tasks. Development is not a straight-line function but is a sequence of functions with a complex set of interrelationships. Impact analysis is critical since no task is stand-alone. For example, the scale of the architecture activity has an impact on two design activities:

- Interface specifications in a directly proportional manner, because the architecture specifies the interrelationship of components
- Implementation design in an indirect manner, because the architectural strategy should impose solution constraints

The implementation design has a proportionally direct impact on the coding. This means that when estimating one must understand all of the interrelationships and the impact of each development phase on another to arrive at a balanced schedule.

It is worth remembering that schedule pressure will only increase the risks and likelihood of failure in some form, such as cost overrun, late delivery, or technical failure.

Nondevelopment activities fall into two categories: task based and productivity based. Task based are those that can be planned easily, such as holidays and training. Retrospectively, sickness can also be treated as a task to show unavailability. Basically any nondevelopment task that can be measured in days per person should be treated as a project task to show unavailability.

Administration is usually productivity based. Most company finance offices track productivity from a financial perspective to assess profit and loss. Most companies average between 65 percent and 75 percent employee productivity, but remember that productivity figures are only as good as those against which they are measured, as proven in studies by DeMarco and others [DeMarco 1987]. Many planning tools, such as Microsoft Project, can use a productivity rate for calculating the workload of a person assigned a task and indicate if they are overutilized for a period given their productivity rate. In addition, they can accept unavailability dates for a project and individual resource levels to take care of fixed unavailability.

"Project leadership recognizes that estimates made during the first half of the project are inherently imprecise and will need to be refined as the project progresses" [McConnell 1998]. Schedules normally are expected to show greater detail for the phase they are in than for future phases. At the beginning of the project you have a very basic schedule, but as you go through the phases the details of the phases become better defined. The further a project progresses through the software development lifecycle the greater the detail and accuracy of the estimates for the remaining tasks should be.

Accurate estimating takes time. Estimating is a mix of thoroughly thinking through all reasonable possibilities in a logical manner and applying experience to the intended tasks. Plan for the work that needs to be done at the level required for the developers to clearly comprehend the timelines and criteria for all the artifacts they need to produce. This should involve the developers so that they can judge the sufficiency of the schedule.

Another important step is to have estimating guidelines for standard tasks, such as the time expected for subsystem and system testing, as defined in Table 4.1. Use previous experiences to establish the guidelines but err on the pessimistic side of the numbers to ensure that it is not an optimistic guideline. Unfortunately, the most common way of identifying optimistic estimates is when the tasks estimated by a person keep overrunning.

When estimating, allow a contingency period for all those inevitable unknowns and ensure that they are part of the template plan used unless you can guarantee that they cannot occur (see Figure 4.4). Unknowns include:

Requirements creep. The requirements incrementally grow in size and scope.

Table 4.1 Sample Standardized Estimates

ROUND	SUBSYSTEM TESTING	SYSTEM TESTING
Initial	5 days per subsystem	12 days
Regression	3 days per subsystem	8 days

Design creep. The design evolves into more than necessary to fulfill the requirements.

Design dead ends. A design strategy proves to be unimplementable in code.

Third-party software workarounds. The development must invest unplanned effort to get third-party software working as required.

Coding creep. The code evolves into more than necessary to fulfill the design.

Defect identification. Time has not been allocated to find the cause of a failure or departure from the required functionality in the software.

Defect correction (bug-fixing). Time has not been allocated to fix defects found in the code during testing.

A timebox is an amount of time that is set for an activity. A timebox is often used because many software development activities will take as much time as made available. Establish a minimum timebox for any activity. This avoids mistakes such as saying it only takes two days to develop a simple program, when in reality it takes much longer to produce a designed and tested program. Unless it's "Hello world!" or something else equally trivial, a two-day timebox is ridiculous. This is because time to state derived functional requirements, design, code, test, fix defects, and retest will by nature of the sequential activities take more than two days. Hewlett-Packard at one time had a rule that no project could be estimated at less than six months because that was the shortest time within which they had ever successfully delivered a product.

Also remember that tasks should be broken down into their lowest common denominator using a technique such as work-breakdown structure. For example, coding usually decomposes to actual programming, engineering testing, defect fixing, and retesting; and producing documentation. The template should identify each of the tasks that make up the development activity (see Figure 4.4).

There are several *do's* and *don'ts* in planning that NASA clearly identifies [NASA Software Engineering Laboratory 1992]. The key ones relating to estimating are:

- Do not plan overtime into a development schedule, but do encourage voluntary overtime at key points in the delivery.
- Do not set unachievable goals; ensure that the developers assist in estimating and buy into the plan.
- Do not overstaff tasks; this will create unnecessary overheads.

Measuring Progress

The baseline schedules should be updated weekly to ensure the appropriate level of visibility that enables planning and to control tasks through accurate information. This will help to identify risks and develop mitigation strategies.

Progress will be measured as an estimated level of completeness of tasks. Completeness should be gross measurements rather than fine measurements, such as tracking in 10 percent steps rather than 1 percent steps. It is far easier to accurately assess that design is 10 percent complete rather than 1 percent complete. When a previous estimate is found to be incorrect the next estimate should rectify that, in which case a reduction in percentage completeness will be the result.

Evaluating the Schedule

Evaluating a schedule requires that several important mechanisms are put into place to ensure that the correct information is available and that the appropriate evaluation mechanisms exist:

- Evaluation mindset
- Evaluation roles
- Project status information

It is critical to have a balanced mindset when evaluating a project and not to expect that just because something is planned it will be automatically produced. Most schedule evaluation criteria are negative because they often measure the lack of the achievement of something that was planned or expected. But given the negative nature of the measurements, late completion of some planned tasks should be expected because that is what is being measured. The time to worry is when there are a large number of negative measurements or a smaller sustained amount. For example, slipping dates should be expected; the time to worry is if slippages are large or happen frequently. Slippages occur for many reasons; some of them were identified previously in the discussion of required contingency planning. When a software development artifact has been produced, it should be treated as a success not just as an expectation.

A software development schedule should be evaluated at several levels within the project and company hierarchy. The frequency and detail of information lessens the higher up in the company hierarchy an evaluator's role is. The three key evaluator roles to consider are:

Senior Developer. A technically experienced member of staff who is deeply entrenched in a project usually focuses on the tasks within a phase. At this level estimates are measured in days and are the lowest level of tasks defined, such as "test and install CD, 0.5 day."

Project Manager/Leader. This individual focuses on the triad of functionality, resources, and time. The functionality achieved, the resources used, and the time taken are all easy to measure against those planned for a given time period. The less tangible aspect of functionality measurement is quality. McCarthy suggests zero defect milestones as a way of achieving a known state and, while this is preferred, often being able to identify defects in a function is a reasonable measure of quality [McCarthy 1995]. The other technical ways of measuring quality that can be applied to delivered code are "ilities": scaleability, reliability, maintainability, performance, and so on.

Project Sponsor/CIO/CEO. Visibility of a software development project is usually in terms of schedule and costs. A project is an investment and is monitored in terms of cost, time, and business benefits. A high-level executive often reviews a traffic light report and then in conjunction with the project manager makes any change to a project timeline measured in months, costs measured in thousands or more of the local currency, or in features.

Project status information is critical to evaluating the progress against the schedule. Many larger companies successfully use a traffic light report on a monthly basis to report the status of a project to their company executive sponsor(s). The report is usually only one or two pages in length and provides a snapshot of the project's health in terms of:

- Progress to plan.
  - Have the scheduled milestones been achieved?
  - If not, what caused the delay?
- Actuals versus planned.
  - Actual costs against projected costs and new estimate for project costs.

- Actual staffing against projected staffing and new estimate for projected staffing.
- Risks and mitigation Strategies.
  - Top five prioritized business risks and mitigation strategies.
  - Top five prioritized technical risks and mitigation strategies.
- Overall assessment.
  - Green light: Currently on schedule, within estimated costs, specified features complete with only minor quality defects, and predicted that this trend will continue.
  - Amber light: Deviation of between 5 percent and 10 percent from predicted schedule, estimated costs or features complete, or predicted deviation in that range in the next month.
  - Red light: Deviation of greater than 10 percent schedule slippage, cost overrun or features incomplete, or predicted deviation in that range in the next month.

Note: It isn't unusual that a project introducing a new technology or a new business solution would receive an amber light rating during the early phases due to the risks associated with inexperience. This should eventually become a green light as the project matures. Using the spiral type lifecycle will reduce the impact of the risks but not stop them from arising.

Updating the Plan

The best form of training to plan, estimate, capture, and replan is practice. A software development lifecycle template can easily be used to give a consistent format and level of detail required to produce a good schedule. To keep it useful requires hard work and experience. By purely planning, estimating, and capturing on a regular basis, the average person will get a lot of experience over the life of a project. Updating a project schedule requires project management to:

- Capture actuals quite frequently
- Reestimate frequently

For the information in a project plan to remain valuable it must be as current as possible. The best way to achieve this is to capture weekly progress against the active tasks for that time period and all other tasks worked on, especially those that have dependencies and those that are on the critical path. This means getting the estimates from those developers doing the actual development and assessing their subjective assessments of progress. This is never easy, but an effective way is to ask the team leader to work out the weekly estimated progress with his or her team from a technical perspective and then persuade the project manager to incorporate those estimates into the project plan schedule with the team leaders.

Validating and producing new estimates should be a regular occurrence, but this need not happen as frequently as capturing against the plan should. There are certain trigger points for reestimating (see Figure 4.6):

Deviation from Planned Tasks. When one or more planned tasks are deviated from in terms of the time period to be worked on or effort required, this task and the dependent tasks should have their estimates reviewed and updated as necessary.

Milestones for Completed Artifacts. At the point that a milestone has been successfully reached, the tasks planned to reach the next milestone should be validated based on the experience of the development staff in reaching the previous milestone.

End of Phase. The end of a software development lifecycle phase is an indicator that more is understood about the specific application or

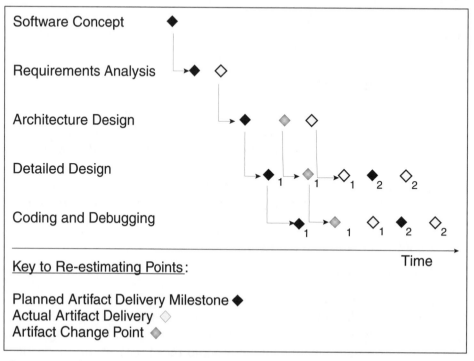

Figure 4.6   Trigger points for reestimating.

product being developed. Based on the experiences in defining earlier phase views, such as requirements or design, the estimates for the next stage should be refined.

Management Plan

"Project plans should be reviewed *and approved* by the people who will carry them out" [McConnell 1998]. This means that the development staff must *own* their part of the estimates, which requires that the plan be public not private so that the developers can add to it, challenge it, and actively participate in its evolution. Changes to the plan should be controlled by the software configuration management's change-control mechanism defined in the initial project plan.

The development plan should be visible to all of the project participants at all times. This can be easily achieved by putting regularly updated copies of plans either up on walls in and around the development area or on a project Web page.

VARIATIONS

There are many variations that all correspond to the level of planning appropriate for the work being undertaken.

An interesting variation is a product or program roadmap plan that is implemented as several project plans. This is usually a feature-level plan that allocates broad date ranges to internal and external delivery of software that needs to be integrated at several stages in its evolution. The roadmap should never be detailed beyond feature delivery dates and integration points and should only be captured against once a particular feature has been fully delivered by a project (see Figure 4.7).

A product or program roadmap should be a multirelease technology plan [McCarthy 1995] so that all development staff can understand the bigger picture and that the particular project on which they are working is but one step in a larger development effort.

EXAMPLE

Three separate examples are used to give a real world instance for each type of poor project management planning that has been identified.

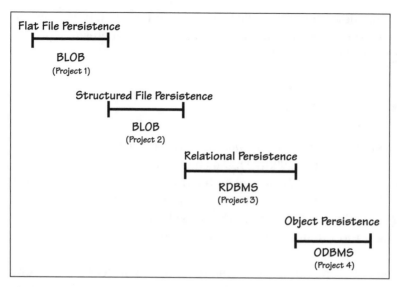

Figure 4.7 A product roadmap for object persistence.

Glass Case Plan

A financial systems integrator decided to build a middleware component not yet available from any major vendors in spite of the international standards that were issued over a year previously. The system integrator produced a detailed schedule in advance of starting any project work to obtain a funding source. The schedule had been based on the view of staff who had not yet delivered this nature of software in anger but had limited experience of demonstration and prototype development. The schedule was technically specific and the estimates were very optimistic because the technology was not properly understood.

This risk was compounded because the schedule was continually referenced by the project manager, but never updated. This resulted in slipping delivery dates due to the lack of knowledge about real progress. The only time that the systems integrator knew that the first round of software delivery dates could not be met was *after* the dates had passed. This was approximately halfway through the project.

After a series of crisis meetings between the system integrator and the customer, it was decided to replace the project manager. The replacement project manager decided that the first job was to assess the delta between the Glass Case Plan and reality. It turned out that not only was the project at a different phase than scheduled, but also there were tasks being implemented that did not exist on the schedule.

The new project manager produced a reality plan of the work achieved and the work in progress against the planned work. After that he worked with each of the team leaders to iterate the project management plan to deal with the technical and management approach, and then with each of the development teams to produce a new project schedule.

The plan was presented to the customer who started to realize that though the systems integrator had fooled both sides with their initial schedule, the chances of successful delivery were greatly increased. The project eventually delivered after a 50 percent time extension with the additional costs being shared between the system integrator and the customer.

Detailitis Plan

An end-user company, in an attempt to control its development to ensure full control of the software development, produces a project plan that has four levels:

- Phases of development
- Components per phase
- Team tasks and effort per component
- Team member tasks and effort per team

The problem is that the inability to track and replan against the detailed schedules without directing considerable focus away from actually delivering the system significantly reduces staff productivity. The management of the plan quickly becomes unrealistic due to the complexity. This was evident in the staff's frustration at being continually distracted from their real work of delivering code.

Eventually the project manager realized that the development was slipping further and further behind and held a crisis meeting with the development team leaders. It soon became obvious that the development staff could not sustain that detailed level of planning and capturing on a weekly basis.

The initial solution that was preferred by the project manager was to plan and capture monthly in an attempt to reduce the required overhead. The problem did not go away, however; it just changed the frequency of the symptoms, with the twist that the fourth week was generally a shambles of making up for not planning and capturing during the previous three weeks.

After a further crisis meeting it was decided to change the level of task definition to reflect:

- Phases of development
- Components per phase
- Team tasks and effort per component

This then meant that the development team leaders were the only staff required to update the plans. As a final twist this initially occurred once every two weeks, but it turned out that it was more timely (and actually was a required part of their job) for the team leaders to update the plans weekly.

Management Plan

Executive management develops a high-level project plan as part of a bid for a large development contract. No actual developers are involved in the estimates because the management does not wish to distract them from their current work. When the project eventually starts, the constraints will not allow active developer participation in any planning since the project budget, delivery dates, and features have already been agreed to as part of the contract. The project appears to progress well through the requirements and architecture phases.

The first sign of any problem is when the team extends the estimates for implementation by a factor of 2 and 3, after they have produced the specification design. The management reacts by blaming the teams for overcomplicating the solution. After a few months of flailing, the management decides that triage (the action of removing out the requirements that have the least chance of surviving the project) is the solution and that the technology is to blame.

The management then proceeds to produce a second management plan, again without input from developers. This time the delta to the management plan estimates is in the order of two to three months, well below a factor of 2. However, the management is still not satisfied and after another three months of flailing the project is cancelled.

 ## RELATED SOLUTIONS

The Lifecycle Malpractice AntiPattern details how to identify an appropriate lifecycle for the specific nature of a software development. The first step in the refactored solution, creating a plan, references the solution supplied by the Lifecycle Malpractice AntiPattern, which should be referenced for more detail on choosing the correct software lifecycle.

APPLICABILITY TO OTHER VIEWPOINTS AND SCALES

While on an individual basis this AntiPattern directly affects the ability to deliver an application, the problem is usually widespread enough in most companies to eventually impact the enterprise since it impacts most applications. This is simply because most companies do not change their approach to planning on a project basis, but adopt a single, companywide approach.

Lifecycle Malpractice

AntiPattern Name: Lifecycle Malpractice

Also Known As: Unicycles are Dangerous

Most Applicable Scale: Application

Refactored Solution Name: A Bicycle Made for Two (or Three)

Refactored Solution Type: Process

Root Causes: Ignorance and Sloth

Unbalanced Forces: Management of Change and Management of IT
Resources

Anecdotal Evidence:
"This waterfall lifecycle can't work for our OO development."
"Maybe we should adopt a spiral (lifecycle) approach to help us
control the risks, but it might blow our schedule."
"The company uses staged delivery for all of its developments. We
don't want to confuse our developers."

BACKGROUND

The Lifecycle Malpractice AntiPattern occurs by failure to pick the appropriate lifecycle for a particular nature of development and the staff skills available. Lifecycle model agility is the key to successfully developing several applications or projects in tandem. This requires that management understand the impact of implementing the various lifecycles in their development culture and technology environment. A dogmatic adoption of a single lifecycle will prevent a more appropriate process set being available for developments of a different nature, resulting in increased costs, reduced competitive edge, and technology malpractice. This is a lifecycle version of the Golden Hammer AntiPattern [Brown 1998].

The basic software development lifecycles are:

- Waterfall Lifecycle
- Sashimi Lifecycle
- Waterfall Subprojects Lifecycle
- Staged Delivery Lifecycle
- Code and Fix Lifecycle
- Spiral Lifecycle
- Controlled Iteration Lifecycle
- Evolutionary Prototyping Lifecycle
- Evolutionary Delivery Lifecycle

Many companies do not understand that a single lifecycle, which worked for one type of development, is not applicable to all development projects. A Waterfall Lifecycle that worked well in legacy COBOL and C applications is misapplied to C++, Java, and DOT software developments. The misapplication of a lifecycle results in increased risks and delays, and often failure to deliver according to requirements, time, and budget.

GENERAL FORM

The major software development lifecycles each have advantages and disadvantages that must be understood to be able to assess their appropriateness to a particular nature of software development. McConnell clearly differentiates the basic lifecycle approaches and their characteristics [McConnell 1996].

Software development projects can be classified as one of the following:

- Demos and proof-of-concept prototyping
- New technology application delivery
- Stable application maintenance

Waterfall Lifecycle

The Waterfall Lifecycle is the oldest of the formal lifecycles and many other lifecycles have been derived from it. The Waterfall Lifecycle has document-driven phases that are nonoverlapping, with the entrance to the next phase of development being gated by the validation and verification reviews at the end of the previous phase (see Figure 4.8).

The pure Waterfall Lifecycle works well for product development in which there is a stable product definition and well-understood and stable development technologies. It minimizes planning overhead since the project plan is produced at the very beginning of the lifecycle. This lifecycle deals well with complexity by forcing it to be dealt with in an orderly manner by strictly sequencing the software development phases. It also works well when quality requirements are a higher priority than cost and schedule

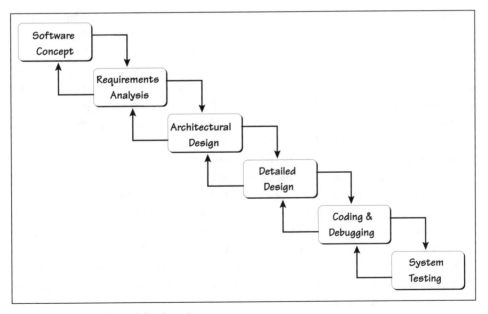

Figure 4.8 Pure Waterfall Lifecycle.

requirements. The pure Waterfall Lifecycle provides requirements stability early on and error reduction throughout, and is structured so different staff can work through the separate phases by the production of extensive documentation. In order to progress to the next stage, the current stage must be thoroughly documented.

The Waterfall Lifecycle makes it difficult to fully plan all the steps of a development, including the prediction of unknowns, at the outset of a development project. It is difficult to fully specify derived requirements at the beginning of a project, since many requirements are derived by early design. Even coding stages uncover the need for utility functions that could not have been logically identified at the time the initial requirements were written. Also, to deal with changes generated from design and coding means reworking back through the lifecycle phase and then forward again to validate and verify the changes; this is very effort intensive. Significant effort is focused on the provision of stand-alone documentation: sufficient documentation that requires no interaction whatsoever with the development staff to assist in fully understanding all aspects of the software. A Waterfall Lifecycle is applicable to stable technology application maintenance.

Sashimi Lifecycle

The Sashimi Lifecycle is the Fuji-Xerox hardware development model (see Figure 4.9). This is unique because it was invented for the purpose of developing computer hardware rather than software. It is easy to issue a patch for released software, but in the case of hardware that is not an option—it either works or it doesn't! There is a strong degree of overlap between the pure Waterfall Lifecycle phases; work continues at decreasing levels of progression on multiple phases at once. So detailed design, for example, will continue after coding and debugging has started, but as coding and debugging tasks increase the detailed design tasks will lessen.

This lifecycle approach reduces the amount of documentation required by the pure Waterfall Lifecycle and the corresponding level of effort by relying more on the continuity of development staff. The Sashimi Lifecycle also overcomes the fact that later software development phases provide a greater insight and corresponding changes to earlier phase artifacts by overlapping the phases, such as design creating more derived requirements. The fact that this approach is successfully used for hardware projects proves that it is robust and practical.

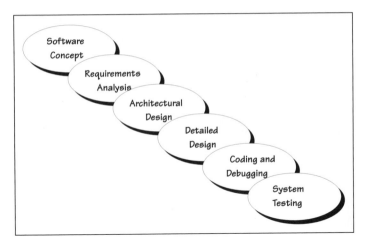

Figure 4.9   Sashimi Lifecycle.

The overlapping of phases in the Sashimi Lifecycle leads to unclear milestones, which makes it more difficult to establish interim artifact deliveries accurately and monitor the progress of a specific artifact. This can lead to inefficiencies because of the lack of a shared understanding of the status of any artifact. The Sashimi Lifecycle is applicable to new technology application delivery.

Waterfall Subprojects Lifecycle

The intent of subprojects is to allow different parts (components) within the product or application that are identified and defined by the architectural design phase to be developed separately. Figure 4.10 details how multiple teams can develop different components of the system in parallel.

This approach allows the rapid development of the better-understood components while the less understood, more complex, or dependent components are progressed at a slower rate. This reduces the risk of developing a component incorrectly or experiencing technical failure.

The Waterfall Subprojects Lifecycle relies on defining a stable and detailed architecture at the beginning of the software development project. Because of this, any unspecified interdependencies or cross-component technology changes will cause significant delays in absorbing the impact and resynchronizing. The Waterfall Subprojects Lifecycle is applicable to new technology application delivery.

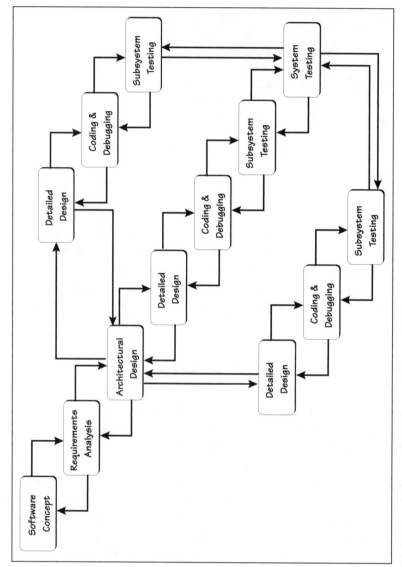

Figure 4.10 Waterfall Subprojects Lifecycle.

Staged Delivery Lifecycle

Staged Delivery Lifecycle delivers software to the customer in successively refined stages by incrementally adding functionality (see Figure 4.11), rather than waiting until the end of the development project as in the pure Waterfall Lifecycle.

The Staged Delivery Lifecycle relies on thorough requirements analysis and architectural design. To change them would impact already delivered software and create rework with corresponding delays. Therefore, any risk of delivering an incorrect solution is caught early. The Staged Delivery Lifecycle is applicable to new technology application delivery.

Code and Fix Lifecycle

The Code and Fix Lifecycle approach starts with a general idea of the product requirements and then uses informal and ad hoc approaches to continually develop the software until it is ready for release (see Figure 4.12). This approach is most applicable to demos and proof-of-concept prototypes.

In this approach there is no overhead of specification, documentation, and quality assurance. The perception is that there is immediate progress because coding begins very early. This approach requires little expertise in any systematic development approach and so has no skills constraints.

The Code and Fix Lifecycle is dangerous because there is no way to assess progress, delivery schedule, quality, or risks. This is because the only artifact produced is the code and the only measurement available is completion. It is notionally great for demos and proof-of-concept prototypes, but it is completely uncontrolled and creates many development and delivery risks.

Spiral Lifecycle

A Spiral Lifecycle reduces risks by regularly performing risk analysis and producing prototypes. As can be seen from Figure 4.13, the lifecycle spirals through its phases to delivery. The incremental, planned risk analysis ensures reduction of risks as the development progresses through the lifecycle and spends increasing amounts of the budget. There is high visibility of risks at an early stage in the development.

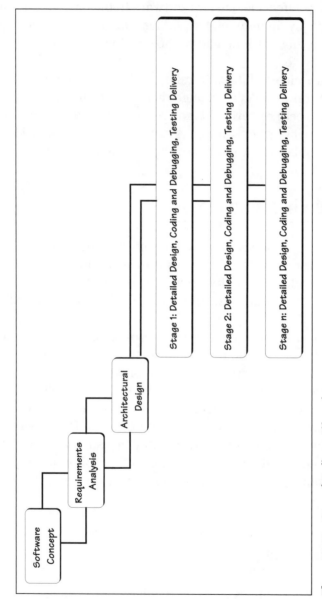

Figure 4.11 Staged Delivery Lifecycle.

The Spiral Lifecycle is a complicated model to implement because of its highly staggered development activities with their complex interrelationships. It relies on experienced management to control its implementation because it is difficult to know when to move onto the next activity due to the lack of a concrete milestone. The Spiral Lifecycle is very appropriate for new technology application development.

Controlled Iteration Lifecycle

A recently invented Controlled Iteration Lifecycle model [Cantor 1998] for object-oriented development (see Figure 4.14) has four phases:

Inception. Gathering of requirements and initial design.

Elaboration. Refinement of requirements and detailed design.

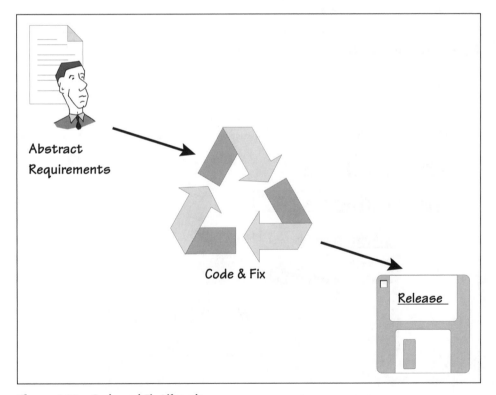

Figure 4.12   Code and Fix Lifecycle.

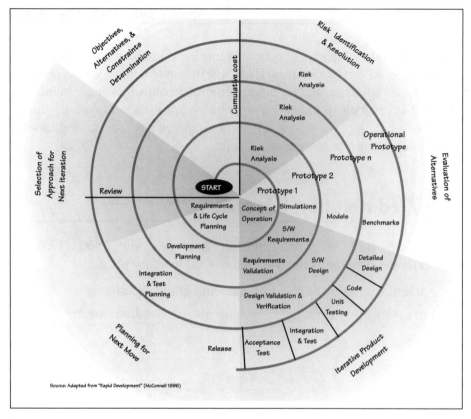

Source: Adapted from "Rapid Development" (McConnell 1996)

Figure 4.13   Spiral Lifecycle.

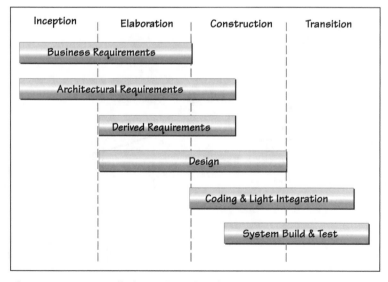

Figure 4.14   Controlled Iteration Lifecycle.

Construction. Further refinement of design and initial coding and testing.

Transition. Refinement of coding through testing and release of software.

The Controlled Iteration Lifecycle allows rapid progress based on the 80/20 rule (if you are 80 percent complete that's good enough) and for the discovery of unidentified derived requirements, which only happens in design when it can be discovered that requirements are functionally incomplete. In addition, this lifecycle has the ability to absorb changes easily because of the iteration of each artifact across multiple phases.

This approach is not easily applicable when an object-oriented development approach is not used. Clear end-of-phase criteria that validate the artifacts before moving onto the next phase are not defined. It is difficult to assess whether the delivered software was what the user specified. The Controlled Iteration Lifecycle is most appropriate for strongly object-oriented or distributed-object new technology application delivery.

Evolutionary Prototyping Lifecycle

The Evolutionary Prototyping Lifecycle develops the application or product concept throughout the lifecycle from initial vague ideas to a concrete product by the development of successive prototypes based on strong customer feedback on the required functionality, as illustrated in Figure 4.15.

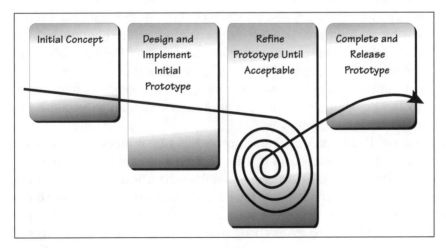

Figure 4.15 Evolutionary Prototyping Lifecycle.

This lifecycle approach is a strongly collaborative way to develop exactly what the customer wants, because of the strong involvement of the customer in the development. It does not require the customer to specify more than a general outline of what the requirements are to start the development process. It begins with prototyping the user interface and then adding core functional code. It avoids overengineering because it provides real development progress in the form of the evolving prototype to the customer on a frequent basis.

The Evolutionary Prototyping Lifecycle suffers from unknown development schedule and costs because it is not possible to plan when requirements are never complete until coding is complete. This lifecycle requires significant customer time for assessment and feedback to work well, and it is difficult to assess progress except by subjective customer comments. There is a major risk that this approach will devolve into a Code and Fix Lifecycle without strong project management. The Evolutionary Prototyping Lifecycle is most appropriate for demos and proof-of-concept prototypes.

Evolutionary Delivery Lifecycle

In the Evolutionary Delivery Lifecycle an initial waterfall is followed, similar to the Staged Delivery Lifecycle, for requirements and architecture design. However, instead of using separate development paths for application components, the evolutionary delivery approach works with the customer to evolve the application (see Figure 4.16) in the same way as the Evolutionary Prototyping Lifecycle.

The Evolutionary Delivery Lifecycle does not require the customer to be able to specify more than a general outline of the requirements, so a rapid start is possible. It also avoids overengineering by regularly showing real development progress to the customer. The Evolutionary Delivery Lifecycle will become more like the Staged Delivery Lifecycle if there is strict change control and limited customer involvement. If the customer is intensively involved in the development then this approach will tend to become the Evolutionary Prototyping Lifecycle.

One common disadvantage to this approach is that it incurs an unknown development schedule and costs if it is allowed to become more like the Evolutionary Prototyping Lifecycle. It requires significant customer time for assessment and feedback to work well and assumes that the basic technology aspects can be defined without any dependence on the application level. Again it is difficult to assess progress except by subjective customer comments.

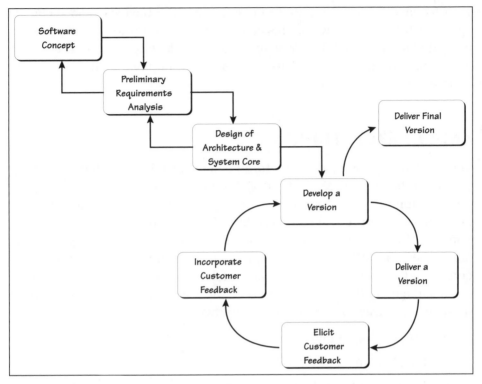

Figure 4.16 Evolutionary Delivery Lifecycle.

SYMPTOMS AND CONSEQUENCES

The primary symptom of implementing an inappropriate lifecycle is the lack of knowledge about the status of the development. The main consequences are unexpected costs and software delivery delays. Without knowing the status of the development, the managers cannot properly manage in the information vacuum and any decisions are entirely subjective and risk laden. When a risk or problem occurs, the lifecycle phase process does not always deal with it in a timely and effective manner. This leads to spending more effort, with associated cost and delay, in resolving the problem.

TYPICAL CAUSES

The cause is the lack of a suitable lifecycle for the nature of the development. This often happens because management picks the lifecycle they wish to have followed without understanding the business and technical applicability of the lifecycle. This can also happen if project developers are permitted to pick what they wish for a software development lifecycle without regard to applicability. This results in the implementation of one or more unsuitable lifecycles.

KNOWN EXCEPTIONS

The main exception to the refactored solution to the usefulness of implementing a lifecycle is a question of the level of maturity of the company implementing it. In other words, a company with an immature software development culture will gain little benefit from a particular lifecycle. The Software Engineering Institute Systems Engineering Capability Maturity Model (SEI SE-CMM) defines the *process areas* in terms of "the practices considered essential to the conduct of basic systems engineering" [SEI 1995] and qualify the effectiveness (i.e., the maturity of implementation) of these process areas according to the following:

Level 0. Not performed

Level 1. Performed informally

Level 2. Planned and tracked

Level 3. Well defined

Level 4. Quantatively controlled

Level 5. Continuously improving

For example, if a company was at level 0 or level 1, the lifecycle adopted would make little difference to their chances of repeated success in delivering software. If a company was at level 2 or level 3, the main advantages and disadvantages of the selected lifecycle would be derived each time they ran a development project.

REFACTORED SOLUTION

The best solution for most development shops is to have a few well-defined lifecycles on hand that fit the different types of development work, such as:

- Demos and proof-of-concept prototyping
- Incremental new technology application delivery
- Stable application maintenance

The more there is in common between the different lifecycles the easier they will be to adopt and to allocate development and management staff flexibly across the differing types of software development projects.

Assuming that most IT companies will eventually mature enough to tackle all three of these types of development, the solution should be to:

1. Identify the three best-suited individual lifecycles.

2. Apply localized refactoring to optimize them.

3. Identify the common phase processes between them.

4. Produce a super lifecycle to understand the points of convergence and divergence from the project planning and skills flexibility points of view.

Step 1: Identify the Best-Suited Individual Lifecycles

Table 4.2 identifies the applicable lifecycle options for each type of development. Specific choices are dependent on the prevalent development work and method of working. The preferred option is always the first listed.

Table 4.2 Lifecycle Options

NATURE OF DEVELOPMENT	APPROPRIATE LIFECYCLE	RATIONALE
Demos and proof-of-concept prototyping	Evolutionary Prototyping	Rapid results for mainly GUIs
	Evolutionary Delivery	Rapid results for non-GUIs
Incremental new technology application delivery	Staged Delivery	Controlled, scoped, prioritized, sequential deliveries
	Waterfall Subprojects	Shared risks across controlled, scoped concurrent deliveries
Stable application maintenance	Sashimi	Rapid version of Waterfall
	Waterfall	Highly manageable and predictable

The reason for not choosing lifecycle options is as important as the reasons for choosing them. In the case of demos and prototyping development, the approach necessarily has to be rapid and involve whatever users or user representatives, such as marketing or sales, are available for a collaborative development. This rules out the nonevolutionary lifecycles, since none of them have these qualities.

The incremental new product delivery projects need to have a lifecycle that supports potentially innovative requirements and architecture, so at least those stages must be done in a sequential manner before launching into the remainder of the development phases. The level of control must be balanced with risk and the ability to accelerate delivery for a market window.

The stable product maintenance projects have little requirements or architectural risk and can use a step-by-step approach that repeats well-understood development processes. Depending on the confidence in the maintenance staff, these processes can be overlapped in a Sashimi Lifecycle manner to achieve a more rapid delivery sequence.

Step 2: Apply Localized Refactoring to Optimize the Lifecycles

Prior to implementing a lifecycle it should be refactored to optimize it. All the lifecycles previously discussed in the Lifecycle Malpractice AntiPattern are covered for completeness.

Evolutionary Prototyping Lifecycle. There is no obvious refactoring to apply to this lifecycle. This has a major role to play in some customer-assisted developments but more usually for the GUI portion of the application used to derive the underlying technical requirements. A variation of this is used for the Evolutionary Delivery Lifecycle model.

Evolutionary Delivery Lifecycle. If the derived requirements were produced in parallel with core technology components then this would mitigate the cost and schedule risks but also remove the main advantage. So, there is no useful refactoring possible. This lifecycle should not be used if cost and schedule are critical or even important factors.

Staged Delivery Lifecycle. At the architectural design phase ensure that all components, their required interactions, and interfaces are produced for all delivery stages. Plan reasonable contingency for each development stage for the possible technical showstoppers that will cause architecture and perhaps even requirements to be revisited, and for some degree of code rework.

Waterfall with Subprojects Lifecycle. Produce a thorough logical and physical architecture that specifies each component, its required interface, and its interaction with other components with a full technology assessment. Where there are suspected technology difficulties, produce and analyze proof-of-concept prototypes as part of the architecture task. This is common where the developers are using a new technology and where innovation occurs.

Sashimi Lifecycle. The disadvantages of this lifecycle can be largely overcome by reducing the amount of overlap to predefined states at which interim artifact milestones can be set. This will give better measurability of progress.

Waterfall Lifecycle. Do not use the pure Waterfall Lifecycle; use one of the variations that keep the advantages but remove most of the disadvantages.

Code and Fix Lifecycle. Never use this lifecycle model since there is no way to assess the result in terms of any serious development that would be based on the proof of concept or demo. Usually demos and proof-of-concept deliveries are built to gain funding for a product development. However, because the approach is largely an ad hoc hacking exercise there is no information deliberately produced on technology assessment or effort required to build as a product.

Spiral Lifecycle. The early steps in the Spiral Lifecycle model can be used to identify business and technical risks during requirements analysis and architectural design. Follow with a more simplified version.

Controlled Iteration Lifecycle. Establish specific criteria for each artifact at the end of each phase to ensure verification and validation. Enforce software configuration management to control creep caused by still deriving requirements during design and coding.

Step 3: Identify Common Phase Processes

This step identifies the common processes shared by the selected lifecycles in Table 4.3.

From this table it seems obvious that most of the phase processes are common. But the degree of process and associated entry and exit criteria to

Table 4.3 Preferred Lifecycle Option Phases

LIFECYCLE PHASE	EVOLUTIONARY PROTOTYPING	STAGED DELIVERY	SASHIMI
Software concept	✔	✔	✔
Requirements analysis		✔	✔
Architectural design	✔	✔	✔
Detailed design		✔	✔
Coding and debugging	✔	✔	✔
System testing		✔	✔

the phases are not the same. By examining Figures 4.15, 4.11, and 4.9 respectively, this becomes apparent.

In Figure 4.15 (Evolutionary Prototyping Lifecycle) the requirements are in more of an abstract or high-level form than derived detail, and design is also higher level rather than detailed. The entry points are not subject to rigorous reviews but are geared to subjective understanding by the staff working on the next phase.

In Figure 4.11 (Staged Delivery Lifecycle) the requirements analysis and architectural design phases are not iterated unless a problem is found later in design, coding, or testing that causes a change to the business and technical requirements. Both of these phases are subject to strict entry and exit criteria to reduce the risks of change later in the lifecycle.

In Figure 4.9 (Sashimi Lifecycle) the phases are iterated constantly and the requirements, architecture, design, and code are continually further developed in synchronization with each other. The entry and exit criteria are geared to ensuring traceability between artifacts in an ongoing manner and rigorous sign-off cannot happen for any phase artifact much before the final delivery of code. The exception to this is if the overlap is reduced, but this introduces the disadvantages of the Waterfall Lifecycle.

Step 4: Produce a Superset Lifecycle to Understand the Points of Convergence and Divergence

A superset lifecycle is the combined view of the multiple software development lifecycles selected. Each lifecycle will likely converge with and diverge from the other lifecycles at some point and this information must be clearly identified. To correctly correlate a superset lifecycle requires the definition of each lifecycle phase at the next level of detail. This process was already started in part in step 3 when the process details and entry and exit criteria for the lifecycle phases are examined. This can be somewhat subjective based on specific corporate preferences. Figure 4.17 gives an example of such a phase-process composition, but should not be treated as a definitive standard.

VARIATIONS

While there are an undefined plethora of minor lifecycle variations, the solution remains unchanged. The key is always to ensure that the best-fit lifecycle is used for the nature of the development and that it is well understood by those who implement it.

EXAMPLE

A major European financial institution centrally imposes the way that software development projects are run. This includes the software development lifecycle and technologies used. The financial institution had not changed its Waterfall Lifecycle approach for the last 15 years based on the success it achieved on previous, now legacy, application developments. However, the technology had changed from COBOL and DB2 to Power-Builder, C++, and Sybase. There was a total lack of awareness by central corporate management and their technical staff that this change of technical direction would have any impact on the way they developed software. This caused significant problems during the changeover to the new technologies.

Most of the institution's development staff at the various sites was well versed in the implementation of the Waterfall Lifecycle. But the new technologies created problems that the Waterfall Lifecycle couldn't handle because there needed to be some time to evaluate and understand the implications of the new technologies.

The financial institution cared deeply about investment levels in software development but always focused on the delivery date as the critical factor. Often additional cash was made available to try to assist a late-running project; quality was rarely ever mentioned at the corporate level.

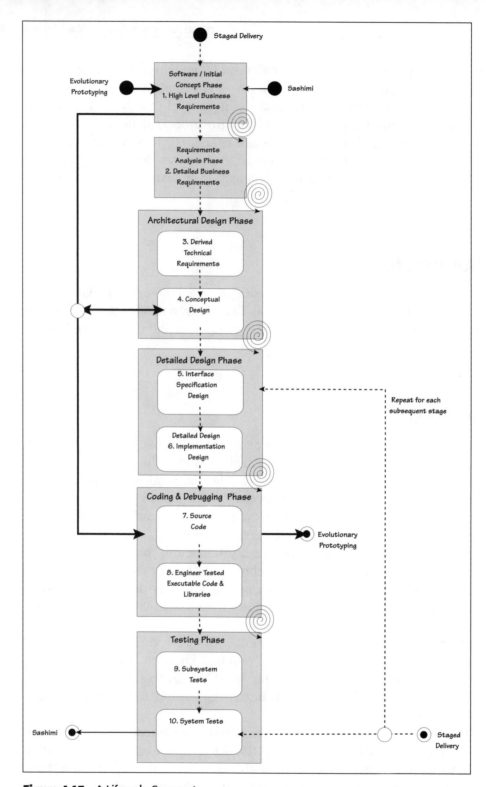

Figure 4.17 A Lifecycle Superset.

WATERFALL ADVANTAGES

The pure Waterfall Lifecycle works well for product development where there is a stable product definition and well-understood and stable development technologies. It minimizes planning overhead since it is all produced at the beginning of the lifecycle. It deals well with complexity by forcing it to be dealt with in an orderly manner. It also works well when quality requirements are a higher priority than cost and schedule requirements. This lifecycle provides requirements stability early on and error reduction throughout, and is structured so that different staff can work through the separate phases by the production of extensive documentation.

WATERFALL DISADVANTAGES

This approach suffers from the difficulty in fully planning all steps of a development, including the prediction of unknowns, at the outset of a development. The practical difficulty of fully specifying derived requirements at the beginning of a project exists because many requirements are derived by early design and even coding discovers the need for utility functions that could not have been logically identified at the time of writing the initial requirements. Also to deal with such changes generated from design and coding issues means reworking back through the lifecycle phase and then forward again to validate and verify the changes; this is very effort intensive. Significant effort is focused on the provision of stand-alone documentation.

The development staff on nine different application development projects was the first to implement the new technology. Although each project recruited some key technical staff to assist with the developments, most of the staff were going through a steep learning curve on the new technologies and the schedules were set by the project manager and agreed to with the customer.

The Waterfall Lifecycle was a root cause of the many development problems encountered because of its mismatch to the nature of the new technology developments (see Table 4.4).

All of the projects generally followed the same pattern of development progression. The software concept phase was performed on time and without any problems because these were all critical projects to the financial institution and had business priority. The requirements analysis phase produced detailed business requirements either early or on schedule.

The architectural design and detailed design phases were not completed on schedule due to the lack of understanding of the new technology. This

Table 4.4 Waterfall Lifecycle Support for New Technology Developments

LIFECYCLE SUPPORT	LIFECYCLE LIABILITY
Stable product definition for well-understood and stable development technologies	No developer knowledge or experience in the new technologies
Minimizes planning overhead	More detailed planning required to control risks

part of the developments broke away from the usual waterfall approach mainly because the staff couldn't cope with the level of detail required since they could not match it with the required level of understanding, as depicted in Figure 4.18. The levels of detail produced fell way short of those required. In light of the reported slippages, the financial institution refused to change its technical strategy of the chosen technologies, blaming the project developments for inadequate skills. Coding and debugging occurred in a fragmented manner for parts of design, while system testing really didn't occur in many cases since the developments did not progress that far.

The developments ended up in a vicious cycle of rearchitecting, redesigning, and recoding each time a developed application component did not

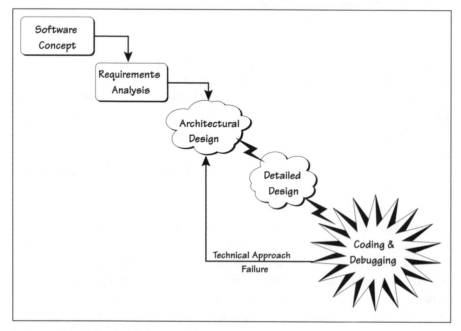

Figure 4.18 Waterfall disintegration.

work due to some perceived technology problem. This caused delays ranging from 50 percent to 150 percent across the nine strategic new technology developments. Seven of the project developments were eventually cancelled and the individual developments were the scapegoats for these failures. The other two projects delivered late, their success being due to better skills and abandonment of the Waterfall Lifecycle after early problems with the architectural design and detailed design phases.

Both projects adopted an evolutionary delivery lifecycle. While both projects constantly hit technology problems due to a lack of experience, the new lifecycle mitigated the risks sufficiently through a better approach to this nature of software development based on the available skills of the staff.

RELATED SOLUTIONS

The Lifecycle Malpractice AntiPattern is strongly related to the Standards AntiPattern that sets the theme for this book. While this AntiPattern considers the application of software development lifecycles, the Standards AntiPattern considers the application of all forms of software development standards.

APPLICABILITY TO OTHER VIEWPOINTS AND SCALES

Although on an individual basis the Lifecycle Malpractice AntiPattern directly affects the ability to deliver an application, the problem is usually widespread enough in most companies to impact the enterprise since it impacts most software developments. This is simply because most companies have continually run with one lifecycle approach regardless of the nature of the development; for example, legacy or client/server. And even if only the more recent client-server- and modern technology-based developments exhibit this problem because the lifecycle is not appropriate, a significant and growing problem is indicated.

The Customer

AntiPattern Name: The Customer

Also Known As: Lesser of All Evils, Too Many Hands in the Soup

Most Applicable Scale: Enterprise

Refactored Solution Name: Customer Focus

Refactored Solution Type: Process

Root Causes: Ignorance, Pride, Narrow-Mindedness, Avarice

Unbalanced Forces: Management of Functionality and Management of Resources

Anecdotal Evidence:
"The customer is always right."
"But the customer wants this! Which customer?"
"The customer is the user. No, the customer is. . . ."
"Yes sir, yes sir, three bags full. One for my master, one for the dame, and one for the little boy who lives down the lane."

BACKGROUND

If you have ever worked in a large corporate information technology (IT) organization you have experienced the Customer AntiPattern. The problem occurs when the project is pulled and pushed in multiple directions by multiple organizations, each attempting to further their interests. Worst of all is when the interests of these organizations are orthogonal to one another or even uncorrelated. Each of these organizations can be identified to the project manager as the customer. The project manager often finds it difficult to satisfy anyone, directing the project first in one direction and then another to satisfy the customer de jour. It truly becomes a lose-lose situation. Often the project manager must sell his or her soul in order to make everyone happy (see Figure 4.19). Sometimes the cost is project failure, but then the definition of failure is dependent on whose interests you didn't satisfy.

The Customer AntiPattern will help the project manager identify when

Figure 4.19 Let's make a project deal.

there are too many hands in the soup and how to recover after he or she is neck-deep in customers that are trying to drive the project.

The analogy of driving the project, as related to this AntiPattern, brings to mind an image of the Three Stooges driving a car, each struggling for the steering wheel, with the dialog going something like this:

Moe: "I've got the wheel."

Larry: "No, I've got the wheel."

Curly: "Hey, I've got the wheel."

The camera shot shows the steering wheel having come off the steering column in the hands of Curly. A look of shock is present on all of their faces. Moe yells to Curly, "You numb skull!" In the last scene a car is going off the cliff, plummeting to certain death.

This analogy is similar to that of the organizations that compete to steer the project in the direction they think it should go. Unfortunately, with their need to steer they don't realize they are driving the project off the cliff, plunging to certain death.

GENERAL FORM

Frequently in development efforts the question is asked, "Who is the customer?" The response reveals that it is not one organization, but several organizations, depending on your perspective. The reason is that often there are various organizational entities that are stakeholders in the project who have something to gain or lose if the project does or doesn't succeed. The predicament for the project manager and the project team is which master do they serve? This can be a confusing and difficult question with severe repercussions if not properly examined and addressed.

The project team typically thinks of the end user as the customer. Most systems engineering approaches the end user as the source for gathering user needs, which translates into user requirements, which translates into functional requirements, and so on. Yet it isn't always simple to discern the end user. In large organizations, ad hoc committees are created to represent the users. These types of committees are especially common when the users are physically disparate. Nevertheless, the ad hoc committees that represent the user base may have an agenda that furthers the interests of the executives steering the group, rather than the actual user population. It is difficult to understand why user requirements are sometimes unilaterally discarded by the ad hoc committee representing the users, when interviewing end users directly captures these user requirements. The project teams can only guess at what politics are taking place.

Unfortunately for the project team, the question of "who is the customer" doesn't end with the identification of the end user. In many large corporate and governmental organizations there is another organization that is responsible for funding the project. Sometimes the funding organization is the recipient of the end user's product, and the whole reason for that organization funding this project is to better enable responsiveness or quality by the organization (end user) providing them with the product. Because this organization is funding the project and has a vested interest, they view themselves as the customer, even if no one else but the project office does. These organizations may threaten a withdrawal or reduction in funding if their requirements are not adequately addressed, regardless of the conflict that may be created elsewhere.

Next there are organizations that have a broader mission within the larger organization and feel compelled to bring their influence to bear on projects. The office of a chief information officer (CIO) is a good example of this type of organization. These organizations feel that they have a charter to ensure that standards are met and that certain areas of technology are being promulgated, even if that technology or application is not ubiquitous throughout the organization. They have a charter to ensure that the project fits into the enterprise and interfaces appropriately. They want to ensure that the project is positioned for the future. These organizations often have some type of approval over projects and can often influence the technical and functional direction of a project by disapproving the project, preventing deployment. This is not always a bad situation. An example of how these organizations can use influence in an appropriate manner could be that they require some assurance of year 2000 testing or certification prior to the deployment of a project. However, some governmental organizations have information technical security offices welding God-like powers over projects and the technical solutions that are employed by the projects. Some of these organizations don't even offer explanations of why certain technologies can or cannot be used. It is unclear whether they are fearful of revealing information that might threaten the organization's security posture or if they are using a shotgun approach because they aren't sure that a potential threat exists.

Finally, there is the management of the project organization. Even if this organization falls under the purview of the CIO's office, the project manager's management typically have an agenda that they are attempting to achieve to ensure their personal success, the success of the organization, and the success of the project or several projects. Sometimes the agendas of these organizations (including the end-user organization) is in conflict, or at least minimally not coordinated with each of the other's requirements. This creates a tremendous amount of pressure on the project office and the project manager, as demonstrated in Figure 4.20.

SYMPTOMS AND CONSEQUENCES

Symptoms and consequences of the Customer AntiPattern are typically revealed incrementally. Lack of progress is normally the first sign. This is due to disagreements with key objectives or even constant changes to the initial planning. While the destructive behavior may be recognized, typically few staff are willing to mitigate their position. Sometimes this behavior is tolerated because each of the parties is either unaware of the damage that

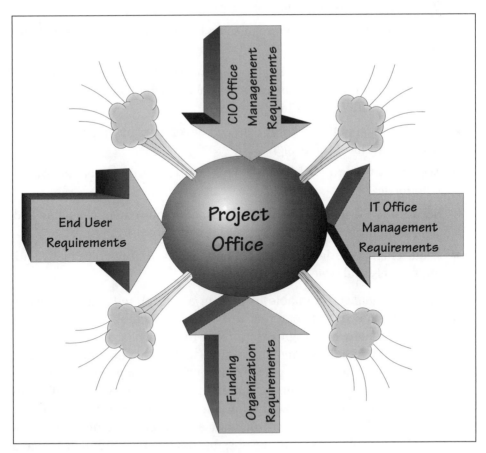

Figure 4.20   Customer project compression.

is impacted on the project by their position or unwilling to address it. Very little is accomplished in meetings because the political climate creates an environment in which technical issues can't be addressed and also because they represent serial discussions of concerns that are regressively covered.

In the worst case scenario, these types of projects exist in a politically charged environment in which few decisions can occur outside of meetings where all participants are represented, precluding timely decisions and actions. Additionally, the political environment results in rescoping project requirements. Often obtaining requirements from the user is abandoned and requirements analysis becomes speculative based on what the development team feels will be amenable to all parties.

Technically the symptoms and consequences are reflected in the inability to move out of the design phase. Specifically:

- Design is overly complex, incoherent, or is excessively defective.
- Documentation is voluminous.
- Convergence and stability are missing from the requirements and the design.
- The development team is unable to prioritize design features by identifying which requirements are essential and which need to be addressed with the next implementation.
- This results in both the architects and developers having conflicting interpretations of the design.
- Eventually the project becomes significantly overbudgeted and over-scheduled.
- Because of the inability to achieve a stable requirements baseline and design, multiple project restarts and rework are prevalent.
- Requirements, design, and implementation issues are continually and regressively addressed.

The project manager is unable to plan in a logical and pragmatic way. Soon the cost exceeds expectations without a predictable end point. The complexity of whatever design exists from the analysis results in implementations that make the system impossible to develop, document, or test. As the project continues to evolve, continually missing milestones, the focus becomes cost rather than the actual delivery. Members from all organizational elements soon realize the imminent danger of project cancellation, and greed takes over further pragmatic decisions. Soon the objective is to protract the project as long as possible and keep it funded to save careers.

The next phase becomes the cover-up phase where the project team attempts to hide and cloud details, blaming others for the failure. The project manager will attempt to feign ignorance of many aspects of the project, making it impossible to review organizations to discern the true status. The project schedule status will most likely be unknown.

The final blow is the failure to deliver. The consequences become continually more apparent to outsiders until finally the project overruns and the typical options are presented. First and most important, additional investment in the project is required. Second, crisis project management is implemented, and third, key personnel that have departed the project are replaced (including the project manager). Usually there is no discovery of the real issues and the project continues to fail until cancellation (unless the refactored solution is implemented).

 ## TYPICAL CAUSES

Causes for the Customer AntiPattern include:

- Lack of project vision and focus. The goal of delivering a product to the customer is diffused.
- Poorly defined goals.
- Planning and leadership lapses.
- Protracted requirements definition and analysis provides little value.
- Poor project oversight.
- Poor project planning and execution.
- Ignorance of basic project planning principles.
- Forced management compliance.
- Planning as a primary objective.
- Attempts to make everyone happy.
- Poor meeting processes marked by ineffective facilitation, including meetings where the loudest person wins the argument.
- Gold plating and requirements creep.
- Undetermined priorities or a software-value system [Mowbray 1997].
- Unseparated concerns and unused reference models [Brown 1998].
- Project management focused on analysis and problem decomposition, rather than design and implementation.

KNOWN EXCEPTIONS

An exception to the Customer AntiPattern is when each of the customers (organizations) has valid requirements that are provided to the project team. If the requirements are provided without political leveraging and presented in a dispassionate manner, then a greater issue is at stake. The problem is not with the project, but rather the corporate strategy. Specifically, this means that there is no common vision or consensus of how the enterprise should operate. This most likely falls into the lap of the CIO and it should be promptly relegated to his or her domain for disposition. The CIO's failure to act in such a situation would result in a greater failure than a single project, most likely an organizational demise.

REFACTORED SOLUTION

The customer is always right. That should be the premise of the project manager. Then all the project manager has to do is define the customer. McConnell defines the customer "[as] the person or persons that the software ultimately must please in order to be considered a success" [McConnell 1998]. The project manager should then proceed to define scenarios that specifically identify the customer for each scenario. But the crux of the Customer AntiPattern is when you have several organizations all acting like the customer. What then?

First, when the project encounters this type of AntiPattern, strict project management and system engineering discipline must be applied. Tight configuration control is especially important because the greatest impact to the project is going to be the technical baseline. The project is primed for analysis paralysis and requirements creep. Actually for this situation a better description of what occurs is requirements ambush. This is when the project office is ambushed by each of the organizations competing to have their parochial and conflicting requirements addressed (see Figure 4.21).

The project manager must choose early on who the end user is and identify those specific requirements pertaining to the end user. More than any other customer, the project needs to accommodate the end user. If the end user is not satisfied the system won't be used and will be absolutely declared a failure. If the remaining customer's requirements aren't addressed, assuming deployment is feasible, the project may be deemed less than successful, but certainly not a complete failure.

More than likely the end user and the funding organization will be closely

Figure 4.21 Requirements ambush.

aligned with their requirements. Attempting to have these two organizations work closely together through the use of a professional facilitator should bring them closer to agreement regarding a requirements baseline. Once these two customers are brought to agreement for the requirements, the project office should move swiftly to baseline. However, there shouldn't be any obvious conflicts with other known organizational directives (e.g., Y2K initiatives). Additionally, if any of the requirements are considered controversial, they should be carefully vetted at a working level to understand what potential repercussions might exist. The requirements baseline developed in this phase should be used as the basis for all following discussions with the remaining customers.

It is also recommended that a spiral development methodology be employed. This allows the initial instantiation to reflect basic requirements, which will most likely not meet any disagreement. The requirements baseline can continue to evolve, incorporating more sophisticated requirements over time and allowing the project office to address more controversial requirements systematically.

The project office should conduct a meeting to baseline the requirements documentation. The meeting should be conducted with designated representatives of each of the customer organizations. Each representative should be fully empowered to approve or disapprove the project artifact. Every attempt should be made to involve no more than five representatives to keep communication clear and effective [Brown 1998]. The proposed baseline should be provided to each of the organizational representatives well in advance of the meeting to allow them ample time to comprehend the documentation. The project office should hire a professional facilitator to conduct the requirements review. This removes the project office from the immediate line of fire and helps to insulate them from any ensuing controversy. It also helps remove any personal conflicts that may exist. The project manager should introduce the facilitator and explain his or her role for the meeting. This is also necessary to ensure that it is clear that the facilitator doesn't have a vested interest in the outcome. Project office technical personnel should be on hand to answer questions, but they should only be senior personnel and should understand the importance of answering questions succinctly and without basis. It should also be clear that the technical personnel do not set the strategy or thinking of the project office, just in case a developer responds emotionally to an answer. This must be done carefully so as not to offend the developer, otherwise the repercussion to the project team is detrimental [Kerzner 1998].

The agenda for the meeting should be clear and concise. The purpose of the meeting should be to approve the requirements baseline and should result in a line-by-line agreement of the requirements. If disagreement occurs and resolution cannot be achieved quickly, the requirement should be noted and the review continued. This may not be possible when certain requirements have collateral impact on the remaining requirements; however, as much as possible, disagreement should be avoided until the end. The objective is to come to an understanding of the many requirements to which the various customers do agree and focus on the success of the effort, rather than getting bogged down in the failure of a single requirement that no one can agree on.

At the conclusion of the meeting, the project office should identify the requirements that prompted disagreement. Depending on the hour of the day and the number of requirements that remain in question, the meeting may be continued the next day or several days later to allow for better preparation. Clear and rested minds function with less confusion and conflict. The facilitator should point out the success of the day, distinctly identify the many requirements that they have agreed on, and minimize the work of the next meeting by highlighting the few requirements that remain in question.

The project office should note the requirements that are in question. For each requirement there should be a clear and understood rationale for the objections, and which organizations made the objections. The project office should develop a matrix of these requirements, identifying the pros and cons of each. Cost, schedule, and impact to the user's ability to accomplish the mission should be specifically identified. This matrix should be reviewed by the project team and then provided to the organizational representatives for review. Another meeting should be conducted to review the requirements that remain in question. All organizational representatives should be present, regardless of whether they take issue with the remaining requirements. Again a facilitator should be employed. The requirements in question should be addressed, one by one, in a logical manner. But, if there is some low hanging fruit, those requirements should be addressed first. A time limit should be established with regards to how much discussion (argument) can be taken for each requirement. The meeting should conclude as the previous one. The facilitator should point out the success of the day, distinctly identifying the requirements that they have agreed on, both this time and at the previous meeting. The facilitator should also minimize the work of the next meeting by highlighting the few requirements that remain in question. This process continues until all requirements are agreed on—this is a win-win moment and should be celebrated. The conclusion should result in the signing of a requirements document that reflects all the agreed to requirements. This document should be reproduced and provided to each of the organizational representatives as a reminder of the agreement.

It is hoped that the customers can agree to all requirements. If not, the project office must decide. This is a difficult time and decisions must be carefully considered. The end user should be considered first, but the political ramifications of each decision must also be studied. There is no one guide to help the project manager at this point. It is a time for good judgment. Whatever the outcome, the document should be signed by all those in agreement and a copy provided to them. The project office should continue to work with any dissenting organizations to mitigate their objections. One option is to incorporate any contested requirement as desired (assuming that the other organizations agree) and then defer the requirement for later implementation. A more underhand method is to include the requirement, with full knowledge that it will fail when tested (because it wasn't implemented). This is not recommended.

Now that the project office has baselined the requirements, it can proceed with the design and development knowing that the requirements will continue to evolve throughout the software development process due to new thinking, new technology, and competition [Whitten 1995]. What is required from here forward is good communication between the project office and the customers. This is critical to the final success of the project.

"Managers and developers who keep project stakeholders informed on a weekly basis, report substantial benefits such as being seen as cooperative, responsive, and conscientious" [McConnell 1998]. Customer involvement is key to the successful deployment and ultimate satisfaction of the customer (see Figure 4.22). To achieve this it is important to keep the same organizational representatives that participated in the baselining of the requirements appraised of the progress, risks, and problems associated with the project.

Finally, McConnell identifies a "Customer's Bill of Rights" in his book, *Software Project Survival Guide.* This is a great guide for project managers involved in any development effort. McConnell's bill of rights follows:

1. To have set objectives for the project and have them followed.

2. To know how long the software project will take and how much it will cost.

3. To decide which features are in and which are out of the software.

4. To make reasonable changes to requirements throughout the course of the project and to know the costs of making those changes.

5. To know the project's status clearly and confidently.

6. To be apprised regularly of the risks that could affect cost schedule or quality and to be provided with options for addressing potential problems.

7. To have ready access to project deliverables throughout the project. [McConnell 1998]

VARIATIONS

The Customer AntiPattern has multiple variations associated with it due to the complexity and diversity of organizations. This varies by the different internal and external roles that act as the customer. Because each enterprise consists of uncommon or dissimilar organizational structures, hierarchies, and elements, this AntiPattern needs to be altered for each specific instance where organizational players are identified as customers.

EXAMPLE

The Customer AntiPattern can occur when the end user doesn't even want the system that is under development. In this example a group of regional

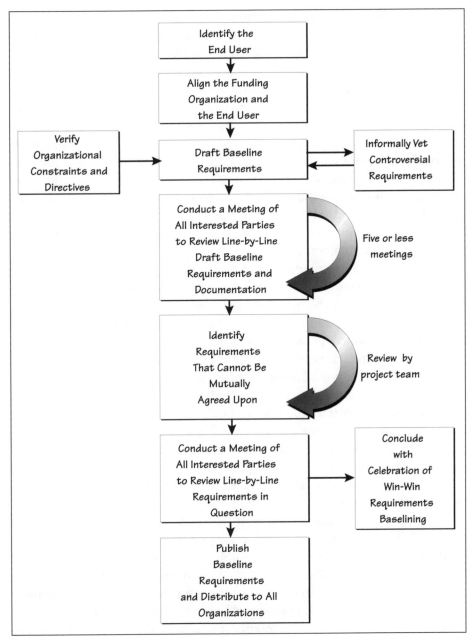

Figure 4.22 Customer refactored solution process.

analysts providing economics reports to investment specialists for international, institutional investing. The analysts' management is convinced that a software tool that has proven successful with one group of analysts is needed by another group. The management is certain that once the analysts get the tool, they will use it and improve the quality and efficiency of their work. Unfortunately, the analysts don't see it that way. They don't want another tool, and they "don't want another system setting on their desk" to accomplish their job. The analysts' requirement is for a single, ubiquitous desktop environment where they can accomplish all of their tasks. Immediately the analysts become hostile toward the development team and resist any progress toward defining user requirements. They make the user-requirements process unbearable for the project team. Additionally they inject ridiculous requirements to ensure that the system will either not be built or fail in its implementation.

At the same time, the management group that has decided the tools are necessary has also decided that they shouldn't have to fully fund the project, and so they call on the benefactors (investment specialists) of the analysts' work to partially fund the effort. This organization has distinct ideas about what they want the analysts' end products to look like and immediately begin redesigning reports and other products, which would require substantial reengineering of business processes. Both the analysts' management and the investment specialists agree that the tool should be developed and deployed no later than the end of the calendar year.

The office of the CIO has clearly stated that there won't be any deployments subsequent to October of 1999 and all new systems must thoroughly undergo Y2K testing to ensure compliance. These requirements compress the development schedule to an incomprehensible three months, with little assurance that the schedule can actually be met.

Finally the project team's management, which supports the development effort and is responsible for providing operations and maintenance, has mandated a specific architecture to help reduce maintenance costs and thereby reduce the costs for the center. Unfortunately, the project team is pursuing an architecture that was used in previous implementations and does not support the management's objectives. The implications of using the architecture mandated by management will impact system performance.

It looked like doom was certain for the project, so the project manager took evasive action. She assumed that she would not be able to satisfy the analysts regardless of what was accomplished, so she took the user requirements from the similar, previously deployed system. She convinced the investment specialists that without modification to the existing reports and products (which would require reengineering) the tool would still have great value to them in achieving better quality and more timely reports from the analysts. The project manager also pointed out that without modifying the existing requirements, she would be able to meet the requirement of deploying before the October 1999 deadline for the CIO's office and, therefore, deploy before the end of the calendar year. She also convinced the CIO's office to provide a staff member who was familiar with the Y2K requirements to participate in the development effort as a consultant to better ensure success of the testing. Finally, the project manager acquiesced on the architecture requirements; however, she asked his management to invest in performance testing to better anticipate the impact of moving to the new architecture. The project is currently in development.

While the project manager wasn't able to achieve a full win-win situation by getting the analysts to buy-in, she did get the remaining parties to reach agreement. The project manager continues to work with the analysts' management to establish better end-user relations.

RELATED SOLUTIONS

Several AntiPatterns are related to the Customer AntiPattern. Project managers should reference and review the refactored solutions for these AntiPatterns to assist in refactoring the solution here. Those AntiPatterns include:

- Analysis Paralysis [Brown 1998] provides a solution to the problem of analysis never completing, which often occurs because the customer is never satisfied.

- Planning 911 includes a solution to planning as used by the customer to control the software development.

- Requirements Jeopardy [Brown 1999] provides a solution for the erratic requirement changes that are caused by the customer.

APPLICABILITY TO OTHER VIEWPOINTS AND SCALES

The Customer AntiPattern is directly applicable to the enterprise perspective, but as in many other AntiPatterns the enterprise-level impact devolves through a few more levels of the software design-level model (SDLM):

- System
- Application frameworks
- Micro-architecture

One Size Fits All

AntiPattern Name: One Size Fits All

Also Known As: Silver Bullet Software Process, Golden Bullet Software Process, Platinum Bullet Software Process, Titanium Bullet Software Process, Turbonium Bullet Software Process

Most Applicable Scale: Enterprise

Refactored Solution Name: Tailor Made

Refactored Solution Type: Process

Root Causes: Ignorance and Sloth

Unbalanced Forces: Management of Change and Management of IT Resources

Anecdotal Evidence:
"We know what we need to do but the 'process' is holding us up!"
"We could have finished coding the demo by now and we're busy developing test plans."

BACKGROUND

Often an IT shop will run many projects of varying size, nature, and complexity. In a well-meaning attempt to support them all in a consistent manner, the IT management decides to institute a single software development process. The rationale is primarily to save money and gain consistency in working practices across software developments while delivering products to market earlier than the competition.

The end-to-end process is never initially sufficient for the needs of all projects, and it is continually added to until it becomes monolithic in an attempt to be the single software development process for all projects.

This has been primarily evident in government- and military-sponsored software development methodologies around the world, such as:

- Technical Architecture Framework for Information Management (TAFIM)
- Structured Systems Analysis and Design (SSADM)
- Capability Maturity Model (CMM)

GENERAL FORM

The problems caused by a single monolithic software process are severe and extensive and increase the risks of:

- Cost overruns
- Premature termination of project
- Development of the wrong product
- Technical failure [Moynihan 1989]

A major risk is the lack of a match of the software lifecycle to the nature of the development, as seen in Figure 4.23. Often the lifecycle adopted is waterfall in nature because managers generally perceive a comfort factor from an apparent high degree of control and detailed, regular production of paperwork. But whatever lifecycle is embedded within the monolithic software development process, it will usually be unsuitable for at least two of the following types of software development project specified in Figure 4.23:

- Demos and proof-of-concept prototyping
- New technology application delivery
- Stable application maintenance

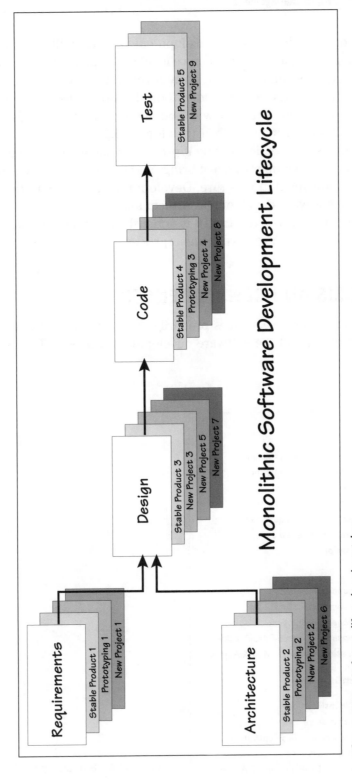

Figure 4.23 Software lifecycle mismatches.

A single monolithic software development process will be too bureaucratic for smaller projects. It will have a level of detail at every phase that is unnecessary for less complex software developments where the business domain and technology is well understood. In those cases the monolithic software development process will add unnecessary activities, directly increasing costs and time to deliver (see Figure 4.24).

A monolithic software development process is usually ignored by project managers and/or developers since it brings no benefits. Lip service is paid to it but actual implementation is rare. Developer teams return to the starting point of each software development project and invent their own software development process; but this time it is under the headings, or phase names, of the monolithic software development process.

SYMPTOMS AND CONSEQUENCES

The symptoms and consequences primarily occur in two stages and impact individual projects and the software development process. The first occurs

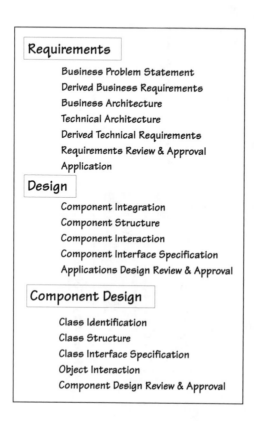

Requirements

> Business Problem Statement
> Derived Business Requirements
> Business Architecture
> Technical Architecture
> Derived Technical Requirements
> Requirements Review & Approval
> Application

Design

> Component Integration
> Component Structure
> Component Interaction
> Component Interface Specification
> Applications Design Review & Approval

Component Design

> Class Identification
> Class Structure
> Class Interface Specification
> Object Interaction
> Component Design Review & Approval

Figure 4.24 Bureaucratic software development process extract.

prior to the full derivation of the monolithic software development process and the second after it is mandated for use by all projects within the enterprise.

The main symptom of the first stage is an insufficient software development process for a project that has to add software development tasks where they need increased process support. This leads to the consequence of extending the planned time and budget. The secondary consequence is an uncontrolled growth of the software development process based on the needs of the latest project.

The main symptom of the second stage is a project that tries to implement an overdetailed and inappropriate process for a project. The initial consequence is that the current project has to invent its own software development process under the phase headings of the monolithic corporate process or, even worse, avoid following one altogether.

The final and ultimate consequences impact at the corporate level, causing delays in getting a product to market or delivering to an internal line of business customer, and the loss of revenue to competition.

 ## TYPICAL CAUSES

Unlike the symptoms, there are three stages of causes. The initial cause is IT management's desire to produce a single software development process that will support all projects. The rationale is usually consistency of process leading to more rapid development and releasing products to market, or internal customer, sooner. Either way the result expected is that the company will be more competitive in the market place.

The second stage is the incremental and partially uncontrolled growth of the software development process when it is found to be insufficient for the needs of the project. This often results from the specific nature of the project:

- Demos and prototyping that need some conceptual modeling to guide the coding, but not detailed requirements, design, or testing.

- New technology product delivery that requires an incremental approach, iterating between the software development phases of architecture, detailed design, coding, and testing.

- Stable product maintenance that needs a sequential waterfall approach repeating a well-understood process for a well-understood product or application.

The final stage is when the IT executive management enforces the single monolithic software development process on all projects because of the symptom of the persistent consequences of projects overrunning the planned time and budget.

KNOWN EXCEPTIONS

The normal exceptions exist when the company is small and has one or two products or applications with no diversity. However, this is not likely to continue if the company is to stay competitive and profitable. The company eventually will need to add more functionality and change to technologies that will move it from stable product maintenance projects to prototypical new technology development.

REFACTORED SOLUTION

The solution is highly similar to the first part of the Lifecycle Malpractice AntiPattern refactored solution. The best solution for most development shops is to have a few well-defined software development approaches that fit the different types of development work.

However, the more there is in common between the different lifecycles the easier they will be to adopt and to flexibly allocate development and management staff. The refactoring process needs to:

1. Identify the nature of the software developments.

2. Identify the candidate software development lifecycles.

3. Identify the best fit software development lifecycles.

Step 1: Identify the Nature of the Software Developments

This step is only simple if the projects examined follow a stated lifecycle or methodology. In most instances it will not be obvious, in which case some judicious investigation will produce the required information:

1. Examine the project plan and schedule for ordering of phases, activities, and tasks. Although scheduling tools such as Microsoft Project support sequential lists, it will be obvious what (if other than a pure Waterfall Lifecycle) is used from overlapping or repeated activities.

2. Examine the software configuration management artifacts for the number of times the configuration identification, configuration control, and audit was implemented. If the configuration identification occurred only once then it is likely to have been a version of the

Waterfall Lifecycle. If the configuration control and audits occurred only once per phase then it reinforces this view. Multiple invocations of these will indicate a more iterative approach.

3. Talk to the senior developers and team leaders about how they have delivered their software in the past. This may well indicate differences in approach but is necessary if the previous information is unavailable or wasn't followed. This activity will lend a sense of reality to any information discovered. Many developers will work in an iterative manner because it is more natural, as depicted in Figure 4.25.

4. Try to classify the projects by lifecycle and purpose, which should be one of:

   ■ Demos and proof-of-concept prototyping

   ■ New technology application delivery

   ■ Stable application maintenance

5. Finally, be aware that many projects will pay lip service to a software development approach while being completely ad hoc in their development activities. Do not assume that because a project manager files a plan and schedule that it automatically represents reality. Confirmation is required. Often a code and fix approach is implemented with any design being more of a reverse engineering exercise. In other words, the design is the result of using a CASE tool to reverse engineer the code rather than a strategic step to specifying the required code.

Step 2: Identify the Candidate Software Development Lifecycles

Table 4.5 identifies the applicable lifecycle options for each type of development. Specific choices depend on the prevalent development work and way of working. The preferred option is always the first listed.

The reason for not choosing lifecycle options is as important as the reasons for choosing them. In the case of demos and proof-of-concept prototyping development projects, the approach necessarily has to be rapid and involve whatever users or user representatives, such as marketing or sales, are available for a collaborative development. This rules out the nonevolutionary lifecycles, none of which has these qualities.

The incremental new technology application delivery project needs to have a lifecycle that supports potentially innovative requirements and architecture, because of using a new technology or dealing with a new business

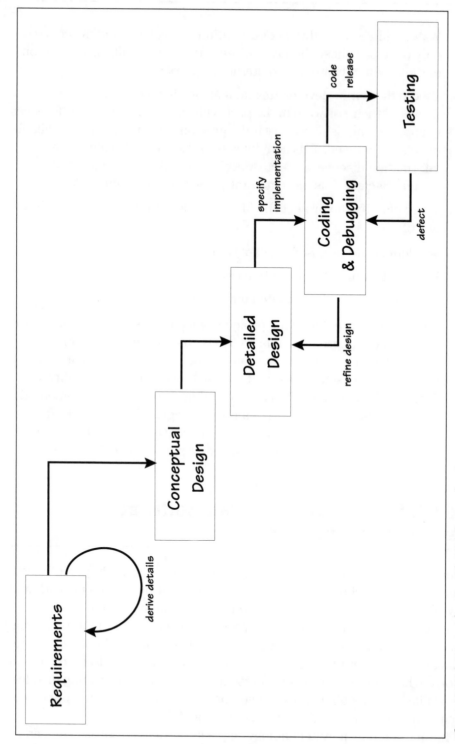

Figure 4.25 A natural approach to software development.

Table 4.5 Lifecycle Options

NATURE OF DEVELOPMENT	APPROPRIATE LIFECYCLE	RATIONALE
Demos and prototyping	Evolutionary Prototyping	Rapid results for mainly GUIs
	Evolutionary Delivery	Rapid results for non-GUIs
New product or new technology delivery	Staged Delivery	Controlled, scoped, prioritized, sequential deliveries
	Waterfall Subprojects	Shared risks across controlled, scoped concurrent deliveries
	Spiral	Controlled risk
Stable product maintenance	Sashimi	Rapid version of Waterfall
	Controlled Iteration	Allows overlapping phases for well-understood changes

domain, so at least those stages must be done in a sequential manner before launching into the remainder of the development phases. The level of control must be balanced with risk and the ability to accelerate delivery for a market window.

The stable application maintenance project has little requirements or architectural risk and can use a step-by-step approach that repeats well-understood development processes. Depending on the confidence in the maintenance staff these processes can be overlapped to achieve a more rapid delivery sequence.

The following identify a useful subset of software development lifecycle approaches that can support at least one of the three project types described previously.

Evolutionary Prototyping Lifecycle. This has a major role to play in some customer-assisted developments but more usually for the GUI portion of the application used to derive the underlying technical requirements. A variation of this is used for the Evolutionary Delivery Lifecycle model.

Evolutionary Delivery Lifecycle. If the derived requirements were produced in parallel with core technology components then this would mitigate the cost and schedule risks but also remove the main advantage. This lifecycle should not be used if cost and schedule are critical or even important factors.

Staged Delivery Lifecycle. At the architectural design phase ensure that all components, their required interactions, and interfaces are produced for all delivery stages. Plan reasonable contingency for each development stage for possible technical showstoppers that will cause architecture and perhaps even requirements to be revisited, and for some degree of code rework.

Waterfall Subprojects Lifecycle. Produce a thorough logical and physical architecture that specifies each component, its required interface, and interaction with other components with a full technology assessment. Where there are suspected technology difficulties produce and analyze proof-of-concept prototypes as part of the architecture task. This is common where the developers are using a new (to them) technology and where innovation occurs.

Spiral Lifecycle. The early steps in the Spiral Lifecycle model can be used to identify business and technical risks during requirements analysis and architectural design. A more simplified version can follow.

Sashimi Lifecycle. The disadvantages of the overlapping phases can be largely overcome by limiting the amount of overlap to predefined states at which interim artifact milestones can be set. These interim milestones should act as preliminary inputs to the next phase.

Controlled Iteration Lifecycle. Establish specific criteria for each artifact at the end of each phase to ensure verification and validation. Enforce software configuration management to control creep caused by deriving requirements during design and coding.

Step 3: Identify the Best-Fit Software Development Lifecycles

To identify the best-fit software development lifecycle it is very important to consider all of the factors, not just the type of project. This includes the future nature of projects and the existing staffing skills.

The future nature of projects should have some level of impact. Consider a large software development company that has survived for decades by producing and selling legacy software. This company knows that it will eventually need to move to more modern technologies to retain and expand its customer base. This means that the future process should be easy to transition to from the initial lifecycle; there should be no major differences between them that could not be implemented as a progression.

Staff skills are a critical ingredient since candidates must be able to successfully implement any software development approach. This will usually involve an investment in training and an increase in initial schedules to overcome the learning curve. A good way to ensure success is to integrate experienced developers in teams with new hires.

VARIATIONS

The main variation of the One Size Fits All AntiPattern is the Building the Perfect Beast AntiPattern where too much time, effort, and money is spent on developing the perfect process. The level of detailed tasking specified by the process is extensive, while the purpose for which it is to be used does not require that level of detail to successfully deliver working software.

An example from the United Kingdom of the One Size Fits All AntiPattern is version four of Structured Systems Analysis and Design (SSADM v4) intended to be used immediately after project initiation and end with system specification (see Figure 4.26) rather than the complete software development process. This government mandated approach tries to cover all types of development with a single lifecycle, yet it is very weak in supporting object-oriented and distributed object development.

Beng Yong Tang, in 'A Brief Introduction to SSADM,' University of Nottingham (UK), provides the following explanation of SSADM.

SSADM consists of a number of stages;
Stage 0: Feasibility
Stage 1: Requirements Analysis
Stage 2: Business Systems Options
Stage 3: Requirements Specification
Stage 4: Technical Systems Option
Stage 5: Logical Design
Stage 6: Physical-Design Stage

Within each stage there is a sequence of numbered steps which in turn are divided up into numbered tasks.

At the bottom level, SSADM consists of approximately 230 tasks, not all of which may be executed in any one implementation of the method.
eg.
Stage 6: Physical Design. . . . consists of
Step 610: Prepare for Physical Design
Step 620: Create Physical Data Design
Step 630: Create Function Component Implementation Map
Step 640: Optimise Physical Data Design
Step 650: Complete Function Specification
Step 660: Consolidate Process Data Interface
Step 670: Assemble Physical Design
Step 620: Create Physical Data Design. . . . consists of
Task 20: Identify the required entry points and distinguish those that are non-key
Task 30: Identify the roots of the physical hierarchies
Task 40: Identify the allowable physical groups for each non-root entry
Task 50: Apply the least dependant occurrence rule

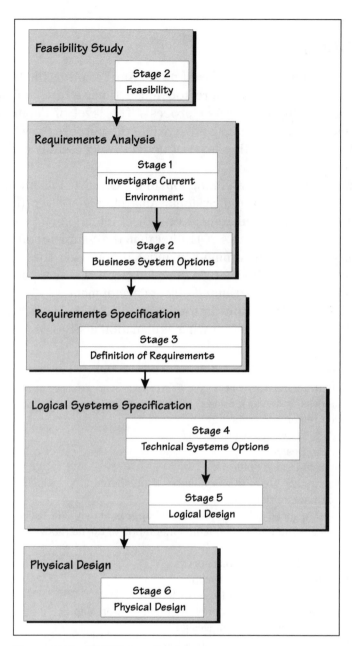

Figure 4.26 SSADMv4 methodology.

Task 60: Deterinine the block size to be used

Task 70: Split the physical groups to fit the required block size.

Task 80: Apply the product specific data design rules for the target DBMS

SSADM does NOT cover project management issues;

Planning

Estimating

Quality Control

Risk Assessment

Capacity Planning

Training

This is a thoroughly detailed sequential process intended to mitigate risks by the level of detail. Interestingly, at the time of its introduction there was no corresponding project management or software configuration management process, and although the Prince approach for these was suggested, there were no synchronized links between the methodologies.

The other problem was that the earlier phases of defining the business case, the business and technical architecture, and the latter phases of coding, testing, and release were all missing and had to be invented by the adopting organization or project. This meant that the methodology could only grow more monolithic.

More recently it has been recognized that SSADM must be usable by software development projects of differing natures and that not all stages are applicable as Sandhill Consultants Ltd. (www.sandhill.co.uk/pware/full/index.htm) point out:

> For a successful SSADM project, YOU MUST TAILOR SSADM TO YOUR PROJECT'S CIRCUMSTANCES. If the Method is used without tailoring, the required system will—at best—take longer and cost more to deliver than is necessary. At worst, the project will be terminated and your career in project management curtailed.

EXAMPLE

One of the largest U.S. insurance companies had three major lines of business, each of which had its own IT department in addition to a central IT department that was responsible for research into new technologies and coordination of enterprise architecture. The problem was that each line of business IT department had its own approach to software development (see Table 4.6).

The executive management believed that economies of scale, cost savings, and more rapid development schedules would be achieved by having a consistent software development process. The first step was for the central

IT department to define the new software development process and the central IT department quickly realized that their process was insufficient for the line of business IT departments. They decided to approach the problem by first combining all the software development approaches used and then refining the result into a well-balanced software development process, as depicted in Figure 4.27.

The central IT department became the corporate police to ensure that the line of business projects properly adopted the silver bullet software development process. Apart from the natural resentment that this created within the lines of business that were subject to the approval of the central IT department, it meant more bureaucracy and software development hurdles. The executive management decided that two years would be a valid period to assess the benefits before fine-tuning their approach.

Over the next two years, about half of the 15 projects came in on or ahead of schedule while the remainder were subject to major delays. Because of the extreme nature of the results, the executive group interviewed the project managers for the evaluation period separately from the overseers in the central IT department.

The executive group found that in the case of the eight successful projects delivered on or ahead of schedule most of the project managers had replaced the monolithic software development process with their own

Table 4.6 Software Development Approaches with Primary Focus

IT DEPARTMENT	SOFTWARE DEVELOPMENT APPROACH
Personal and Casualty	Evolutionary Delivery Lifecycle with the primary focus on: ■ Business concept ■ Requirements analysis ■ Architectures
Home and Business	Staged Delivery Lifecycle with the primary focus on: ■ Detailed design ■ Coding and debugging ■ Subsystem testing
Motor and Marine	Staged Delivery Lifecycle with the primary focus on: ■ Business concept ■ Requirements analysis ■ Architectural
Central	Evolutionary Prototyping Lifecycle with the primary focus on: ■ Technology concept ■ Architectures

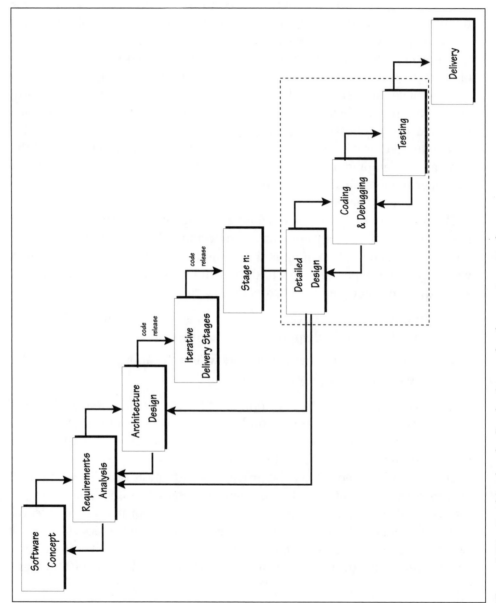

Figure 4.27 Combined and refined software development approach.

process. Their project plans and schedules showed the correct phase headings but the actual development tasks were invented locally by each project. Since the central IT department controls were paper-based this was relatively easy to do but potentially hazardous to the careers of those project managers who put professionalism above blind obedience.

The exception in three cases was where the monolithic software development process had been successfully followed and had delivered. In the case of these three successful projects, they were legacy maintenance projects where the staff well understood the technology and business application, and the application had already been thoroughly documented. The remaining four project managers had also faithfully followed the monolithic software development process and their projects had suffered from cost overruns and technical failure, with a few being terminated due to overruns of more than 100 percent.

This made no sense to the executive management, so they brought in a management consultancy company to determine the causes of success and failure. At the end of two months the consultant report identified that there were two basic types of projects during the two-year period and that the successful ones adopted the correct approach:

- Minor extensions to existing applications where a waterfall-like lifecycle of a sequential approach was appropriate.

- Implementation of new technology where the approach needed to be incremental and highly iterative.

The monolithic software development process worked reasonably well for the first but poorly for the second. The proposal recommended two distinct software development processes that were specific to those two types of software developments (see Figure 4.28).

The executive management approved the adoption of this two-process approach with the software development process selection made by project managers. The central IT department returned to its normal role of research into new technologies and enterprise architecture coordination. The result two years later was that over two-thirds of projects were delivered on time, with the remainder overrunning schedule and budget by less than 100 percent.

 # RELATED SOLUTIONS

All of the related solutions have as the common theme a single monolithic solution to a perceived problem with an aspect of software development. It is same thinking that causes the One Size Fits All AntiPattern.

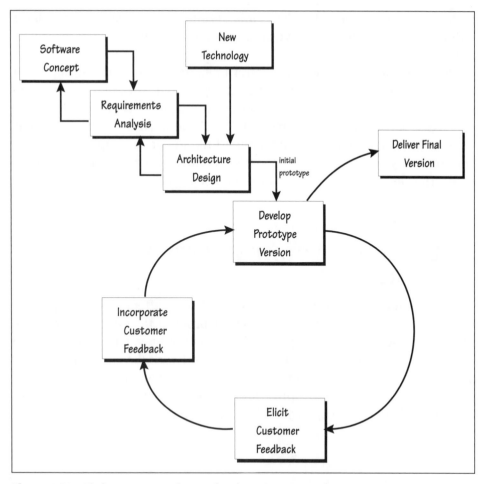

Figure 4.28 Fit-for-purpose software development approaches.

The Blob AntiPattern [Brown 1998] investigates the problem of how procedural-style design leads to one object with a lion's share of the responsibilities and most other objects holding only data or executing simple processes. The solution includes refactoring the design to distribute responsibilities more uniformly and isolating the effect of changes. This is a code version of the One Size Fits All AntiPattern, and the Blob AntiPattern can sometimes be caused by implementation of a Waterfall Lifecycle on a new technology project.

The Golden Hammer AntiPattern [Brown 1998] is used when a familiar technology or concept is applied obsessively to many software problems. The solution involves expanding the developers' knowledge through education, training, and book study groups that expose developers to alternative technologies and approaches. The Golden Hammer AntiPattern is similar in nature because of the obsessive application of a single strategy regardless of the nature of the project.

The Lifecycle Malpractice AntiPattern illustrates the problem that many companies do not understand: A single lifecycle that worked for one type of development is not applicable to others. Lifecycle-model agility is the key to success in being able to develop several applications or projects in tandem. This requires management to understand the impact of implementing the various lifecycles in their development culture and technology environment. The One Size Fits All AntiPattern is a subset of the Lifecycle Malpractice AntiPattern.

APPLICABILITY TO OTHER VIEWPOINTS AND SCALES

While in general the One Size Fits All AntiPattern affects the enterprise in the form of all projects that use the magical process, the direct impact is initially on those individual projects. The scale starts at an enterprise level with the production of the enterprisewide software development process and then moves to the application level as individual projects use the process. As more and more projects use the process the scale increases through system back to enterprise for the full impact of the problem.

The Domino Effect

AntiPattern Name: The Domino Effect

Also Known As: Crap Rolls Downhill, Chaos Theory

Most Applicable Scale: Enterprise

Refactored Solution Name: Reverse Domino Tilting or Strategic Domino Removal

Refactored Solution Type: Process

Root Causes: Multiple

Unbalanced Forces: Management of IT Resources

Anecdotal Evidence:
> "Hey Rick, your project is doing great! Listen, we've decided to pull Ben from your team for just a couple weeks to help out on Jerry's project. I know he's your best Java guy, but it's only for a little while, and Jerry's project really needs some help. Besides, your guys are doing really great work, and you're a little bit ahead of schedule, so pulling Ben may even help you out by giving some of your junior developers a chance to show some leadership! So talk to Ben about it okay . . . he'll have to delay that vacation he's planned, too, because they want him to start with Jerry this afternoon."

BACKGROUND

As authors we are always on the lookout for new and variations of published AntiPatterns that are part of the software development maelstrom. We get a lot of feedback from readers who have experienced both. Some of the stronger feedback concerned a variation of the Firedrill Mini-AntiPattern [Brown 1998].

The line of thinking prompted by our readers was that the Fire Drill AntiPattern is often just a consequence of a much larger problem that was really an aggregate AntiPattern, which eventually leads to several project-level firedrills. We had already identified the interaction of AntiPatterns across many projects (see the AntiPattern Collision AntiPattern), but this was somewhat different. Fascinated by the concept, we started looking for this potential combinatorial AntiPattern, and we are indeed sad to report that it is highly frequent and truly devastating (see Figure 4.29).

This AntiPattern is found in many failed projects where one problem in the guise of a solution was repeatedly, with increasing frequency, implemented to solve a problem that it was exacerbating.

Figure 4.29 The domino effect.

GENERAL FORM

The conditions that foster the Domino Effect AntiPattern typically occur in organizations that are performing multiple, somewhat isolated tasks simultaneously. These tasks may be closely related, but for the AntiPattern to be present there must be separate teams for each task. Furthermore, these teams must be largely independent of each other and usually in competition against each other for key resources.

Where these conditions are present, a senior manager who has authority over several projects typically tilts the first domino of this AntiPattern by treating the resources for each separate project collectively and interchangeably. Moving them about willy-nilly like chess pieces, this manager believes that he or she is providing "big picture" thinking (see Figure 4.30). The manager believes that he or she can maximize progress (or minimize problems) by temporarily moving resources (the term often used by such managers for people) from one project that's doing well to a faltering project. The manager mistakenly believes that this will bolster the troubled project, and that once it is back on track he or she can move the resource back to its original project.

Figure 4.30 The manager's chess set.

The unfortunate and unintended result of this action is the true domino effect, namesake of this AntiPattern. The individual dominoes that are tilted as a result of this first action fall like the proverbial snowball rolls downhill in a sickening trend of disasters as each project in the organization is eventually touched. As each project in the chain is tapped for a key resource to support a more critical project, each project is placed into extremes, and performing project teams become generally disenchanted with the process. The lesson is that to get staff a team must first fail and the reward for success is to have key resources borrowed from the team. The domino casualties are many:

- Project team motivation, attitude, and unit cohesion
- Key staff forced to jump from critical project to critical project
- Project schedules
- Cohesive support
- Cohesive project management
- Project team's willingness to exert extra effort
- Trust and confidence in leadership and management

The single most costly domino is also the most difficult to quantify, for it is truly priceless and extremely difficult to obtain. This ultimate cost is the organization's collective sense of purpose and concept of meaning, which can only be achieved through successful completion of challenging efforts. Top developers and engineers who sense that they are in dead-end situations will leave in droves and quickly spread the word. Those who stick around are typically lacking in marketability and hence pretty much useless without the spark previously provided by those who have left in search of a job or project they can be proud of.

SYMPTOMS AND CONSEQUENCES

The following symptoms and multiple consequences can occur in different sequences with a symptom being a consequence of an earlier symptom, so they are relatively indistinguishable. One common sequence is:

1. No single project stays on schedule or goes smoothly.
2. A general state of crisis management exists for all projects within a particular IT department.
3. Cross-project managers frequently move key contributors from project to project to avert crises.

4. Retraction of developers into defensive posture that eliminates collaboration and sharing [McConnell 1998].

5. Frequent personnel crises spark expensive personnel searches.

6. High personnel turnover (especially among top developers, engineers and project leaders).

7. Strong pressure on project leaders to get deeply involved in development to cover for lost critical staff members.

8. A general defeatist malaise sets in because developers no longer identify with their project and no longer really care about success.

9. Increasing "blame-storming" and faultfinding as projects tailspin toward failure.

 ## TYPICAL CAUSES

There are many specific causes of the Domino Effect and the most common are:

- Rapidly expanding or growing organization that has taken on increased workload beyond its present capability with the idea that it can juggle projects and quickly build up the staff needed to support them all.

- Organizations simultaneously working on multiple isolated tasks with separate, independent teams for each task.

- Inability to build up an experienced staff to support increased contracted workload, especially exacerbated by the failure to anticipate the high cost of hiring "ready to run" expertise overnight.

- Key staff members "matrixed" across multiple projects, spreading them so thin that they are rendered effectively useless and moot.

- Projects in competition for key staff members.

- Senior manager with authority over several projects who treats individual project staff members collectively and interchangeably.

- Managers and project leaders (those with significant development expertise) being tapped to support the development effort, leaving critical (but not immediately critical) project management to be caught up on later.

- Dependence on a single person critical to the success of multiple projects where each project requires a large portion of that individual's concentration and focus.

A'S HIRE A'S

Building a quality staff is a "chicken and the egg" kind of challenge. For this example let's rate people generally on an overall scale of excellence from A to C. A's are those truly excellent managers who lead and inspire their staff through sincere dedication to their needs, and overall excellence in keeping commitments and following through. C's are the average-quality managers who generally do a fair job.

What you'll find is that in an interview and hiring situation, A's hire other A's, and B's hire C's. Why is this so? Our guess is that the high-quality managers have excellent self-esteems and are therefore not at all threatened or challenged by other excellent persons. In fact, they seek them, and even attract them to themselves. However, B's and C's tend to be more easily intimidated by those whom they perceive to be more capable or confident than themselves. These people tend to hire others whom they find less threatening. The results are easy to see. Check for yourself. [Dillingham 1999]

KNOWN EXCEPTIONS

Research indicates that the Domino Effect AntiPattern is the norm for many fast-growing technology firms. In fact, the more successful of these firms typically accept the symptoms of the Domino Effect and use mitigation strategies automatically as a matter of normal business routine. Where this is the case, and where the most damaging consequences can be held at bay, many smaller companies find themselves rapidly expanding and quickly gaining credibility. One company uses the term *creeping validity* to describe their strategy of gradually taking on and succeeding different kinds of tasking, resulting in a gradual but constantly gaining level of corporate credibility, which in turn improves the company's ability to attract and hire quality staff.

However, in spite of your best efforts at planning, anticipation, and mitigation, the dominoes sometimes get out of hand quickly, and crises do actually happen. When this happens, triage is the only reasonable response. While it's risky to plan on leveraging a superhuman effort (see the Fire Drill AntiPattern [Brown 1998]), people often do rise to the challenge and overcome amazing or even impossible obstacles. So, if you absolutely must move a key person to another project in order to save it and if the risk to the second project is worth the chance of salvaging the first, then go for it. Just be sure to read the refactored solutions provided here and start taking action to remove some dominoes, or else you may lose the whole chain.

 REFACTORED SOLUTION

There are two types of refactored solution. The first is prevention and the second is that of recovery.

Prevention Strategies

The best and most effective solution to the Domino Effect AntiPattern is, as with most AntiPatterns, avoiding it entirely. If you recognize the symptoms of the Domino Effect but have not yet tilted that first domino, there are three prevention strategies that you can try. Time is of the essence, so you really *must* use one of them immediately to have any reasonable hope of neutralizing the potential disaster. You should also take great care not to allow that first domino to be tilted until the chosen strategy has been implemented. Each strategy is listed here in order of difficulty:

1. Strategic Domino Removal
2. Strategic Domino Blocking
3. Domino Rearrangement

Prevention Strategy #1: Strategic Domino Removal

When you find yourself facing an impending Domino Effect AntiPattern, you can prevent it by entirely putting off or delaying select at-risk projects to ensure the success of those that are doing well (see Figure 4.31). Later, as the organization grows in capability, these projects can be revived or reborn as necessary to support the organization's objectives.

The selection of projects to delay or cancel outright is an organization-wide decision that should be made with great care and considerable analysis and planning. The fact that you are in this position indicates that the delaying or canceling of any particular project will risk serious negative consequences and can damage an organizations reputation as a result of failure to provide a deliverable at the contracted delivery date. However, by taking action early, the resulting negatives can be weighed against each

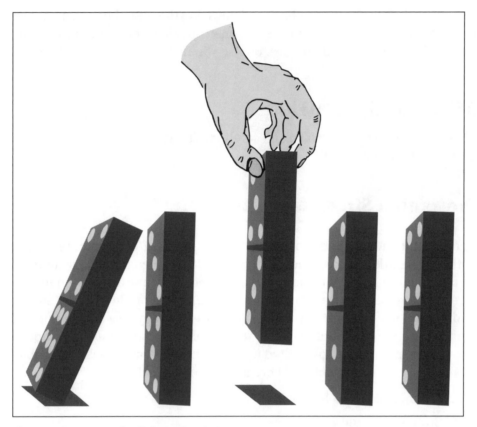

Figure 4.31 Removing links in the chain.

other and against the organizations larger objectives to choose the so-called lesser of evils and to focus on the larger returns.

Prevention Strategy #2: Strategic Domino Blocking

As with an actual row of dominoes, if you can place a physical barrier between any two dominoes, you can stop them from tilting into each other (see Figure 4.32). In project management terms, you do this by barring cross-project transfers of personnel. In each case where a cross-project manager desires to move an individual from a project that's going well to a troubled project, you can insert the physical barrier of a formal review process. This will ensure that such transfers do not take place without careful consideration of the impact on all affected projects.

Furthermore, where the transfer of personnel is allowed to occur, it must be carefully planned and both projects' schedules must be reevaluated and adjusted *sanely*. Be very careful that you do not burn out your key staff by robbing them of success anticipated on their previous project. In any case, take proactive measures to ensure the continued success of the first project and be absolutely certain to remember early contributors to that project when accolades, bonuses, and recognition arrive.

Prevention Strategy #3: Domino Rearrangement

In cases where you truly cannot delay or cancel any single at-risk project and cannot prevent the transferring of key resources from less troubled to more troubled projects, you have only this remaining prevention strategy. This strategy is the most difficult and the most risky, for as with an actual row of dominoes, you can often rearrange them such that if any one falls it will not knock over an adjacent one. However, in doing so, you may accidentally bump one of the dominoes over, thereby actually *starting* the Domino Effect that you were trying to prevent.

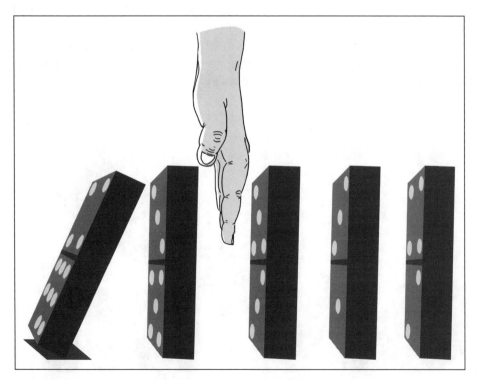

Figure 4.32   Building barriers.

The process of rearranging dominoes is accomplished by reducing cross-project dependencies on isolated staff members (see Figure 4.33). This is tricky, but one way of doing this is to arrange for a special intense training of other project team members to double up on certain critical skills. A good example is when a unique, single-day, *very expensive* instructor is contracted to provide a highly customized training course for all project developer staff to reduce dependency on the small number of project experts. The associated risk involved is the time to organize the training by a critical individual because she was the only one with the expertise required to identify and plan the specific instruction needed. This took time away from work, robbing her of critical project-specific focus during that time and thereby temporarily placing the project at risk.

Other methods of reducing interproject staff criticality are to add new, experienced staff to the *successful project* before reassigning key members from that project to another troubled project. The reasoning behind this method is based on the same reasoning that prompts the transfer (and resulting Domino Effect AntiPattern) in the first place. By replacing the critical person ahead of time, you may be able to leverage the experience of the key member in the form of mentoring, and if you get the chemistry right, you provide a channel for the original expert to indirectly remain involved with the first project through that protégé. The keys here are time and chemistry. The mentor and her protégé must have time to bond and transfer knowledge, and they must become friends or else the protégé is likely to lose contact once the mentor is pulled away.

Figure 4.33 Rearranging things.

Recovery Strategies

Typically the opportunity for prevention is often past history by the time an AntiPattern is recognized and identified. In the case of the Domino Effect, once the dominoes have begun tilting, you need to act fast to mitigate further damage down the line. There are three triage strategies to choose from in this case.

1. Spartan Domino Blocking
2. Immediate Domino Removal
3. Reverse Domino Tilting (Fireblock)

Triage Strategy #1: Spartan Domino Blocking

In a situation where the dominoes are already falling and you lack the time necessary to take strategic action, you can still stop the chain of events if you can place a physical barrier between any two dominos (see Figure 4.34). In project terms, you do this by immediately barring all cross-project transfers of personnel without exception, letting the chips fall as they may.

Figure 4.34 Holding your ground (the Spartan software manager).

At this point you will be pressured from many fronts to yield "just in this special case" because of some absolutely critical need, but like the legendary Spartans you must hold your ground. However, as with the Spartans, you will be placing yourself at great personal risk because if you are overruled by higher management or if too many projects (maybe just one) fail, you will be blamed and most likely become the scapegoat.

But if you can hold your ground, you will both stop the Domino Effect in its tracks and force those projects in trouble to seek an alternative remedy that does not cause cascading Fire Drill AntiPatterns. At this point, you can implement the Strategic Domino Blocking prevention strategy and be heralded throughout the land as the hero who saved the company (or at least be allowed to keep your job and thereby keep up with your mortgage payments).

Triage Strategy #2: Immediate Domino Removal

When the dominoes are already falling, you can stop the chain of events immediately by snatching away the next one or two dominoes about to be knocked over. It is illogical to even consider the actual domino (project) because it is lost either way, and by sacrificing it you can stop the Domino Effect cold, buying time to take more considered action. You do this by immediately stopping work, canceling or delaying at-risk projects, and focusing immediate effort on projects that are going well—making sure that they continue to succeed. Managers who understand the need to succeed will understand the necessity of triage [McCarthy 1995], while those who don't are risks in themselves.

At this point, one or more of the prevention strategies should be selected and put into effect to reduce the likelihood of future catastrophe.

Triage Strategy #3: Reverse Domino Tilting (Fireblock)

If you have a little time to consider your actions, and recognize that the immediate at-risk project is critical and therefore cannot be cancelled or delayed, then you can instead look down the line for a project that can be canceled with less impact. Then instead of removing it, tilt it the other way against the domino flow from above, as illustrated in Figure 4.35. This strategy is similar in many ways to the time-honored forest-fire-fighting technique of preburning areas of the forest in a controlled manner to separate an uncontrolled forest fire from the rest of the forest, or "fighting fire with fire." However, as with forest fires, the prevailing winds are unpredictable and can go against you, such as if your selection of projects to sacrifice contradicts the hindsight of your superiors (but that's why you're in charge and get the big bucks).

If you time it just right, you may be able push staff up from lower projects to bolster the projects to be robbed of staff. In this way, you "backfill" the necessary staff for each project. The risk is high and it far less desirable than the Immediate Domino Removal strategy.

VARIATIONS

Variations of the Domino Effect AntiPattern can take many forms. This includes the AntiPattern Collision AntiPattern that examines the common problem of one AntiPattern causing another. This is a form of the Domino Effect AntiPattern. Consider Figure 4.36, where the AntiPatterns can cause another AntiPattern, that is, tilt the next domino. It can happen in a horizontal sequence going across the lifecycle or vertically through the layers of software development responsibilities of management, architecture, and development.

Figure 4.35   Reversing the flow.

Vertical collision is harder to identify usually because the causes are hidden at a different level of role responsibility. Each role will only see the AntiPattern, or domino, at its level.

Another variation is prune and conquer. Sometimes when the dominoes are already well under way, an organization can intentionally divide itself, passing failing projects to one side and successful projects to the other. The result of this action, if the division is truly irrevocable (such as the forming of separate corporations), can be one where a smaller cadre rises to the occasion and gains strength from the challenge. This is a direct result of people's reactions to the sudden explosion of opportunity that the newly pruned staff in both parts experiences. People formerly resigned to their present position with only distant hope for major career advancement are suddenly lit with the excitement and perceived increased potential for advancement in the now smaller company. This may be enough to quickly generate the critical motivation, synergy, and superhuman effort needed to pull off an amazing feat.

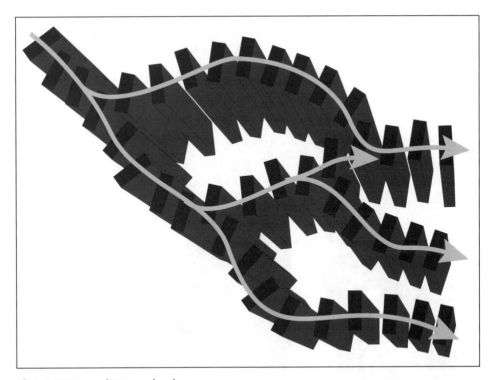

Figure 4.36   AntiPattern dominoes.

EXAMPLE

A senior program manager at an East Coast company related the following example of the Domino Effect AntiPattern in practice. This manager, whom we'll call Troy, is responsible for several critical projects at his fast-growing systems engineering company of about 40 to 50 persons. Company goals include doubling in size within the next two years, which results in an intense motivation on the company's part to develop revenue and new business. This force is countered by an intense shortage of high-caliber software talent in the company's region. These two factors produce tremendous strain on the company's current staff.

A typical situation starts as a company wins new contracts. Almost immediately, the new contracts require high-caliber management to begin interfacing with the customer and gain their confidence. Unfortunately, these people are currently fully engaged on another customer's projects and were keys to gaining that customer's confidence; pulling them off suddenly would be of great concern to the customer. At Troy's company, however, this is anticipated and every project manager is expected to be prepared. Troy's company successfully uses the Domino Rearrangement prevention strategy. Their ace in this case revolves around two key factors:

- A very strong human resources ethos that hires only top-notch staff.

- A "no surprises" policy that prepares current customers for staffing adjustments as far ahead of time as possible. In Troy's words, "We telegraph our punches."

One specific example involved a new key project in a critical new business area that required Troy to give up his right hand engineer completely. Troy found that he personally had to compensate for a lot of the activities previously handled by his former engineer, such as day-to-day operations, test direction, equipment management, test planning, logistics, and other very time-intensive activities. Troy had to let some of his normal tasks slide in order to make deadlines, and his manager was able to buffer for him similarly.

Additionally, they leveraged part of prevention strategy Strategic Domino Removal by coordinating with a current customer to delay one complete piece of work for three months until the new contract was on an even keel.

The result was that Troy's company succeeded on a new contract that expanded the company's demonstrated area of capability and provided many new venues for future revenue to be pursued.

What else can we learn from Troy's experience? A lot. Troy said that the net effect on morale each time they manage to pull off another challenging project is very positive. People take increased personal ownership and find greater self-esteem as a team. A large part of this is the way Troy's company recognizes its staff with generous overtime compensation and bonuses, and with sincere written recognition in the form of personal letters from the company president. These factors, when implemented by an excellent management team (see *A's Hire A's*) who is deeply involved and therefore able to watch for employee burnout (see *How to Prevent Burnout*), result in continued success at Troy's company, in spite of an ever-looming Domino Effect AntiPattern.

RELATED SOLUTIONS

The Antipattern Collision AntiPattern discusses the problems of one AntiPattern causing multiple other AntiPatterns within the same project. The AntiPattern Collision AntiPattern solution deals with how to identify the various AntiPatterns and find the true cause of the multiple AntiPattern effect. AntiPatterns can occur at managerial, architecture, or software development levels in terms of their main impact, causing apparently unrelated AntiPatterns at other levels and phases of the project. The Antipattern Collision AntiPattern solution is highly relevant to solving the Domino Effect AntiPattern.

APPLICABILITY TO OTHER VIEWPOINTS AND SCALES

The scale is already enterprise, so the domino effect will always be applicable to the lower scales of system and application because of the impact on individual software development projects.

The domino effect symptoms are at a project level while the main cause is at the enterprise level. Both of these symptom types occur within a project starting at the task level (affecting everything from daily development work up to major deliverables) and eventually involving the project itself.

HOW TO PREVENT BURNOUT

How do you handle early-to-mid 30s hard chargers who seek increased responsibility and live to earn the laurels of high accolade from their company? Pile it on, you say? Absolutely! To do anything else would risk discouraging them, almost as if you were saying, "You can't handle any more." It would seem to them like a failure.

But watch out! Staff have limitations, and the more you pile on, the closer you'll come to overloading them and risking burning them out. You'll have to pay close attention without seeming to doubt their capabilities, but if you miss the signs of burnout, or detect them too late, you'll risk loosing some of your most valuable team members.

Early signs of burnout can include:

- Noticeable increase in sick days over a short period.
- Sudden shift in work schedule, such as coming in later and staying even later.
- Interpersonal flare-ups where it was generally harmonious before.
- Change (usually for the worse) in dress habits or grooming standards.
- Increased or intensified dissatisfaction with other staff members' performance.

So what do you do when the early signs of burnout appear? Take immediate steps, but do so in a calm, normal, everyday way. You absolutely do not want to let on that you see them straining—it would also be acknowledgement of failure. Instead, find a "critical mission" for them that requires them to hand off their current work for a while.

One example we've seen is to send them on a business trip where they can provide critical help on someone else's project for a while, but make sure that the trip duration exceeds the time really necessary for the job. Ideally, the trip should be to someplace really nice. One company sends their top performers to the Bahamas to accompany system-testing teams [Dillingham 1999].

Myopic Delivery

AntiPattern Name: Myopic Delivery

Also Known As: Delivery Zone

Most Applicable Scale: Application

Refactored Solution Name: Get Out of Town

Refactored Solution Type: Process

Root Causes: Ignorance, Pride, and Narrow-Mindedness

Unbalanced Forces: Management of Resources

Anecdotal Evidence:
> "What is the difference between management and a terrorist? You can negotiate with the terrorist!"
> "Nine women can't make a baby in one month."
> "I don't care about the schedule anymore, just do it."

BACKGROUND

Imagine, if you will, a project manager of a high visibility software development effort. Imagine that this project manager has done all the appropriate planning, scheduling, and staffing. After months of skillful project management execution, he learns that he's going to miss the delivery date, no fault of his own. Suddenly his management no longer cares about proper project management techniques. His management wants him to deliver to the original date. His managers just want him to do it—make it happen. For your inspection, one Joe Schamukatelli, project manager. Joe thought he was coming to work on a project with reasonable management. Little did Joe know that he has just entered . . . The Delivery Zone. (Can you hear the music?)

Slipped schedules can generate project compression faster than water running through a sieve. Project compression creates a gap in the space time continuum allowing the incomprehensible to be accomplished in the minds of management. It causes all logical, pragmatic, rational, reasonable thinking to fly out the window. Management will do anything to meet the delivery date. No one's life is unexpendable. Everyone will suffer. Nothing is more important than the delivery date.

The Myopic Delivery AntiPattern will discuss what happens when the schedule slips and yet management demands the original delivery date (see Figure 4.37).

GENERAL FORM

Management demands project managers perform in accordance with all of the appropriate corporate guidelines, policy, standards, and data reporting. All of a sudden there is an unanticipated problem with the technology, a key programmer leaves, requirements change, or the market demands an earlier delivery than originally scheduled. Eventually management panics, giving in to their worst fears and directs the project team to do whatever it takes to get the product to market. This typically occurs at a point where the project is sufficiently into the project lifecycle so that there is not enough time to modify the schedule and still achieve the original delivery date. The result is that the project manager dispenses with proper project management techniques and starts hacking to get something out the door.

The worst scenario is when the management, knowingly or unknowingly, causes the schedule compression. This can happen when management asks

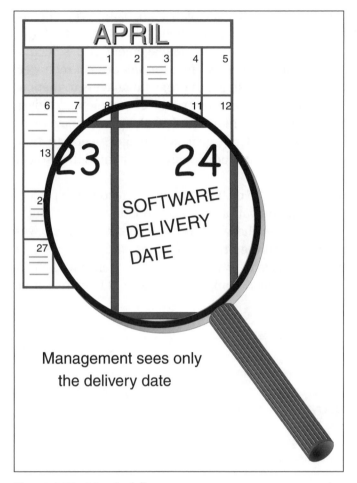

Figure 4.37 Myopic delivery.

the project team to take on more risk by incorporating the latest technology or programming methodologies, reducing staffing, reducing funding, and so on. Yet somehow management expects the project manager to maintain the original delivery date without compensation for the increased risk that the project has assumed. Sounds unreasonable, but it happens.

What can be most frustrating for the project manager is when he or she anticipates the slip and alerts management. However, management fails to hear the cautioning words of the project manager and asks, "Can it be done?" The project manager replies something like this, "Yes, it can be done, but I'll have to evaluate the impact on schedule and cost and get back to you." Management hears nothing after the word "but" and the result of the management-listening filters produces an outcome something like this,

"Yes, it can be done, but blah, blah, blah, blah, blah, blah, blah." Project managers must especially be aware of the management "blah, blah, blah" syndrome (see Figure 4.38). This occurs when management has selective listening and memory, and it should be a red light for any project manager. In fact, this red light should be a clear signal to project managers to meticulously keep all project documentation until after project completion. This is called building your paper foxhole. It will be needed when the management team starts lobbing accusations and the project manager needs to take cover, using the documentation that has judiciously documented the project manager's warnings.

At the next project review, after the change has been effected, the project manager identifies the risks and mitigation strategies relating to the change. Management will tend to gloss over these as they did when the change was originally levied on the project and the project manager warned of possible risks. The reason is because management will only lend credence to the risk if a discussion ensues. By passing over them, the management team reaffirms

Figure 4.38   Blah, blah, blah.

that the risks are not real or are insignificant. Management is concerned with the delivery date and nothing else. They assume that risks will be handled as required.

In between project reviews, the risk become a real live problem and the schedule is impacted, costs increase, or—worst of all—project delivery feasibility goes to zero. A good project manager will alert the management before the next project review; however, if the management responds as they have in the past, the project manager may think that he or she is no better off by alerting management now, rather than at the next project review. This violates Thomas' rule: "Bad news doesn't get better with time." This rule holds true even with bad managers. Bad managers are no less upset than good managers, and so, it is better to inform them earlier rather than later when things are going south.

Now with the realization that the project delivery schedule is imminently threatened, management panics. They ruthlessly demand that the project delivery date be maintained despite the problem(s) that have developed. This typically results in a volley of accusations between the project manager (or team) and the management team. Even when documentation is produced vindicating the project manager, some managers remain totally unreasonable and ignore the obvious (it is still important to keep all documentation). This arguing can go on for hours before someone gives in. Typically the project manager acquiesces once again and sets out to resolve the situation. The project manager states that the job can be done, but they will have to cut corners to get to the original delivery date. The management team agrees to do what is necessary by cutting corners to get the product delivered. The project team takes this as carte blanche to do whatever, eliminating whatever. The management team doesn't have the same interpretation.

The next project review is no better. Management demands to know why the project is no longer having formal reviews, since they have forgotten or misunderstood the agreement to cut corners discussed at the last meeting. They demand to see the formal documentation and basically jump up and down wondering what happened to the formal processes. Once again management heard only, "Okay, we'll meet the original delivery schedule, but blah, blah, blah." Tensions and emotions run high and now there tends to be no give and take, only bad feelings. Morale sinks and in most situations the project only worsens, because now there is not only low morale but the initial problem precipitates more problems. This is referred to as the *swamp effect*. It references the fact that there are a finite number of alligators in a swamp; however, if you compress the swamp into a smaller area, just as you compress the project schedule, you increase the likelihood of being eaten by an alligator (see Figure 4.39).

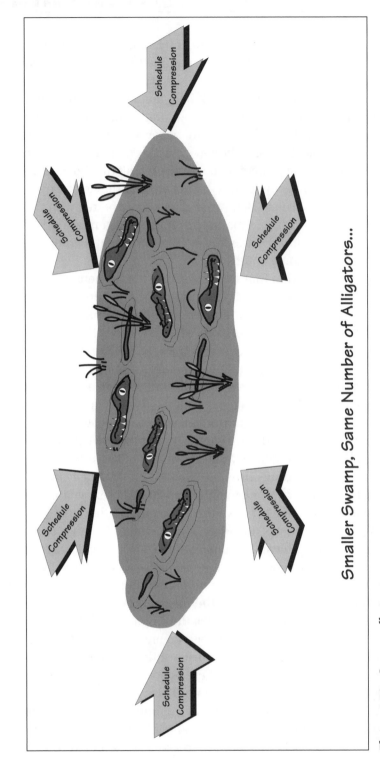

Smaller Swamp, Same Number of Alligators...

Figure 4.39 Swamp effect.

The project team abandoned the schedule after the last meeting when the management team agreed to cut corners. This creates additional fear on the part of management (and rightfully so), because now the project team no longer has a viable schedule. The project team is now spending an inordinate amount of time preparing for more frequent project reviews because the management team has lost faith in their ability to control the schedule.

Finally, after weeks of disparate positions, the management team recognizes the futility in arguing and no longer cares how the project team gets it done, they just want the job finished. Whatever it takes to get the product delivered. Now the project team, with less time, possibly fewer resources (attrition through bad morale), and more problems, throws all planning and project management techniques out the window and starts to hack away at a solution. This is the kiss of project death. It is the wrong solution and the wrong time. It's as bad as it gets on a project, because now there is no control on a project that is out of control. Control is never regained and the project is virtually doomed.

SYMPTOMS AND CONSEQUENCES

There are many symptoms to watch out for in the Myopic Delivery AntiPattern; however, they must be in the context of the environment that is described in the General Form. Otherwise the symptoms can be confused with other AntiPatterns. Still other symptoms are ubiquitous to poor project management and not necessarily associated with an AntiPattern:

- Management control of the project or micro-management
- Demands by management that additional risk be assumed without compensation
- Management with selective hearing and memory about:
  - Changes they imposed upon the project
  - Identified risks arising from those changes
  - Agreements regarding schedule, cost, and resources
- Incremental crisis project management or little project management and control
- Spending inordinate time on project review meetings and schedules to convince management of project control
- Increased project team frustrations and low morale
- Weak project leadership

The consequences are ultimately severe; however, the Myopic Delivery AntiPattern is incremental and can be halted before the worst of the consequences occur. The consequences that occur before the final demise of the AntiPattern are:

- Many problems in a compressed period of time—the swamp effect
- Low morale and high attrition
- High stress and emotions
- Invalid or unrealistic schedule
- Missed delivery date and project cancellation
- Delivery date is missed and the project is extended with additional funding, then canceled after failing to make delivery the second and third times
- Delivery date is missed and the project is extended with additional funding and then is successful after project leadership is installed
- Delivery is met with the project achieving limited functionality
- Delivery is met with the project achieving limited functionality and poor reliability
- Project is successful in achieving the delivery date, full functionality, and reliability (not likely)

TYPICAL CAUSES

Causes for the Myopic Delivery AntiPattern are probably obvious from the discussion in the General Form. The typical causes include:

- Management attempts to control the project, rather than letting the project manager do his or her job
- Delivery becomes the focus of the project, at the expense of all other objectives
- Abandonment of project management principles
- Planning and leadership collapse
- Ignorance of basic project planning principles and management principles
- Forced management compliance
- Attempting to make management happy without regard for the project

KNOWN EXCEPTIONS

There should never be an exception to the Myopic Delivery AntiPattern, even though it is allowed to occur far too often.

REFACTORED SOLUTION

The refactored solution must be presented for the various states of the Myopic Delivery AntiPattern. For simplicity consider the states to be the beginning, the middle, and the end.

The Beginning

When the Myopic Delivery AntiPattern first raises its ugly head it's time to take action before it progresses. First, as the project manager you may need to consider changing jobs. The reason is that there is little you can do to change the tracks that the management train is riding on. Consider the options, you can voluntarily leave the project now or wait until the end and have management arrive at the same conclusion before your resume is updated.

Okay, so leaving is not an option. What do you do then? Consult with your project team and document your findings. When you meet with management be honest, strong, and stand your position, but be absolutely sure that you have considered the consequences. The project manager must be adamant about not making substantial changes to the project without compensation to the schedule or other resources (see the Chaos AntiPattern).

Additionally, you must get management to become stakeholders in the project. Attempt to lead them to arrive at the same decisions and outcomes that you and the project team have. One method of doing this is to invite management to participate in some of the discussions that take place at the project level. In most instances if you are experiencing the Myopic Delivery AntiPattern, your management is micromanaging anyway. If management members insist that they are too busy, tell them you'll arrange the meeting to accommodate their schedules. If this doesn't work then during the course of the project reviews engage management in the discussions that led you to these decisions and outcomes. Ask for their advice on the matter in such a way that they give you the solution you presented to them.

Micromanagers can't get enough information. The key is getting them to arrive at the same conclusion you have. If you can do this often enough, you will probably gain their confidence.

The Middle (Swamp Effect)

So you didn't see it coming and now you're smack in the middle of the Myopic Delivery AntiPattern. Leave now, it's still not too late.

Okay, leaving still is not an option. Then, if you haven't implemented the beginning state of the refactored solution, that should be your first step. Next, don't agree to anything that you don't believe is accurate. Don't acquiesce. Watch out for the "blah, blah, blah" management filter. If your management seems to have selective hearing and memory, you need to document your concerns, issues, and meeting results and e-mail them to your management. If possible mail them to a larger audience (the next level of management). This will better substantiate your position and also lessens the likelihood of selective hearing and memory of your management.

Project managers need to keep management informed and up to date. Too much information is not an option. On the other hand, attempt to keep the project team isolated from the wrath of management. Keep the project team morale high and focus on the successes of the team.

Most important, stick to fundamental project management and system engineering principles. These cannot get you into trouble. If asked if you can meet the schedule by cutting corners reply, "No!" Cutting corners can only get you deeper into trouble. Keep in mind the transmission commercial of a previous decade, "Pay me now or pay me later." The commercial should have stated, "Pay me now or pay me a lot more later" because whatever you put off today will cost more, later in your process. Also, don't commit to schedules that are dependent on third parties. If you do, make sure that you have plenty of slack.

Finally, try to keep perspective. Remember that there is more to the project than just meeting the schedule. This can be hard to do when management has become myopic. Helping management remember that there is more to the project is important too. Often they lose sight of what is really important, which is making the customer happy.

The End

This state couldn't be more appropriately named. In most cases that is exactly what it is—the end. The end of projects, jobs, and careers. If the

Myopic Delivery AntiPattern has progressed this far, bail out as quickly as possible.

There is one other option. But you may have to risk becoming a martyr. Determine what you can safely and reliably deliver on the promised date, and deliver it. Something is better than nothing. Delivering something will likely save the project and probably more important your job. But be prepared for the worst. You may end up as the sacrificial lamb. Whatever you do, don't blame your management. By now it is too late and you will suffer the consequences (see Figure 4.40).

VARIATIONS

The Myopic Delivery AntiPattern can occur at various levels in the organization, including within the project organization. If project managers micromanage individual tasks and drive the schedule and efforts of individuals that work for them, mini versions of this AntiPattern could also be realized within the project. The Myopic Delivery AntiPattern can also be seen at a higher levels in the organization where strategic planning is performed. When the AntiPattern occurs at this level the results can be disastrous for the entire enterprise.

Additionally, there are variations to the root of the AntiPattern. That is, rather than simply being myopic about the delivery date, the management

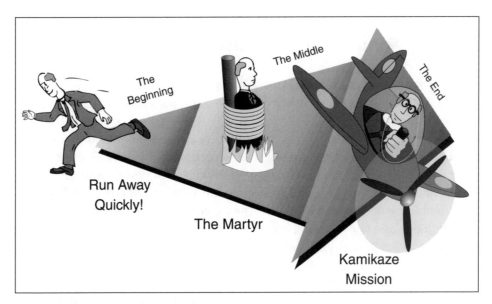

Figure 4.40   Refactored solution stages.

can also be myopic about planning, funding, personnel, or functionality. Each of the variations drive the project management to lose focus of a balanced project management approach.

EXAMPLE

This is a real-life example of how the wrong set of ingredients can result in a miserable project. The ingredients include the following:

- High visibility software development effort with a tight schedule
- Inexperienced project manager with weak technical skills
- Overbearing micromanager who wants to gain recognition

The initial major milestones of a project (referred to as project X) were presented to management and accepted. These milestones presented major functionality that was to be incorporated into the baseline over time. The first of these milestones had been achieved and the project was lauded for its accomplishment. With the initial success of project X, more customers were now demanding the system.

At the same time a competitor arrived on the scene with broad claims. Specifically, greater functionality was planned for the competitor's system and would be available at nearly the same time as project X. These claims were doubtful; however, they were widely marketed.

Delivery Minus Nine Months

During a marketing and management meeting with the future customer of project X, the customer confronted project X management with the claims of the competitor. Management panicked. Without thought or consultation with the project manager, the management promised increased functionality within the same time frame as the original product. Management returned to tell the project manager of the revised schedule and increased functionality. The project manager took the news rather lightly, thinking that it could be accomplished. When the project manager informed the system engineer and task leaders, havoc ensued. The system engineer insisted that this was an impossible feat, with unanimous agreement from the task leaders. The project manager was prodded by the project team to met again with management to inform them of the bad news. This meeting resulted in an ultimatum for the project manager, "Do it or we will find someone who can." At the same time management was now broadly marketing the new delivery schedule and increased functionality.

Delivery Minus Eight Months

The project manager took the system engineer and task leaders off-site to attempt to find a way to "make it happen." After three days of laboring over the issues, with consultants and commercial vendor support, a strategy was devised that would produce the functionality promised to the customer on the original date. The strategy was heavily burdened by a number of assumptions, to which management had agree to make it happen.

Delivery Minus Seven and a Half Months

A meeting was arranged between the project team and the management to discuss the assumptions that were devised by the off-site project meeting. Management was happy to learn that the project team could accomplish the delivery date with the required functionality, with little focus on the assumptions. Nevertheless, management agreed to the assumptions. A state of euphoria erupted. It would be the last time.

Delivery Minus Six Months

The assumptions had stated that six months prior to delivery a critical component of the system had to be delivered by a third party. It was not delivered. Any slip would result in a slip in the schedule. Moreover, the resources that were requested as part of the assumptions were still not provided as promised by management.

At the monthly project review the project manager insisted that the original plan for deploying functionality be reinstated. Management was livid and blamed the project team for not doing enough to make the third-party delivery happen. But more unbelievably, the management team took the offensive. Management accused the project team of not taking on more risk and insinuated that even more functionality be added. The project team was shocked and amazed at the response of management and left the meeting in total disbelief.

Finally, management insisted that key members of the project team participate in corporate development efforts to design business processes for acquiring new business. This had nothing to do with the project except to drain it of valuable resources.

Delivery Minus Five Months

The project team, responding to management requests to provide detailed schedules and detailed status reports at the monthly project reviews, complied. The project team was spending approximately 40 hours per week per month preparing for monthly project review meetings because of the rigor and detail that management demanded.

At the next monthly meeting the project team presented a schedule that reflected a one month slip in the schedule. The management team went ballistic. Anarchy prevailed and for three hours the two groups berated each other, at times getting personal. Emotions were very high. The project system engineer saw no way out except to offer a solution to make it happen by the promised date. The arrangement was that the management team would allow the development team to cut corners with the development effort. The project manager reiterated that the schedule as well as other technical aspects of the project were still high risk. Management was relieved that the project team had once again agreed that they could accomplish the schedule, deaf to anything else that was stated.

Delivery Minus Four Months

At the next monthly project meeting an abbreviated schedule was presented. It reflected that there would no longer be any formal reviews. Management again went ballistic. One manager demanded that a critical design review be conducted. The system engineer replied that the project team did not know what the design was because it was unsure whether the third-party solution would be available, requiring a change to the architecture.

The practice of not having formal reviews was considered unacceptable. Management announced that there was corporate policy and standards to follow. The project team was shocked. The project team believed they were fully in accordance with the agreements of the last meeting—to cut corners. Once again anarchy ensued with no relief this time. The meeting concluded with management assuring the project team that they were there to help and accordingly would begin conducting weekly project reviews requiring detailed schedules and reports. Subsequently a task leader resigned.

Delivery Minus Twelve Weeks

The third-party solution was still unavailable. Finally, management agreed, after being convinced by the project manager and the system engineer, that the functionality associated with the third-party solution could not be incorporated into the baseline if the project was to make the delivery date. Management scolded the system engineer for not making this risk known earlier. The system engineer walked away in disbelief.

Delivery Minus Eleven Weeks

Management was now concerned about the morale of the project team (perhaps rumors were circulating). The next weekly meeting was conducted in a more conciliatory manner. The management team asked to see the interface. The project team announced that coding had just begun. Management was skeptical of the project team's last report, which continued to promise the delivery date.

Delivery Minus Ten Weeks

The management team was concerned about the interface. Consequently management tasked two junior developers, without the knowledge of the project manager, to browse the Internet looking for cutting-edge Web pages to leverage into the project interface.

The weekly project meeting was conducted. Tensions remained high. The assistant project manager was reprimanded by management for not having a more detailed schedule.

After the weekly project meeting the assistant project manager complained to the system engineer that the management team wanted too much detail. The system engineer agreed that the management team might be asking for too much detail; however, when the system engineer asked where the development effort stood, the assistant project manager could only reply that she didn't know.

Delivery Minus Nine Weeks

At the weekly project meeting management was convinced again to withdraw another key component of functionality. Only one piece of new functionality remained in the system.

Delivery Minus Eight Weeks

The system engineer realized that the application development environment will not allow the last key component of functionality to be implemented with the current security constraints. For two days engineers and developers meet to discuss alternative solutions. It is decided to implement the solution and reduce the security of the system (a key reason for purchasing the system by many customers). Management is not told of the development until the weekly meeting. Management throws up their hands telling the project manager to deploy the system doing whatever it takes to meet the deployment date. Weekly project reviews are canceled. The project team throws all caution to the wind, along with all known project management and development practices. Unit testing is stopped. Developers are told to "just code."

Delivery Minus Four Weeks

Testing, scheduled to begin at delivery minus seven weeks, is delayed because an adequate test environment cannot be stood up. This was a result of not being able to adequately define the architecture and then procure the appropriate hardware far enough in advance to create the test environment. All of this was the effect of delaying the project for the third-party solution.

Delivery Minus Three Weeks

Test execution is abysmal. Significant deficiency reports are generated.

Delivery Plus Five Weeks

The system is still not delivered. The project manager is fired. The project is overhauled. A new schedule is created.

 ## RELATED SOLUTIONS

There are several AntiPatterns that are related to the Myopic Delivery AntiPattern. Project managers should reference and review the refactored solutions for these AntiPatterns to assist in refactoring the solution for this AntiPattern. Those AntiPatterns include:

- The Brawl AntiPattern deals with poor leadership and its impact on software development, which is a central cause of the Myopic Delivery AntiPattern.

- Chaos AntiPattern covers the problems that occur with continual change to aspects of a software development as exemplified by Myopic Delivery AntiPattern.

- Fire Drill Mini-AntiPattern [Brown 1998] deals with management driving a development by creating constant firedrills and not allowing successful progression through the software development process.

APPLICABILITY TO OTHER VIEWPOINTS AND SCALES

The Myopic Delivery AntiPattern is applicable at the system perspective and the enterprise perspective, depending on the level at which management intrusion occurs. At the system and enterprise levels it commonly occurs because of the poor corporate culture.

AntiPattern Collisions

Colliding AntiPatterns exist when multiple AntiPatterns interact to create more severe problems than those caused by a single AntiPattern. The scenario of multiple AntiPatterns occurring within a single software development is fairly common but often not recognized.

Consider that a management AntiPattern can cause an architecture AntiPattern, which in turn can cause a development AntiPattern, but it is the development AntiPattern that is visible. For example, the Planning 911 AntiPattern can cause the Architecture By Implication AntiPattern [Brown 1998] resulting in the Blob AntiPattern [Brown 1998]. The Planning 911 AntiPattern produces a Glass Case Plan that is never updated and results in an inaccurate schedule with no project control. This causes the Architecture By Implication AntiPattern where the architecture phase is not properly controlled, resulting in insufficient architecture being defined and causing design flails in the next phase. The Blob AntiPattern then produces unstructured code because there is no design to specify the code structure. If the development AntiPattern is the only one tackled, the other two AntiPatterns will cause accumulated software development consequences, which may cause further AntiPatterns to emerge. It is critical to identify all of the AntiPatterns and deal with each of them in the order that will remove them as rapidly as possible.

The greatest cause for concern is that the nature of AntiPattern interaction may not be apparent. Inability to identify the causes, symptoms, and consequences that exist between or across AntiPatterns can be fatal for a software development project. Once the AntiPatterns have been identified and the causes traced back to the primary cause, then refactoring can begin.

The *AntiPattern Collision AntiPattern* identifies the nature of AntiPattern interactions and interdependencies and provides guidelines to finding the primary AntiPattern—not just the localized one—and tips about how to refactor the complex set of causes.

AntiPattern Collision

AntiPattern Name: AntiPattern Collision

Also Known As: The AntiPattern's AntiPattern, The Death March, The Goliath

Most Applicable Scale: Enterprise

Refactored Solution Name: AntiPattern Management

Refactored Solution Type: Software, Technology, Process, and Role

Root Causes: Haste, Apathy, Narrow-Mindedness, Sloth, Avarice, Ignorance, Pride, Responsibility (the universal cause)

Unbalanced Forces: Management of Functionality, Management of Performance, Management of Complexity, Management of Change, Management of IT Resources, Management of Technology Transfer, Risk (the underlying force)

Anecdotal Evidence:
"One thing goes wrong after another. No sooner do we solve one problem and move on, and then another problem surfaces. You'd think they were all linked or something!"
"I know that the original lack of planning led to a hack and slash approach but we fixed that, started over and now we are stalled in analysis, trying to imply that the architecture and the project schedule haven't been updated to show what's really happened!"

BACKGROUND

AntiPatterns rarely occur in isolation. Particularly over the extended time-line of a full software development it is likely that more than one AntiPattern will occur. Because the phases and activities within them are integrated, the consequence of an AntiPattern can have a wider secondary impact on other phases and activities that they primarily affect.

It is important to understand the relationship of known AntiPatterns to the phases and activities throughout a software development lifecycle and the major cross-AntiPattern interrelationships of causes, symptoms, and consequences.

Figure 5.1 identifies the fact that causes, symptoms, and consequences can exist within a hierarchy. Also a symptom or consequence in one scenario can be a cause in another. This richness of AntiPattern interrelationships must be understood when it exists to more rapidly and effectively solve all problems, rather than deal with the problems piecemeal.

Risks will move to the next phase, activity, and task of the software development process that is not sufficiently under control. The reason for this is that any part of software development that does not have a well-understood,

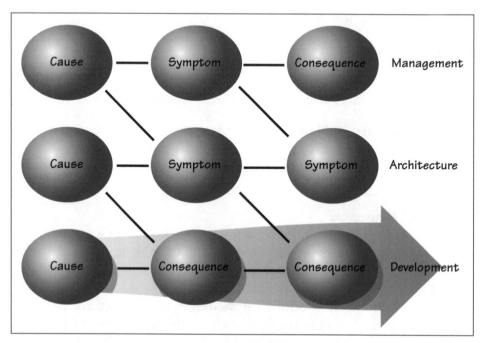

Figure 5.1 Hierarchy of causes, symptoms, and consequences.

pragmatic process incurs the risks of a development activity not being performed as required. This includes the people factor of not having the right project staffing structure and required individual skills.

GENERAL FORM

Because the scope of the AntiPattern Collision AntiPattern is a subset of the published AntiPatterns, including some of those specified within this book, they must be viewed as aberrant practices occurring within the software development lifecycle.

To avoid confusion it is best to initially view the impact using the rich, sequential software development phases of the Waterfall Lifecycle, supported by a software configuration management process and project management process (see Figure 5.2).

The software development AntiPatterns that are referenced in this section are the most common. There are many other AntiPatterns that overlap these at the same or different scales. It is not the intent of this book to exhaustively document the complex interrelationships of all published AntiPatterns but to show the nature of interaction between key AntiPatterns and the larger impact on software development. For a simple guide to identifying the existing relationships between each AntiPattern the Related Solutions section in each AntiPattern identifies the primary ones. The interrelationships need to be identified horizontally across the software development phases and vertically with relevant activities within the software configuration management and project management processes. First, it is necessary to enumerate the AntiPatterns in sequence in each of the three categories: software development AntiPatterns, software configuration management AntiPatterns, and project management

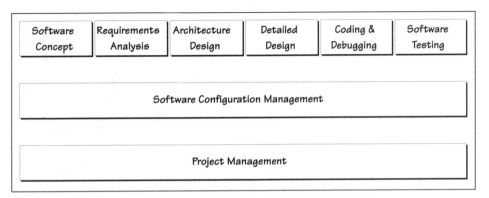

Figure 5.2 Software development lifecycle processes.

AntiPatterns. Note that architecture has been included under the first category of software development. Also note that the descriptions are brief; for a full understanding of each AntiPattern, please refer to the source indicated.

Software Development AntiPatterns

The AntiPatterns here are a selection of those that are both common and critical to overcome. They have been drawn from the books, *AntiPatterns: Refactoring Software, Architectures, and Projects in Crisis* [Brown 1998] and *AntiPatterns and Patterns in Software Configuration Management* [Brown 1999]. Figure 5.3 shows their focus within the software development process.

Requirements Jeopardy AntiPattern

Overconfident development teams and inexperienced program managers are frequently the cause of the Requirements Jeopardy AntiPattern [Brown 1999]. This AntiPattern is often revealed during a user demonstration of the prototype system, when the users begin to question why specific functionality isn't incorporated. A spirited discussion between the development team and the

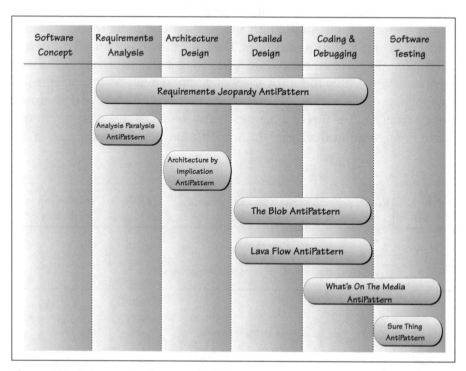

Figure 5.3 Software development AntiPatterns.

users ensue, with the embarrassed program manager acting as referee. Later, the program manager will learn upon conferring with the development team that the requirements weren't documented or, even worse, the users were never solicited for requirements. The inability of the project team to produce a document that identifies the requirements baseline appears to the users as confirmation that the project team didn't record the requirements, regardless of the veracity of the users' claims. Ultimately the development team assumes responsibility for having overlooked the missing requirements and the program manager's only hope is that the development team's vision and the users' visions aren't too far apart. The discovery of the AntiPattern at this time is fortunate since a demonstration of this system to the users occurs before deployment and allows for the incorporation of the refactored solution.

Analysis Paralysis AntiPattern

Analysis Paralysis [Brown 1998] occurs when the strive for perfection and completeness of the analysis phase is excessive. Analysis Paralysis involves turnover and revision of the models and the generation of detailed models that are less-than-useful to downstream processes.

Many developers new to object-oriented methods do too much up-front analysis and design. Sometimes they use analysis modeling as a exercise to gain comfort in the problem domain. One of the benefits of object-oriented methods is developing analysis models with the participation of domain experts. It is easy to get bogged down in the analysis process if the goal is to create a comprehensive model.

Analysis Paralysis usually involves waterfall assumptions: that detailed analysis can be successfully completed prior to coding, that everything about the problem is known a priori, and that the analysis models will not be extended nor revisited during development. Object-oriented development is poorly matched to waterfall analysis, design, and implementation processes. Effective object-oriented development is an incremental process where incremental and iterative results of analysis are validated through design and implementation and used as feedback into later system analysis.

Architecture by Implication
AntiPattern

The Architecture by Implication AntiPattern [Brown 1998] is characterized by the lack of architecture specifications for a system under development. Usually, the architects responsible for the project are experienced with previous system construction and assume that documentation is unnecessary because of their competence and experience. This overconfidence leads to exacerbated risks in key areas affecting system success. Missing architecture definitions occur in one or more of these areas:

- Software architecture and specifications including language use, library use, coding standards, memory management, and so forth.

- Hardware architecture, including client and service configurations.

- Communications architecture, including networking protocols and devices.

- Persistence architecture, including databases and file-handling mechanisms.

- Application security architecture, including thread models and trusted system base.

- Systems management architecture, including system administration and operating requirements.

The Blob AntiPattern

The Blob AntiPattern is characterized by a class diagram comprised of a single complex controller class surrounded by simple data classes [Brown 1998]. The key problem is that the majority of the responsibilities are allocated to a single class. In general, The Blob is a procedural design even though it may be represented using objects notations and implemented in object-oriented languages. A procedural design separates process from data. An object-oriented design merges process and data models, and partitions. The Blob contains the majority of the process and the other objects contain the data. Architectures with The Blob have separated process from data, that is, they are procedural-style architectures rather than object-oriented.

The Blob can be the result of inappropriate requirements allocation. For example, The Blob may be a software module that is given responsibilities overlapping most other parts of the system for system control or system management. The Blob is also a frequent result of prototypical development, where proof-of-concept code evolves over time into a prototype and eventually a production system. This is often aggravated by the use of primarily GUI-centric programming languages, such as Visual Basic, that allow a simple form to evolve its functionality and therefore purpose during incremental development or prototyping. The allocation of responsibilities is not repartitioned during system evolution so that one module becomes predominant. The Blob is often accompanied by unnecessary code, making it difficult to differentiate between the useful functionality of the Blob

Class and no-longer-used code as described in the Lava Flow AntiPattern [Brown 1998].

The Lava Flow AntiPattern

The Lava Flow AntiPattern is commonly found in systems that originated as research but ended up in production [Brown 1998]. It is characterized by the lava-like "flows" of previous developmental versions strewn about the code landscape that are now hardened into a basalt-like, immovable, generally useless mass of code, which no one can remember much, if anything, about. This is the result of earlier (perhaps Jurassic) developmental times while in a research mode where developers tried out several ways of accomplishing things, typically in a rush to deliver some kind of demonstration and therefore casting sound design to the winds and sacrificing documentation.

The result is several fragments of code, wayward variables, classes, and procedures that are not clearly related to the overall system. In fact these flows are often so complicated-looking and spaghetti-like that they seem important, but no one can really explain what they do or why they exist. Sometimes an old gray-haired hermit-like developer can remember certain details, but everyone has decided to "leave well enough alone" since the code in question "doesn't really cause any harm and might actually be critical, and we just don't have time to mess with it."

What's on the Media AntiPattern

The What's on the Media AntiPattern [Brown 1999] is a common occurrence of the independent-testing phase being put at risk due to the lack of documented requirements, design, and so on. When an integration-test or system-test team receives software, they should have significant prior knowledge, in the form of documentation, to prepare and be able to begin testing the day the product media is received.

Often software is "thrown over the wall," that is, passed from developer to tester with no interaction and with little or no accurate documentation in the form of design, programmer/reference/user manual, or complete test cases. This leads to multiple unplanned activities. The receiver of the software has to resort to code mining to find out what has been delivered before preparing to integrate scripts and test cases. Too much reliance is then placed on unit tests received from development, which by their very nature are only intended to test up to the level of isolated components. The test coverage is very thin with no ability to measure development unit test coverage because of little or no documentation and a shrinking allotted integration and test period to produce integration tests.

Sure Thing AntiPattern

The Sure Thing AntiPattern occurs when testing does not occur because it is thought unnecessary. Testing is critical to a system, regardless of size or complexity [Brown 1999]. It ensures that the design and implementation reflect the requirements and that the system will operate in a manner consistent with what the users expect. Moreover, testing provides some assurance of the reliability and the availability of the system when it is deployed. Testing mitigates the risk of development by evaluating the system in an attempt to find defects.

Many development efforts use commercial off-the-shelf (COTS) applications as the foundation for creating customized programs that are tailored to a single user's need. While these projects appear to be small efforts, frequently these projects become popular and through increased demand, scale to become an enterprisewide system. In other circumstances, the initial requirement is for an enterprise application built upon a COTS product. In either case, the need for testing exists. However, often the project team (especially the development team) feels that they are doing little more than providing minor enhancements to the COTS product and, therefore, testing is not required because the COTS developer has already tested the product. Alternatively development efforts are viewed as small and insignificant or noncomplex. The project team believes that testing such a small system is overkill and bureaucratic.

Software Configuration Management AntiPatterns

The software configuration management AntiPatterns under this category are all from *AntiPatterns and Patterns in Software Configuration Management* [Brown 1999], which primarily focused on software configuration management. Figure 5.4 shows their focus within the software configuration management process.

Silver Bullet AntiPattern

The Silver Bullet AntiPattern deals with the problem of relying on a tool rather than a process to provide adequate software configuration management [Brown 1999]. The lack of experience in software configuration management often leads to impractical solutions that don't work and eventually cause project failure. The most common form of an impractical solution is to rely on a software configuration management tool to implement a soft-

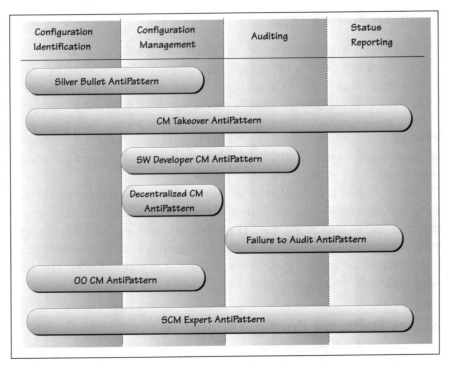

Figure 5.4   Software configuration management AntiPatterns.

ware configuration management program. This hard lesson is not well learned by software project teams and the hype from the software configuration management product companies encourages the belief that a tool will not only solve all of the problems but also provide a comprehensive software configuration management program [McConnell 1996].

A software configuration management tool is seen as the only solution necessary to achieve full software configuration management. Specifically the elements defined in the Configuration Management Organization Pattern must be addressed:

- Enterprise processes that define software configuration management
- Configuration identification and control
- Software configuration management standards
- Status accounting and auditing

Total reliance on a tool cannot establish the software configuration management program [Brooks 1995] and ensure its integration within the development processes.

CM Takeover AntiPattern

The CM Takeover AntiPattern occurs when the configuration management (CM) manager takes control of the software development project with software configuration management as the only focus [Brown 1999]. Usually software developments suffer when a person other than the project manager controls the delivery process and resources. In this case an overdomineering CM manager can misappropriate resources, reducing emphasis on other parts of software development and ignoring the plan [McConnell 1996].

A CM manager has a critical role to play in software development. The role spans the entire development lifecycle and assists with the delivery of software in a highly useful manner. However, sometimes the CM manager becomes a controlling force outside of the planned role and areas of focus. This CM manager dictates the delivery sequence and dominates all other processes and their resources.

Developer-Software Configuration Management AntiPattern

The essence of the Developer-Software Configuration Management AntiPattern [Brown 1999] is to empower the development team to perform the role of software configuration management. The result is typically a system that ends in disarray because software configuration management is not performed or at least not performed in the manner in which it should have been. This AntiPattern frequently results in multifaceted problems, not the least of which is an unsuccessful development.

This AntiPattern is frequently realized in development meetings or project meetings, when it is discovered that a developer or subgroups within the development team unilaterally decided to change the design without any software configuration management. The software configuration management process for processing a change is sidestepped and the configuration control documentation to facilitate the change in design and interface specifications is not promulgated, so the project team is unaware of the current design implementation.

Decentralized Configuration Management AntiPattern

The Decentralized Configuration Management AntiPattern is recognized by the inability to share critical development information [Brown 1999]. Many developments have significant problems when it comes to sharing and controlling information; this results in incorrect assumptions and delivery delays. Yet a repository is a natural feature of most CASE tools, which can often be used for more than just design. For example, many CASE tools allow entry of requirements and testing details that can be attached to one or more symbols or diagrams. This offers a common place for development information to be shared. Repositories are an essential key factor in information sharing and reuse, within single developments and across multiple developments up to the enterprise level [Brown 1995].

This means that the requirements and architecture [Coplien 1995] need to be available in a controlled manner that would allow other developers to read everything, but only the specific owners of architecture, requirements, and design to create and update specific items. To this end it is necessary to understand the different repository organizations that will affect what can realistically be done in terms of shared information access, control of that information, and computer assistance, as in CASE.

Failure to Audit AntiPattern

The Failure to Audit AntiPattern [Brown 1999] exposes the risks when the auditing of software, as part of the software configuration management, is omitted. While the foundation of configuration management is widely accepted to consist of four elements, that is, configuration identification, configuration control, status accounting, and audit, the last of these is often not performed. The rationale that may be applied by a project manager is that if the current software development effort is going smoothly and the software configuration management program is otherwise good, why is an audit or technical review necessary? That is when the three software configuration management elements of configuration identification, configuration control, and status accounting are performed in a satisfactory manner, but the auditing of the software is considered an unnecessary overhead. It is also possible that the audit function is not performed because of lack of resources or schedule compression, or rationalized as unnecessary because of the magnitude of the effort. Regardless, performing an audit is instrumental to achieving confidence in the system and configuration documentation. It is a verification of the documentation that is used as a basis for development, maintenance, and configuration control throughout the lifecycle. Finally, an audit or technical review can point to strengths and weaknesses in the software configuration management and software development processes.

Object-Oriented Configuration Management AntiPattern

The Object-Oriented Configuration Management AntiPattern focuses on the software configuration management issues raised by implementing an object-oriented technology solution [Brown 1999]. Software configuration management must happen at the detailed level of interaction of objects and at the higher level where component interfaces are really a sequence of invocations of its objects' public methods. Versioning at both levels is critical and must be part of the software configuration management process.

There is confusion in how to apply software configuration management in a highly iterative and incremental development environment, where macro and micro software changes take place.

To add to the complexity of the problem it is usual to have a version of the executable code that has been released to integration and system test, the version of the associated source code, and an under-development version of the source code.

Software Configuration Management Expert AntiPattern

The Software Configuration Management Expert AntiPattern deals with an inexperienced software configuration manager and the problems that are caused [Brown 1999]. It isn't uncommon for an individual to volunteer or is asked to perform CM responsibilities without any experience with actually performing configuration management. Developers, between projects, looking for a break, or otherwise willing to volunteer for the CM role, believe that their CM experience as developer qualifies. System engineers having a broad perspective of the process believe that they can easily fill the role as well, with little comprehension of the details. Still others believe that because they fundamentally understand software configuration management and have read about it, they are qualified to perform it. It is the perception of what CM is and their exposure to CM that leads to the belief that anyone can be a configuration manager.

The Software Configuration Management Expert is anything but an expert. This usually results from a lack of experience rather than from a lack of knowledge. Worst of all, the expert is unaware of her own limitations and presents herself as being fully knowledgeable and experienced. Not knowing but believing she does know is perhaps the greatest problem for the project manager, and it is his job to convince the expert that she's not an *expert*.

Project Management AntiPatterns

The following AntiPatterns are from this book and our two previous works:

- *AntiPatterns: Refactoring Software, Architectures, and Projects in Crisis*
- *AntiPatterns and Patterns in Software Configuration Management*

These AntiPatterns provide rich descriptions of project management processes that are critical to implement for guaranteed success. Figure 5.5 illustrates their focus within the project management process.

Corncob AntiPattern

The Corncob AntiPattern [Brown 1998] examines the impact of a manipulative project member who has a personal agenda and uses the software development project as a vehicle to achieve it. A difficult person (the corncob) causes problems through destructive behaviors for a software development team or, even worse, throughout an enterprise. This person may be a member

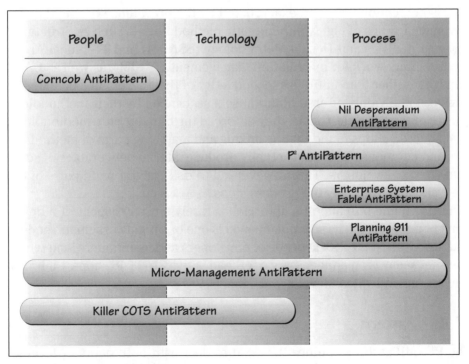

Figure 5.5   Project management AntiPatterns.

of the team or external senior staff (such as a technical architect or development manager) who adversely impacts the team through various means: technical, political, and personal. When dealing with corncobs, it is important to remember that "politics is the exercise of power." Corncobs focus much more on politics than technology. Corncobs are usually experts at manipulating politics at personal or organizational levels. Technology-focused people can become unwilling but easy victims of the corncob's political manipulations.

In all cases, the key solution is the withdrawal of management support for the destructive behaviors. By eliminating management support at tactical, operational, and strategic levels, the problem person loses support and the best interests of the software development team can dominate.

Nil Desperandum AntiPattern

The Nil Desperandum AntiPattern refactors the chronic problem of bureaucratic development methodologies that incur severe software delivery risks [Brown 1999]. Failure to engineer software is commonplace, as is development project failure. Many IT/IS shops, their customers, and individual developers do not see the need for formal process steps and their interim deliverables.

This perception has been exacerbated by the prevalence during the 70s, 80s, and early 90s of highly bureaucratic methodologies, such as Structured Systems Analysis and Design Methodology (SSADM) and Technical Architecture Framework for Information Management (TAFIM), as well as CASE tools that rather than fulfill the second letter of their acronym (A = aided or assisted) really only offered notation sets sequenced by their methodology phases of the lifecycle; that is, they enforced the bureaucratic methodology.

Many IT/IS shops found that by mixing and matching parts of methodologies and notations they could actually produce interim deliverables of some value to the developers. This however led to risks migrating to parts of the lifecycle not covered by the process steps.

Ironically the bureaucratic approaches rarely left any aspect of a development uncovered. The solution needed is one of a highly pragmatic end-to-end process that meets the needs of developers and maintainers, and which does not seem as an unnecessary overhead activity to IT/IS shops, their customers, and individual developers.

P² AntiPattern

The P^2 AntiPattern examines the need to deal with both people (development staff) and process in tandem rather than as isolated aspects of a software development project [Brown 1999]. Software developments rely on skilled people following a pragmatic process in an appropriate organizational structure. It is critical for large-scale, distributed developments to focus on these criteria to achieve success.

People and process must be tackled together, not as two separate things. Neither one will independently achieve success on a large-scale, software development project. The problem is exacerbated as soon as the development is split over multiple sites. In practice it makes little difference whether the other site is in the building, across the street, or hundreds of miles away. There is more than just a long drive or a short plane ride to this because the more remote the people and process, the more severe the problems.

Enterprise System Fable AntiPattern

The Enterprise System Fable AntiPattern [Brown 1999] deals with the commonly occurring problem of the lack of real enterprise application integration. Very few, if any, companies achieve any level of enterprise systems because they are controlled by their lines of business (LOBs). If they change the way they approach enterprise systems, they can successfully achieve reusable enterprise components and integrated views across their systems.

The Stovepipe AntiPattern and the Enterprise Stovepipe AntiPattern [Brown 1998] are two of the classic AntiPatterns in the management of software development. These identify and refactor the problems caused by stand-alone legacy systems that offer no interoperability with other corporate systems, at a system or enterprise scale. The only truly successful way to deal with the causes is at an enterprise level.

Failure to achieve enterprise systems occurs because the company does not tackle the strategic root of the problem in a corporate manner. Instead, they offer tactical solutions that will build better stovepipes. The overriding consequence is the continual drain on corporate funds to build endless LOB-driven stovepipe solutions that cannot be fully effective. The equally significant consequence is the failure to meet the business needs of an enterprise view of critical data and provide access to remote system transactions.

Planning 911 AntiPattern

Software planning is intended to be the representation of the reality of software development. Many projects fail from either overplanning or underplanning; in other words, an inappropriate level of planning will ultimately lead to growing risks, delays, and often failure to deliver.

The Planning 911 AntiPattern deals with how to plan your way out of trouble when no one knows what the reality of delivery is. It explains how to plan your way out of the Detailitis Plan [Brown 1998], the Glass Case Plan [Brown 1998], and the Management Plan. In the Detailitis Plan the project schedule attempts to capture too much detail throughout the development. In the Glass Case Plan the project schedule is produced prior to beginning development but never captured against. In both cases it is impossible to use the project schedule to visibly show the actual status of the development. The Management Plan exists when the software development schedule is completely produced by senior management who have no direct, day-to-day contact with the senior development staff and thereby no information as to the reality of the state of the software development. The management then attempts to drive delivery by surprise firedrills according to their management plan.

Micro-Management AntiPattern

The Micro-Management AntiPattern is recognized by the project manager managing the project staff at a task level rather than at an activity level. Many project managers do not understand how to manage people, technology tasks, or process improvement well. They are sometimes excellent technical staff who are promoted or line managers given a change of role. Development success should be attributed to the developers who do the right thing in spite of their managers, but success is often attributed to the project managers' skills. Any failures can be blamed on the developers' lack of skills.

A project manager needs to understand how to balance people, technology, and process. He or she must have skills in each of these three areas as well as the ability to appropriately balance them as necessary to overcome development problems and different skill levels among those working for them.

Project managers often overmanage a particular aspect of people, technology, and process, either because they are weak in that particular skill and believe that a microfocus will mitigate risks or because it is the one skill area that they have.

Batteries Not Included AntiPattern

The Batteries Not Included AntiPattern covers the impact of poorly choosing development-time and runtime COTS applications. Unreliable COTS vendors can cause users to have to cope with version management of erratically evolving software and the embedded costs of continuing its inclusion in their application or product.

A key technology area that requires serious risk assessment by the project management and senior technical staff is that of COTS software because often its stability is poor, the interoperability weak, and the rate of codebase change frequent.

Bad compromises in the adoption of COTS software limit future product functionality with the result of replacing software based on the earlier decision to use more stable software that is rapidly becoming dated.

AntiPattern Perspectives

There are three critical perspectives for software development AntiPatterns: the roles responsible for the AntiPattern, the nature of cause within the organization, and the software development process scope (see Figure 5.6). These perspectives can also be the causes.

Roles

The roles are those that commonly are used for perspective of the problem and refactored solution:

Managers. Project managers, software configuration managers, testing manager.

Architects. Line of business architects, technology-specific architects, Enterprise Application Integration (EAI) architects.

Developers. Designers, technology layer programmers (e.g., GUI, server application logic, or database), language programmers (e.g., Smalltalk, C++, or Java).

Nature

The nature is measured in terms of the nature of the following organizational causes:

People. Managers, architects, and developers.

Process. Software development lifecycle processes.

Technology. What is used to provide a solution.

Corporate. Cultural aspects that shape the organization.

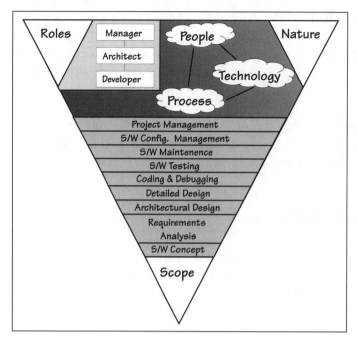

Figure 5.6 AntiPattern perspectives.

Scope

The scope can be specific to one or more software development lifecycle phases or much broader, such as project management, which affects all of the phases:

Software concept. Includes business goals.

Requirements analysis. Includes derived business requirements.

Architectures design. Includes derived technical requirements, conceptual design, and initial interface design.

Detailed design. Includes finalization of interfaces and implementation design.

Coding and debugging. Includes engineering testing.

Software testing. Includes subsystem and system testing.

Software maintenance. Includes new requirements analysis through to software testing.

Software configuration management. Includes configuration identification, configuration control, audit, and status accounting.

Project management. Includes lifecycle selection, planning and control, and risk management.

SYMPTOMS AND CONSEQUENCES

The symptoms and consequences are more than just those exhibited by each of the listed AntiPatterns. They are a cumulative effect on the software developments within single projects and across the enterprise. Table 5.1 identifies the key symptoms and consequences for each AntiPattern. The commonality is strong, which means that based purely on the nature of symptoms and consequences it is not possible to isolate the AntiPattern(s). Therefore, AntiPattern recognition requires more detailed investigation to correctly identify the refactoring required.

Corporate Symptoms and Consequences

The corporate symptoms and consequences are common to most projects that share the same bad development culture, as indicated in Table 5.2.

Horizontal Symptoms and Consequences

Horizontal symptoms and consequences are concerned with the individual software development phases impacted, including those of project management and software configuration management, as defined in Table 5.3. The abbreviated headings include:

- RA = requirements analysis
- AD = architecture design
- DD = detailed design
- CD = coding and debugging
- ST = software testing
- SM = software maintenance
- SCM = software configuration management
- PM = project management

It can be assumed that if an AntiPattern is not refactored during the phase it initially occurs within, then it will continue to affect the rest of the software development lifecycle. The X in Table 5.3 indicates the phase that the

Table 5.1 People, Process, and Technology Symptoms and Consequences

ANTIPATTERN	SYMPTOMS	CONSEQUENCES
Requirements Jeopardy	Delays in delivery	Cost overruns + missing functionality
Analysis Paralysis	Design decisions in analysis phase + delays in delivery + repeating work already done	Cost overruns
Architecture by Implication	Abstract or incomplete architecture + increased design effort + delays in delivery	Cost overruns + lack of software integrity + technical failure
The Blob	Monolithic software modules (classes or functions)	Increased development and maintenance costs
Lava Flow	Obsolete code (no-longer-used interfaces and implementations)	Increased development and maintenance costs
What's on the Media	Lack of test coverage + delays in delivery	Cost overruns + technical failure
Sure Thing	Lack of test coverage + delays in delivery	Cost overruns + technical failure
Silver Bullet	Integration failure + redeveloped components	Cost overruns + technical failure
CM Takeover	Delays in delivery + frustrated developers	Staff attrition + cost overruns
Developer-Software Configuration Management	Delays in delivery + uncontrolled software configurations	Cost overruns + software version incompatibilities
Decentralized Configuration Management	Integration failure + user dissatisfaction	Technical failure + wrong product
Failure to Audit	Increased testing + cost overruns	User dissatisfaction + delays in delivery
Object-Oriented Configuration Management	Integration failure	Cost overruns
Software Configuration Management Expert	Missed functionality + integration failure	Cost overruns + technical failure

(Continues)

Table 5.1 *(Continued)*

ANTIPATTERN	SYMPTOMS	CONSEQUENCES
Nil Desperandum	Delays in delivery + user dissatisfaction + frustrated developers + integration failure	Wrong product, technical failure, cost overruns, or premature termination
P²	Delays in delivery + integration failure	Cost overruns + technical failure
Enterprise System Fable	Stovepipe systems	Non-interoperable systems + lack of shared business information
Planning 911	Crisis project management + developer frustration + delays	Cost overruns + loss of key staff + project termination
Micro-Management	Wrong product + technical failure + delays + cost overruns	Staff attrition + project termination
Batteries Not Included	Changing embedded software outside of normal maintenance cycle	Repeated technical failure

AntiPattern initially occurs in and the right-pointing arrows indicate the remaining phases affected by the AntiPattern.

TYPICAL CAUSES

Table 5.4 identifies the causes in terms of the organizational criteria of people, process, and technology. Given that the project manager is ultimately responsible for successful delivery (of requirements, on time, and within

Table 5.2 Corporate Symptoms and Consequences

SYMPTOMS	ASSOCIATED CONSEQUENCES	EXTREME CONSEQUENCE
Repeated, unsuccessful activities	Developer dissatisfaction	Staff attrition
User dissatisfaction	Missing functionality	Development of the wrong product or technical failure
Delays in delivery	Cost overruns	Project termination

Table 5.3 Horizontal Symptoms and Consequences

	LIFECYCLE PHASE							
ANTIPATTERN	RA	AD	DD	CD	ST	SM	SCM	PM
Requirements Jeopardy	X	➢	➢	➢	➢			
Analysis Paralysis	X							
Architecture by Implication		X	➢			➢		
The Blob		X	➢	➢	➢	➢		
Lava Flow		X	➢	➢	➢	➢	X	
What's on the Media					X	➢	X	X
Sure Thing					X			X
Silver Bullet		X	➢	➢			X	X
CM Takeover							X	X
Developer SCM							X	X
Decentralized CM							X	
Failure to Audit							X	
OOCM							X	
SCM Expert							X	X
Nil Desperandum								X
P^2								X
Enterprise System Fable		X	➢	➢	➢			X
Planning 911								X
Micro-Management								X
Batteries Not Included		X	➢	➢	➢	➢		X

budget), the role of project manager is indicated when the responsibility lies directly with the project manager, rather than a subordinate role. Otherwise the alternative responsible role is listed.

The lack of technology as a root cause in most cases is highly interesting. And although there are many other AntiPatterns that could be explored, the majority of causes relate to people and process.

Note that where a lack of software development processes is stated as a possible key cause, this usually indicates that there is no software develop-

Table 5.4 People, Process, and Technology Causes

ANTIPATTERN	PEOPLE	PROCESS	TECHNOLOGY
Requirements Jeopardy	Inexperienced or overconfident developers + inexperienced project manager		
Analysis Paralysis	Inexperienced project manager and analysts	Lack of analysis process (including exit criteria)	
Architecture by Implication	Inexperienced project manager and architects	Lack of architecture process (including exit criteria)	Complex, undocumented technology
The Blob	Inexperienced architects and developers	Lack of architecture process (including exit criteria)	
Lava Flow	Inexperienced SCM manager, architects and developers	Lack of architecture process + lack of SCM process	
What's On the Media	Inexperienced project manager	Lack of, or ignored, software development processes + lack of project management process	
Sure Thing	Inexperienced or overconfident developers + inexperienced project manager	Lack of project management process	
Silver Bullet	Inexperienced project manager, SCM manager and architects	Lack of architecture process + lack of SCM process + lack of project management process	Technology benefits less than marketing hype
CM Takeover	Inexperienced project manager	Lack of project management process + lack of software development process ownership	
Developer SCM	Inexperienced or overconfident developers + inexperienced project manager	Lack of software development processes (including SCM process)	

(Continues)

Table 5.4 *(Continued)*

ANTIPATTERN	PEOPLE	PROCESS	TECHNOLOGY
Decentralized CM	Inexperienced SCM manager	Lack of SCM (configuration identification and control) process	
Failure to Audit	Inexperienced SCM manager	Lack of SCM (audit) process	
OOCM	Inexperienced SCM manager	Lack of SCM (configuration identification and control) process	
SCM Expert	Inexperienced SCM manager	Lack of SCM process + lack of software development processes	
Nil Desperandum	Inexperienced project manager	Lack of software development processes + lack of project management process	
P²	Inexperienced project manager	Lack of software development lifecycle + lack of project management processes	
Enterprise System Fable	Inexperienced project manager	Lack of consistent software development processes + lack of enterprise project management process + lack of enterprise integration architecture process	
Planning 911	Inexperienced project manager	Lack of project management process	
Micro-Management	Inexperienced project manager	Lack of project management process	
Batteries Not Included	Inexperienced architects	Lack of proof-of-concept research and development	Lack of stable COTS applications

ment lifecycle being followed, which would prompt the definition and inter-action of each development phase.

Corporate Causes

The corporate causes are the driving force of the people, process, and technology causes. These are much less visible because they are embedded in the corporate culture. They are natural business objectives that are poorly implemented in the development of supporting information systems. They are abstract in nature although the corporate executives will often label them as corporate objectives:

Profitability. Making money is more important than how effectively the information technology supports corporate goals; all corporate deci-sions are guided by this philosophy.

Increased margin. Either doing less work on a software development or requiring project staff to work regular overtime to finish the project in a shorter period.

Time to market. The quickest way to deliver the software, by ignoring overhead activities such as software configuration management, detailed design, and testing.

KNOWN EXCEPTIONS

The singular exception is simple and slightly tongue in cheek: Don't develop software! If you develop any software at any scale, several of these AntiPat-terns will eventually occur. The realistic exception is to so thoroughly understand both the business problem to be solved and the technology to be used, and to be in control of the project plan at all stages, that only one AntiPattern will occur.

REFACTORED SOLUTION

The refactored solution scope is the correct identification of the existing and imminent AntiPatterns within one or more related software development projects. The nature of project relationship will usually be as part of a pro-gram of projects delivering interdependent software. The activities vary somewhat depending on whether single or multiple projects are under inves-tigation.

You will notice that the steps here are intended for complex problems that do not reveal themselves as an AntiPattern. In most cases it is expected, based on experience of others using the *AntiPatterns: Software, Architectures, and Projects in Crisis* book, that the Antipattern identification will be simpler. These steps are a formal way to improve risk management using AntiPatterns as the core to the approach.

Single Project

The simplest case to refactor is one in which the scope of the problems is a single software development project. The following refactoring steps should be followed to identify the AntiPatterns occurring, after which the refactored solution for each identified AntiPattern should be applied:

1. Identify prevalent problems.
2. Identify problem causes, symptoms, and consequences.
3. Identify AntiPatterns.

Identify Prevalent Problems

The first step is to identify what appears to be wrong. This is certainly not trivial because at any time many problems may appear to be significant only to be easily resolved in a week or two. Appearances can be deceptive because often people have a knee-jerk reaction to what they see as a problem and make a mountain out of a molehill. This is why rapid investigation and clarification is required. A problem is something more persistent that can be isolated as a risk and must be mitigated.

If a Spiral Lifecycle is followed then at least risk analysis is a consistent part of each phase that enforces some discipline to seek and mitigate risks. However, risk analysis should be an integral part of every software development process set. It is part of what should be considered project management analysis and mitigation of business and technical risks. The top risks would be reported in a monthly traffic light report as suggested in the Planning 911 AntiPattern. To produce a traffic light report the actual data should be collected weekly as part of the risk management activities, and those lists should be as long as required to capture all of the known and candidate risks.

A risk should be identified as either a business risk or technical risk. As soon as it has been identified, it needs to be investigated. The usual time limit for the investigation is by the next week's meeting, where the level of risk (from none to extreme) must be set and the risk prioritized for action. The choices will range from "wait and see," delay the mitigation, or aggressively resolve the risk. Table 5.5 presents an outline for capturing risk information.

Table 5.5   Risk Identification Categories

BUSINESS RISK	TECHNICAL RISK
Software concept (completion and stability)	
Requirements (completion and stability)	
Business architecture (completion and stability)	Technical architecture (completion and stability)
	Detailed design (completion and stability)
	Technology (COTS or proprietary) stability
	Staff technical skills
	Software failure
Software acceptance	

Unless a wait and see approach is adopted to see if the risk does not naturally resolve itself, the next step should be immediately pursued by the risk management team. This should be either to deal with the risk immediately or to review it weekly until it is time to deal with it.

Identify Problem Causes, Symptoms, and Consequences

For each business and technical risk that is treated as active, a problem should be investigated further to clarify the prevalent symptoms and consequences as well as any likely future consequences. This should be straightforward since the only way a risk can be identified is by the prevalent symptoms or consequences. It is more a matter of clarifying the scope of these factors to ensure that the overall risk is understood.

If the risk is a cause, such as a lack of a detailed architecture, then there is a need to establish its current level of impact in terms of symptoms and consequences. On the one hand, such a cause could easily be recognized without the need to suffer symptoms and consequences and should be caught by reasonable phase exit criteria. However, if a symptom of increased design effort and design delays already exists, then the risk is much higher that the consequences of cost overruns, lack of software integrity, or other technical failure may occur. The state of the problem in terms of cause, symptoms, and consequences must be clearly understood to identify the necessary actions to take to refactor the problem.

If the risk is a symptom, such as frustrated developers, then the action should be to interview the developers to identify the real nature of the problem. Common sense has to be used here because it is possible that frustrated staff will take the opportunity to vent about all of their hot spots. Look for a common recent experience that is primarily causing the frustration. This should now identify the likely causes and symptoms. But it may not yet be possible to see the consequences because they may be in the very early stages of occurring.

If the risk is a consequence, such as various forms of technical failure, then it is usually much harder to identify the causes because there may be many. The first step is to identify the symptoms associated with each consequence. If the symptoms are developer frustration, increased design effort, and design delays, then the possible causes will be narrowed down to where specific causes can be identified. This is an iterative activity and should not be rushed, otherwise the risk arises that the wrong problem might be tackled. This will then create a problem where none previously existed, in addition to the existing problems.

The output of this step should be an extension of Table 5.5, detailing the known causes, symptoms, and risks for each active risk as outlined in Table 5.6.

Identify AntiPatterns

This step should be easy since most of the identification work appears to have been done in the previous steps. However, that assumption is based on there being a clean matchup between a published AntiPattern and its identified causes, symptoms, and consequences.

Table 5.6 Risk Causes, Symptoms, and Consequences

BUSINESS RISK	CAUSES	SYMPTOMS	CONSEQUENCES
Requirements unstable	Lack of rigorous analysis process and weak project management	Repeated analysis tasks and unstable analysis artifacts	Continual analysis delays and cost overruns

TECHNICAL RISK	CAUSES	SYMPTOMS	CONSEQUENCES
Detailed design incomplete	Lack of detailed architecture	Developers inventing architecture and coding dead ends	Delays to design and coding and associated cost overruns

The previous steps may lead to the identification of new AntiPatterns that have yet to be publicly documented. There are plenty of these to keep software developers going for as long as software will be around. So if a match cannot be made to a published AntiPattern, congratulations!

Not all the details of the causes, symptoms, and consequences may be known. It may also be the case that a new AntiPattern is identified or that a vertically or horizontally overlapping AntiPattern is discovered. Also depending on the state of the AntiPattern, it could be very difficult to identify (see Figure 5.7).

Partially Identified AntiPattern

In this case it is expected that one of the causal states has been identified with the associated symptoms and consequences. It is often the case that causes incrementally grow and at each stage have new symptoms and consequences, such as the Micro-Management AntiPattern causes, symptoms, and consequences listed in Table 5.7. It is necessary to identify the current cause and any previous causes with associated symptoms and consequences to better ascertain the correct AntiPattern, rather than one with similarities.

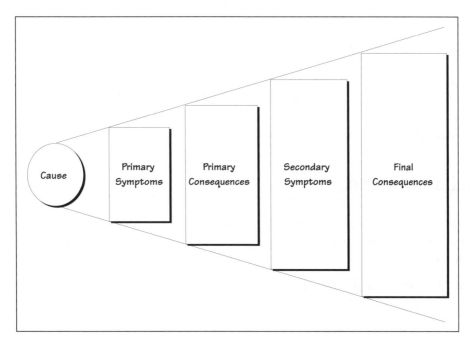

Figure 5.7 AntiPattern states.

Table 5.7 Cause, Symptom, and Consequence States of the Micro-Management AntiPattern

CAUSES	PRIMARY SYMPTOMS	PRIMARY CONSEQUENCES	SECONDARY SYMPTOMS	FINAL CONSEQUENCES
Lack of project management skill and experience	People management failure	■ Development of the wrong product ■ Cost overruns	Micro-Management AntiPattern	■ Staff attrition ■ Premature termination of project
	Technology management failure	■ Technical failure ■ Cost overruns		
	Process management failure	■ Development of the wrong product ■ Cost overruns		

Vertically Overlapping AntiPattern

Vertical AntiPattern overlap is where one AntiPattern exists within another. This hierarchy is usually causal and relatively easy to identify as shown in Figure 5.8. The overlap can be within a single project or across related projects.

Horizontally Overlapping AntiPattern

Horizontal AntiPattern overlap is concerned with common software development phases that are impacted, including those related to project management and software configuration management defined in Table 5.3. A horizontal overlapping AntiPattern is people and/or process oriented.

Related Projects

In the case of related projects, the problem is more complex and needs additional steps to correctly identify what AntiPatterns exist and require refactoring:

- Identify project interrelationships
- Identify individual project status
- Follow the steps for a single project

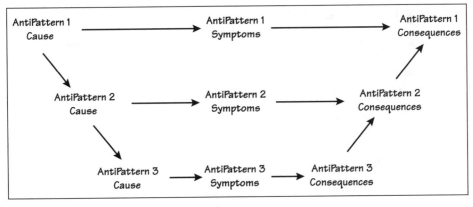

Figure 5.8   Vertically overlapping AntiPatterns.

Identify Project Interrelationships

AntiPatterns can easily occur across multiple projects, either as the same AntiPattern at a different stage of occurrence or an associated AntiPattern that has the same root cause. Tables 5.1, 5.2, 5.3, and 5.4 will help you to identify some of the AntiPattern relationships.

The steps used to identify project interrelationships must identify the physical dependencies between projects and then assess the phase of development for each dependent project. This will establish the likelihood of a cross-project AntiPattern existing.

The first step is to identify the specific project relationships, which will be based on specific dependencies. The main dependencies are software and related documentation. For example, a project will always have one of the following dependencies to a related project:

- Documentary dependencies
  - Requirements
  - Architectures
  - Design
- Software dependencies
  - Reusable component libraries or executables
  - Framework or embedded components

Once the nature of the physical dependency is identified the next step can be initiated to complete the picture.

Identify Individual Project Status

Each project state must be identified by asking the following questions:

- What phases have been completed?
  - What problems were encountered?
  - What problems were resolved?
  - What was the mitigation for problem resolution?
- What is the state of progress of the current phase?
  - What are the prevalent problems?
  - What are the mitigation options?
- Has the dependent deliverable from another project been delivered?
- What problems are related to the deliverable from the other project?
  - What are the mitigation options?

The answers to these questions will ensure that the interdependencies and states of each project, in terms of risks, are understood before any further internal project risk management is undertaken. This is because the solution may not lie within the project being focused on, but rather the project it is dependent on. Alternately, the problem may exist across several interdependent projects. The problems must be identified at a level of scale before they can be successfully tackled.

Establishing whether a dependency has been successfully consumed by the dependent project initially identifies the scale of the problem. The scale is within the dependent project. However, if there are problems with successfully consuming the deliverable from the producer project then the dependency still exists and the scale is multiproject.

A variation of this is not tied to deliverables but management. If there is a hierarchical management team then the problem could be management caused. This should be identified by common project management problems identified across the management-related projects, as identified in Tables 5.3 and 5.4.

Follow the Steps for a Single Project

The previously defined steps for a single project should now be followed:

- Identify prevalent problems
- Identify problem causes, symptoms, and consequences
- Identify AntiPatterns

If the scale is multiproject then the steps must be followed at that scale (see Figure 5.9). Again when the AntiPatterns have been identified their specific solutions should be applied.

EXAMPLE

An insurance project was undertaken to provide a centralized view of customer data via a Web server. A management team and two development teams (see Figure 5.10) were responsible for Web server services and connectors to the legacy systems.

The software development process started as a fairly typical waterfall sequence of development phases. There was an allowance for some limited overlap between the end of one phase and the beginning of the next. The planned software development phases included:

- Software concept
- Requirements analysis
- Architectural design

Refactored Solution Step	Project 1						Project 2						Project 3					
Identify Project Interrelationships	People																	
	Technology																	
	Process																	
Identify Individual Project Status	Phase																	
	Progress (Problems)																	
	Deliverables (Problems)																	
Identify Prevalent Problems	Business Risk			Technical Risk			Business Risk			Technical Risk			Business Risk			Technical Risk		
Identify Problem Causes, Symptoms, & Consequences	Cause	Symptom	Consequence	Cause	Symptom	Consequence	Cause	Symptom	Consequence	Cause	Symptom	Consequence	Cause	Symptom	Consequence	Cause	Symptom	Consequence
Identify AntiPatterns	AntiPattern	Related AntiPattern	AntiPattern	Related AntiPattern	AntiPattern	Related AntiPattern	AntiPattern	Related AntiPattern	AntiPattern	Related AntiPattern	AntiPattern	Related AntiPattern	AntiPattern	Related AntiPattern	AntiPattern	Related AntiPattern	AntiPattern	Related AntiPattern

Figure 5.9   Steps and scales in AntiPattern identification.

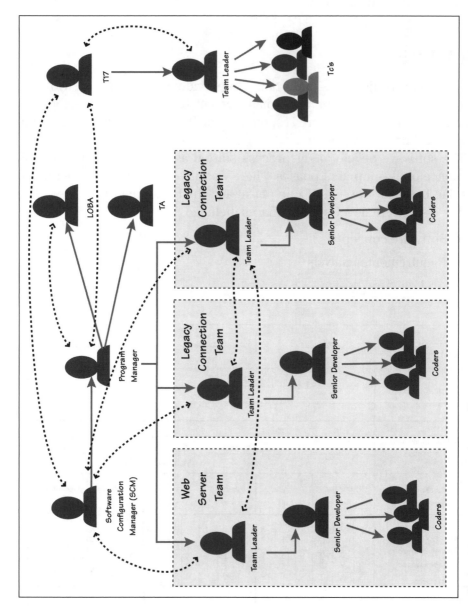

Figure 5.10 Insurance project staffing structure.

- Detailed design
- Coding and debugging
- Software testing

Phase 1: Software Concept

There were no initial problems in establishing the software concept business goals, strategies, and associated business processes. Nor were there any problems producing an initial project plan or building the project team.

Phase 2: Requirements Analysis

The requirements analysis phase was intended to produce the derived business requirements in a one and a half-month period. All project staff were to be involved at various levels of requirements gathering and validation to ensure a thorough understanding of what requirements had to be met.

The first problem noticed by the project manager was that after one month the requirements were still in a state of flux, which indicated the likelihood of not finishing on schedule.

The users were specifying requirements outside of the scope set by the software concept document. This had not been enforced by anyone and so the requirements had crept significantly with users trying to add their personal favorite requirements under the guise of the software concept headings.

The project manager decided that this was a software configuration manager issue and when he confronted the software configuration manager about this he found that the software configuration manager had had little experience in software configuration management, being newly promoted from a developer role.

With the known facts, the project manager produced a cause, symptom, and consequence table, outlined in Table 5.8, based on the order in which he assembled the information.

Table 5.8 Identifying Causes, Symptoms, and Consequences in Requirements

CAUSES	SYMPTOMS	CONSEQUENCES
■ Inexperienced software configuration manager	■ Lack of SCM process ■ Requirements scope creep	■ Requirements instability ■ Predicted delays to changing requirements

This indicated three possible AntiPattern matches. The symptoms and consequences indicated aspects of both the Analysis Paralysis AntiPattern and the Requirements Jeopardy AntiPattern. The cause indicated the Software Configuration Management Expert AntiPattern.

This was enough information for the project manager to take action. In the case of the Requirements Jeopardy AntiPattern and the Software Configuration Management Expert AntiPattern, the answer was to institute a strong SCM process. This meant that the Project Manager had to lead the SCM process and use the software configuration manager as an assistant so that he could learn on the job.

The Analysis Paralysis AntiPattern showed the lack of a strong analysis process and lack of leadership of this phase. Since the project manager had just increased his workload, he appointed the senior team leader for the Web services team to lead the analysis phase. Her first tasks were to reestablish the scope of the analysis and then reinforce the analysis process.

Phase 3: Architectural Design

The technology architect and business architect struggled to produce the level of detail required by the architectural design. They had produced initial but not derived technical requirements. They had developed a conceptual architecture and design without any associated interface definitions. This had raised concerns from the senior designers but this received little attention because the architects owned this phase. Consequently, the problem was not visible to the project manager and went unnoticed, particularly since the architecture documents were delivered on the scheduled date.

Phase 4: Detailed Design

Two months into the detailed design process, the team leaders started reporting slippage against schedule to the project manager. These warnings were not taken seriously until this had continued for another month. At that time the project manager held a series of project review meetings. The architects said that the designers didn't understand the architecture and were "doing their own thing." The designers complained that the architectures were not of sufficient detail to be useful. The risk of delays and cost overruns was obvious to the project manager who identified the problem, as shown in Table 5.9.

Table 5.9 Identifying Causes, Symptoms, and Consequences in Design

CAUSES	SYMPTOMS	CONSEQUENCES
Lack of agreed architectures exit criteria	Disagreement between architects and designers about usefulness of architecture	Predicted delays to finalizing interfaces and producing implementation design and subsequent coding

The project manager readily identified the Architecture By Implication AntiPattern and with a tiger team consisting of the architects and senior designers defined the refactored solution:

- Establish the architecture artifacts
- Establish the exit criteria for each architecture artifact
- Finalize the architecture
- Modify the detailed design

It was estimated that the rework could cause a two-month delay in delivery of the detailed design. But the project manager believed that some time would be made up during the next phase because the detail of the design would reduce the coding effort.

Phase 5: Coding and Debugging

This phase started late but initial coding proceeded according to schedule. However, midway through this phase the detailed design was revisited to update it with utility classes and additional class methods that had not been anticipated during the main design phase.

As soon as the project manager discovered from the team leaders that this was occurring he panicked, thinking that the design was about to be reworked. He did not understand the necessary iterative nature of design and coding. However, the team leaders assured him that this was not an additional activity but a normal activity and that they had included time for this in their estimates.

The coding and debugging phase now seemed as if it would take the scheduled time to complete, although it would be a month and a half later than originally scheduled because of the architecture problems. Suddenly the Web software stopped working when the Web server services team switched to a new version of the Web server COTS product. This prompted a technical risk assessment that identified that the new COTS product was not fully backwards compatible (see Table 5.10).

Table 5.10 Identifying Causes, Symptoms, and Consequences in Coding

CAUSES	SYMPTOMS	CONSEQUENCES
Implementation of new COTS version release	Changing functionality supported	Changing design and code as well as retesting

The Batteries Not Included AntiPattern was identified along with the following refactored solution:

- Evaluate the COTS application
- Adapt existing software
- Integrate with existing software

The estimate for this was an additional month and a half. However, despite the delays, the users insisted on the new version that promised greater ease of use. The project manager had realized his mistake in allowing the new COTS software to be adopted without allowing time for any technical difficulties, but based on the users' insistence managed to negotiate a one and a half month extension to the final delivery. This covered the incorporation of the new version of the Web server COTS product, but not the slippage of detailed design.

Phase 6: Software Testing

The knock-on effect of the month and a half delays so far reduced the time available for integration, subsystem, and system testing from three months to one and a half months. This meant doing more in less time. The testing manager complained to the project manager that there was simply not sufficient time for them to finish writing their tests and then run them and the engineering tests that the developers had produced during coding and debugging. The time compression would allow for a subset of testing only. So the project manager and testing manager produced the risk assessment in Table 5.11 and identified that they were suffering from the What's On the Media AntiPattern.

The options were to ask the users for an extension, and suffer the penalties under the service level agreement, or deliver on schedule with partially tested software that could easily have undetected fatal or severe defects. The project manager and testing manager met with the users and agreed to deliver in two stages to facilitate more complete testing of the software:

Table 5.11 Identifying Causes, Symptoms, and Consequences in Testing

CAUSES	SYMPTOMS	CONSEQUENCES
Compressed timescale	Insufficient time to write and run planned tests	■ Predicted test coverage incomplete ■ Predicted technical failure undetected

- Web server and services one month late
- Legacy connectors over a staggered period between one to two months late

Project Review

The corporate project review identified two further problems that were not visible to the project management team (see Table 5.12).

This prompted the company to investigate two additional AntiPatterns:

- Lifecycle Malpractice, identified by the cause of an inappropriate software development lifecycle followed
- Micro-Management, identified by a weak project management process

RELATED SOLUTIONS

The related solutions will always be those of other AntiPatterns that can be caused by the visible AntiPattern, or the AntiPattern that initially caused it. This is relatively open ended, with no definitive patterns of AntiPattern occurrences yet evident.

Table 5.12 Identifying Causes, Symptoms, and Consequences in Project Management

CAUSES	SYMPTOMS	CONSEQUENCES
Inappropriate software development lifecycle followed	Insufficient overlapping and iteration between phases	■ Cost overruns ■ Delays in delivery
Weak project management process	Imbalance of people, process, and technology management	■ Cost overruns ■ Delays in delivery

APPLICABILITY TO OTHER VIEWPOINTS AND SCALES

Within the enterprise, the Collision AntiPattern will affect all viewpoints (manager, architect and developer) and all levels:

- Object scale focusing on the definition and management of objects
- Micro-architecture scale involving patterns of interdependent classes and their cooperating objects
- Framework scale involving individual components and design patterns for them
- Application scale dealing with multiple components and software layers
- System scale involving the integration several applications

Ultimately this complex hierarchy of AntiPatterns will extend beyond the enterprise and have a more global effect. When many of the existing and emerging systems have suffered from these AntiPatterns the released software will often have unidentified flaws. When that software developed by different global companies is eventually connected, then the problem has started to grow towards the global scale.

Conclusions
and Resources

Project Management Best Practices

It may seem conflicting for a book on project management AntiPatterns to have a project management best practices section. After all, the premise of this book is that as project managers, regardless of our preparation, the real world is still going to sneak in and wreak havoc with the project. This shouldn't mean that you throw all caution to the wind, roll the dice, and wait for the next project catastrophe. Tactful use of knowledge and skills is always recommended and therefore this section is provided as a summary of helpful actions that may be leveraged. It is in no way intended to be the end-all or consummate list of best practices; rather, as with all lists, consider it a jumping-off point.

In truth *best practices* are nothing more than the dos and don'ts of project management. They might be referred to as *keys to success* or *rules of project management*. The list presented here is organized to correlate with the text: people, technology, and processes. Relevant AntiPatterns are included in parenthesis throughout, as a reference.

People

Nearly all of the experts in the field of software project management agree that people are your most valuable resource and will make or break your project. In fact, the software is the project team.

The best practices presented here should help you achieve a better project through your people. The practices for people are separated into three areas: staff, psychology, and external. The staff breakout refers directly to staffing your project. The psychology breakout covers the cerebral, emotional, and cognitive aspects of people, and finally the external breakout identifies those people aspects that are external to the project.

Staffing

The area of staffing software developments is often mismanaged and needs to be handled in a pragmatic manner.

Start with a Small Senior Staff

Begin by getting together an initial cadre of senior staff who will act as project leaders and are responsible for planning and managing specific activities including the staffing plan for the remainder of the team. The senior leadership should agree on strategies, priorities, and project organization. If a specific individual is a problem on the team, you probably want to consider removing him early on [NASA 1992]. Always try to hire people better than yourself and don't overlook older developers; they have the experience the hot shots don't.

Don't Over- or Understaff

Overstaffing can cause morale problems, and morale problems result in all kinds of bad things. It is acceptable to be slightly overstaffed at the beginning of the project, when you are unsure of the project direction. However, idle hands are the work of the devil, and this is true for software projects. Idle staff create new (busy) work, they come up with new ideas (out of scope), generate new requirements, and distract the productive developers. As quickly as you can, discern the appropriate level of staffing required and release all unneeded staff.

Understaffing has obvious problems as well. Effects include failure to meet schedule and burnout of your limited staff, and without rapidly fixing the situation you'll have problems. Try to remember the nursery rhyme, *Goldilocks:* "This porridge is too hot, this porridge is too cold, but this porridge is just right!"

Qualified and Experienced Staff

To have a successful project you need qualified and experienced staff. This is especially true of the senior project leaders for development, testing, training, and customer interface. While many other professions can lay claim to the same challenge, software development and deployment is a different kind of animal that requires individuals of high caliber with the experience of having "done it right" in the past. One of the reasons that software development is different is that software technologies change so rapidly. New releases of Java occur at very short intervals, which is frustrating to say the least [Strauss 1998]. Developer (and tester) training should also be considered an integral part of your risk mitigation strategy for leading and bleeding-edge development projects [Software Development Magazine 1999].

Too Little Too Late

Fred Brooks in *The Mythical Man-Month* [Brooks 1995] nailed this one on the head, "Adding manpower to a late software project makes it later." Of course the other popular saying is, "Nine women can't make a baby in a month." These are great quotes to get you into trouble when management is pushing to compress your schedule (Myopic Delivery AntiPattern). There may be exceptions to this practice, but for the most part it is true.

Vapor Staff

Every project should be broken down into definable tasks and assigned to responsible individuals. If you find that many of your tasks are being assigned to nonexistent, soon-to-be-hired staff, you're looking at some serious problems in the very near future. The first problem will be the failure to meet schedule milestones, the next will be staff burnout and attrition, and finally, project failure—in that order.

Encouraging Interaction

When a group of developers applies their differing levels of knowledge and experience to implementing a software development process they can often bring noncontiguous views that appear competitive. But positive challenging is the mechanism for facilitating learning and real project progress. People need to be able to discuss different solutions when problem solving factors such as architecture, design, and coding, thereby contributing to a better solution because it has been validated through positive challenging. This should occur not only within peer groups but also up and down management chains.

Psychology

The ability of staff to work well together is largely dictated by a positive work environment and culture.

Empower Staff

Empowering the staff means that people should be allowed to accomplish what they were hired to do and should also be responsible and accountable for their successes and failures. The project manager has the responsibility to communicate project goals, methodologies, and standards that are to be used as well as job-specific goals, including deliverables and schedules. Empowering your people results in more effective, efficient, and well-motivated staff. However, empowering must be accomplished carefully and gradually. The amount that an individual is empowered to accomplish should depend on the specific individual. It should be explained that empowering doesn't mean making renegade, unilateral decisions.

Motivation

Studies have found that the single largest impact on productivity and quality of a software project is motivation [Boehm 1981]. But how many organizations focus on motivating their people? Some organizations, only looking at the hard cold facts (read that, dollars), implement management decisions that create morale problems and in the long run negatively affect the bottom line of the project.

Team Spirit

Esprit de corps. This is certainly not simple or easy. There are specific things that project managers can do to foster team spirit, including paying for lunches and parties. Everyone loves free food and, even on the worst of projects, it puts people on their best behavior. During these sessions don't talk about work; rather, focus on outside interests (movies tend to be popular with developers). Observing and celebrating successes is especially important. While individual accomplishment should be recognized, the project manager should be careful to ensure that it is well deserved (as viewed by peers), otherwise jealousy can wreak havoc. Recognition of birthdays and baby showers help people to better know one another on a personal basis.

Problem Employees

It is imperative that management deal with a problem employees. This is the most common complaint that team members have about their leaders. While this symptom is not specific to software projects, it is clear that software projects are not immune. Ineffectively dealing with problem personnel will likely result in poor morale and potentially attrition [IEEE 1996]. Worst of all, it may promote bad practices by others. It only takes one person—that is, one bad apple, as in the Corncob AntiPattern [Brown 1998].

In the same vein, projects are destined for catastrophe if they have individuals who want to transfer off the project but are prevented from doing so. Let them go, because the individual will probably leave the project one way or another, and if they don't, others will probably leave because of the miserable conditions that result.

Naysayers

Listen to those who say the sky is falling—it just might be. While it is easy to find fault, complain, and look for the negatives, it is important to listen and filter out the shaft. Even the naysayers may have something. Discuss the issues that are brought to the surface with the senior leadership and discern if there is any weight to the allegations.

Office Conditions

People like to be treated with dignity and respect, and developers are no different. Developers may appear to be animals, but they are really human. Throwing them into a cage and expecting them to perform efficiently and effectively just isn't going to happen. Developers in noisy, crowded, low-budget office space perform significantly worse than those in quiet, private offices [DeMarco 1987]. If you are surprised by reading this, you need to go work in a sweatshop.

Respect

Staff are usually loyal and hardworking when their role and contribution is recognized. High attrition is common among companies that treat their development staff as mushrooms, that is, they cover them with fertilizer and trample all over them. The real benefit gained from respecting the views and opinions of staff is that communication and productivity increase because people are allowed to say their piece and contribute to working practices and problem solving.

External

Dealing with those people on the periphery of a project and buffering the developers is a hard task, particularly when the external people have a direct say in project matters, such as customers and bosses.

Communication

Communication is imperative. Up, down, and sideways—communicate. Make sure that it is open. You'll never find out what the problems really are if you don't listen to those actually doing the work. Moreover, you need to make sure that you have open communications with those organizations and projects you are interfacing. Finally, be sure to communicate with management both the good and the bad news. No one likes to deliver bad news, but bad news doesn't get any better with time.

Meetings

Communication is imperative, but meetings should be minimized. This appears to be conflicting. However, the point is that focused communication is the objective. When you conduct a meeting make sure you have all the right people there, but no more. Generally, people want to be productive, but making them sit through meetings is tortuous if they don't need to be there. For large projects you may find that a weekly review of project status, accomplishments, and upcoming events (e.g., demonstrations, reviews, management meetings) is appropriate. Keep these general meetings to a maximum of an hour. Make sure that the presentations and discussions remain focused, and if a more detailed discussion is required, table it and conduct a separate meeting [Strauss 1998].

User Input

Developers are infamous for creating technically exquisite products that users love to hate. It is too easy to incorporate the user, from the beginning through the end, and develop what they want. The truth is that developers don't like to involve the user because it takes much of the creativity out of the project for them. Nevertheless, user involvement is the number one reason that projects succeed [IEEE 1996]. "Involving the user throughout the project is a critical software project survival skill" [McConnell 1998].

Know Your Customer

Identify and know your customer. This can be an extremely difficult thing to do (that is why we wrote The Customer AntiPattern to address this problem). Basically, you need to know who the stakeholders are and identify what they are trying to achieve. If there are multiple customers find out who has the biggest club so that you don't get clobbered by it. That said, look for the win-win situation and work toward a solution, but understand that you must first know the players and their objectives [Johnson 1998].

Technology

The best practices presented in this section should help you achieve a successful project through the use and implementation of technology. The practices for technology are broken down into two areas: standards and product. The standards breakout identifies those practices that are used to develop the product and the product breakout focuses on technology-implementation-specific practices.

Standards

Standards actually help make software development easier if they are adopted in a pragmatic manner.

Standards versus Time and Money

Sometimes in a fit of panic, standards are relaxed to achieve schedule or cost. This is akin to selling your soul to the devil. Don't do it. The reasons are obvious and shouldn't require any additional discussion, but just in case you're a neophyte the following explanation is given: There was an obvious reason for instituting the standards on your project and to deviate in a single instance from the standards is akin to opening the door to a world of chaos. Soon there will be a need for another exception and then another. Finally, there won't be any need for standards and specifications because no one will be using them. Subsequently, all hell breaks loose and the project begins its death spiral.

Specifications

Specifications must be appropriately tailored for the project. Too much detail can result in overconfidence, while not enough detail doesn't provide the necessary direction for developers and testers (Standards AntiPattern).

Documentation Doesn't Guarantee Success

Make sure that the formality and the level of detail of the documentation is appropriate for your project. Don't assume that if you have volumes of great documentation your project will succeed. Scale your efforts to the magnitude of the effort, the duration of development, the intended lifecycle of the project, and the number of users.

Product

Product development management requires a good understanding of technologies and development processes.

Gold Plating Failure

Most projects experience about a 25 percent change in requirements from the point at which the requirements are baselined until the system is deployed [IEEE 1996]. If 25 percent is the average, imagine the worst case scenario. The idea here is to keep your baseline as stable as possible by incorporating new requirements and changes into the next baseline release. You are more likely to meet schedule, stay within budget, and achieve quality goals if you only do what is required. Don't let managers, users, architects, or developers convince you that they can add a little more for nothing. There is no such thing as a free change (Gilding the Lily AntiPattern).

Silver Bullet Syndrome

The silver bullet syndrome is the belief that a single tool, technology, or methodology will achieve project success. It doesn't work. The reason it doesn't work is that the tool, technology, or methodology never lives up to its claims. One side effect of the silver bullet syndrome is the elimination of so called unnecessary engineering disciplines and practices due to the claims of the silver bullet.

Stable Software Baseline

Attempt to achieve a stable baseline as early as possible. If it appears that some requirements have not been addressed, identify them and assign a priority (e.g., categories 1 through 4, where 1 is critical and 4 is cosmetic). Determine which category 1 (or 2) requirements must be addressed in the existing baseline before the delivery. Assign specific individuals to close those actions and monitor them closely. Attempt to minimize changes to the baseline by deferring noncritical changes until the next release. All proposed changes to the baseline should specifically identify cost and schedule impact.

Better Is the Enemy of Good Enough

Developers are optimistic and believe that they can solve any problem. Like monkeys, given enough time, developers can solve any problem; however, the real difficulty is solving the problem within the time frame and cost constraints. The time and cost variables add a level of complexity that requires something greater than superhuman developer strength. Therefore, limit the scope of the software project to something that is manageable by lesser humans, with the given constraints of time and money. Just as a footnote, it won't be the problem that the developers thought they could solve that will bite them in the bum, it will be the one problem they hadn't anticipated.

It is also important to remember that perfection is not necessary for a software project. Remind the development team that "better is the enemy of good enough." Sometimes it is better to get the software out the door and get some real feedback, rather than tweaking it in the sandbox.

Codependencies

There are certain combinations that just weren't meant to be. Alcohol and cars, alcohol and guns, and alcohol and matches. In the software development domain, performing two (or more) dependent software development projects at the same time can have essentially the same disastrous results as those in the previous examples. Similarly, software development efforts that have substantial dependencies on other organizations to gain approval or even to provide key infrastructure is very dangerous.

Like most things, try to keep it simple. This is especially true of projects that have compressed time schedules, because no one will find it as important to accomplish the necessary tasks for deploying your product as you do. You may wait days for network connectivity and firewall access before you can test, just because the network guys are backlogged. Try to eliminate these dependencies; however, if you do have dependencies, attempt to pre-coordinate activities well in advance of your delivery date.

Product Performance

It seems that projects don't identify performance requirements these days. This is most likely a result of many products being built on top of commercial applications. The thought process is that the product's dependency on the application's performance characteristics precludes focusing on something you can't control. However, that isn't the case. Too often the product is delivered for system test only to find out that it's slower than molasses on a cold day in Vermont. Users are extremely intolerant about performance, and it is no longer acceptable to boot up an application and go make a pot of coffee. Address performance and size requirements for all major modules of the product and reserve resources for unanticipated problems [Software Development Magazine 1999].

Process

The process section of the Best Practices will help you identify those practices that will enable a smoother project. The process section is divided into three areas: planning, scheduling, and status and reporting to coincide with the three primary process activities.

Planning

Planning is a critical aspect of software development that provides sufficient information on a frequent basis to control and coordinate development activities.

Develop and Adhere to a Development Plan

At the beginning of the project develop a plan that establishes project goals, organization, and responsibilities. The plan should identify specific milestones and deliverables for each milestone. The final deliverable should be defined by specific terms for achieving success. Processes, including the development methodology, should be identified. The plan should be updated as the project progresses to reflect revised milestones, deliverables, identified risks, and changes to personnel. If the plan isn't used, then you didn't do it right (either the plan or the implementation).

Abandoning Planning under Pressure

When the going gets tough, management panics. When panic sets in, suddenly all of the practices that were necessary to manage a controlled project are no longer required to manage an out of control project. Huh? Stick to the fundamentals and do what you've been taught; it may be the only thing that does save the project (Myopic Delivery AntiPattern and Process Disintegration AntiPattern).

Reestimate Regularly

Nothing stands still, especially on a project, and as your project takes on new requirements, new customers, additional funding, and additional (or fewer) developers, you must reestimate your schedule, cost, and staff requirements. It is impossible to accurately know before the project started what was required: Yes, you gave an estimate, but hopefully you explained to management you would be revisiting them from time to time with updates. While you probably don't want to go back to management on a monthly basis, you do want to reestimate on a monthly basis [NASA 1992]. Identifying trends is helpful to you and management.

Front-End Loading

Spending too much time in the front end of a project can be just as devastating to the project as trying to eliminate some of the back end. "Ready, Fire, Aim" is more than appropriate, it is crucial because most of the time spent performing up-front planning is thrown out the window later. This is because at least half of the obstacles that are encountered in a project are unknown until you are well into the development effort. While the statistics may be overstated, the fact remains that the project path is unknown, otherwise we would never have AntiPatterns.

Unreasonable Goals

No goals are better than unreasonable goals [NASA 1992]. Unreasonable goals typically result in burnout, attrition, poor performance, and team demoralization. Most project staffs will work like devoted dogs in an attempt to meet the project goals, doing whatever it takes; but when the goal is not achieved, it is extremely discouraging. Too many unobtained goals and you have project failure and staff burnout (if any staff at all).

Scheduling

Knowing how to schedule pragmatically is a key skill for a project manager. The pitfalls are many and the consequences disastrous.

Aggressive and Unrealistic Schedules

Most projects with aggressive schedules never make it. They depend on optimism, but unfortunately optimism doesn't produce code. Even if you achieve the aggressive schedule, you usually don't have the quality product you had hoped for. Basically, the saying goes, "If you want it bad, you get bad." Pushing the envelope of time is something that only Rod Serling and George Lucas have been successful at achieving (Myopic Delivery AntiPattern).

Tyrannical Scheduling—Power to the Team

If management is dictating schedule, it is fair to assume that the schedule is not real or achievable. The project team should be responsible for generating the schedule. If management is dissatisfied with the project team's schedule, then management should be responsible for justifying how the changes to the schedule will be achieved (more time, money, or people). Nevertheless, the project team's schedule should be the baseline.

Fat Reduction

This is what project managers think they are doing when they start looking at the engineering disciplines or activities they believe aren't required to deliver the product. Unfortunately, what appears to be unnecessary at the beginning of the project will ultimately become necessary upstream and at a 10 to 100 times greater cost [Boehm 1988]. "If you don't have time to do it right the first time, how are you going to find time to do it over?" (The Sure Thing AntiPattern [Brown 1999]).

The Devil Is in the Detail

High-level schedules don't do anyone any good. High-level schedules fail to identify sufficient detail to discern early on if the project is slipping. It is important that the appropriate level of detail be incorporated into a project schedule, including milestones and reviews, as well as time planned for holidays and vacations. The schedule should provide enough detail to ensure that the project manager and task managers have sufficient insight to determine if the schedule is being achieved.

Too much detail requires the project team to spend an inordinate amount of time maintaining the schedule, and it doesn't ensure any more success in achieving the schedule.

Competing Schedules

Project managers should not be keeping two sets of schedules: one for the project team and one for management. Sometimes this is done to motivate the project team to achieve early successes. However, if the second schedule is discovered it can lead to mistrust and poor morale. Open communications and project team involvement in the schedule is critical to building a team that can work together, make informed decisions, and track progress.

Hiding the reality of a schedule from management has much more substantial consequences if the project manager is caught.

Absorbing Slippage or We'll Make It Up

Frequently when there is a problem and the solution is rendered, temporary euphoria sets in. Suddenly the project team is capable of doing anything, including recovering the lost time for developing the solution to the problem. The battle cry is issued, "We'll make it up." *No you won't.* You're not going to make it up, even if you work weekends and evenings. Your team is not going to be able to accomplish what no one else has ever accomplished. Never trade a bad date for an equally bad date.

The corollary to "we'll make it up" is in the bin for deficiencies entitled, "Fix it, if you have time." *You won't have time* [Software Development Magazine 1999].

Configuration Management

Apply configuration management 101. Every change has a impact; there is no such thing as a free change (if for no other reason than you should regression test). Every change proposal should be taken before a engineering review board and a decision made as to whether or not to pursue the recommended change based on the impact to functionality, performance, schedule, and cost. It should also be clear which baseline the change will affect.

Slack Time

Slack time should be used for incorporating fixes, not for adding functionality or completing functionality that is behind schedule. If you have difficulty developing or integrating functionality, then the schedule should be slipped. You will still need the originally planned slack time to incorporate the fixes for the deficiencies.

Status and Reporting

The ability to schedule well, adjust processes for maximum effect, and control technology risks depends on accurate, up-to-date information.

Periodic Evaluations of Project Status

There must be some measure of a project's success. The inability to accurately assess the health of the project will most likely result in delays or failure. People will rise to the level of what is expected from them, and if you don't inspect they will disappoint you (not always, but frequently). There are several means for tapping into the status of the project. Testing (including unit and integration testing), configuration audits, and design reviews. If you detect or unveil problems, the project should be stopped, accessed, and a solution refactored for getting it back on track.

Reporting and the Blame Game

Project managers should not accept the inability of a responsible team member to accurately and adequately report on the status of a task or the project. Frequent requests to delay status reports or reports that excuse details or regularly blaming others as well as factors outside of their control is simply unacceptable. Team members should be identifying risks and mitigation strategies and divulging the facts, not playing the blame game. If you suspect that individuals are holding out on information or blaming others, dig deeper. Chances are there is a reason that the information isn't forthcoming.

Failure to Observe Milestones and Reviews

Project milestones should be clearly identified, both in terms of schedule (date) and in terms of what is considered project success at that milestone. It is easy to quickly dismiss a slipped or missed milestone but worse than that is the attempt of the project team to fool themselves into believing that they have achieved a project milestone with less than adequate criteria to evaluate if success has been achieved.

Lack of a Daily Build

Build your software daily. This may seem like overkill, but if you are able to achieve this practice on a daily basis you will most likely meet schedule, and once into the rigor of performing it daily, the effort is hardly noticeable. To achieve a good build you need to merge code, build and test a development baseline, check it with configuration management, create the build and test, and fix deficiencies immediately [McConnell 1998].

Try It, You'll Like It

If at all possible, the project team should attempt to use the product that they are developing. This is almost better than getting user input because now the project team understands the user's problems.

Track Metrics

You've got to know how you are doing on the project and metrics are important to discern pending success or failure. Metrics are an impartial view of your progress; however, as with all things, balance is important. Specifically don't become overly focused on the metrics and lose the focus of the project. Make sure that you identify project metrics up front and make sure that they are meaningful to tracking progress; otherwise, you will lull yourself into a false sense of security by measuring artifacts that don't reflect status. Metrics should be tracked at regular intervals (at least monthly) and published.

Summary

As with any general recommendation, such as those previously discussed, it is important to remember that not only should you be selective in applying the appropriate best practice for your project, but also you may need to tailor the practice to your specific project. After all, you are getting paid the big bucks to be the project manager and make decisions. If it were as simple as implementing the preceding recommendations a monkey could do the job (and we have all worked for project monkey managers).

AntiPattern Synopsis

The AntiPatterns that appear in this book are summarized in Table B.1. The chapter column (far right) indicates the chapter in which the AntiPattern is defined. The chapters each represent a different perspective:

Chapter 2: People

Chapter 3: Technology

Chapter 4: Process

Chapter 5: Combined perspectives of people, technology, and process

The AntiPatterns are identified by name and the subsequent columns identify the AntiPattern solution (the bad practice that is commonly repeated) and the refactored solution (the good practices that are used to replace the bad ones).

Table B.1 Project Management AntiPattern Synopsis

ANTIPATTERN NAME	ANTIPATTERN SOLUTION	REFACTORED SOLUTION	CHAPTER
AntiPattern Collision	AntiPatterns rarely occur in isolation and often an unseen primary AntiPattern can cause others that become the visible problems. However, refactoring the secondary AntiPatterns does not remove the primary cause.	Identify the visible problems in terms of causes, symptoms, and risks. Use these to identify the AntiPatterns. Check if the causes may be symptoms of other AntiPatterns either earlier in the software development lifecycle or at a project management level. Refactor the AntiPatterns based on severity of risk.	5
Batteries Not Included	The impact of poorly choosing development-time and runtime COTS software can cause system integrators and application developers to cope with version management of erratically evolving, unstable software, and the embedded costs of continuing its inclusion in their product or application.	Implement a strict COTS software (COTSS) adoption and maintenance process: ■ Define the purpose for the COTSS ■ Define the acceptance criteria for the COTSS ■ Evaluate the COTSS ■ Adapt the COTSS to the requirements ■ Integrate the COTSS ■ Maintain embedded COTSS	3
Chaos	Nearly one third of all software projects are canceled and over 80 percent of all software projects are deemed failures. In most cases the reason for the high failure rate in software development was not because the project was poorly planned, but rather that the project didn't execute as planned. The projects were unable to adapt to changes and failed to meet their goals.	A change process is critical to ensure that change can be accommodated and controlled: ■ Understand change ■ Plan for change ■ Prepare for change ■ Reactive planning	2

Table B.1 *(Continued)*

ANTIPATTERN NAME	ANTIPATTERN SOLUTION	REFACTORED SOLUTION	CHAPTER
Corporate Craziness	Cliques and management hierarchies control the working environment for most developers. The hierarchies are often based on personal relationships and favorite opinions of how the company should manage software development. Frequent changes to the organization of the management hierarchy occur. This results in inconsistent management and little developer support.	Establish management teams: ■ Forming ■ Storming ■ Norming ■ Performing Set the correct management roles: ■ Driver ■ Originator ■ Coordinator ■ Monitor ■ Supporter ■ Implementer ■ Finisher ■ Investigator	2
Distributed Disaster	Integration of legacy and new technology systems is the current EAI trend. Complexity is added by dealing with the DOTs that often provide the interconnectivity. The main problem is how to integrate applications written in different programming languages that use different data typing and associated functionality in an integrated manner with the DOTs that are meant to provide distributed interconnectivity.	The three refactoring tools are those of architecture planning, proof-of-concept prototyping, and software configuration management. The architecture must be thoroughly defined to drive implementation. The implementation must be proven to work in prototypical form to ensure that the architecture are achievable. The architecture configuration will change as a result of the proof-of-concept implementation and must be strictly managed.	3
Gilding the Lily	Software sometimes gains a life of its own and grows beyond the original functional intention. This often happens under the informal guise of improvements. The	A project manager must anticipate and control the pressure phase and damage phase. Part of this is the need for requirements identification, control, status accounting, and audit; that is, configuration	3

(Continues)

ANTIPATTERN NAME	ANTIPATTERN SOLUTION	REFACTORED SOLUTION	CHAPTER
	result is often unusable software.	management.	
Killer Demo	Demonstration software can become an end in itself rather than the eventual application or product for which it is proving the concept. Its initial success encourages the addition of new features. The demonstration turns into a software development of its own, not just a proof-of-concept phase of a full software development.	The first step in refactoring is to have a prevention strategy that includes setting expectations for the demonstration software. It is also often necessary to have an aggressive recovery strategy that deliberately disables the demonstration and returns the focus to the main software development.	3
Lifecycle Malpractice	There are basically three types of software development: ■ Demos and prototyping ■ Incremental new product delivery ■ Stable product or application maintenance Traditionally software development organizations stick to a single software development lifecycle that is inappropriate for two of the types of software development. This causes risks of technical failure, cost overrun, and project termination.	A software organization must first identify the nature of its software developments and then: ■ Identify the best-suited individual lifecycles. ■ Apply localized refactoring to optimize the lifecycles ■ Identify common phase processes ■ Produce a superset lifecycle to understand the points of convergence and divergence.	4
Micro-Management	Project managers that don't understand how to provide balanced management of people,	The project manager must focus on each of the three areas of people, technology, and process and then on	2

ANTIPATTERN NAME	ANTIPATTERN SOLUTION	REFACTORED SOLUTION	CHAPTER
	technology, and process are likely to cause project failure. They tend to micro-manage their area of weakness, causing unnecessary developer problems.	how to balance the management of all three. Success is achieved by such actions as: ■ Catalyzing the formation of management and development teams ■ Involving everyone in planning. ■ Performing runaheads ■ Adopting developer-friendly tools ■ Developing pragmatic project management ■ Establishing software development controls	
Myopic Delivery	When a well-planned software development falls behind schedule for unavoidable reasons, the disciplined process of project management is usually dropped and a panic management mode is activated. This impacts the remaining deliveries by compressing the remaining schedule and making its achievability more unlikely.	This problem can be tackled at any of three stages: the beginning, the middle, or the end of a project. Any project adjustments must have compensatory schedule and resource adjustments. Up-to-date, accurate project status information is critical to making good decisions. Finally, triage of requirements becomes an option if the schedule cannot be slipped.	4
One Size Fits All	Often a single software development process is expected to be successful for all software developments, although it is either not detailed enough to be useful or covers so many optional steps that it is too bureaucratic.	The solution involves the basic lifecycles chosen, the detailed software development process followed, and the skills of the staff. The first steps: ■ Identify the nature of the software developments undertaken ■ Identify the candidate software development lifecycles	4

(Continues)

ANTIPATTERN NAME	ANTIPATTERN SOLUTION	REFACTORED SOLUTION	CHAPTER
		■ Identify the best fit software development lifecycles	
One-Shot Deal	Many software development projects are treated as special cases and not as repeatable software development activities. This is demonstrated by the one-shot deal project needing to produce a special deliverable to be able to be successful, such as: ■ An application demonstration ■ A code development tool ■ Retrofitting a temporary solution	There are two steps that can be taken. The first is prevention, by recognizing that the project isn't unique but can follow a repeatable software development process. The second step is a cure if the software development is already suffering from the problem. The cure is to sell the idea to management that the special deliverable really is useful and should have a project of its own.	3
Planning 911	Project plans tend to the extreme and may be one of the following: ■ A Glass Case Plan, which is produced at the beginning of a project but never updated ■ A Detailitis Plan, which expects endless details of all tasks on a highly regular basis ■ A Management Plan, which is a management-only view of what should be happening, not what is happening	The solution is basically the same for all three types of misplanning: ■ Choose a software development lifecycle ■ Develop a schedule template ■ Create a balanced plan ■ Establish a baseline ■ Estimate the tasks ■ Measure progress ■ Evaluate the schedule ■ Update the plan	4
Process Disintigration	Management can often misuse processes deliberately to	A pragmatic software development process must be	2

ANTIPATTERN NAME	ANTIPATTERN SOLUTION	REFACTORED SOLUTION	CHAPTER
	control what they believe are dissident groups of developers. The processes usually have so many detailed steps that they are bureaucratic and unusable, leading to wholesale process abandonment and out-of-control software developments.	implemented and honored by both managers and developers. The process must not be used as a management club to control developers but as a structured way for management and developers to communicate effectively and cooperate in the software delivery.	
Size Isn't Everything	Adding additional developers in an attempt to speed up delivery has been a long-standing myth in software development. It must be understood that there are optimal sizes for teams and projects to best succeed.	Staffing for software development should be added incrementally, allowing time for some early progress without warm bodies sitting around. The staffing needs to be based on the software lifecycle requirements and the schedule.	2
The Brawl	There are two distinct aspects to being a project manager: leadership and management. While management skills are important, a lack of leadership makes a critical difference in the success or failure of a software development.	Understanding leadership skills is the key. It is also critical that the project manager comprehends the difference between management and leadership. A successful leader must: ■ Diagnose ■ Adapt ■ Communicate	2
The Customer	Often it is unclear who the customer is; for example, the funding organization, the end user, or the executive steering group. This leads to instability of requirements, overly complex designs, and	The project manager must identify the customer. Otherwise requirements will be specified by a different group than the one constraining the money to be spent capturing them. The solution is to have a single cooperative	4

(Continues)

Table B.1 *(Continued)*

ANTIPATTERN NAME	ANTIPATTERN SOLUTION	REFACTORED SOLUTION	CHAPTER
	bureaucratic levels of documentation, causing cost overrun and the risk of technical failure.	executive steering group of all interested parties and follow a Spiral Lifecycle to have regular checkpoints and strong risk control.	
The Domino Effect	Managers often move key resources between software development tasks on different projects to fill any gaps. Unfortunately every move exacerbates the situation by creating another gap. This frustrates developers and reduces confidence in management.	The prevention strategies: ■ Strategic Domino Removal ■ Strategic Domino Blocking ■ Domino Rearrangement The recovery strategies: ■ Spartan Domino Blocking ■ Immediate Domino Removal ■ Reverse Domino Tilting	4
Wherefore Art Thou Architecture	Ever-evolving reference architecture can impact software development schedules by changing during the software development lifecycle of a project and requiring the technical requirements, design, and code to be altered in an attempt to adhere to the corporate reference architecture.	It must be acknowledged that the reference architecture will change at a different rate than project delivery cycles. A project should adopt only a single version of the reference architecture. This can be addressed by: ■ Architecture definition ■ Architecture management ■ Planning and scheduling architecture implementation ■ Management of architecture implementation	3

AntiPatterns Cross-Reference

The book purpose of the first book, *AntiPatterns: Refactoring Software, Architectures, and Projects in Crisis*, was to introduce the concept of AntiPatterns and the template for defining them in a consistent manner and to examine some of the commonly occurring AntiPatterns in the areas of software development, software architectures, and software management. It provides strong references to published Patterns as the seminal works for identifying and proposing solutions to some of the problems.

The purpose of the second book, *AntiPatterns and Patterns in Software Configuration Management*, was to primarily identify the AntiPatterns that commonly occur in the poorly understood area of software configuration management. In addition, there was some examination of the areas of software management, software development processes, software requirements specification, and software testing. Some of the topics were addressed as patterns.

This book focuses on commonly occurring project management problems and offers refactored solutions to avoid the identified problems and to recover from their occurrence. The project management problems are classified as people, technology, or process related in an attempt to focus on a specific part of the necessary project management discipline. We also examine how a project manager must manage all three of these aspects of a software development in a synchronized manner.

Table C.1 is a cross-reference of AntiPatterns that are related to the project management patterns covered in this book. The table lists the project management AntiPattern, the name of the related AntiPatterns, the book number and the type classification for each of the related AntiPatterns. The sources of the related AntiPattern type are as follows:

- *AntiPatterns: Refactoring Software, Architectures, and Projects in Crisis* [Brown 1998]
  - Software
  - Architecture
  - Project Mgmt
- *AntiPatterns and Patterns in Software Configuration Management* [Brown 1999]
  - SCM
  - Mgmt & Process
  - Reqts & Testing

Note that the AntiPattern Collision AntiPattern has not been included because it would be the ultimate treatise on all of the possible interactions between all published AntiPatterns. It would be easier to just read all three books and use the combined knowledge for real-world instances as they occur than to exhaustively document all of the relationships. Also note that in a few cases instead of an AntiPattern a related Pattern is indicated. These are from our second book, which included some Pattern solutions.

Table C.1   AntiPatterns Cross-Reference

PROJECT MANAGEMENT ANTIPATTERN	RELATED ANTIPATTERN	BOOK NUMBER	RELATED ANTIPATTERN TYPE
Batteries Not Included	Golden Hammer	1	Software
	Stovepipe System	1	Architecture
	Vendor Lock-In	1	Architecture
	Postmortem Planning	2	SCM
Chaos	Analysis Paralysis	1	Project Mgmt
	Death by Planning	1	Project Mgmt
	Irrational Management	1	Project Mgmt
	Requirements Jeopardy	2	Reqts & Testing
	Sure Thing	2	Reqts & Testing

Table C.1 *(Continued)*

PROJECT MANAGEMENT ANTIPATTERN	RELATED ANTIPATTERN	BOOK NUMBER	RELATED ANTIPATTERN TYPE
Corporate Craziness	Design by Committee	1	Architecture
	Corncob	1	Project Mgmt
	Irrational Management	1	Project Mgmt
	CM Takeover	2	SCM
	Detente	2	Mgmt & Process
Distributed Disaster	Stovepipe Enterprise	1	Software
	Stovepipe System	1	Software
	Architecture by Implication	1	Architectures
	Decentralized CM	2	SCM
	OOCM	2	SCM
	P² (Pattern)	2	Mgmt & Process
Gilding the Lily	The Blob	1	Software
	Golden Hammer	1	Software
	Analysis Paralysis	1	Project Mgmt
	Failure to Audit	2	SCM
	P² (Pattern)	2	Mgmt & Process
	What's on the Media	2	Reqts & Testing
Killer Demo	The Blob	1	Software
	Analysis Paralysis	1	Project Mgmt
	What's on the Media	2	Reqts & Testing
Lifecycle Malpractice	Project MisManagement	1	Project Mgmt
	P² (Pattern)	2	Mgmt & Process
Micro-Management	Death by Planning	1	Project Mgmt
	Nirvana	2	Mgmt & Process
Myopic Delivery	Irrational Management	1	Project Mgmt
	Sure Thing	2	Reqts & Testing
	Great Expectations	2	Reqts & Testing
One Size Fits All	Project MisManagement	1	Project Mgmt
	Nil Desperandum	2	Mgmt & Process
One-Shot Deal	Golden Hammer	1	Software
	Project MisManagement	1	Project Mgmt
	Silver Bullet	2	SCM
	Enterprise System Fable	2	Mgmt & Process

(Continues)

Table C.1 *(Continued)*

PROJECT MANAGEMENT ANTIPATTERN	RELATED ANTIPATTERN	BOOK NUMBER	RELATED ANTIPATTERN TYPE
Planning 911	Death by Planning	1	Project Mgmt
	Project Mismanagement	1	Project Mgmt
	Nil Desperandum	2	Mgmt & Process
	P² (Pattern)	2	Mgmt & Process
Process Disintigration	Cut and Paste Programming	1	Software
	Irrational Management	1	Project Mgmt
	Postmortem Planning	2	SCM
	Nil Desperandum	2	Mgmt & Process
Size Isn't Everything	Project Mismanagement	1	Project Mgmt
	P² (Pattern)	2	Mgmt & Process
The Brawl	Corncob	1	Project Mgmt
	Irrational Mgmt	1	Project Mgmt
	CM Takeover	2	SCM
	Nirvana	2	Mgmt & Process
The Customer	Corncob	1	Project Mgmt
	Irrational Management	1	Project Mgmt
	Software Configuration Management Organization (Pattern)	2	SCM
	Requirements Jeopardy	2	Reqts & Testing
The Domino Effect	Irrational Management	1	Project Mgmt
	Project MisManagement	1	Project Mgmt
	P² (Pattern)	2	Mgmt & Process
	Nirvana	2	Mgmt & Process
The Standards AntiPattern	The Blob	1	Software
	Lava Flow	1	Software
	Golden Hammer	1	Software
	Spaghetti Code	1	Software
	Cut and Paste Programming	1	Software
	Architecture by Implication	1	Architectures

Table C.1 *(Continued)*

PROJECT MANAGEMENT ANTIPATTERN	RELATED ANTIPATTERN	BOOK NUMBER	RELATED ANTIPATTERN TYPE
	Death by Planning	1	Project Mgmt
	Project MisManagement	1	Project Mgmt
	Software Configuration Management Expert	2	SCM
	Failure to Audit	2	SCM
	Silver Bullet	2	SCM
	OOCM	2	SCM
	Nil Desperandum	2	Mgmt & Process
	P² (Pattern)	2	Mgmt & Process
	What's on the Media	2	Reqts & Testing
Wherefore Art Thou Architecture	The Blob	1	Software
	Lava Flow	1	Software
	Golden Hammer	1	Software
	Spaghetti Code	1	Software
	Poltergeists	1	Software
	Architecture by Implication	1	Architecture
	Design by Committee	1	Architecture
	Reinvent the Wheel	1	Architecture
	Stovepipe Enterprise	1	Architecture
	Nil Desperandum	2	Mgmt & Process
	Enterprise System Fable	2	Mgmt & Process
	Information Integrity Management (Pattern)	2	Reqts & Testing

Bibliography

Belbin, Meredith. *Management Teams: Why They Succeed or Fail.* London, UK: Heinemann, 1981.

Bennatan, E.M. *On Time Within Budget: Software Project Management Practices and Techniques.* New York: John Wiley & Sons, 1995.

Bennett, Douglas. *Designing Hard Software: The Essential Tasks.* Greenwich, CT: Prentice Hall, 1997.

Bennis, Warren G. *On Becoming a Leader.* Los Angeles, CA: Perseus Press, 1994.

Bennis, Warren G. and Robert Townsend. *Reinventing Leadership: Strategies to Empower the Organization.* New York: Simon and Schuster, 1996, Audiocassette.

Boehm, Barry. *Software Engineering Economics.* New Jersey: Prentice Hall, 1981.

Boehm, Barry and Papaccio. "Understanding and Controlling Software Costs." *IEEE Transactions on Software Engineering.* October 1988.

Brooks, Jr., Frederick P. *The Mythical Man-Month.* Anniversary Edition. Reading, MA: Addison-Wesley, 1995.

Brown, William J., Hays W. McCormick III, and Scott W. Thomas. *AntiPatterns and Patterns in Software Configuration Management.* New York: John Wiley & Sons, 1999.

Brown, William J., Raphael C. Malveau, Hays W. McCormick III, and Thomas J. Mowbray. *AntiPatterns: Refactoring Software, Architectures, and Projects In Crisis.* New York: John Wiley & Sons, 1998.

Brown, William J. and Thomas J. Mowbray. "Technocratic AntiPatterns." *Distributed Computing.* Vol. 1, Issue 3, March 1998.

Cantor, Murray R. *Object-Oriented Project Management with UML*. New York: John Wiley & Sons, 1998.

Carnegie Mellon Software Engineering Institute. *A Systems Engineering Capability Maturity Model*, version 1.1. Pittsburgh, PA: Carnegie Mellon Software Engineering Institute (www.cmu.edu), 1995.

Carnegie Mellon Software Engineering Institute. *Capability Maturity Model for Software*, version 1.1. Pittsburgh, PA: Carnegie Mellon Software Engineering Institute (www.cmu.edu), 1993.

Carnegie Mellon Software Engineering Institute. *COTS-Based Systems*. Pittsburgh, PA: Carnegie Mellon Software Engineering Institute (www.cmu.edu), 1999.

Carnegie Mellon Software Engineering Institute. *People Capability Maturity Model*. Pittsburgh, PA: Carnegie Mellon Software Engineering Institute (www.cmu.edu), 1995.

Constantine, Larry L. *Constantine On Peopleware*. New Jersey: Yourdon Press, 1995.

Coplien, James O. and Doug C. Schmidt. *Pattern Languages of Program Design*. Reading, MA: Addison-Wesley, 1995.

DeMarco, Tom. *The Deadline: A Novel About Project Management*. New York: Dorset House Publishing, 1997.

DeMarco, Tom and Tim Lister. *Peopleware: Productive Projects and Teams*. New York: Dorset House Publishing, 1987.

Goodland, Mike with Caroline Slater. *SSADM Version 4: A Practical Approach*. Berkshire, England: McGraw-Hill, 1995.

Hersey, Paul and Kenneth H. Blanchard. *Management of Organizational Behavior: Utilizing Human Resources*. 7th ed., Englewood Cliffs, NJ: Prentice Hall, 1996.

Hilliard, Richard, Dale Emery, and Tom Rice. *Experiences Applying a Practical Architectural Method in Reliable Software Technologies: Ada Europe '96*, Lecture Notes in Computer Science, Vol. 1088, ed. A. Strohmeier. New York: Springer-Verlag, 1996.

Institute of Electrical and Electronics Engineers (IEEE). *Best Practices*, IEEE Software, Vol. 13, No. 5, September 1996.

"Is Your Project Out of Control?" *Software Development Magazine*. September 1999.

Johnson, Col. Wayne M. "Rules a Program Manager Can Live By: Getting Back to Basics." *Crosstalk, the Journal of Defense Software Engineering*. July 1998.

Kerzner, Harold. *In Search of Excellence: Successful Practices in High Performance Organizations*. New York: John Wiley & Sons, 1998a.

Kerzner, Harold. *Project Management: A Systems Approach to Planning, Scheduling, and Controlling*. New York: John Wiley & Sons, 1998b.

Kidder, Tracy. *The Soul of a New Machine.* London: Penguin Books, 1992.

King, David. *Project Management Made Simple.* New Jersey: Yourdon Press, 1992.

Kitchenam, Barbara. *Software Metrics.* Cambridge, MA: Blackwell Publishers, 1996.

Larson, Carl E. and Frank M.J. Lafesto. *Teamwork: What Must Go Right; What Can Go Wrong.* Thousand Oaks, CA: Sage Publications, 1989.

Managing the Journey: Understanding and Implementing Change with Dr. Ken Blanchard. 0210-LF-020-4700. 86 min. Blanchard Training and Development, Inc. VPH1 (Video Publishing House Inc. of Blanchard Management Corp.). Videocassette.

May, Lorin J. "Major Causes of Software Project Failure." *Crosstalk, the Journal of Defense Software Engineering.* 1998.

McCarthy, Jim. *Dynamics of Software Development.* Redmond WA: Microsoft Press 1995.

McConnell, Steve. *Rapid Development.* Redmond, WA: Microsoft Press, 1996.

McConnell, Steve. *Software Project Survival Guide.* Redmond, WA: Microsoft Press, 1998.

Moore, James. *Software Engineering Standards: A Users Road Map.* Los Alamitos, CA: IEEE CS Press, 1998.

Mowbray, Thomas J. "The Seven Deadly Sins of Object-Oriented Architecture." *Object Magazine.* March 1997.

Moynihan, T., G. McCluskey, and R. Verbruggen. "Riskman 1: A Prototype Tool for Risk Analysis for Computer Software." *Third International Conference on Computer-Aided Software Engineering.* London, 1989.

NASA. *Cost and Schedule Estimation Study Report.* Greenbelt, MD: NASA Software Engineering Laboratory, 1993.

NASA. *Managers Handbook for Software Development* (revision 1). Greenbelt, MD: NASA Software Engineering Laboratory, 1990.

NASA. *Recommended Approach to Software Development* (revision 3). Greenbelt, MD: NASA Software Engineering Laboratory, 1992.

NASA. *Software Measurement Guidebook* (revision 1). Greenbelt, MD: NASA Software Engineering Laboratory, 1995.

NASA. *Software Process Improvement Guidebook.* Greenbelt, MD: NASA Software Engineering Laboratory, 1996.

Peters, Tom. *Liberation Management: Necessary Disorganization for the Nanosecond Nineties.* New York: Fawcett Books, 1994.

Shaw, M. *Comparing Architectural Design Styles.* IEEE Software, November 1995.

Shaw, M. *Software Architectures.* Englewood Cliffs, NJ: Prentice Hall, 1996.

Strauss, Janice. "The Softer Side of Project Management." *Crosstalk, the Journal of Defense Software Engineering.* July 1998.

Tichy, Noel M. *Managing Strategic Change: Technical, Political, and Cultural Dynamics.* New York: John Wiley & Sons, 1983.

Tichy, Noel M. and Mary Anne Devanna. *Managing Strategic Change.* New York: John Wiley & Sons, 1990.

Tuckmann, B.W. and M.A.C. Jensen. "Development Sequences in Small Groups." *Psychological Bulletin*, Vol. LXIII, No. 6, 1965.

Whitaker, Ken. *Managing Software Maniacs: Finding, Managing, and Rewarding a Winning Development Team.* New York: John Wiley & Sons, 1994.

Whitten, Neal. *Managing Software Development Projects: Formula for Success.* New York: John Wiley & Sons, 1995.

Wysocki, Robert K., Robert Beck Jr., and David B. Crane. *Effective Project Management: How to Plan, Manage and Deliver Projects on Time and within Budget.* New York: John Wiley & Sons, 1995.

Yourdon, Ed. *Death March.* New Jersey: Prentice Hall PTR, 1997.

Zigarmi, Patricia, Drea Zigarmi, and Kenneth H. Blanchard. *Leadership and the One Minute Manager: Increasing Effectiveness Through Situational Leadership.* New York: William Morrow & Co, 1985.

Index